The Psychology
of
Classroom Learning

An Inductive Approach

The Psychology
of
Classroom Learning

An Inductive Approach

Richard M. Gorman

Charles E. Merrill Publishing Company
A Bell & Howell Company
Columbus, Ohio

The author and publisher wish to thank the following for permission to reprint:

From *Verbal Behavior* by B.F. Skinner. Copyright © 1957 Appleton-Century-Crofts, Inc. Reprinted by permission of Appleton-Century-Crofts, Educational Division, Meredith Corporation.

From *Cooperative English Test.* Copyright © 1953 by Educational Testing Service. All rights reserved. Adapted and reproduced by permission.

"Acceptance," from *The Poetry of Robert Frost,* ed. Edward Connery Lathem. Copyright 1928, © 1969 by Holt, Rinehart and Winston, Inc. Copyright © 1956 by Robert Frost. Reprinted by permission of Holt, Rinehart and Winston, Inc.

Excerpted from John W. Atkinson, "The Mainsprings of Achievement-Oriented Activity," in John D. Krumboltz (ed.), *Learning and the Educational Process,* © 1965 by Rand McNally and Company, Chicago, pp. 29, 31.

From *Science of Education and the Psychology of the Child* by Jean Piaget. English translation. Copyright © 1970 by Grossman Publishers. Reprinted by permission of Grossman Publishers. © by Editions Denoel-Gonthier, 1969.

Published by
Charles E. Merrill Publishing Company
A Bell & Howell Company
Columbus, Ohio 43216

Library of Congress Catalog Card Number: 73-89606

ISBN: 0-675-08847-X

3 4 5 6 7 8 / 78 77 76

Printed in the United States of America

Contents

Preface   vii

To the Student   ix

1   Introduction   1

part one   Human Abilities   19

2   The Nature of Intelligence   21

part two   Learning: Basic Considerations   61

3   Theories of Learning   63

4   Current Issues in Learning   95

5   Motivation   122

part three   Learning: Products   147

6   Verbal and Factual Learning   151

7   Concept Formation   184

8   Relations and Structures   211

part four   Learning: Processes   245

9   Comprehension   247

10   Creativity   269

11   Problem Solving   292

12   Critical Thinking   323

part five   Learning: Skills and Attitudes   339

13   Skill Learning   341

14   Attitudes and Values   364

part six   Retention, Transfer and Evaluation   381

15   Retention and Transfer   383

16   Evaluation of Learning   410

Appendix A   The Structure of Intellect   438

Appendix B   Summary of the Taxonomy of Educational
                    Objectives: Cognitive Domain   440

Appendix C   Statistical Techniques   442

Bibliography   445

Index   461

Preface

This introduction to educational psychology is different. With over seventy educational psychology texts currently available, it would in justice have to be. I submit that it is different in a number of ways:

1. It proceeds as much as possible from the concrete to the abstract, from practice to theory (and then again to practice).
2. It emphasizes an explanation of *how* students learn as well as the conditions that influence their learning.
3. It encourages students to become involved in learning through guided discovery exercises at many points in each chapter.
4. It integrates theory and practice by showing how actual teaching situations are related to theories of learning and by making these theories functional for teachers.
5. It usually presents at least two theories or points of view on an issue and encourages the student to compare them and formulate his own position rather than simply accept the position of the author.
6. It continually relates intelligence and learning by specifying the intellectual abilities that are involved in each type of learning.
7. It relates learning and evaluation closely by suggesting specific evaluation techniques that are appropriate for each type of learning.
8. It includes an extensive treatment of several important contemporary topics that are usually given little or no attention in educational psychology texts: structure, critical thinking, and Piaget's view of learning.

In the evolution of the text from first draft to final form, I am deeply indebted to Meryl Englander, Glenn E. Shelbecker, and Douglas Muller, whose valuable and constructive criticisms helped prevent the work from becoming "just another educational psychology text."

There are others whom I wish to thank publicly: primarily my wife Betty, for being the inspiration behind the endeavor; my former students at the University of New Mexico, who first used the guided discovery materials in their experimental form; and finally Denny Rea and Bev Kolz of Charles E. Merrill, who helped bring the project to fruition.

Richard M. Gorman

To the Student

The purpose of this book is to help you gain an understanding of the processes that are involved in classroom learning and be able to apply this knowledge in your own teaching.

You will soon notice that this is a different type of book: it contains both text and exercises, each of which is of equal importance in helping you understand the topics treated. If you are the type of student who likes specific examples for what you are studying, or if you are the type who likes to know how to apply the more theoretical points in actual practice, I would strongly advise you to do each of the exercises as well as read the text. For maximum benefit, do them at the points at which they are included in each chapter.

For the most part the exercises serve two purposes: (1) they provide you with a concrete background to better understand the more theoretical treatment in the text, and (2) they offer you many suggestions for applying the theory and research presented in your own teaching.

A word regarding the text part of the book. It has been deliberately made as concise and direct as possible. The more theoretical sections, while a little more abstract than you will usually find in an educational psychology text, are nevertheless important for an understanding of the learning processes. If you work at them in conjunction with the appropriate exercises, you should not find them difficult.

Educational philosophers and psychologists from John Dewey to Jean Piaget have stressed the importance of activity and interaction in our efforts to learn anything. The whole idea of this text is to encourage you to be active and to interact with the topics presented. My hope is that your interaction with them will allow you to better understand the processes involved in the various types of classroom learning and will eventually make your own classroom more conducive to effective learning.

The Psychology
of
Classroom Learning

An Inductive Approach

Introduction

EXERCISE 1-1. Essential Background for Teaching

Why study educational psychology? Will it help you in your teaching?

Suppose that on your first day of student teaching you are called on to teach the history of the English language to junior high students. The topic as outlined in the text that all students have is as follows:

> Origins of English
> > Indo-European family
> > German root
> > French contributions
> > Other languages

What questions about the *teaching* of this topic can you think of? What basic concerns—not about the content but about the teaching of it—would you wish to clarify before you taught it?

Here are a few possible questions or concerns; check which ones you think are important.

_____ 1. What value does the topic have for students?
_____ 2. What is the purpose for including this topic in the course?
_____ 3. What should I aim at specifically as I teach this topic?
_____ 4. How should I approach the teaching of the topic?
_____ 5. How will students best learn this topic?
_____ 6. How can I motivate the students for a lesson on the topic?
_____ 7. How will I order the material to be covered?

_____ 8. What specific teaching technique will I use?

_____ 9. What activities can I involve students in to have them learn effectively?

_____ 10. How can I be sure that the students have learned what I intended them to learn?

Actually, you might very well ask any of the above questions as you prepare to teach the topic.

The questions regarding the value (1), the purpose (2), and the specific aim (3) of teaching the history of the English language are the province of philosophy of education.

The questions of how students learn most effectively (5) and how to evaluate student learning (10) are two of the main problems considered in educational psychology. The questions on specific technique (8) and activities (9) are treated in a methods of teaching course.

The remaining questions, i.e. the approach (4) and the order to use (7), plus how to motivate students (6), can be considered either in educational psychology or in a methods course—usually in both. In educational psychology these questions are treated from the point of view of how students learn most effectively; in a methods course they are treated from the point of view of the specific ways there are to present material and involve students.

It seems, then, that many of the concerns that you as a teacher might have as you prepare to teach a topic are treated in educational psychology (learning, motivation, evaluation, etc.); and that therefore a study of educational psychology may be worth your while.

How do students learn? What abilities do they bring with them to the act of learning? How can their learning be made more effective? How can we be sure that they have actually learned something? These are some of the questions that teachers are often concerned with and that educational psychology attempts to answer. They are also the main questions we will be concerned with in this book.

Just what is educational psychology? How can it help you as a prospective teacher? And what about this present text in educational psychology: what does it treat and how does it proceed? These are the specific questions that we will be concerned with in this brief introductory chapter.

The Nature of Educational Psychology

What is educational psychology? With what kind of knowledge does it provide us?

Educational psychology is the science of classroom learning and its correlates. It is concerned with the student particularly as a learner, but also as a developing, behaving human being in a classroom, with abilities, motives, and achievements that are very much his own. As much as possible it considers these further aspects of the student as they relate to him as a learner.

Educational psychology is at the juncture of psychology and education. It is a branch of psychology that deals mainly with human learning; it is a branch of the study of education that provides scientific knowledge about what goes on in the classroom. (See figure 1-1.)

A Branch of Psychology

Scientific psychology, the study of man's behavior, has many specific branches, some pure or experimental, some applied, some both. Educational psychology is both an experimental and an applied science. Educational psychologists conduct research on students in classrooms, and they also take many insights from other branches of psychology—experimental, developmental, personality, psychometrics—and apply them in their analysis of classroom learning.

Even in their classroom experimentation, some educational psychologists study how students learn and the characteristics of their personality and development with a view simply to understand better the process of learning or how development and personality relate to learning. They are engaged in basic research and their findings contribute to the pure or academic side of educational psychology. Other researchers are more interested in the relative effectiveness of different instructional procedures or in trying out specific learning materials with a view to improving classroom learning and teaching. They are engaged in applied research and their findings contribute to the applied side of educational psychology.

The field as a whole, then, consists of the results of both basic and applied research plus the applications of relevant findings from several other branches of psychology. It should be mentioned that the balance among these sources of knowledge is continually changing. In the early decades of educational psychology, there were more applications made from other branches of psychology than there were conclusions based on research data within the field. Today there is an abundance of educational research data regarding many types of classroom learning, but educational psychologists have formulated very few significant theories as to how these types of learning actually occur. For explanations of the process of learning, they still depend on theories taken from other branches of psychology, particularly the experimental psychology of learning. Hopefully in the next few decades, through a greater emphasis on basic research and theory construction, educational psychology will offer some viable theories of its own that will be more relevant for classroom learning than those it now borrows from other areas.

A Branch of Education

Education also has several branches: some concerned with aims and objectives, some with methods of teaching and the curriculum, and some with scientific research on the life of the student in the classroom. For the most part the latter is coterminous with educational psychology. Let's consider the various branches of the field a little more at length.

To give you, the prospective teacher, an adequate background for your profession, some consideration of the aims and objectives of education, a

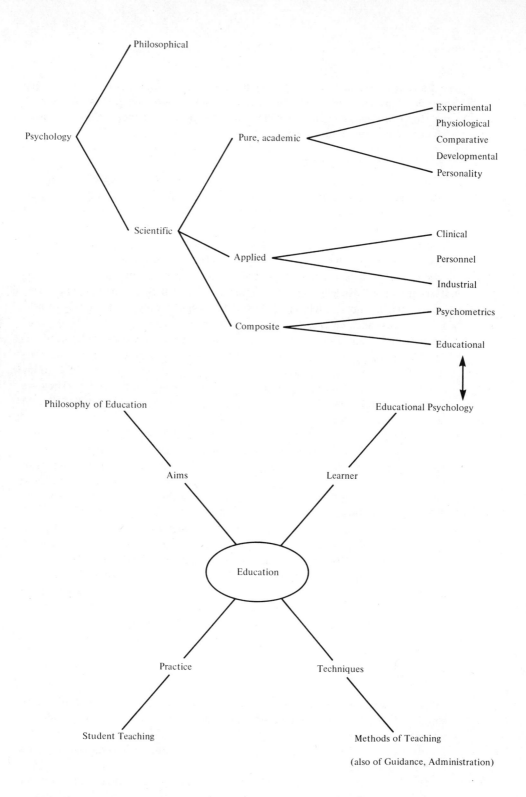

Figure 1-1. *The Fields of Psychology and Education*

knowledge of the student and the learning process, and an awareness of the various techniques of teaching relevant to your field plus some skill in using them are usually considered essential. Aims are examined in the philosophy of education,[1] the learner in educational psychology, and how to teach in methods courses and student teaching. Although you should not divorce the study of the learner from why and how to teach him, neither can you expect to study everything about education in one semester or one book. In the present book we will not be treating objectives or at what the teacher should aim, nor will we be treating methods or how the teacher should teach; we will limit ourselves to an analysis of the learner, and specifically to what his abilities are, how he learns and how to evaluate his learning.

Would that the human condition would allow for a more panoramic view of the educational process all at once! Actually it does, but it takes both time— more than one semester—and a broad knowledge—more than one course. Let me suggest a few ways that the three main areas in the study of education can be related; then you can work out your own, more global view later—sometime before you begin to teach. Consider the following examples.

Aim	The Learner	Techniques
To develop the ability to think critically	Critical thinking abilities Nature of critical thinking Conditions favoring the improvement of critical thinking	Group discussion Debate Questioning
To have students gain a knowledge of the main aspects of reality	Intellectual abilities The learning process Conditions favoring the learning of concepts, relations, structures	Informal lecture Group discussion Project method Emphasis on structure in the curriculum
To develop a well-rounded person	Nature of personality Causal influences on personality Behavior and adjustment	Student-centered discussion Discipline

Through your philosophizing about education you arrive at certain conclusions as to what the educational process should accomplish, i.e. its aims. In relation to each of the aims, educational psychology can contribute some

---

1. Many—if not most—teachers base their instructional objectives on their own educational experience and on school policies and requirements plus perhaps some ideas gleaned from curriculum courses or developmental psychology. The fact that this *is* frequently the case does not mean that these are the best bases for educational aims and objectives. On the contrary, aims and objectives *should* be based on the nature of the learner, of society and of the education process, in a word, on philosophical grounds.

insights on the nature of human abilities, on how we learn, and on the conditions influencing our learning. On a more concrete level, a methods course will offer some helpful suggestions on how to use some specific techniques of teaching that relate to each aim and how to organize your subject matter for effective instruction.

Two important points to keep in mind are (1) that our present study of educational psychology will not try to establish objectives but on the other hand will serve you well once you have established them on a philosophical base; and (2) that educational psychology will not tell you how you should teach or how you should organize your subject matter, although once you understand the nature of the learning process you should be able to assimilate the many specific suggestions of your methods courses much more intelligently.

The Content of Educational Psychology

Although we have defined educational psychology as the study of school learning and its correlates, you should not get the impression that it has always been—or even is—an integrated discipline. Quite the contrary. It grew more by accretion than design, with the result that it is a compound of several loosely related areas. Edward Lee Thorndike (1874-1949), who more than anyone can be called the "father of educational psychology," was interested mainly in learning but also in measurement and human abilities. The interest of G. Stanley Hall (1844-1924) in child study alerted early educational psychologists to the importance of considering the developmental aspects of children and adolescents in school. As clinical psychology grew in this country, educational psychologists gradually included personality and mental health as essential topics to be treated in relation to the learner in the classroom. More recently, the area of the social interactions in which students engage in the school have been added to the topics treated, largely due to the insights on the social dimension of human behavior contributed by social psychology.

Educational psychology today, then, is a compound discipline that includes the following six areas: learning, human abilities, development, personality, social interactions, and measurement, all as they relate to the student in the classroom. This focus on the student offers whatever possibility there is of unity in this complex field. For instance, we might order the various topics of educational psychology as shown in figure 1-2.

The student is a human person with intellectual and physical *abilities* plus the quality we call *personality* (temperament and character). All of these facets of the individual *develop* in a particular *social*-economic-cultural context. Largely through social interaction the person can *learn* various skills, ideas, and behavior that are related to these several facets of himself as a human being. Finally, both the learning outcomes and the initial qualities of the person can be *measured.*

In this book we will try to keep the focus on the student and in this way provide some unity to the multiplicity of topics we will treat. We will not be able to examine all of the above aspects of the student. In fact we will only

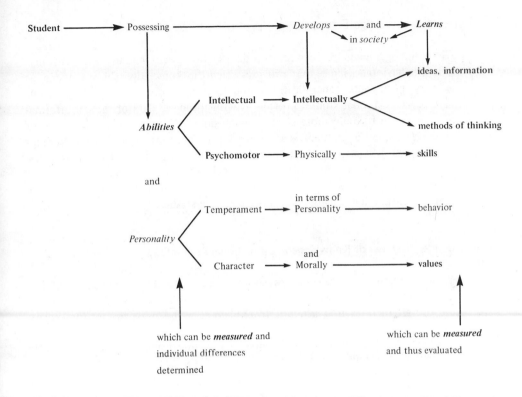

Figure 1-2. *Schema of Topics Treated in Educational Psychology*

attempt to treat several of them—and for good reason. The main purpose of a textbook in any field is to present the important research, theory, and practice of that field in a comprehensive, orderly way. However, the phenomenal growth of educational psychology during the past two decades—both in terms of quantity and quality of research—has led several recent attempts to present a comprehensive coverage of the field to exceed eight hundred pages.

It is impossible to provide more than a superficial treatment of all phases of educational psychology within a book of workable size. Two solutions to this impasse have emerged. One is to treat only one of the six phases in a relatively small volume. The other is to treat half of the field and leave the remaining half to others. This latter solution is the one chosen here. We will, for the most part, include only learning, human abilities, and measurement as we focus on the student in the classroom. An insight into his personality, his development, and the social dimensions of his life in school will have to be gained elsewhere.

In the meantime it is important to realize how the topics that we will be examining fit into the whole discipline of educational psychology. In the above schema, the facets of the student that we will be treating here are printed in bold type; those that deserve your study elsewhere are in regular type.

The Type of Knowledge Educational Psychology Provides

What kind of knowledge does educational psychology provide us with? Basically, it is a behavioral science that provides scientific knowledge about students as learners: both facts, generalizations, and theories. Individual experiments, surveys or correlational studies provide us with the basic data or factual information on which to build more general conclusions.[2] Once a sufficient amount of research data on a problem is available, a generalization regarding the findings can be made. Finally, as more and more generalizations are derived from the research, a theory can be constructed to explain them on an even higher level of inclusiveness. The theory in turn helps to suggest further problems that can be examined through experiments and correlational studies.

EXERCISE 1-2. Degrees of Knowledge in Educational Psychology

When you study educational psychology, you acquire knowledge that has varying degrees of generality: specific facts, generalizations based on many facts, and overall theories that attempt to explain several generalizations (and many facts).

Given below are some sample statements in educational psychology. Indicate whether you consider each to be a specific fact (F), a generalization (G), or a broader theory (T).

	F	G	T
1. The correlation between scores on the Lorge-Thorndike Intelligence Test and the Torrance Tests of Creative Thinking was found to be .32.	___	___	___
2. There is a rather low correlation between creativity and intelligence.	___	___	___
3. Intelligence is a complex of many abilities: cognition (traditional "intelligence"), creativity, critical thinking.	___	___	___
4. The group that was taught the principle of refraction of light succeeded in hitting the lowered target in an average of 2.4 trials; the group that was given practice only took an average of 8.5 trials.	___	___	___
5. Understanding a principle results in greater transfer of learning than does rote learning.	___	___	___
6. Transfer of learning occurs through a process of generalization: when we understand a principle we can apply it generally to all instances of that principle.	___	___	___

Examples of fact resulting from specific research studies are: (1) the .32 correlation between the two tests, and (4) the difference of 6.1 between the two groups in the refraction of light experiment.

---

2. Exercise 1-3 at the end of the chapter will explain these research methods more fully.

Examples of broader generalizations derived from these and similar facts are the statements that (2) there is a low correlation between creativity and intelligence, and (5) understanding brings greater transfer.

Illustrations of theories derived from the generalizations are: (3) intelligence is a complex of many abilities, and (6) how transfer of learning occurs, viz. through generalization.

As scientific knowledge, educational psychology tells us what *is*, not what *should* be. In other words it is speculative[3] rather than practical knowledge. However, since most practical knowledge is based on scientific knowledge, we can make applications from what we find out about the learner and the learning process to our teaching. Bear in mind, though, that when we do this we are leaving the strict realm of behavioral science and are attempting to draw reasonable implications from our speculative knowledge.

To a large extent, the research in educational psychology—at least in the three phases of it that we will be considering—tells us something about the *conditions* of learning, e.g. whether distributed or massed practice is more effective for learning a skill, whether all positive instances are better than some positive and some negative instances in learning a concept, whether a student's awareness of what his creative thinking abilities are will help him to improve in creativity, etc. In other words, the available research itself offers us mainly some facts and generalizations regarding what makes for the effective learning of skills, concepts, creative thinking, etc.

To a lesser extent some of the research in educational psychology will offer an insight into certain aspects or variables relating to the *process* of learning itself. But for the most part our knowledge of the internal processes involved in learning is gained from the theories that are *derived* from research, particularly laboratory but also classroom research. As you can imagine, there may be competing theories on a specific type of learning, depending on who formulates the theory and what his research base is (experiments with animals or men, using verbal associations or principles, etc.). But a knowledge of one or more major theories that attempt to explain the learning process is just as valuable to you as a teacher as is the knowledge of what the research has found on the conditions of learning. And so even in this introductory text we will treat theories as well as conditions of learning.

The Structure and Approach of This Book

There are several basic things that a teacher should know about the learning process:

---

3. Speculative: pertaining to what is or what happens; from the Latin *speculari*, to observe. N.B.: "speculative" is best thought of as a type of knowledge; it has nothing to do with "sheer speculation."

What exactly it is that is learned (the outcome);

How it is learned, i.e. what goes on in the act of learning (the process);

What can make the learning more effective (the conditions).

It will be helpful to you as well to have some awareness of what intellectual abilities are involved in the learning act and also a knowledge of how you can evaluate your students' learning. Finally, you as a prospective teacher will not be satisfied with simply a scientific knowledge of the learning process plus the other aspects that relate to it; you will also want some indication of how you can apply that knowledge in your own teaching.

The Topics Treated

All of the above considerations are in fact the aspects of the learning process that we will examine in this book. A typical chapter among those that treat the types of learning will include the following sections:

1. a definition and explanation of what is learned;
2. an analysis of one or two of the leading theories that attempt to explain the learning process;
3. an indication of what intellectual abilities are active in the specific type of learning;
4. some generalizations based on the relevant research regarding some of the conditions that make for more effective learning;
5. some suggestions for how you can help students learn based on the research and theory presented; and finally,
6. some examples of evaluation techniques that you can use for determining the quality of your students' learning.

What specific topics will we be treating in this text? As mentioned above: human abilities, learning, and evaluation. We will begin with human abilities, specifically the current views on the nature of intelligence and a brief consideration of the development of intellectual abilities (our only venture into the area of development). Then we will examine some basic topics regarding learning: several theories of learning in general, two current issues that are directly related to those theories, and the question of motivation for learning. Our analysis will then focus on the main types of learning that go on in the classroom and will include: (1) the many *products* of learning that we can acquire—facts and language, concepts, relations, structures, psychomotor skills, and, later, attitudes and values; and (2) the several thought *processes* that we can learn to improve—comprehension, creativity, problem solving, and critical thinking. Finally, we will treat several topics that follow upon learning, viz., retention and transfer of what we have learned, plus some technical considerations on the evaluation of learning outcomes.

If we incorporate these topics into our earlier outline of topics treated in educational psychology, we will have the expanded schema (figure 1-3) that hopefully will provide some unity to our study. (Again, the phases and topics that we will be treating are printed in bold face.)

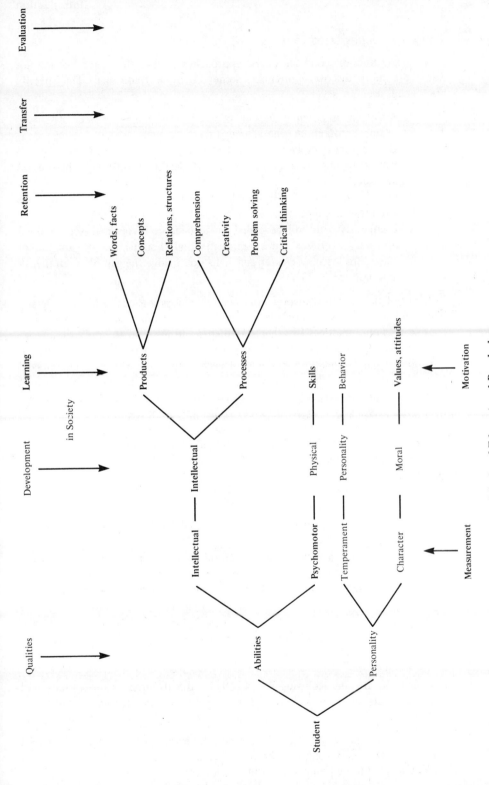

Figure 1-3. *Topics to Be Treated in Relation to Whole of Educational Psychology*

The Approaches Used

Is there anything different about the approaches used in this text? Yes and no. Some are more discovery oriented, some are more traditional. The specific approaches used are several:

1. As often as possible we will proceed from some concrete classroom examples to a more general analysis.
2. Rather than simply be exposed to one point of view (mine), you will usually be encouraged to compare two leading positions or theories on an issue.
3. Much of the time I will present explanations, analyses, generalizations from research plus suggestions for teaching and evaluating.
4. Frequently you will be called on to become involved in some guided discovery exercises and experiments that should make the analysis of classroom learning clearer and help you bridge the gap between theory and practice.

Some of the exercises involve your analyzing class sessions or informal lesson plans and deriving aspects of the learning process from them. Others contain capsule teaching practices or other statements and ask you to apply the theory that you learned in a chapter. Still others consist of experiments that pertain to the topic at hand. Finally, at the end of each chapter you are often encouraged to plan a class session that will apply the main insights gained about the learning process in that chapter. All of the exercises are an integral part of the text as a whole and play a very important role in your interaction with it.

I would urge you to do the guided discovery exercises at the point at which they occur in the text. They have been placed there on the conviction that you will profit most from them if you complete them before reading on in the regular text.

EXERCISE 1-3. Types of Research Studies in Educational Psychology

What are some of the basic research methods used in educational psychology? How do they differ? Do they support a causal connection between variables?

Presented below are summaries of three recent research studies in educational psychology, each one using a different research technique. Read through the summaries and see if you can discern what the general method or approach is in each. (So as not to overwhelm you, only part of the data from each study is given here.)

1. Green, R. B. and Rohwer, W. D. 1971. SES differences on learning and ability tests in black children. *American Educational Research Journal* 8: 601-9.

The goal of the study was to examine intellectual performances that might illuminate the relationship between socioeconomic status (SES) and school performance within a population of black children.

Hypothesis: abilities to do associative tasks (level I) are distributed equally across SES groups; abilities to do conceptual tasks are not.

Subjects: 60 fourth-grade pupils, divided into low, lower-middle and middle SES groups.

Tasks: Paired associates (dog-gate), digit span (61395), Raven Progressive Matrices (reasoning).

Results:

Table A. *Mean Performance as a Function of SES and Tasks*

| | Task | | |
SES	Paired Associates	Digit Span	Raven Matrices
low	24.10	16.50	17.75
low-middle	25.25	23.15	21.75
middle	24.75	25.45	22.85

For paired associates there was no difference among SES groups. On Digit Span the low SES group was significantly below the low-middle and middle groups. Similarly on the Raven, the low SES group scored significantly below the other two groups. There was no difference between the low-middle and middle groups on any task.

Conclusion: Substantial SES differences were found on two tasks: an immediate memory task and a complex problem-solving measure.

Comment: The hypothesis (Jensen's theory of level I and level II intelligence) was partly supported, partly contradicted.

2. Reilly, D. H. 1971. Auditory-visual integration, sex, and reading achievement. *Journal of Educational Psychology* 62: 482-86.

The purpose of the study was to investigate auditory-visual integration skills as they relate to reading success.

Subjects: 225 pupils in grades 1-4.

Measures: Gates-MacGinitie Reading Test; individually administered Auditory-Visual Integration Test.

Method: Correlations of Auditory-Visual Integration Score with Vocabulary, Comprehension, and Total Reading score by grade.

Results:

Table B. *Correlations between AVIS and Reading Scores*

Group	n	AVIS-Vocab.	AVIS-Compreh.	AVIS-Total Reading
Grade 1	60	.23*	.14	.21
Grade 2	56	.65**	.71**	.70**
Grade 3	51	.42**	.34**	.40**
Grade 4	58	.25*	.30**	.30**
Total	225	.30*	.61**	.50**

Note: *Significant at .05 level.
**Significant at .01 level.

For grade 1 AVIS correlated significantly with vocabulary but not with comprehension or total reading score. For all other grades AVIS correlated significantly with all three reading achievement scores.

Conclusion: Ability to integrate auditory and visual stimuli is significantly related to reading achievement. When the total group was examined, AVI ability appeared to be more closely related to comprehension scores than vocabulary scores.

Comment: The results suggest that AVI ability be given serious attention in any attempt to understand the means by which reading ability—particularly comprehension—is developed.

3. Mathis, R. W. and James, W. H. 1972. Internal-external control as an environmental variable in listening. *Journal of Experimental Education* 40: 60-63.

The purpose of the study was to investigate the effects of the internal-external personality variable upon the improvement of listening skills. (Internally oriented: perceiving control over events as within one's own influence; externally oriented: believing that major events are outside one's control, i.e. due to luck or fate.)

Hypothesis: Students will demonstrate greater improvement in listening skills when operating under an induced attitude that is toward the internal end of the I-E continuum.

Subjects: 60 male college freshmen from a rural area, divided into two groups equated on general ability using ACT scores.

Treatment: A five-week reading improvement course using Educational Development Laboratory program.

Internal group: Skills represented constantly as up to individual.

External group: Skills represented constantly as under control of experimenter.

Measures: Listening achievement tests in EDL program.

Results:

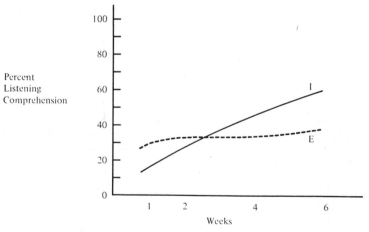

Figure A. *Comparison between I and E Ss on general listening skills over the experimental period*

General listening skill increased to a significantly greater degree under the internal situation than under the external situation.

Comment: Internal-external continuum of the setting is an important variable affecting the quality of more complex learning.

Indicate which study is characterized by each of the following descriptions.

_____ Groups of students are exposed to two or more specific kinds of treatment and then tested to see if the treatment(s) have resulted in any measurable differences.

_____ Students are given tests or other measures and the results analyzed to see if there are any differences among various categories of students.

_____ Students are given tests or other measures and the results analyzed to see if there is any connection or relationship between or among the scores.

The study that dealt with the effect of internal and external control on learning of listening skills involved dividing the students into two groups, exposing them to two different kinds of treatment and finally testing them to see whether there is a difference between the groups attributable to the different treatments. This type of study, which is a genuine *experiment,* uses several ways of controlling the important variables involved. First of all, the groups are equated on such variables as intelligence, educational background, sex, etc. Second, the experimental treatment is carefully described, e.g. in this case five weeks of constant reminders what the main cause of improvement is, through verbal statements, attitude toward workbook exercises, evaluation, etc. Finally, one or more common tests or other measures are given to both groups at the end of the experiment, with the group averages compared to see whether there is an appreciable difference between (or among) the groups.

Statistical Note 1. Statistical Significance

Does a large difference on the final measure in an experiment mean a real superiority of one treatment over the other? Does a small difference mean that it could easily be due to chance and sampling error? In sum, how large a difference between groups do you need to be sure that it is due to the experimental treatment and not to chance?

The question arises because only a sample of students (not all students) is used in an experiment; hence we are dealing with probability (not certitude) in any assertion that one treatment is superior to the other. To establish the degree of probability we must take into account (1) the number of students in the groups (a reasonably large number will help reduce the chance factors involved in a small sample); (2) the size of the difference in group scores on the outcome measure (the greater the difference the less likely it is due to chance); and (3) to what extent the scores of individuals among the two groups overlap (if too many in the lower group score above the average in the higher group, it is an indication that there is no real difference between the groups).

There are statistical techniques available that will take into account these three elements, i.e. number in groups, size of difference in group scores, and degree of overlap or variability among scores, techniques that will allow an experimenter to determine the degree of probability that his results possess. For example, through a technique called analysis of variance, a researcher may find that the difference he obtained between the groups can be expected to occur 95 times out of 100 because of a genuine superiority of the one type of treatment and only 5 times out of 100 because of chance involved in the use of a sample of students. Thus the experimenter—and his readers—are 95 percent sure that one treatment is more effective than the other. In statistical terms we speak of his degree of confidence as being at the 0.05 level (1.00 [always] − 0.95 [most often] = 0.05 level of confidence) or of his results as being "significant at the 0.05 level."

By common agreement, researchers require a 95 percent level of probability (i.e. a 0.05 level of significance) before they will make any claims about their results being due to something other than chance.

The study conducted to determine whether black students of different SES levels perform differently on different types of tests involves the simple collection of data with a measuring instrument and its analysis, with students being divided into various categories, in this case three levels of socioeconomic status. In this type of study, which is generally termed a *survey*, data can be collected by any one of several measuring instruments: tests, inventories, questionnaires, systematic observation. In the study, the students are not actually divided into separate groups, only their test scores are divided or categorized according to some basis that permits a meaningful analysis of data. Often in this type of study there will not be as much emphasis on the control of variables as in the strict experiment. For instance, in the present study, educational level was the same for all, but intelligence was not clearly controlled.

The study conducted to investigate auditory-visual integration skills as they relate to reading achievement involved the administration of two tests to a group of students plus a comparison of the test scores to see the relationship between them. In this *correlational* type of study, usually two or more measures are given to the same group and the scores analyzed to see whether there is, not a difference, but a "going togetherness" or correlation between them. For the most part, controls are not as much a concern as in the experimental or even the survey method, as long as the group is somewhat homogeneous on key variables such as age, intelligence, and the like.

Statistical Note 2. Correlation

Correlation is the "going-togetherness" of two variables, whether they be height-weight, intelligence-achievement, physique-temperament, etc.

A coefficient of correlation is a mathematical index of the "going-togetherness" of two variables. Scores of individuals are obtained on two measures and then each individual's relative position on both measures is compared using a mathematical formula. The result is a coefficient of correlation which indicates the overall degree of relationship between the two variables on a scale of 0 to 1.00.

For most situations the following mathematical-verbal equivalents are valid:

.80 to .99	high correlation
.60 to .80	substantial correlation
.40 to .60	moderate correlation
.20 to .40	low correlation
0 to .20	little or no correlation*

*Negative correlation (e.g. − .45) indicates an inverse relationship, i.e. one variable goes together with the absence of the other.

How about the question of causality? From the results of the studies above can we infer any causal connection between any of the variables studied? Check those in which there is a causal relationship.

_____ Internal-external oriented environment determines learning.

_____ Socioeconomic status determines performance on certain tasks.

_____ Auditory-visual integration skill determines reading ability.

The only study in which we can legitimately infer causality is the first, the experiment on internal-external oriented environment. Since the only difference between the two groups was the imposed environmental factor of internal versus external orientation, we can conclude that the difference between the groups on the final tests was due to the difference in treatment, i.e. that the internal-external dimension has a causal influence on the learning of listening skills.

In the SES study, it is not possible to say whether the difference in performance on the several tasks was due more to socioeconomic level or to degree of basic intelligence. In other words, there are too many uncontrolled variables for us to say for sure whether there is a causal connection between SES and task performance.

How about in the auditory-visual integration and reading study? Probably not. Correlation says nothing in itself about one variable causing another, only that they go together to a certain extent. Sometimes causality can be reasonably inferred, e.g. in the correlation between intelligence and achievement; but sometimes the relation is probably due more to a common cause, e.g. the correlation between math and English achievement is due to a common cause— intelligence; at other times it isn't due to anything, e.g. the positive correlation between enrollment figures and the price of lunch in the cafeteria (both went up over the years, but . . .). In the present study it would be unwise to posit a causal relationship, certainly to the extent that some of the correlations might suggest. Further experimentation would have to be done to establish a genuine causal connection.

Suggested Reading

Herbert, J. and Ausubel, D. P., eds. *Psychology in Teacher Preparation.* Toronto: Ontario Institute for Studies in Education, 1969.

part one

Human Abilities

This book is mainly concerned with learning in the classroom. But before we consider the nature and types of classroom learning, it is essential that we examine the intellectual abilities that students bring with them as they engage in learning. We begin with an analysis of intelligence: both what it is in general and what specific intellectual operations we can expect our students to be able to perform as we attempt to teach them.

2

The Nature
of Intelligence

What mental abilities do students bring with them to the act of learning? What are the main intellectual processes of students that a teacher can involve in the various types of classroom learning? Teachers who want to make their classes effective and stimulating will want to know the answers to these questions.

But there are other things regarding intelligence that are also important for a teacher to know. For instance: What kinds of mental operations can students perform at various grade levels? What are the intellectual processes and abilities that can be improved by training and practice? How can intelligence be measured? These are some of the questions that we will be treating in this chapter on the nature of intelligence.

Before we try to answer these questions, do this preliminary exercise. It should make our discussion much more concrete.

EXERCISE 2-1. Intellectual Processes in the Classroom

You are teaching a topic in your field (select any topic). What kinds of questions can you think of to ask your students regarding the topic, particularly questions that will require them to think in different ways?

Here are some questions that an English teacher who was teaching the "Secret Life of Walter Mitty" asked his students. What type of intellectual abilities are called upon by each question?

1. What is the main theme of the story?
2. Is Thurber's delineation of Walter Mitty effective? Why or why not?
3. Why did Walter Mitty have a secret life?

4. You are relaxing in your favorite chair. Your wife comes in and suggests that you mow the lawn. What would some of your daydreams be at that point?

Match each question with a type of intellectual ability or process listed below.

_____ Understanding of main ideas
_____ Memory ability
_____ Ability to get at the reason for something
_____ Ability to think critically
_____ Ability to engage in free, open-ended thinking

A history class is studying nationalism. During one class session the teacher asked the following questions. What intellectual processes or abilities should they activate in his students? Again, match each question with one of the types of abilities listed above.

5. What is nationalism?
6. During what century did nationalism develop in Europe?
7. Why has the center of power shifted away from Western Europe?
8. Did nationalism help or hinder the development of Africa?
9. What changes can you foresee if the trend toward nationalism continues?

The first question in each set, i.e. "What is . . ." (1 and 5), calls for an understanding of a main idea. The question on when nationalism developed (6) calls for memory.

The ability to put data together and to come up with the reason for something is activated through the "why" questions in each set (3 and 7).

Critical thinking or evaluation is required in questions 2 and 4 that deal with how effective a story or a policy was.

Finally, the questions regarding your own thoughts on a matter (4 and 9) are more open-ended and call for a freer and more creative type of thinking.

In teaching a topic thoroughly, you as a teacher will involve several intellectual processes or ways of thinking in your students. What these processes are form an important preliminary consideration to any treatment of classroom learning.

There are at least two reasons why a teacher must be aware of the intellectual processes and abilities that students bring with them as they engage in learning. First, in all types of learning a variety of intellectual functions are actively engaged; hence a full analysis and understanding of the different types of learning require that we identify the intellectual processes and abilities that are active in each type. Second, some types of learning, viz. the learning of processes as distinguished from products, entail the improvement of the intellectual processes themselves, and so a teacher must have a thorough knowledge of what these processes are if he is to attempt to improve them in his students.

We will try to gain an understanding of the nature of intelligence by examining three main headings: (1) the main definitions of intelligence that psychologists hold, (2) some of the principal scientific descriptions or theories of intelligence, and (3) an analysis of what intellectual operations students can perform at various age levels.

These three sections represent three different approaches to the study of intelligence: (1) definitions—a rational approach that attempts to define intelligence more on the basis of logical analysis than scientific research; (2) scientific theories—a quantitative approach that uses objective measures of intelligence and bases an analysis of the nature of intelligence on the data obtained from these measures; and (3) developmental levels—a qualitative approach that attempts to identify the characteristics of intellectual activity at different age levels through an examination of how children and adolescents solve problems that are presented to them.

Following our treatment of the nature of intelligence, we will consider several points regarding its measurement.

Definitions of Intelligence

How can we define intelligence? Although psychology has more to contribute to an understanding of intelligence by way of analyzing and describing it rather than attempting to define it in the strict sense, it will be of interest to examine the main types of definitions that psychologists have suggested. The definition you prefer will depend as much on your philosophical persuasion as on your leanings in psychological theory.

We will examine three broad traditions: the behaviorist, the pragmatist, and the operational views, and attempt to identify both the definition of intelligence held by each and also the philosophical background that each definition is based on.

The behaviorists, those psychologists who demand that all principles of behavior be closely tied to observable behavior, consider intelligence to be a system of responses to the stimuli of the environment. Intelligent behavior is reflected in an individual's capacity to learn and to use what he has learned in a variety of situations. In a related tradition, Edward Lee Thorndike defined intelligence as "the power of good responses from the point of view of truth or fact." In his view, a person's intelligence depends on the number of stimulus–response or problem–solution connections that he has formed and how well he can apply these to new situations.

This type of definition of intelligence is rooted in the philosophical tradition of the British empiricists who held that ideas are "things implanted in a man's mind." Man's intellect is like a "blank tablet," and knowing is simply a process of imprinting the mind with the images and ideas of things outside it.

A definition held by many American psychologists is that intelligence is man's problem-solving capacity. In the same vein Claparède, the great Swiss psychologist, defined intelligence as "conscious adaptation to new situations." The emphasis here is on man consciously adapting or adjusting to the problematic situations in the environment.

The philosophical tradition to which this view is directly related is that of pragmatism. This distinctly American philosophy, which is ultimately based on the general theory of evolution, considers ideas to be hypotheses that we use in our solving of problems. Successful ideas, those that work out through our experimenting, are selected as solutions (the "survival of the fittest").

Many contemporary psychologists hold an operational view of intelligence that emphasizes the interaction of man's mind with his environment. Piaget, for instance, defines intelligence in terms of a complex system of operations that "constitute genuine actions, being at the same time something produced by the subject and a possible experiment on reality." Guilford considers intelligence to be a complex structure of mental abilities through which man discovers and deals with information. In this same vein, Lewis Terman thought of intelligence as the ability to do abstract thinking, for instance to relate in the mind various objects that exist in the environment.

The operational view is rooted in a philosophical relativism which considers ideas to be the product of an interaction between a person's experience and how he orders these experiences in his mind. It is closely related to a traditional Aristotelian view which holds that ideas result from an interaction between mind and reality: we grasp the essence of things with our minds, and things exist intentionally in our minds when we know them.

EXERCISE 2-2. Definitions of Intelligence—Some Criticisms

A thorough evaluation of the several main definitions of intelligence is more a philosophical than a psychological matter; however, some attempt at critical analysis is appropriate here. The definitions that were examined above were:

    A. Behaviorists: a system of responses.
    B. Pragmatists: problem-solving ability.
    C. Operational view: the interaction between mind and reality.

To which of the views do each of the following criticisms apply?

	A	B	C
1. Its mentalistic flavor infers more than is warranted on the basis of observation—a behaviorist criticism of . . .	___	___	___
2. It is too narrow and does not take into account much of man's behavior—a pragmatist criticism of . . .	___	___	___
3. It is too one-way in that it takes into account only the aspect of man's reacting to his environment—an operational criticism of . . .	___	___	___

4. It is limited because it stresses just one of the intellectual
   processes—an operational criticism of . . .   ____ ____ ____

> 1. Behaviorists consider the operational view to be too "mentalistic"; but the
> latter in turn accuse the behaviorists of not getting at the essence of man's
> intelligence because they are too constricted by "observation of overt behavior."
>   2. Pragmatists consider the behaviorist "system of S-R connections" to be
> narrow and not to include the main type of activity of the problem-solving
> organism that is man.
>   3. The operational psychologists criticize the behaviorist view as involving a
> unilateral relation between environment and man, i.e. $S \rightarrow R$. They prefer a
> reciprocal relation in which the environment provides input which is processed
> and incorporated by the person, i.e. $S \leftrightharpoons R$.
>   4. The operational view also considers the pragmatists to limit themselves to
> only one of the several intellectual processes, i.e. the problem-solving process,
> and hence to give only a part of the whole picture.

Which view you prefer depends largely on your personal preferences regarding
the nature of man, his mind, and his behavior. My own conviction is that the
most significant insights concerning the nature of man's intelligence have been
provided by those who hold an operational view. It is this view that we want to
consider more specifically as we examine some of the current scientific descriptions of intelligence. But first to get a glimpse of how psychologists have thought
of intelligence over the past fifty years or so, do exercise 2-3.

EXERCISE 2-3. Intelligence as Measured by Tests

Some psychologists state: "Intelligence is that which is measured by intelligence
tests." Although this seems to be a cautious, almost circular definition, in an
important sense it is very true. In the scientific study of intelligence we are
dependent on the measures of intelligence that are available to us. Let's examine
some of those measures now.

   Skim through the following sample items taken from some of the more
popular intelligence tests used during the past five decades. How would you
characterize each test? Try to trace a developing view of intelligence that the
tests exemplify. To do this, key on the general view of intelligence represented
by each test, not on the specific test items themselves. Finally, you might
consider the practical point of which test would be more usable in schools.

1. *Otis Quick-Scoring Mental Ability Tests.* Copyright 1920, 1936, 1954 by World Book
   Company.
   A tape measure is to distance as a clock is to
     a. its hands   b. an hour   c. time   d. a watch   e. school

If 3 1/3 yards of ribbon will make 25 badges, how many badges will 10 yards make?
    a. 250   b. 33 1/3   c. 75   d. 10   e. 50

The opposite of general is
    a. specific   b. ordinary   c. prevalent   d. inferior   e. subordinate

A rosebush must have
    a. roses   b. thorns   c. roots   d. fertilizer   e. buds

Score: I.Q. (mental age/chronological age)

2. *American Council on Education Psychological Examination.* Copyright 1924 (many revisions through 1948) by Educational Testing Service.

Select the word at the right which means the same as or the opposite of the first word.
    famous   a. renowned   b. faithful   c. renewed   d. destined

Think of the word that fits the definition. Then mark the first letter of that word on the answer sheet.
    A mark remaining after a wound is healed.
      F J N S V

Find the correct answer to each problem below.
    Lemons sell at 3 for 10 cents. How much will 1 1/2 dozens cost?
      a. 30¢   b. 40¢   c. 45¢   d. 50¢   e. 60¢

Find the rule in each problem below.
    6 9 7 10 8 11 9
      a. 7   b. 10   c. 12   d. 13   e. 14

Scores: L (linguistic) and Q (quantitative) in percentiles (what percent of students score below an individual)

3. *Differential Aptitude Tests.* Copyright 1947, 1963, 1971 by the Psychological Corporation.

Verbal Reasoning

_____ is to one as second is to _____

A. two   – middle
B. first   ,– fire
C. queen – hill
D. first   – two
E. rain   – fire

Numerical Ability

Add   13
       12

A. 14   B. 25   C. 16   D. 59   E. none of these

Abstract Reasoning

The four Problem Figures make a series. Which of the Answer Figures would be next in the series?

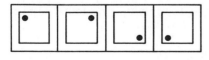
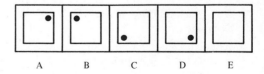

                  A   B   C   D   E

Clerical Speed and Accuracy
Underline at right the symbol which is underlined at left.
A7   7A   B7   <u>7B</u>   AB   7B   B7   AB   7A   A7
Mechanical Reasoning
Which weighs more? (If equal, mark C.)

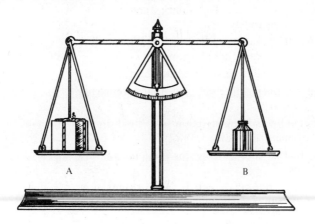

A   B

Space Relations
Which figure can be made (folded) from the pattern shown?

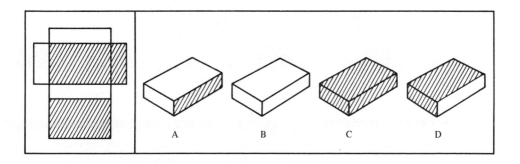

A   B   C   D

Profile of Scores: in percentiles

	Verbal Reason-ing	Numer-ical Ability	VR + NA*	Abstract Reason-ing	Clerical Sp. & Acc.	Mechan-ical Reasoning	Space Rela-tions	Language Usage	
								Spelling	Grammar
Percentile									

*The equivalent of a scholastic aptitude or general mental ability score.

For each of the following statements indicate whether it is best exemplified by the Otis, the ACE Psychological, the DAT, or none of the tests.

	Otis	ACE	DAT	None
1. A test that includes many types of items, all contributing to one score.	____	____	____	____
2. A test that measures several abilities and reports the score for each separately.	____	____	____	____
3. A test that differentiates two of the main intellectual abilities necessary for school learning.	____	____	____	____
4. A test that measures a person's innate ability.	____	____	____	____
5. A test that reflects the early view that intelligence is something unitary.	____	____	____	____
6. A test that reflects the conviction that intelligence is a complex of many abilities.	____	____	____	____
7. The test that is most usable for grouping in various subject fields.	____	____	____	____
8. The test that reports scores in a way that gives a counselor the most complete view of a person's abilities.	____	____	____	____

The Otis test, one of the leading traditional measures of intelligence, contains items of varying types, all of which contribute to one I.Q. score (1). This was in keeping with the common view held in the first few decades of the century that intelligence was a unitary function (5).

The famous American Council on Education Psychological Examination was one of the first intelligence tests to distinguish between verbal and numerical abilities, based on the thinking that separate scores in these two broad areas would be more helpful in predicting scholastic achievement in the related subjects than would simply one I.Q. score (3). This represented the initial differentiation among intellectual abilities.

The Differential Aptitude Test, one of the most widely used of the tests that measure and report scores for several intellectual abilities (2), reflects the conviction derived from the factor analytical work of the 1940s that intelligence is a complex function consisting of many different abilities (6).

In terms of usage in schools, the DAT with its profile of scores gives the teacher and counselor a relatively complete view of the students' abilities in relation to school subjects; it is thus more usable than the earlier measures for grouping in various subject areas (7) and for both educational and vocational counseling (8).

Note: actually no intelligence test measures innate ability (4); what they measure is present mental ability or innate ability as developed.

Scientific Theories of Intelligence

Factor Analysis

The most productive work using the quantitative or intelligence test approach to the analysis of intelligence has been that of the factor analytic psychologists. Factor analysis is a mathematical procedure whereby a large number of diverse measures are sorted into subgroups of highly similar measures. The subgroups are called factors. The procedure involves (1) administering many types of tests to a group of subjects, (2) correlating each test with every other test, and (3) applying complex mathematical procedures to the correlations, such as matrix algebra and rotation on axes. The result is (4) a series of subgroups of tests together with the extent to which each test correlates with each subgroup (some correlate to a greater or lesser extent, others not at all); finally (5) the tests that cluster together in each subgroup can be examined and a name given to the factor that is descriptive of the common characteristic of the tests in that subgroup.

The purpose of factor analysis is to simplify the description of data by reducing the number of variables, i.e. to sort the various tests or other measures into a lesser number of groupings or categories. The correlations among test scores are analyzed mathematically in such a way that several underlying categories are identified. These categories in turn can be said to represent the basic dimensions of ability or behavior that are measured by the many tests that have been used.

There are several basic considerations that are necessary for a more complete understanding of the nature of factor analysis; at the same time they may suggest some built-in limitations of the technique. First, factor analysis is based on the assumption that similarities in test scores are due to similar abilities being measured, i.e. if scores on two tests are positively correlated with one another, they measure more or less the same abilities. Before accepting the factor analytical approach, one has to decide whether this assumption is a reasonable one.

Second, the nature of the factors resulting from a factor analysis depends on the tests that are put into it and on the type of mathematical procedures that are used. In other words, the factor analysis technique sorts the tests that have been fed into it and sorts them in a way that is determined by the specific statistical procedures that have been chosen. (This fact in part explains why, as we will see shortly, factor analytic psychologists differ in their views of intelligence.)

Finally, the factors that result from the mathematical analysis are basically groupings or categories of tests. On the surface level, therefore, a factor represents a statistical construct, namely a functional grouping of similar tests or test items. If one desires—and if his theoretical persuasions allow—a person can make the further judgment that factors also represent underlying functions in the mind, i.e. the intellectual abilities needed to do well on certain similar tests. (Most behaviorist-oriented psychologists, for instance, hold the "statistical construct" view; whereas many operational psychologists allow for the "underlying ability" interpretation.)

One result of the factor analytical approach that is of major interest to the teacher is the construction of several theories of intelligence. These theories attempt to describe intelligence systematically by using a model designed to show the order and interrelationship among the various factors or intellectual abilities.

The two main theories of intelligence are (1) the British view—first Charles Spearman and currently Cyril Burt, Philip Vernon, among others, and (2) the American view—originally L. L. Thurstone and now J. P. Guilford. In both instances the earlier factor analytical work primarily stressed the identification of the basic factors comprising intelligence and was not really interested in any ordered schema of the abilities identified. The contemporary approaches continue to be interested in the further identification of factors but are more concerned with the construction of a workable model or way of structuring intelligence. Let us consider the earlier work briefly and then get into a more detailed examination of the two main contemporary views.

Earlier Theories

Spearman.   On the basis of an early type of factor analysis in which only four measures were analyzed at a time, Charles Spearman (1863-1945) formulated a two-factor theory of intelligence.

Spearman found that practically all tests had something in common. He called this universal factor *g* and explained it as being similar to mental energy; we can think of it as general intelligence. He explained the portion of a test not due to *g* as representing a "special" factor that varied from test to test and denoted this specific aspect of each test as *s*. For most mental functions Spearman considered *g* to be a more important factor than *s*.

Thurstone.   In America, L. L. Thurstone (1887-1955) and others used more sophisticated techniques of factor analysis and identified a series of broad group factors that seemed to explain most mental activity.

The group factors were those that were found to be present on a group of tests, i.e. they were common to some tests but not to others. Thus they are somewhere between Spearman's *g*, which is universal and found on all tests, and *s*, which are specific and measured by only one or two tests. Group factors, those found on several different tests but not on others, are also referred to as common factors or, by Thurstone, as *primary mental abilities*.

Thurstone's original list of primary mental abilities contained the following factors: verbal comprehension, word fluency, number (computation), space, associative memory, perceptual speed and general reasoning (inducing a rule).

Through the years as factor analytical psychologists identified additional common factors, Thurstone's original list increased to several dozen distinct mental abilities.

Contemporary Theories

Burt, Vernon.   The contemporary British view of intelligence, one that follows directly in the tradition of Spearman, organizes the various intellectual abilities into a hierarchical structure with *g* as the most important factor.

> What is now known of mental activities suggests a far more complex and systematic type of structure (than that of Spearman or Thurstone); it goes far to confirm the notion that the mind is organized on what may be called a hierarchical basis. There is first a comprehensive general factor, covering all cognitive activities; next a comparatively small number of broad group factors, covering different activities classified according to their form or content; these in turn sub-divide into narrower group factors; and the whole series appears to be arranged on successive levels, the factors on the lowest level being the most specific and the most numerous of all. (Burt 1949, pp. 198-99)

> In eight analyses, g was found to cover more than twice as much variance as all group factors combined. . . . After the removal of g, tests tend to fall into two main groups: the verbal-numerical-educational on the one hand (referred to as v:ed factor), and the practical-mechanical-spatial-physical on the other hand (referred to as k:m factor). If the analysis is sufficiently detailed, i.e. if sufficient tests are included, these types themselves sub-divide. The v:ed factor gives minor v and n (number) group factors. In other analyses k:m splits similarly into mechanical information, spatial, and manual subfactors. Thus a first approximation to mental structure is provided by a hierarchical diagram resembling a genealogical tree. (Vernon 1950, pp. 22-23)

The basic model of the hierarchical view of intelligence is presented in figure 2-1. The British factor analytical psychologists thought that the best way to integrate their (and the Americans') findings regarding common or group factors with Spearman's g was through a multilevel hierarchical classification ranging from the most general factor (g) through major group factors (v:ed and k:m) and minor group factors (the main "common" factors) to specific factors, e.g. rote memory for spelling, computational accuracy in multiplication, etc.

A unified view of intelligence is achieved by structuring the factors around g, the factor that is found in a significant degree on practically all tests; all other factors are related to g through subclassifications on the basis of degree of generality-specificity. The model, similar to a genealogical tree, is based on the distinctions and divisions that seem to be warranted from the many factor analytic studies conducted by the British psychologists, i.e. after the general factor is removed, the remaining correlations always fall into two main groups: the verbal-educational group and the spatial-practical-mechanical group. These two main complexes include the respective "common" factors as indicated in the diagram (note that many of the common factors are similar to Thurstone's "primary" factors).

Always interested in the educational implications of their theory, Vernon and his associates have studied the abilities necessary for various school subjects; their findings are as follows. The g and v:ed factors are basic to all subject fields. More specifically, the verbal factors are important for the languages, literature, history, and social studies: verbal comprehension for understanding the ideas involved, verbal reasoning for manipulating these ideas in problem solving and grasping relationships. The numerical factors are important in math-related subjects: numerical reasoning in algebra, geometry and other branches of mathe-

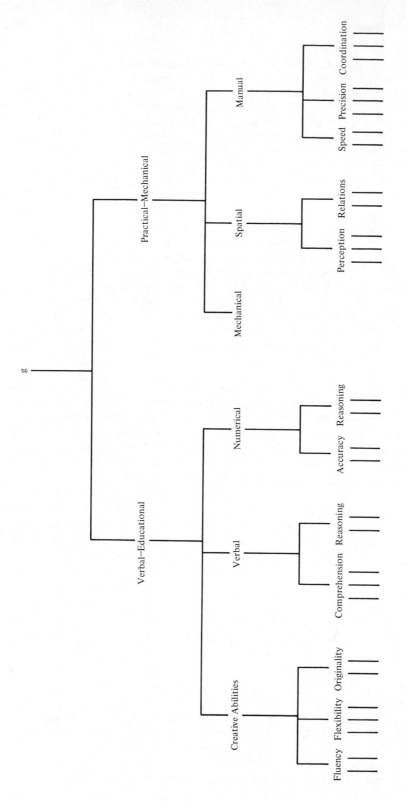

The common factors (fluency, comprehension, etc.) can be further subdivided into more specific or *s* factors.

Figure 2-1. *British Hierarchical Theory of Intelligence*

matics, and to a lesser extent in the mathematically oriented sciences such as physics and chemistry; numerical accuracy in the computational phase of math, e.g. arithmetic. The $k:m$ factors (manual, spatial, mechanical) affect a student's performance primarily in the crafts and technical subjects plus handwriting and drawing. Music and the arts are not as closely related to the group factors but have been found to involve mainly specific factors plus g.

As far as testing is concerned, Vernon claims that on the average about 40 percent of the variance in human abilities can be attributed to g and only about 20 percent to the group factors (with the remaining 40 percent to specific factors). In practice this means that fairly good predictions concerning academic success can be made from general intelligence tests, with multiple aptitude tests contributing some, but not much, additional information.

A teacher or counselor following the British view would much prefer to give a general intelligence test with its one I.Q. score than bother with a differential aptitude battery that provided a profile of scores. He would also use the general intelligence score more than aptitude test scores for dividing students into homogeneous groups.

Guilford. The work of identifying the many factors of intelligence begun by Thurstone was continued in America by J. P. Guilford and his associates. Through his factor analytical studies he has discovered eighty or more common mental abilities, not just those of Thurstone and others, but also such factors as originality, redefinition abilities, sensitivity to problems, memory for semantic implications, etc. More significantly he has constructed a model that gives organization and structure to these many abilities.

EXERCISE 2-4. Measures of Basic Intellectual Processes

Before we get into an explanation of Guilford's model of intelligence, it will be helpful to have some background in the types of tests that he used in formulating it. Some of the tests that he employs in his work are the same as those used by Thurstone and others years earlier; but in addition Guilford and his colleagues have constructed other, newer types of tests that have been productive in identifying the many different abilities that comprise intelligence.

Here are some sample items from those newer tests. Do the items and then try to analyze what type of thought processes were active while you were doing them. Again bear in mind that our concern is not with the test items themselves but with the view of intelligence derived from them. Recall that the main scientific theories of intelligence are based on tests and how test scores correlate with one another. Therefore, if we want to understand a theory, it is worth knowing something about its basis, in this case different types of tests.

1. What letter belongs at the place of the question mark?

2. Study material: Gold is more valuable than iron.
   Diamonds are harder than coal.

   Test item: Coal is _____ than diamonds.

   a. softer   b. blacker   c. less valuable

3. Take away three matches leaving six triangles.

4. You arrive on Mars and notice that the Martians wear emblems to show what each person's job is. You notice one Martian wearing the emblem shown below. Jot down as many possible jobs as you can that might be indicated by the emblem.

5. From which object could you most likely make a needle?

   a. a cabbage   b. a steak   c. a fish   d. a paper box

6. Classify the following words into three meaningful groups, using no word in more than one group.

   1. airplane
   2. bicycle
   3. cabin
   4. car
   5. hotel
   6. house
   7. knapsack
   8. suitcase
   9. tent
   10. trunk

A.	1	2	4	–	3	5	6	9	–	7	8	10
B.	1	5	8	–	3	4	6	10	–	2	7	9
C.	1	4	5	6	–	3	9	10	–	2	7	8

7. Which class name best fits a class represented by the four given class members?

   Class members   Class names
      CAT   a. Farm animals
      COW   b. Four-legged animals
      MULE   c. Domestic animals
      MARE

8. Which of the alternative conclusions follows from the statement given?

   Given statement: In the mid-Pacific, on Buna-Buna, the game of ticky-ticky is played out-of-doors.

   Alternative conclusions:

    a. People in Buna-Buna like to play games.
    b. Ticky-ticky is a difficult game to play.
    c. There is an island called Buna-Buna.

First the answers.

1.

2. softer

3.

4. Any jobs that are actual occupations, e.g. electrical engineer, light bulb manufacturer, bright student, etc.

5. fish

6. A. means of travel, types of shelter, things to carry belongings in

7. Domestic animals. Farm animals is too restrictive—cats are found elsewhere than on farms; four-legged animals is much too general. Domestic animals is broad enough yet sufficiently restrictive.

8. C. From the statement only the fact that there is an island called Buna-Buna can be validly inferred.

What type of mental process would you say you went through in answering each question. Here are some characteristics of the main types of intellectual processes; match each item above with one of the characteristics.

_____ Understanding the meaning or order among things
_____ Retention of something (fact, meaning, relation, etc.)
_____ Given data or a problem, arrive at the one correct answer
_____ Given a topic or problem, think of a variety of answers
_____ Judge whether alternatives satisfy some criterion or not

The first question involves the discovery and understanding of the underlying principle behind the order of the letters. The question about coal, diamonds, etc., required the retention of the relation between the various minerals.

The next four questions involved thinking in two different directions: in the needle and categories questions, you started with some data and proceeded to arrive at the one correct answer; in the triangle and possible jobs questions, you started with a topic and proceeded to think of as many different answers as you could.

Finally, in both the class name and the Buna-Buna questions, you had to make a judgment about whether the given alternatives satisfied some standard or criterion, in these cases a class title that is both sufficiently broad and restrictive and an inference that can be logically drawn from given information.

Regarding his theory of intelligence, Guilford states:

> When the writer first faced the problem of organizing the intellectual factors into a (unitary) system, almost forty such factors had been demonstrated. . . . Almost no one (in the U. S.) reported finding a *g* factor. The factors appeared to be about *equally general* in that they are strongly represented by small numbers, and relatively equal numbers, of tests. . . . The absence of a *g* factor and the apparently comparable generality of all factors did not give support to a hierarchical conception of their interrelationship. . . .
>
> It was found however that many factors had obviously parallel properties. Three distinct, parallel *content* categories were recognized and called by the terms figural, symbolic and semantic. Even before these distinctions as to content became evident, there had been some tradition for classifying the intellectual factors in another way, i.e. according to the kind of *operations* involved: creative thinking, memory, evaluation, etc. A third way of looking at the abilities and of classifying them came to view more slowly. It came about because of the need for taking into account the parallels that appeared across both the content and the operation categories; (it was termed the *product* dimension). A way was found to integrate all these parallels by putting the known intellectual factors into a single, solid model, with the five operation categories arranged along one dimension, the three content categories along a second dimension, and the six product categories along the third dimension. Thus content, operation and product became three parameters of a three-dimensional model. (Guilford 1967, pp. 60-62)

In constructing his model of intellect, Guilford observed that many intellectual abilities had certain things in common. One thing they had in common was the kind of intellectual process or operation that certain abilities seemed to involve. He noticed that some factors such as verbal comprehension and inductive reasoning involved the *understanding* of the meaning of something or of the order among things, etc. Other factors such as associative memory, rote and logical memory were similar in that they involved the *retention* of what had been learned. Of the many abilities that have to do with the production of new knowledge from given information, some of them seemed to involve thinking in a *variety* of different directions, e.g. word fluency, originality. On the other hand some of them required the type of thinking that leads to *one correct* or best answer, e.g. deductive reasoning, the classification abilities. Finally, it was clear to Guilford that some abilities entailed making a *judgment* about the logic, correctness, adequacy, and similarity of anything.

Under these categories—which he termed cognition, memory, divergent thinking, convergent thinking and evaluation—he was able to group all of the common factors that he had identified to that point. These five categories, which represent the basic intellectual operations or processes that a person engages in, form the main dimension of the model that Guilford used to structure the intellectual abilities of man.

Similarly, Guilford observed that the many tests used in his factor analytical studies contained different types of content: some involved figures or pictures, e.g. $\bigcirc$, $\perp$, $\textcircled{Q}$; some involved symbols such as A, 569, X, \$, >, $\int$, H_2; many involved material that had to do with ideas or the meaning of something, e.g. hammer, starting a business, reciprocity. All of the forty or more identified factors could be classified according to whether they had to do with one or the other type of content—which Guilford called figural, symbolic and semantic respectively. A fourth type of content—behavioral, having to do with human interactions—was hypothesized at the time Guilford constructed his model; to date only a few behavioral abilities have been identified, all in the cognition category.

Looking at the many common abilities from another point of view, Guilford classified them in still a third way, according to what resulted when an operation was applied to a certain kind of material. This third way of classifying human abilities has to do with the different kinds of knowledge or information that results from our intellectual activity. These products of our mental activity are specifically: (1) a single figure, symbol or word, e.g. π; (2) a class having some property in common, e.g. grass, fern, flower = plant; (3) a relation between two things, e.g. $\square$ is to $\triangle$ as $\square$ is to $\diagdown$; (4) a structure or system that involves order or interrelationships, e.g. 1 2 4 7 11 16 (adding one more each time); (5) a change or modification in meaning or order, e.g. an orange and apple are alike in various ways (soft, edible, seeds, tasty, etc.), each of which involves a change in the basis for the similarity; (6) implications of given information, e.g. all tennis players are swimmers; some tennis players are skiers; how many swimmers are skiers? (some or all).

Guilford called these products of intellectual activity: (1) units, (2) classes, (3) relations, (4) systems, (5) transformations, and (6) implications.[1]

He combined the three ways of classifying the intellectual abilities—process, content and product—to form a three-dimensional matrix which he entitled "the structure of intellect" (figure 2-2). His model is basically a cross classification of factors into intersecting categories, rather than into categories within categories as in the hierarchical model. Each cell in the matrix represents a certain kind of ability that can be described in terms of process, content and product, for instance cognition of semantic units, evaluation of symbolic transformations, etc. Thus through the insight of "process applied to content resulting in product" Guilford provided unity and structure to the many intellectual abilities that he and others had identified through factor analysis.

---

1. If you would like some further examples of test items measuring the various products, look back at exercise 2-4. Classes were measured in 6 and 7, relations in 2, systems in 1, transformations in 3 and 5, and implications in 4 and 8.

If you want some examples of units, recall exercise 2-3. Cognition units are measured by the vocabulary (verbal comprehension) items in the ACE. The Clerical Speed and Accuracy test of the DAT measures units in the evaluation category.

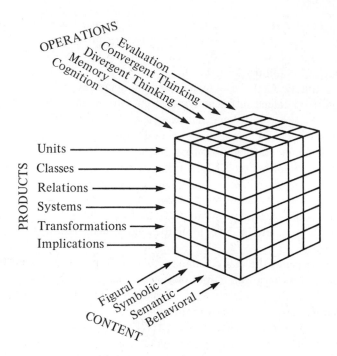

Figure 2-2. *A Cubical Model Representing the Structure of Intellect*

A summary of the three dimensions of the "structure of intellect" is as follows:[2]

1. Process: intellectual operation, action or function

   cognition: understand, discover, recognize, realize, be aware of, compre-
        hend
   memory: remember, retain, recall, acquire lasting knowledge
   convergent thinking: draw conclusions from data, classify or order given
        data, think rigorously, arrive at the correct solution
   divergent thinking: think in different directions, think creatively, indepen-
        dently, inquire or search in a free, open-ended way
   evaluation: think critically, judge, assess, decide as to the similarity, cor-
        rectness, truth, adequacy, goodness, etc. of something

2. Content: type of material involved in intellectual activity

   figural: concrete, visual or auditory
   symbolic: in the form of signs, symbols
   semantic: verbal, having to do with ideas, meaning

3. Product: form in which information occurs, way of knowing

   unit: thing, fact, word

---

2. A schematic presentation of the specific abilities included in the structure of intellect
model is provided in Appendix A.

class: set of objects with one or more common property

relation: connection between two things, ideas, classes

system: a complex pattern, an organization of interdependent or interacting parts, a plan, outline, program

transformation: an item of information becoming something else, going
over into another state

implication: something expected, anticipated, predicted from given information, one thing suggesting another

With regard to education the structure of intellect model offers many possible applications. Guilford suggests the following relationships between the content and process dimensions and the various school subjects.

Figural content is most closely related to the manual and industrial arts, mechanical drawing, the fine arts, home economics, engineering, and physics. The abilities involving symbolic content are important in subjects such as mathematics, accounting, linguistics, symbolic logic, chemistry, and physics. Semantic or ideational content is involved in all school subjects but is particularly emphasized in language, literature, history, social sciences, and philosophy.

The processes of cognition and memory are necessary for all school subjects as are also (hopefully) productive thinking, both convergent and divergent, and evaluation. More specifically, the rigorous type of thinking involved in convergent production is especially called for in such areas as mathematics, science, logic, engineering, and law. Divergent thinking is especially important in any area that emphasizes creative production: art, music, writing, science, architecture, home economics, and, in a way, anything that involves planning, composing, inventing, and theory building.

On a more practical level a teacher who is aware of the complexity of his students' intelligence will not expect every student to do equally as well—or poorly—in each of his subjects. He will look for his strengths and build on these. For example, a poor reader who has above average figural and symbolic abilities but low semantic abilities should probably be encouraged to take more math and technical subjects than English and humanities. If, as is often the case, his interests match his abilities, an English teacher will probably find that the student will do better in reading if he provides him with reading material in the area of mechanics or science fiction rather than the usual literary topics. An elementary student who seems to be doing poorly in grammar, spelling and basic history facts may not be "dumb" but simply a more divergent thinker who is turned on by creative activities and individual projects but is bored by drill work and repetition.

With regard to testing, Guilford suggests that the rather low correlations among the main intellectual processes (e.g. about .30 between cognition and divergent thinking) result in the need to measure each of the processes if we want to get an adequate idea of a student's intellectual abilities. General intelligence tests measure mainly cognition and to a lesser extent convergent thinking. Measures of divergent thinking and evaluation as well as memory should also be given to obtain a complete view of a person's intelligence.

EXERCISE 2-5. Theories of Intelligence—Evaluation

The two main contemporary theories of intelligence are the hierarchical view of Cyril Burt and Philip Vernon and the structure of intellect model of J. P. Guilford. Which do you prefer and why? To help you decide, listed below are some points of criticism regarding the two theories.

A. Indicate which theory each of the following statements criticizes.

	Vernon	Guilford
1. A g factor simply does not occur in analyses that use a sufficient number and variety of tests.	____	____
2. Intellectual ability has been fractionated into more and more factors of less and less importance.	____	____
3. The model is not sufficiently comprehensive: it should include all of the common factors that have been identified.	____	____
4. The model is *too* complete: it includes factors that result from specially designed tests, whereas it should be limited to those that are important in education and daily life.	____	____

B. In your opinion:

	Vernon	Guilford
5. Which model provides a view of intelligence that is more in keeping with your own experience and reflection on the nature of human intelligence?	____	____
6. Which model is more suggestive of practical applications for teaching strategies and curriculum design?	____	____

1. Guilford claims that when a sufficient number and variety of tests are used in a factor analysis, no factor universal to all of the tests occurs. He also states that many of the British studies tend to find a g factor because they do not adequately control age, education, or sex. For instance, if age varies, intelligence test scores will be correlated with age, all of the intercorrelations will be raised, and a g factor will appear. Vernon, on the other hand, prefers to use a lesser number of tests and a "fairly representative population" in his analyses. In so doing he usually finds g to be a major factor.

2. Vernon quotes Quinn McNemar, an American exponent of general intelligence tests, to the effect that Guilford has fragmented intelligence into too many ability factors and has lost the unity that is human intelligence. Guilford counters that intelligence is a complex unity, one that is best understood when we distinguish among the several main processes and the many common abilities that comprise it.

3. Guilford feels that *all* of the factors that are common to several tests should be included in a comprehensive theory of human intelligence. The hierarchical model as constructed by Burt and Vernon is not flexible enough to incorporate all of the identified common factors; in addition Vernon has decided to omit from his model any factor that does not account for more than 5

percent of the variance in intellectual ability among individuals. In Guilford's view, these are limiting aspects that contribute to making the hierarchical model not sufficiently comprehensive.

4. On the other hand, Vernon claims that a meaningful model of intelligence should include, not all of the identified factors, but only the factors that are important in education and the daily life of a person. He says that Guilford's view has resulted as much from specially designed tests constructed to fit the structure of intellect model as from measures that are related to the ordinary intelligent behavior of individuals. In this sense it is *too* complete.

5 & 6. The question of which contemporary theory of intelligence is closer to what intelligence really is is open for debate; and similarly for the question of which view offers more practical applications for teaching and the curriculum. If Guilford's view seems to be emphasized in subsequent exercises in this chapter as well as in other chapters of this book, it is because I believe that not only is his view more comprehensive and satisfying but also his theory contains the most possibilities for applications to classroom learning and the curriculum.

EXERCISE 2-6. Intellectual Processes and Teaching Strategies

Teachers who realize that intelligence is a complex of many types of abilities tend to use a variety of strategies or approaches in their teaching, appealing sometimes to understanding or cognition, sometimes to creative or divergent thinking, etc.

Look at the sample teaching strategies given below. Try to relate them to one of the processes in Guilford's structure of intellect; indicate which process will mainly be activated in students through each approach. The examples in turn should suggest some ideas for varied teaching strategies in your own field.

	Cogn.	Mem.	Div.	Conv.	Eval.
1. A discussion on modern versus traditional art is held in a humanities class.	___	___	___	___	___
2. An English teacher provides a first line and then has the class as a group compose a poem.	___	___	___	___	___
3. A math teacher has the students arrive at the concept of π using circles of various sizes.	___	___	___	___	___
4. An English teacher holds a recitation session on rules of grammar.	___	___	___	___	___
5. A science teacher explains mitosis using visual aids.	___	___	___	___	___
6. An English teacher gives the students a list of sentences and has them classify them into simple, compound, and complex.	___	___	___	___	___
7. A history teacher asks the class what it would be like today if the colonists had lost the War of Independence.	___	___	___	___	___

	Cogn.	Mem.	Div.	Conv.	Eval.
8. Students are asked to criticize (+ or –) an essay written by one of the class.	____	____	____	____	____
9. A social studies teacher has the students try to find out the main purpose of the Marshall Plan.	____	____	____	____	____

As we have seen, cognition is the process that involves understanding, recognition, or discovery of something. In (3) the students come to an understanding of π using an inductive approach; in (5) the teacher's aim is to have the students understand mitosis.

Memory emphasizes retention and recall. The all too familiar textbook-recitation method or the recitation session in (4) are examples of approaches that activate memory more than anything.

Divergent thinking is a productive process that involves independent, creative thinking, especially thinking up various or original ways of doing things. For instance, in (2) the students create their own poem and in (7) they come up with a variety of ideas on what the country would be like *if*. . . .

Convergent thinking involves either classifying data into given categories or arriving at the best or correct conclusion from data that is given or obtained. For example, (6) requires classifying into basic types, and (9) involves examining the data and arriving at the main purpose of the Marshall Plan.

Evaluation entails making a judgment about the truth, goodness, similarity, or adequacy of anything. In (1) students are judging whether modern or traditional art better measures up to the criteria they have selected, and in (8) the students evaluate an essay on the basis of some norms either stated or implied (clarity, originality, style, etc.).

You may have judged that more than one process is involved in several of the approaches; for example, cognition is a prerequisite to evaluation in (1), convergent thinking could be involved in (3) if it were set up as a problem, but mainly cognition if the emphasis is on discovery of meaning or understanding. Similarly in (9), the process used largely depends on how the question is phrased. If the students have data on the Marshall Plan available and then are told to determine what the main purpose was, they will think more in terms of convergent production of one correct answer. If several purposes have been treated and the students are asked to decide which was the main one, they will use evaluation more than anything. Finally, if students have read a chapter on the Marshall Plan in which the main purpose is clearly stated, a question on the main purpose would simply entail the process of memory.

A knowledge of the main views of intelligence can make teachers aware of the many intellectual abilities and processes they can appeal to in treating most topics of a course. It can also make them aware of their students' basic intellectual processes that warrant further developing. Finally it can help to make their classes both varied and stimulating through the use of strategies and questions that involve not just understanding, memory and problem solving, but also the creative and critical thinking processes as well.

Through the use of multiple aptitude tests that reflect the most current thinking on the nature of intelligence, both the strongest and weakest ability areas of students can be identified and developed: the strongest so as to allow each person the satisfaction of fulfilling himself to the utmost and thus be able to make a contribution to society; the weakest—and those in between—so that each person will be well balanced and not deficient in any of the main intellectual functions.

Intellectual Operations at Different Age Levels

It is not only important for teachers to realize what intellectual operations their students can perform in general, but it is also essential that they be aware of what operations they can perform at different age levels. The most helpful research on this question is the qualitative study of the thought processes conducted by the Swiss psychologist Jean Piaget and his associates. Piaget has studied the thinking of children from birth through adolescence and has provided data not only on the characteristics of their thought processes in general but also on the development of such concepts as number, time, space, physical causality, and morality.

In this brief summary of Piaget's contributions to the classroom teacher, we will limit ourselves to the school years and to the thought processes in general. To get a more complete idea read one of the introductions to Piaget listed at the end of the chapter plus some of Piaget himself.[3]

The Elementary School Child

What operations or internal manipulations of data can the elementary school child perform? What are some basic characteristics of his thinking? How is his thinking different from the pre-school child? And how does all of this apply to teaching strategies and the curriculum?

Two simple experiments will illustrate the operations proper to the elementary school child (and by contrast show what the pre-school child—and many first-graders—cannot do).

In the first problem the child is asked, "Are there more boys or children in your class?" A typical five-year-old will answer, "Boys," whereas most seven-year-olds will say, "There are more children." The seven-year-old was able to do a mental manipulation or operation that the five-year-old was not, namely to group boys and girls together into the class "children," to put parts together into a whole, in a word, to classify.

In the second experiment the child is given ten rods of varying lengths (e.g. one each of the Cuisenaire rods is convenient) and told to put them in order from smallest to largest. Whereas one six-year-old might put a very short rod with a medium one, another medium rod with a very long one, a short with a fairly long, etc., another six-year-old may put them in order from the shortest to

---

3. E.g. Piaget and Inhelder 1969; Inhelder and Piaget 1958.

the longest. The first child thinks in terms of "short," "long," i.e. absolute values; the second is able to relate things into an order or series.

The two operations that children can perform in elementary school—at least most second graders can and even many first graders—are *classifying* and *ordering*.

A third experiment will illustrate several further characteristics of the child's thought processes. Twelve poker chips are laid on a table, six in one row an inch apart and six in the second row right below the first (a). The chips in the top row are then spread out so that they are four inches apart (b), and the question is asked: "Are there more here (top) or here (bottom) or are they both the same?" The five-year-old will say "More here (top)." The seven-year-old will probably say something like "They're the same." Why? "You just moved them; you didn't add any."

(a)   (b)

What the seven-year-old was able to do that the five-year-old couldn't was (1) *decenter* his thinking from just the arrangement and take into account two aspects of the situation at once, i.e. quantity and arrangement; (2) *coordinate* these two aspects and see how they are related (i.e. a change in one does not change the other); so as to be able to (3) *conserve* quantity or number even though arrangement was changed.

A final characteristic of the elementary school child's thinking—Piaget considers it central and most important—is illustrated by a simple example of the balance with a one ounce weight on either side (a). A three ounce weight is added to the left side (b) and the question posed: "How can you balance the scale again?" Some six-year-olds will still say, "Put another weight on (the right)," and will put a one or two ounce weight on the right—and remain puzzled. Some sixes, many sevens and most eights will say either, "Take the (larger) weight off" or, "Put the same (three ounce) weight on the other side."

(a)   (b)

The latter children have been able to come back to the starting point (the scale in balance) by either negating an operation (taking the three ounce weight off) or making up for it (putting an equal weight on the other side). In either case they reverse an operation or its effect; in other words their thinking is characterized by *reversibility*.

In all of these examples the elementary school children—except for many first graders—are able to perform internal manipulations of data, but the data must be perceptible or concrete, not purely verbal or abstract. For this reason, Piaget termed this level of cognitive development *concrete operations*.

It should be added that the type of reasoning proper to the child at this level is inductive: from particular instances to a generalization, from observable data to a conclusion.

Ordinarily concrete operational thought begins to emerge in first or second grade and reaches a certain maturity in the middle grades, at which point pupils can perform the different types of groupings, reversibility, etc. with ease and assurance.

To review briefly, the basic operations that elementary school children can perform are classifying and ordering; some further characteristics of their thought processes are: decentering of thought and coordination of aspects plus the resulting conservation of such attributes as quantity, number, weight and length through changes in shape, position or the like; and finally reversibility. Their thinking is always related to the concrete, perceptible realm, and their reasoning is mainly inductive.

How does all of this apply to teaching? First of all, a first or second grade teacher will want to make sure that a child is able to do operational thinking before she attempts to teach him arithmetic or even reading—at least through the traditional phonetic approach. Even the simplest arithmetic operations require: (1) an awareness of number, i.e. that number remains the same through changes in arrangement, and (2) the operations of classifying and ordering, since to understand $1 + 2 = 3$ the child must realize that 2 and 3 are groupings of units (ones) and that the order of the number system is 1, 2, 3, etc. (3 is 2 places after 1). If the child has not yet achieved these insights, the teacher should work with him until he does, rather than proceed directly into arithmetic operations.

In reading instruction that uses the traditional alphabet, the child must be able to realize that a letter is the same even though its sound changes. For example, he must conserve the letter a through changes of $\bar{a}$ to $\breve{a}$ to $\ddot{a}$—to say nothing of the visual change from a to A. Unless the child has developed the ability to decenter his thinking and to conserve one aspect of something while another changes, he can be expected to have considerable difficulty in learning how to read by the traditional approach. The Initial Teaching Alphabet with its one symbol for each of the forty-four basic sounds of the language does away with this problem and can be used even before the child arrives at the stage of operational thinking.

Concrete operational thought with its capacity to reverse an operation or its effect makes the child's thinking much more flexible. He can revert back to the original problem after a trial or two has led nowhere; in math he can grasp that division is the inverse of multiplication; in the arts he can realize that one thing can compensate for another, e.g. that a brighter color can make up for a smaller area as far as the intensity of a painting is concerned.

If a child is not yet in the stage of concrete operations, a first or second grade teacher can give him some exercises such as the ones in the experiments above to challenge him into operational thought. If he is on the verge, these will probably be effective; if he is nowhere near this stage (if he has too much difficulty with them), it would be better to discontinue them temporarily and wait for him to mature some more before attempting to challenge him into it.

The Junior and Senior High Student

Beginning in about junior high school the young person's thinking makes some dramatic advances over the time when he was in elementary school. What are these advances in his thinking? How do the thought processes of the high school student differ from those of the elementary pupil? What implications can be drawn for teaching and the curriculum?

Several characteristics of the thinking of pre-adolescents and adolescents are illustrated in the following experiment. The subject is presented with a series of rods attached to the edge of a basin of water, parallel to the water (a). The rods differ in several ways, including length, thickness and type of material; in addition, different weights can be screwed onto the end of the rods (b). The task is to determine whether the rods can be made to touch the water and how. The subject's explanation is of primary importance.

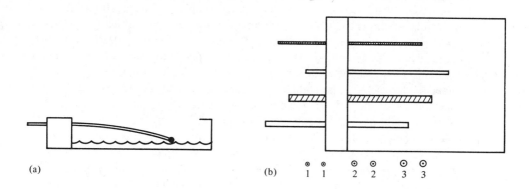

(a)   (b)   1 1   2 2   3 3

A ten-year-old girl (Sonya), after bending each of the rods with her fingers, says, "These two (the thinner rods) can bend because they are lighter; but these two (the thicker ones) are heavier so they can't bend as well." "Can you show this?" the experimenter asks. She puts a one ounce weight on one thin rod— which happens to be longer—and a one ounce weight on a thick one—which is shorter. "There, this one (thin, long) touches the water." How about length, does that have anything to do with it? "Let's see." She puts the same weights (one ounce) on the same two rods (long thin and shorter thick). "Yes, the longer the rod the more it is able to bend."

A fifteen-year-old girl (Linda) begins, "Whether they bend enough to touch the water could depend on several things: the thickness, the heaviness of the weight attached, the length of the rod, and maybe the material. Is this brass and the other steel?" "Yes," states the experimenter. "Can you demonstrate any of these possibilities?" She puts a one ounce weight on a thick and a thin steel rod, both eighteen inches long. "There, that proves that the thinner the rod the more likely it is to touch the water. For the length all you have to do is shorten this one (the thin steel rod with a one ounce weight); when it's long it touches, when it's short it doesn't. The same way with the weight (as she compares one ounce and three ounce weights on the same steel rod). Now the material; let's see." She takes two thick rods, one of brass, one of steel, puts a three ounce weight on each and compares them at the same length.

The characteristics of the thinking of the high school student can be seen both by an analysis of the second transcript (Linda, 15), and also by contrasting the two transcripts to see what the younger student (Sonya, 10) could not do.

First of all, the high school student can begin solving a problem by stating hypotheses or possible solutions: "it could depend on thickness, length, etc." By contrast, the elementary school child starts with the data, with the observable, i.e. the real as opposed to the possible. This new relationship between the real and the possible, with a student able to start with possibilities and reason from there and with the real able to be subordinated to the possible, is one of the most distinctive features of the thinking of the high school student. Piaget calls it *hypothetico-deductive* thinking.

A second characteristic of the pre-adolescent's and adolescent's way of thinking is that he can prove his statements by giving a genuine reason or demonstration. Proceeding systematically, he can verify his hypotheses by showing the necessity of the proof; on the other hand the elementary school child doesn't give a real proof nor does he proceed systematically. Rather he tries out one thing at a time. Also he attempts to provide some data in support of his statements, but it is not convincing as a genuine proof; he uses "because" but more in terms of constancy or correspondence (lighter—bend) than in terms of necessity.

Finally, the high school student is able to separate and control the several variables involved in a problem. He examines each variable separately while holding others equal, e.g. he controls weight, length and material while examining thickness. The elementary school child by contrast can't control the variables but confuses them, for instance, by trying to examine thickness without holding length constant.

Some further characteristics of the high school student's thought processes can be derived from the following simple example used earlier. The problem is given: All tennis players are swimmers; some tennis players are skiers. What is the connection between skiers and swimmers? Jim, ten years old, replied, "They're tennis players." Who? "The swimmers and skiers." Joe, a fourteen-year-old, thought some and then concluded: "Some swimmers are skiers."

It is rather obvious that the ninth grader could operate on a purely verbal and abstract level, whereas the fifth grader could not. Similarly, an ability available to the high school student, and not to the elementary, is that of forming pure abstractions, e.g. the concept of relative density or "the weight of an equivalent amount of water" (which is not a perceivable entity but a pure abstraction). He can also form "second order" concepts, i.e. abstracted not from concrete instances as regular or first order concepts are, but from regular concepts that are already abstract to some degree. Second order concepts such as allegory, relativity, mass ($\frac{force}{acceleration}$) are more abstract than first order concepts because they are twice removed from their concrete underpinnings. For instance, to grasp the allegorical or symbolic meaning of a story a student must first abstract the basic meaning from what happens in the story and then in turn abstract the symbolic meaning from the basic meaning.

Another characteristic that can be derived from the above example is that the high school student is able to draw a conclusion from the premises as much on the basis of the *form* of reasoning as on the given content. This ability to distinguish form from content and to analyze and evaluate the form of reasoning as distinct from specific content is so characteristic of pre-adolescent and particularly of adolescent thinking that Piaget termed the thinking of this level *formal operations.*

For a final and very important quality of the thought processes of the high school student, consider the following illustration. A miniature see-saw with blocks of various weights is given to the subject. A large (two ounce) block is put half way on one side (a) and the question asked: "Can you balance the see-saw again and how?" Mike, age nine, says, "Put the same on the other side" (b). Any other way? "Take it off" (c). Can you think of any other ways? (Pause) "How about putting a small one at the (other) end" (d). How is that? "It weighs more if it's further out."

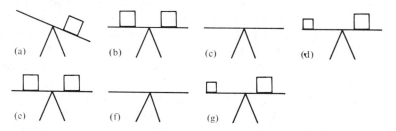

Ken, age 13, states: "There are several ways: you can balance it by putting an equal block on the other side (e), or by just taking the first one off" (f). Are there other ways? "Yes, you can also balance it by putting a lighter weight further out on the other side" (g). How is that? "Well, the further out it is the less weight you need; the distance makes up for the weight. It's the same with the weight: the heavier the weight the less far out it has to be." Can you put that together in one statement? (Pause) "A lighter weight further out is the same as having a heavier weight closer in." What would you say the relation is between increasing and decreasing the weight and the distance? "Increasing the weight has the same effect as increasing the length in the same way that decreasing the weight has the same effect as decreasing the length."

The younger student (Mike, 9) can perform the two types of reversibility: negation ("take it off") and compensation or reciprocity ("it weighs more if it's further out," i.e. the distance makes up for the lighter weight). He can also see simple relationships, for example, putting a smaller weight further out has the same effect as putting a large weight half way in.

But the older student (Ken, 13) can do much more. He not only has a better understanding of compensation or reciprocity ("the distance makes up for the weight") but he can also combine the actions of increasing weight and increasing length (from the fulcrum) and the transformations of decreasing weight and decreasing length into a systematic and interrelated whole, i.e. $+W$ is to $+L$ as $-W$ is to $-L$. Similarly he can see that increasing the weight is related to decreasing the weight in the same way as increasing the length is related to decreasing the length ($+W$ is to $-W$ as $+L$ is to $-L$) or by crossed products: "A lighter weight further out is the same as having a heavier weight closer in" ($-W \times +L = +W \times -L$). In other words, he can grasp the interrelationship among variables in terms of proportionality. (Similarly in mathematics, an elementary school child can handle ratios, e.g. 3/8, but it takes a junior high student to do proportions, e.g. 3 : 8 :: 15 : ?.)

There are other qualities of the pre-adolescent's and adolescent's level of thinking, but these represent most of the principal ones. Again, they are: hypothetico-deductive thinking or the ability to start with possibilities and reason from there, the providing of proof in terms of necessity, the control of variables, abstract and formal thought, proportionality and a systematic whole of operations and transformations.

Formal operational thinking usually begins about age twelve—give or take a year or two—and reaches a level of relative maturity about fifteen or sixteen; however, young people continue to improve in abstract thinking up through college and beyond.

How can the junior and senior high teacher apply some of these insights in his own teaching? First of all, the ability to do hypothetico-deductive thinking makes possible several basically new and different approaches in the discussion of issues and in solving problems. Students are now able to consider various positions on an issue as possible solutions and then through an examination and evaluation of evidence arrive at the most tenable conclusion. In the same way, the ability to start with hypotheses plus the ability to control variables and operate in terms of "other things being equal" allows the high school student to use the strict experimental method in the sciences and social sciences.

Second, the adolescent's concern for reasons and proof should lead teachers to expect students to demand reasons and evidence for statements that teachers make; in the same vein, teachers should require students to give proof and reasons for mathematical procedures, literary and philosophical positions, and scientific conclusions.

Finally, the ability to do abstract and formal thinking opens up many new possibilities for teaching and learning. More verbal and abstract manipulation of ideas and relationships are possible, which for one thing allows students to formulate their own structures or systems of interrelated and ordered knowledge. Although inductive and discovery-oriented approaches are still appropriate, especially for new and unfamiliar subject matter, more verbal teaching can now be effective if it is not purely expository but allows for an active manipulation of ideas on the part of the student.

Students can be much more critical in their thinking and reading since they can now perceive fallacies and contradictions in an argument or line of reasoning. However, teachers should not expect formal and abstract thinking to

develop automatically. Experience and even specific exercises in abstract thinking are necessary if students are to be expected to reason in a formal, abstract
way. These are particularly called for if a student's socioeconomic background is
such that the type of thinking that he is regularly exposed to is concrete rather
than abstract. It should be noted that the best time to encourage any developing
ability is when it begins to emerge; if it is not given an opportunity at that time,
it will be more difficult to develop as years go on. This means that experience in
logical and critical thinking as well as in abstract manipulation of ideas should be
provided certainly in senior high or better still in junior high if formal operational thought is to develop readily.

Summary of Intellectual Operations

Now that we have analyzed the thought processes of elementary and high school
students separately, it may be helpful to juxtapose the characteristics of the
thinking of the two levels and clarify them further through comparison and
contrast.

	Concrete	*Formal*
Operations	Classifying: he can group objects into a class.	Hypothetico-deductive thinking: he can start with possibilities and reason from there.
	Ordering: he can relate objects into an order.	Proportionality: he can relate relationships into interrelationships.
Characteristics	Concrete: his thought is dependent on the concrete, real world.	Abstract: he can think on a purely abstract, verbal level.
	Decentered: he can take into account more than one aspect of something.	Formal: he can consider the form of reasoning aside from specific content.
	Coordination: he can coordinate two aspects of something.	Control of variables: he can isolate and control variables or aspects of something.
	Conservation: he is aware that one aspect of something remains the same even though another aspect is changed (and knows why).	Verification: he has a need for explaining and proving his statements.
	Reversibility: he is able to revert back to the starting point of an operation either by a. cancelling it out by an inverse operation (inversion) b. making up for it by a compensating operation (reciprocity).	Systematic whole: he is able to relate basic operations and their reversibilities into an integrated and interrelated system.
Reasoning	Inductive: forming a generalization from particular instances.	Deductive: drawing a further conclusion from one or more generalization(s).

The concrete operational thinker can take data and group it into classes or
into an order or series. The formal operational thinker does not have to begin
with data but can set up several (or many) possibilities and operate deductively
drawing implications from the hypotheses. The relationship between the real and

the possible is different in the two cases: whereas the younger child is limited by the real, the older student can subordinate the real to the possible and consider the former as one among several possibilities.

While the concrete thinker can order and form relationships, only the formal thinker can relate relationships into laws or interrelationships, e.g. proportionality.

The elementary school child's thinking is always based on and related to concrete data, either what he currently perceives or what he has perceived in the past. He learns best when something is related to his experience. On the other hand, the high school student can form pure abstractions that are not directly based on the perceptible realm of things. He can also learn through a purely verbal presentation and discussion of ideas.

Whereas the concrete operational child can decenter his thinking from the most noticeable aspect of something (shape, position, etc.) to take into account two aspects at once, e.g. shape and quantity, the formal operational student can decenter his thinking from the content of a statement and take into account both the content and the form of reasoning, and then analyze and evaluate the latter.

While the younger child can coordinate two aspects of something and can grasp that changing one does not necessarily entail a change in the other, the adolescent can isolate various aspects of something and make sure that other variables remain constant while he changes or examines one variable.

The true conserver (e.g. of quantity when shape is changed) on the concrete level can give a reason for his judgment: "it's the same" (identity) or "you can put it back just as it was" (reversibility). But the formal thinker is much more concerned with verifying his (and others') statements and is able to give genuine proofs in terms of necessity.

The concrete operational thinker can perform the transformations of inversion and reciprocity, the two reversibilities; but only the formal operational thinker can combine these transformations with other (positive) operations into a systematic whole and grasp the interrelationships among them, e.g. through proportionality.

Finally, the elementary school child for the most part reasons inductively, from particular instances to a generalization; the high school student can reason both inductively and deductively, from a generalization to further conclusions.

EXERCISE 2-7. Applications of Developmental Levels of Thought Processes

Teachers will emphasize different approaches on different grade levels depending on the developmental level of their students. Listed below are some specific approaches used in various subjects. Indicate whether they are more appropriate for the elementary school or the high school, i.e. for the level of concrete or formal operational thought.

	Concrete	Formal

1. A math teacher uses first pebbles and other objects, and then a number line and an abacus in teaching arithmetic operations. ____ ____

2. A math teacher has students work out proportion problems and algebraic equations requiring that they be able to give proof at each step of a solution. ____ ____

3. A math teacher has students measure different geometric forms and classify them as two- and three- dimensional or as three-, four-, or poly-sided figures. ____ ____

4. A math teacher juxtaposes addition–subtraction and multiplication–division to show the reversible relationship between them. ____ ____

5. A history teacher often shows filmstrips, pictures, takes his class on field trips, emphasizes famous persons and important events in history. ____ ____

6. A history teacher emphasizes causes of major events and important trends; he constantly asks questions about the significance and implications of different events and trends. ____ ____

7. A social studies teacher stresses the characteristics of peoples of different cultures as well as comparisons and relationships among them. ____ ____

8. A social studies teacher stresses the conflicts and interaction among environmental factors, economic forces, military strength, and human decisions in the study of contemporary international affairs. ____ ____

9. A social studies teacher has students play a city management game: given a certain amount of tax money, a specific population distinguished into socioeconomic groups, plus definite problems and issues facing the city council, what decisions should be made. ____ ____

10. A social studies teacher asks the following types of questions regarding proposed solutions to a problem facing the local community: how are the solutions similar; how are they different; which would be more effective and why? ____ ____

11. A science teacher has a variety of objects available for students to weigh, compare and put in order, to classify in various ways, to drop into a container of water to see if they sink or float. ____ ____

12. A science teacher encourages students to do experiments to discover what factors affect the growth of organisms, setting up hypotheses and testing them out. ____ ____

13. A science teacher has students classify animals and plants in various ways, forming their own taxonomy and even making cross classifications. ____ ____

14. An English teacher shows films of some great stories in literature and then has students discuss the theme of each story and what type of story it is. ____ ____

15. An English teacher stresses character analysis and the underlying, symbolic meaning in discussions of stories. ____ ____

Concrete   Formal

16. An English teacher has the students analyze the basic structure
of the sentences they have written and then has them make
some transformations, e.g. into passive, interrogative, etc.   ____   ____

17. An English teacher has the students analyze and make comparisons among the various figures of speech in literature, e.g. irony,
metaphor, paradox.   ____   ____

On the level of concrete operations, genuine learning depends on concrete, sensible experience. The elementary teacher, respecting the characteristics of this level, will use such techniques as: concrete objects, abacus (1), pictures, field trips (5) and the like. He also stresses famous persons and events (5), stories and their themes (14), and the characteristics of peoples of different cultures (7) rather than more abstract considerations.

Since the characteristic operations of elementary students are those of classifying and relating, the teacher has them classify things (3, 13) and examine relationships and comparisons between things (7, 11). In addition, they are not only able to study grammar and perform arithmetic operations, but they can also understand the basic transformations or reversibilities and so can transform sentences (16) and grasp reversible relationships between computations (4).

On the level of formal operations, students are conscious of proofs, causes, and reasons for what they are studying. Therefore high school teachers can well stress the causes and significance of events (6), the proof of solutions to problems (2), and the reasons for a character's actions (15).

More abstract thinking and the interrelating of variables is also possible, allowing for the study of symbolic meaning (15) and figures of speech (17) in literature, proportions and algebraic equations in math (2), and the interaction of various factors or influences in social studies (8).

Hypothetico-deductive reasoning plus the ability to control variables is also characteristic of the formal level and makes possible true experiments in science (12), if-then type activities (9) and the examination of possible solutions to problems (10) in social studies.

Conclusion

Combining the theories and research of both Guilford and Piaget, we can draw several conclusions. A teacher can expect elementary school pupils to be able to perform all of the intellectual processes: cognition, memory, divergent and convergent thinking plus evaluation. He will find that they will feel more at home with figural-concrete content, but that they can handle symbolic and semantic content if it is related to the concrete, perceptible realm of things. In terms of the product dimension of Guilford's schema of intellect, pre-school children and all first graders will be able to handle "units" of words, facts, etc.; but only those on the level of concrete operations will be able to group things into genuine classes and relations.

Although elementary school children can induce simple "systems," perform transformations and draw implications to some degree, the ability to handle more advanced interrelationships and systems such as proportionality plus more involved transformations and implications is developed only on the junior and senior high school level (Guilford states that hypothetico-deductive thinking mainly involves the cognition and production of implications). Similarly, the high school student can operate much more easily with symbolic and semantic content than the elementary pupil can; in fact purely symbolic and semantic material can only be grasped and manipulated by the student on the formal operational level.

The Measurement of Intelligence

What can you as a teacher do to measure the intelligence of your students? What should you be aware of in regard to any testing program that includes measures of intelligence?

First of all, by way of clarification, you should realize that general intelligence tests, scholastic aptitude tests and general classification tests are for all practical purposes the same thing. Intelligence tests that are used mainly for predictive purposes in a school are called scholastic aptitude tests; similarly when such tests are used to classify recruits in the armed services they are called general classification tests. Distinct from general intelligence tests, which usually provide only one or two scores, are the intelligence tests that measure several different abilities such as verbal comprehension, numerical reasoning, spatial relations, perceptual speed, and associative memory. They are called multiple aptitude batteries and provide a whole profile of scores for an individual.

For the most part, both the general intelligence tests and the multiple aptitude batteries that are currently available measure only cognition and to a lesser extent some convergent thinking or memory abilities. As we have mentioned earlier in the chapter, to get a full idea of intelligence, we should also use some measures of creative and critical thinking.

Although a counselor usually administers intelligence and aptitude tests, a teacher should be aware of some important points regarding intelligence testing so he can provide knowledgeable input into any decisions regarding the measurement of his students. In addition he himself can use some informal techniques for certain purposes. In this brief treatment, we will consider a few general principles plus some specific suggestions for measuring intelligence.

The first and most important consideration is that the *purpose* for which you want to use any measure determines the specific measure you use. This should be the guiding principle for both you and the counselor in any decisions regarding the testing of your students.

For instance, in the first grade if you would like to have some basis for dividing the pupils into reading groups, you would probably do better to use a reading readiness test rather than a strict intelligence test. You are mainly interested in finding out what their background and aptitude for reading is, and it is largely a reading readiness test that will tell you this.

The Metropolitan Readiness Test, for example, will provide you with scores on the following abilities of each pupil (plus others):

> Word meaning (a picture vocabulary test)—identifying the picture of a thing that the examiner names.
>
> Comprehension of sentences—selecting a picture that portrays a situation the examiner describes briefly.
>
> Visual discrimination—WAS | ASK WAS SAW (matching identical letter combinations).
>
> Knowledge of the alphabet—Mark the *m:* n   m   a   w

All of these factors are important for learning how to read and so you will want information on how your pupils rate on each of them. There are other important abilities as well, but the point is that scores on these types of abilities tell you more for your purpose than will "an I.Q. of 96." As a bonus, the Metropolitan includes a draw-a-man test which will allow you to get some indication of each pupil's general ability.

Again in the first or second grade, if you want to find out whether your pupils are ready to study arithmetic, you would do best to identify what abilities are necessary for arithmetic operations and then test accordingly. You will probably get more valuable information from a few simple Piaget-type measures than you will from an intelligence test score. With a little practice you can actually administer these measures to your pupils yourself (individually).

For instance, to understand any arithmetic operation, the pupil must have developed the genuine concept that number remains the same through a change in arrangement. A good way to measure the conservation of number is as follows:

1. Using stones, poker chips or pennies, arrange two rows of six items (a).
2. Get pupils to admit that there are the same items in both rows.
3. Spread top row out (b).
4. Ask "Are there more here (top) or here (bottom), or are they both the same?"

(a)   (b)

The child who fails to grasp the conservation of number is going to need more readiness work in conservation before he tackles arithmetic. Also since arithmetic computations require the operations of classification and ordering, you will want to test for these as well (but some further reading and practice is called for before you attempt to use the Piaget-type measures extensively).

In the middle grades, if you would like to group students for instructional purposes, you should first decide which is more important for this purpose: an indication of past achievement or a measure of basic aptitude. Since measures of past achievement have traditionally correlated more highly with course achievement than aptitude test scores have, you may prefer to group on the basis of school grades or a standardized achievement test rather than by intelligence test scores. Of course, since aptitude scores do predict achievement to some degree, you will do better to group on the basis of both measures, with greater emphasis on achievement than on intelligence test scores.

If you do decide to use an intelligence test, you should be aware of certain limitations, especially:

1. their white, middle-class orientation, which puts less economically advantaged students and members of minority groups at a distinct disadvantage;
2. their dependence on the reading ability of students, which puts the below average reader at a disadvantage;[4]
3. their moderate accuracy, which usually results in scores that are approximate rather than exact, e.g. an I.Q. of 110 usually means "Somewhere between 100 and 120";
4. their limited coverage in terms of intellectual abilities, i.e. they usually measure mainly cognition abilities and usually units, classes, and relations rather than systems, transformations, and implications.

With these considerations in mind, you will probably want to recommend that your counselor:

1. use an intelligence test that has a nonverbal as well as a verbal section; and
2. use additional measures, e.g. creative and critical thinking, to get a more complete picture of your students' intelligence (in the full sense).

For instance, the Lorge-Thorndike Intelligence Tests, which can be used from K-12, contain the following types of items (specifically on the test for middle grades), and give both a verbal and a nonverbal I.Q. score.

Verbal

Sentence completion: There's no book so _____ but something good may be found in it.

A. good   B. true   C. beautiful   D. bad   E. excellent

Verbal classification: find the word that belongs with
                    cotton   wool   silk

A. dress   B. sew   C. fibre   D. linen   E. cloth

Verbal Analogies: then → now: yesterday →

A. tomorrow   B. time   C. today   D. here   E. past

---

4. This point applies to the group paper-and-pencil tests that are used in schools, not to individual tests.

Vocabulary and arithmetic reasoning (word problems) subtests are also part of the verbal section.

Nonverbal

Figure classification: find the drawing that goes with the first three

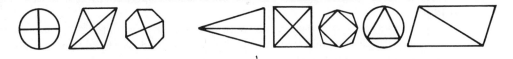

Number series: find the number that comes next in the order 2 4 3 5 4 →
A. 2   B. 3   C. 4   D. 5   E. 6
Figure analogies:

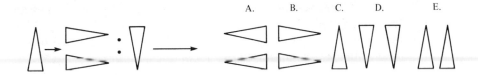

The Lorge-Thorndike is actually among the two or three best group intelligence tests available; it is also one of the few that give both a verbal and nonverbal I.Q. score. Again, if there is doubt about the language or reading ability of some of your students, you would do better to use the nonverbal score as a better estimate of their intelligence than the verbal score.

For a measure of divergent thinking see the suggestions on evaluating creative thinking ability in chapter 10. At present the available measures of critical thinking are extremely limited (cf. chapter 12).

In junior and senior high you may want to use (or recommend) a measure of several important aptitudes that relate to the various courses that your students are or will be taking. Your purposes could include: guidance of students in their selection of courses, grouping students into sections of a course (again in conjunction with achievement tests in the subject), and planning for individual differences in ability in your subject (enrichment or remedial work). The best available measures for your purpose will probably be the Differential Aptitude Tests for senior high, and their counterpart, the Academic Promise Tests for junior high. You have already seen some sample items from the DAT in exercise 2-2. You will want to give measures of creative and critical thinking in addition to the mainly cognition tests of the DAT.[5]

---

5. Some recent research has shown that transformation abilities are very important for many school subjects (Hoepfner 1969; Hoepfner, Guilford and Bradley 1970). Convergent production of transformations is measured for instance by the "needle" item in exercise 2-4, p. 34; however, tests for intellectual abilities involving transformations are not generally available in published form.

EXERCISE 2-8. Systematic Observation of Intellectual Processes in the Classroom

Observe a class on any level—elementary, secondary or college—concentrating on the teacher question—student answer sequences. Categorize the questions—answers according to whether they activate cognition, memory, divergent thinking, convergent thinking, or evaluation. The summary of the process dimension of Guilford's schema on page 38 plus the examples on pages 21-22 will be of help to you.

In arranging to observe a class be certain that you stress to the principal and especially the teacher that you are simply analyzing and categorizing question—answer sequences; you are not evaluating the teacher in any way.

In class your instructor may wish to:

1. have students give examples of questions—answers for each process with a view to clarifying the meaning of each as well as seeing further how each is applied in practice;
2. discuss whether some questions could or do activate more than one process;
3. tabulate the frequency with which the five types of questions are used in the classrooms sampled.

EXERCISE 2-9. Application of Intellectual Processes in Teaching

Select a topic in your field. Describe in a paragraph for each how you would teach it:

1. if you wanted to stress mainly cognition
2. if you wanted to involve mainly memory
3. if you wanted to engage your students' divergent thinking abilities
4. if you felt the topic would be better taught by supplying data and having students think convergently
5. if you wanted to involve mainly their evaluation abilities.

EXERCISE 2-10. Application of Developmental Aspects of Intelligence

Select another topic in your field. Describe how you would teach it:

1. if you were teaching an average class of fourth-grade pupils
2. if you were teaching tenth-grade students of average ability.

List the activities that you would use in each case, basing them on the characteristics of the thought processes on either level.

Suggested Readings

Quantitative Analysis of Intelligence

Anastasi, Anne, ed. *Individual Differences.* New York: Wiley, 1965.

Anastasi, Anne. *Psychological Testing.* New York: Macmillan, 1968.

Guilford, J. P. *The Nature of Human Intelligence.* New York: McGraw-Hill, 1967.

Vernon, P. E. *The Structure of Human Abilities.* London: Methuen, 1961.

Qualitative Analysis of Intelligence

Elkind, D. *Children and Adolescents: Interpretative Essays on Jean Piaget.* New York: Oxford, 1970.

Flavell, J. H. *The Developmental Psychology of Jean Piaget.* Princeton, N. J.: Van Nostrand, 1963.

Ginsburg, H. and Opper, S. *Piaget's Theory of Intellectual Development: An Introduction.* Englewood Cliffs, N. J.: Prentice-Hall, 1969.

Gorman, R. M. *Discovering Piaget: A Guide for Teachers.* Columbus, Ohio: Merrill, 1972.

Inhelder, Barbel and Piaget, J. *The Growth of Logical Thinking from Childhood to Adolescence.* New York: Basic Books, 1958.

Piaget, J. *Psychology of Intelligence.* London: Routledge & Kegan Paul, 1950.

Piaget, J. and Inhelder, Barbel. *The Psychology of the Child.* New York: Basic Books, 1969.

part two

Learning:
Basic Considerations

Now that some insight into students' intellectual abilities and operations has been gained our attention may be turned to learning, specifically to the many aspects and types of learning that are important in education.

In this section several basic considerations regarding classroom learning will be treated: the nature of the learning process in general, some contemporary issues regarding approaches to classroom learning, and the all important question of motivation for learning. These basic questions are treated first because to a large extent they underlie all of the specific types of learning that will be considered later.

3

Theories of
Learning

A teacher is mainly concerned about helping students learn. But what is learning? How can we define it? How can the learning process best be explained? And if there are differing explanations, how do they differ? Even more important for us, how does an explanation or theory of learning work in the classroom?

The Nature of Learning

You have learned many things during your lifetime: knowledge, information, skills, how to react in different situations, how to solve problems, etc. Taking into account all of your learning experiences, how would you define learning?

You would probably include in your definition at least some of the following elements: (1) learning as a process, (2) the acquisition of knowledge and skills, (3) a change in behavior, and (4) self-activity.

Although in everyday speech we sometimes speak of "a man of learning" and "much learning" as a product of man's activity, in the context of psychology learning is defined and treated as a *process* that goes on within the person.

To be comprehensive and encompass all of the different kinds of learning, learning must be defined in a way that will include both the *acquisition* of knowledge and skills and a *change* in behavior.

Finally, learning is accomplished basically through the *activity* of the learner, e.g., practice, observation, thinking, and sometimes with the help of another (a teacher). It is distinguished from growth and development which is a process in which our abilities change mainly as a result of the natural process of maturation, rather than through our own efforts.

Learning then can be defined as the process by which knowledge and skills are acquired and behavior is changed through self-activity.

Learning Theories in General

Although most psychologists agree on a broad definition of learning, they are frequently in disagreement when it comes to explaining the learning process. Explanations or theories of learning are valuable, however, for they serve many functions: (1) they attempt to explain how learning takes place; (2) they summarize a large amount of experimental knowledge about learning; (3) they provide a framework for further research on learning; and (4) they provide a basis for various approaches and methods used in teaching.

EXERCISE 3-1.   Learning Theories in Classroom Practice

Traditionally there have been two different approaches used in classroom learning, each one based on a different theory of learning. Below are several contrasting strategies representing each of the two approaches to learning. Analyze the various strategies and identify the characteristics of the different approaches.

I	II
Area of a rectangle is taught by giving students the formula: Area = base X height	Area of a rectangle is taught stressing the number of square inches in the rectangle:

I	II
In first-grade readers, the most commonly used words are repeated several times in a story.	In first-grade readers, the stories are made as interesting as possible, sometimes made up by the pupils themselves.
Grammar rules are stated; students are questioned on them and then given workbook exercises to do.	In grammar, rules are induced from specific examples and then related to the several main functions of language.
In science, students follow instructions in lab manuals for experiments.	In science, students experiment and discover relationships.
In arithmetic, the students study the multiplication table.	Students use an abacus to understand arithmetic computations.
In geography, important facts about major cities are identified and learned.	In geography, the nature and characteristics of cities are analyzed, then important facts related to the characteristics.
In poetry, the types of imagery and rules for meter are given and then applied.	In poetry, students write their own poems and then analyze the meter and imagery involved.

Listed below are several characteristics of the approaches exemplified above. Check whether each is related more to the approaches in column I or those in column II.

	I	II
Understanding, explanation emphasized	___	___
Formulas, material given	___	___
Thinking processes involved	___	___
Memory stressed	___	___
Facts, specifics, rules emphasized	___	___
Relationships, generalizations, reasons stressed	___	___
Discovery-oriented	___	___
Exposition-oriented	___	___
Students are active, creative	___	___
Students are receptive, directed	___	___

The approach exemplified in column I above emphasizes specific facts and concepts, rules to be remembered, material presented by the teacher who is expository and directive in the learning process. The approach illustrated in column II emphasizes understanding, relationships, thinking, discovery, and activity on the part of the student.

The type of learning theory that underlies the approaches in column I is the stimulus-response theory of the behaviorists and connectionists. The type of learning theory underlying the emphases illustrated in column II is the cognitive theory of the Gestalt psychologists and others.

On the basis of what you have induced so far, see if you can identify certain characteristics of the S-R and cognitive theories.

	S-R	Cognitive
1. Learning is behavior change or habit formation: we learn responses.	___	___
2. Learning is mainly the acquisition of knowledge: we learn ideas, relationships.	___	___
3. Processes between a stimulus object and our knowledge of it are stressed, particularly that of organizing.	___	___
4. Connections between situations and our responses to them are stressed.	___	___
5. The organism is active in learning; we interact with objects in the environment.	___	___
6. The organism is neutral in the learning process; we react to stimuli in the environment.	___	___

Statements 1, 4 and 6 are characteristic of the S-R theories; statements 2, 3 and 5 are representative of the cognitive theories.

For each of the two main families of learning theories that are of current interest and relevance to classroom learning, we will consider the philosophical and scientific background of the theory and the general view of the learning process proposed by the theory. Then we will examine two representative theorists within each family and show how each position works out in practice. Finally, it might be helpful for you to consider a few possible ways of reacting to the multiplicity of views about the learning process.

Stimulus-Response Theory

The stimulus-response approach to learning has its roots in the philosophy of associationism held by John Locke, Thomas Hobbes, Alexander Bain, and other British philosophers of the empiricist tradition. Several key tenets of association-ism are the following:

1. Our knowledge is derived from sense experience.
2. Ideas are objects implanted in the mind; they form the elements of mental activity.
3. Ideas can be combined through association according to the laws of contiguity, similarity, and contrast.[1] For example, seeing a sailor might remind you of ocean travel (contiguity) if you have been on a ship before, or perhaps of a soldier (similarity), or maybe of a landlubber (contrast).

The scientific background of the stimulus-response theory is found mainly in the work of the Russian physiologist Ivan Pavlov (1849–1936). Pavlov was concerned with studying animal reflexes, not only natural reflexes such as the knee jerk, but also reflexes that could be introduced into an animal's behavior through a process he called *conditioning*. For instance, in his famous saliva experiment with dogs, he would ring a bell just before food was presented; after a number of trials, the dog would salivate when the bell was rung even though food was not given. Hence through the process of conditioning, salivation (conditioned response) was now elicited by the bell alone (conditioned stimulus).

In their emphasis on connections or associations, the S-R theorists are direct descendants of the British associationists; in their claim that connections occur through a conditioning process most of them are also indebted to Pavlov.

Learning, according to the S-R theorists, consists in forming a connection between a stimulus and a response. A stimulus may be a sensation, a situation, or a problem; a response is any observable behavior. The connections between them are called by a variety of names, such as bonds, habits, or conditioned responses.

S-R theorists concentrate mainly on responses emitted by an individual and on the conditions that influence those responses. For them, learning is basically

---

1. These laws of association were first expressed by Aristotle and taken over by the British empiricists; however, they represent a very minor part of Aristotle's philosophy of man and knowledge, so that the stimulus-response theory cannot really be said to be based on Aristotle as some have claimed.

a matter of habit formation: we learn responses. Although not entirely passive, the learner for the most part reacts to the stimuli in the environment.

The S-R theorists allow for understanding of what is learned, but in their formal analysis of the learning process they do not usually include such terms as "understanding" or "knowledge" for at least two reasons: (1) they want to explain learning in the simplest, most economical terms possible, and (2) they are convinced that more complex human processes can be understood best in terms of the simpler elements of which they are composed.

Within the S-R family of learning theories there are several emphases: (1) learning simply through the stimulus and response occurring together, (2) learning primarily through being rewarded, and (3) the many factors that influence learning and behavior.

The first view, expounded chiefly by Edwin R. Guthrie (1886–1959), is rather simplistic and has not offered as many insights for classroom teaching as some of the other emphases. The third view, the systematic theory of Clark L. Hull (1884–1952), has been extremely productive in terms of laboratory experimentation but has provided few practical applications for education. The reward-centered position on the other hand, originally formulated by Edward Lee Thorndike and currently championed by B. F. Skinner, has offered many significant applications for classroom learning. This position will be examined more fully later.

Cognitive Theory

The cognitive approach to learning has its roots in the philosophical tradition of Aristotle. Some of the relevant tenets of this tradition are the following:

1. Our knowledge is derived from sense experience.
2. Ideas result from our abstracting the natures (what things are) from things that we have experienced with our senses.
3. Knowledge consists in the understanding of the relationships between ideas.

The scientific source of at least some cognitive learning theories is the work of the Gestalt[2] psychologists in the field of perception. Through such experiments as the following the Gestaltists identified some major principles of perception.

Figure perceived as a triangle to illustrate closure

Dots perceived as a pattern to illustrate perception of wholes or groups

Ambiguous design to illustrate figure-ground relationship

2. "Gestalt" means form or shape, pattern, configuration.

Some of the major laws of perception derived from such experiments are:

Closure: things are seen as a totality and not piecemeal

Similarity: things that are alike tend to be perceived as wholes or to fall into groups

Figure-ground relationship: a thing is perceived against a background, i.e. in a context.

In sum, the Gestaltists hold that the organism perceives organized wholes—not just elements or parts—and that these wholes, since they possess organization, represent more than just the sum of their parts.

The carry-over of the Aristotelian emphasis on understanding and the Gestalt findings regarding the perception of organized wholes is evident in the cognitive approach to learning. Learning, according to the cognitive theorists, involves the understanding of relationships and interrelationships among ideas. A relationship consists of two or more ideas united in a way that gives them meaning; an interrelationship is simply an ordered group of relations, ideas, and things (most often it is called a structure).

Cognitive theorists are mainly interested in the internal processes that man uses in dealing with the complexity of his environment and in the resulting cognitive structures that exist in his mind. For them, learning is basically the acquisition of knowledge: we learn ideas, relations, and structures. The learner is very active as he interacts with and organizes the objects in his environment.

Unlike the S-R theorists, the cognitive theorists attempt to explain the learning process mainly in terms of its larger, more complex components. They will include such terms as "understanding" and "organization" at the heart of their theory, claiming that even though these terms may not have a directly observable referent, they are necessary to explain adequately their research findings on the learning process.

The most important of the early cognitive theorists was the classical Gestalt group of Max Wertheimer (1880–1943), Wolfgang Kohler (1887–1959), and Kurt Koffka (1886–1941), plus the "field theorist" Kurt Lewin (1890–1947). Although they taught and worked in Germany originally, they all in turn eventually settled in the United States. Of the several leading contemporary cognitive theorists, the most outstanding is Jean Piaget (1896–   ).

Since Wertheimer, more than any of the Gestalt triumvirate, was interested in classroom learning, we will examine his views as an example of an early cognitive theorist. Even though Piaget is not really a learning theorist, he has delineated several important concepts regarding the learning process more clearly than any other cognitive theorist; hence we will also examine his position on learning as representing a contemporary view in the cognitive tradition.

EXERCISE 3-2. Classical Learning Theory in Action

Examine this brief sequence in which two students grapple with a new problem in arithmetic. See if you can discern what approaches and processes are at work in either case.

Pupils who have previously studied addition and subtraction with one- and two-place numbers and multiplication with one-place numbers are given the following problems:

Multiply	Multiply	Multiply
32	43	34
23	22	26

| I | II |

I

S. We haven't had these before. Let me see. (He tries adding 32 + 23 and gets 55.)

T. No. You have to multiply.

S. (Multiplies 3 × 2 and then 2 × 3, getting 66, and in the second problem 2 × 3 and 2 × 4, getting 86, and in the third 6 × 4 and 2 × 3, getting 624.) Is that right?

T. No.

S. Well, I can't figure it out. I don't know what to do.

II

S. This is quite complicated. Can I try an easier problem, like 14 × 3?

T. Yes.

S. Now if I have 4 × 3, this means 4, 4, 4, or 12. This is the same as 10 + 2 only put together differently, 4 + 4 + 2 plus 2. Now 14 × 3 means the same thing as 10 × 3 plus 4 × 3. If you do, you get 30 + 12 or 42.

Now let's see, the first problem, 32 × 23. It means 2 × 3 and 30 × 3; 6 and 90 is 96. Then with 20: 2 × 20 and 30 × 20; 40 and 600 or 640. Added together you get 736. So 32 × 23 is 736. You can do the others the same way.

Check which sequence possesses the following characteristics.

	I	II
1. Approaching a problem looking for the inner relationships.	____	____
2. Approaching a problem in terms of what the student has learned previously.	____	____
3. Seeing the relation between whole and parts.	____	____
4. Emphasizing the elements in the situation without relating them to the whole.	____	____
5. Responding to the problem by using responses that the elements of the problem evoke.	____	____
6. Solving the problem through a realization of what "being equal" entails, i.e. you can change a number without changing its arithmetical amount.	____	____

The first student approached the problem in terms of what he had learned previously, i.e. addition and one-place multiplication (2). He keyed on the elements of the situation (4) and responded in a way that these elements led him to (5).

The second student approached the problem looking for inner relationships, viz. the relation between two-place numbers and the one-place numbers he was more familiar with (1). He saw that the whole could be broken down into parts and solved the problem accordingly, always with an ultimate eye on the whole (3). Specifically, he was able to solve the problem through the realization that he could change a number around without affecting its basic value (6).

This particular example plus the above analyses are taken from the writings of the two classical learning theorists that we are now about to examine. The original problems, how the first student attempted to solve them, plus the analysis of his efforts are based directly on Thorndike's *Educational Psychology*, 1913. The second student's solution of the same problems plus the analysis of the process were taken from Wertheimer's *Productive Thinking*, 1945. Let's take a more systematic look at the positions of each of these theorists.

Classical Learning Theorists

For each of the classical learning theorists mentioned we will (1) provide a sample of the experimental basis for his position, (2) examine his basic view of the learning process, (3) explain some further characteristics or laws of learning that are an integral part of his position, and (4) draw some implications of his theory for education.

Thorndike's Connectionism

Edward Lee Thorndike was the founder of educational psychology; he was also a pioneer in the field of intelligence testing. But above all he was an outstanding researcher and theorist in the realm of animal and human learning. As such, he did more to influence the course of classroom learning in America than any other man, probably even more than his colleague at Teachers College, Columbia University, John Dewey.

Thorndike derived his view of learning from some interesting experiments with animals. His best known study was done with a cat in a puzzle box similar to that shown in figure 3-1.

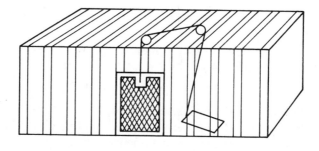

Figure 3-1. *Puzzle Box Used by Thorndike in Animal Experiments*

He put a hungry cat in the box with a small piece of fish or meat just outside. The cat's "task" was to get out of the box by depressing a lever or some other device. At first the cat would try to squeeze through the slats, claw at the door or the wire grate, etc. Eventually she would step on the lever (seemingly by accident), the door would slide up and she would get out. The experiment would be repeated with the cat behaving as she did in the first trial only tripping the lever much sooner. After several trials the cat's activity would center around the lever and the useless clawings would be eliminated. After about twenty trials, she would trip the lever immediately. A typical learning curve for this type of experiment is shown in figure 3-2. From this and similar experiments with dogs, chickens, monkeys, and other animals, Thorndike derived a basic learning pattern that he said underlay all learning.

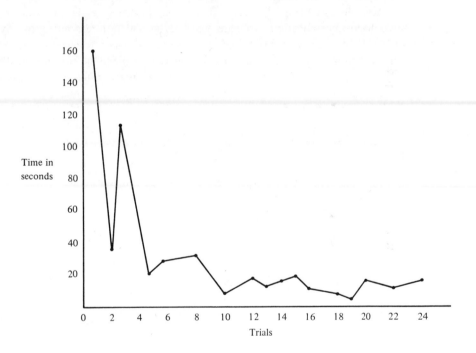

Figure 3-2. *Learning Curve of a Cat*

The factors involved in this sort of learning, called connection-forming, are:

a situation or problem,
an organism whose inner conditions can be changed,
multiple responses or trials,
selection of the correct or appropriate response,
association and connection of this response to the situation. (Thorndike 1913)

Learning for Thorndike—both animal and human—was a matter of establishing connections or "bonds" between a situation and an impulse to action, between a problem and a solution. The most characteristic form was trial and error learning or learning by selecting and connecting. The pattern again is:

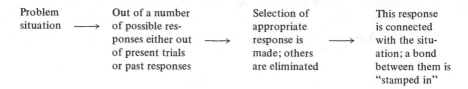

| Problem situation | $\longrightarrow$ | Out of a number of possible responses either out of present trials or past responses | $\longrightarrow$ | Selection of appropriate response is made; others are eliminated | $\longrightarrow$ | This response is connected with the situation; a bond between them is "stamped in" |

How does this relate to classroom learning? Recall the example of two-place multiplication given above.

According to Thorndike, the first child, like most children, could not do two-place multiplication problems because he had not responded to anything like it before and so did not possess the bonds necessary to respond correctly to the situation. Even if the child had solved the problems he would have done so because he applied the already acquired rules for place-value and multiplying. In sum, for Thorndike, all learning consists of selecting and connecting.

What are some of the factors that influence learning? The main factor is reward which results in satisfaction, which in turn strengthens the connection. As Thorndike says:

> When a modifiable connection is made between a situation and a response and is accompanied or followed by a satisfying state of affairs, the strength of that connection is increased. When an annoying state of affairs goes with or follows a connection, the strength of that connection is decreased. (Thorndike 1913, p. 71)

For example in the classroom, the question of state capitals is being studied:

T. What is the capital of North Dakota?
S_1. Fargo.
T. No.
S_2. Bismark.
T. Right.

      A week later:

T. What is the capital of North Dakota?
S_2. Bismark.

The "right" of the teacher served as a reward and set up a "satisfying state of affairs" in the student. The result was a strengthening of the bond between state and capital, as witness the correct answer the following week.

Thorndike called this principle the *law of effect*. Although in his earlier writings this was just one among several basic laws of learning, in his later writings it became the major law of learning, with other factors dependent on it for their effectiveness. Also, in his later writings, he eliminated the negative or "annoying" phase of the law and emphasized simply that rewards bring about learning.

A second factor that can influence the forming of connections is practice or "exercise." As Thorndike states: "When a modifiable connection is made between a situation and a response, the strength of that connection is, other things being equal, increased; if it is not made over a length of time, its strength is decreased" (adapted from Thorndike 1913, p. 70). It should be emphasized that practice alone, without reward, will be ineffective; only rewarded practice will strengthen a bond.

There were other subsidiary laws of learning such as readiness, belongingness, and associative shifting (conditioning), but they are not essential enough to Thorndike's theory to go into here. In fact his theory of connection forming can be summed up as he himself did in suggesting a general rule for education: "Put together (and exercise) what should go together, and reward desirable connections."

In practice, Thorndike's theory of learning resulted in several widely used approaches in the classroom.

1. The emphasis on specific connections to be formed led to a detailed analysis of the facts, words, and specific skills that are to be learned. In reading, the most frequently used words are identified and used over and over again. Thorndike and Lorge's famous list of basic words and the basal readers which used these words repeatedly are direct applications of this aspect of the theory. In arithmetic, the specific facts of addition, subtraction, and multiplication are identified, memorized and practiced without emphasis on the understanding of the processes involved or without attention to the meaning of number, sets, types of numbers, etc.

2. The law of effect led to the liberal use of concrete rewards, stars, turkeys, Christmas trees and the like stamped on papers, points given for good work, plus the constant use of "That's right," "That's good," etc.

3. The law of exercise led to much repetition, practice, and drill in all subjects: spelling, grammar, history, as well as reading and arithmetic.

Classical Gestalt Theory

Of the major Gestalt psychologists, Wertheimer, Kohler and Koffka, the one who has dealt most directly with the kind of learning that goes on in the classroom is Max Wertheimer. His work was at once a rebuttal of the elementistic analysis of the learning process championed by Thorndike and an exposition of a more holistic approach to learning that was in keeping with the Gestalt research on perception. In his *Productive Thinking*, Wertheimer presents several experiments on learning, which are more analyses of his experiences and those of others (Galileo, Gauss, etc.) than actual experiments. The most famous of these is the area of the parallelogram.

Wertheimer gives the account of the teacher who first taught his students to find the area of a rectangle by multiplying the two sides together, and then taught them how to find the area of a parallelogram. He dropped perpendiculars from the two corners (a), established the equality of the respective angles and lines, and concluded that the area is equal to the base times the height—as in the case of the rectangle. Then he had the class do a number of similar problems, which they completed successfully and without difficulty.

But Wertheimer was not satisfied that the students really understood what they were doing. He was troubled: had they grasped the idea or simply repeated the formula blindly? He asked the teacher if he could give them a problem. The teacher, obviously proud of his class, consented. So Wertheimer drew a parallelogram on the board (b).

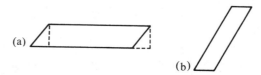

Most of the students were stumped. In trying to find the area, some dropped the perpendiculars (a); others claimed that the area was equal to the base times the height (correct, but they couldn't explain it); finally, a few turned their papers, dropped perpendiculars (b), and solved it in their usual way. The teacher believed that the problem was unfair because it was so different (actually it was the same figure turned 45 degrees).

To a second class Wertheimer himself taught the area of the parallelogram in another way. He handed out pieces of paper in the forms of parallelograms (c) and asked the children if they could find the area. After some thought, several of the children asked for scissors: one cut the left side and put it on the right (d) to make a rectangle; another cut it in the center and made a rectangle (e). Other children simply drew lines and "transferred" one side to the other in their minds and solved it (f).

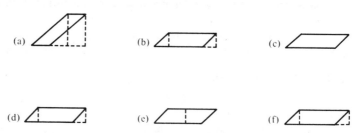

What was involved in this second approach? Wertheimer explained it in terms of a process that involves the following factors and operations: There was a

> regrouping with regard to the whole, a reorganization or fitting; the factors of inner relatedness and of inner requirements were discovered, realized and followed up. The steps were taken, the operations were clearly done in view of the whole figure and the whole situation. They arose by virtue of their part-function, not by blind recall or blind trail; their content, their direction, their application grew out of the requirements of the problem. Such a process is not just a sum of several steps or operations, but the

growth of one line of thinking out of the gaps in the situation with a view to getting at the good inner relatedness. (Wertheimer 1945, p. 49)

Learning, then, according to Wertheimer, involves: (1) a grouping into organized *wholes,* (2) a realization of the inner-relatedness or *structure* among the parts of that whole, and (3) an awareness of the meaning and function of the parts of the whole or of the steps to the solution—in a word, *understanding.* The most characteristic form of human learning is the understanding of relationships, or as the Gestaltists call it, "insight."

The pattern of the learning process is as follows:

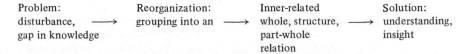

Problem: disturbance, gap in knowledge $\longrightarrow$ Reorganization: grouping into an $\longrightarrow$ Inner-related whole, structure, part-whole relation $\longrightarrow$ Solution: understanding, insight

Recall the second student in the above multiplication example who figured out the solution by realizing the relation between one- and two-place numbers. According to Wertheimer, if a child learns arithmetic operations, not through recipes and blind connections, but by being aware of the meaning and the results of the operations, then he will learn them with understanding, i.e. he will grasp the inner relation between the operations and their results. In sum, all genuine human learning involves insight or the understanding of relationships, particularly the relationships between parts and whole and between means and consequences.

What are some of the other characteristics of the learning process? First, learning situations usually start with a problem and hence give rise to a certain disturbance or tension at the gap between the problem and the solution. Second, the laws of perception suggest some further qualities of the learning process, although it should be noted that the Gestaltists tend to apply them without too much concern about establishing them directly as laws of learning.

The law of pregnance,[3] for instance, suggests that the striving for solution tends toward a "good gestalt," an organized pattern, a clear and orderly explanation. In this connection, Katona's famous experiments (inspired by Wertheimer) showed that when a person understands the organizing principle underlying a problem, his retention of what he learns is improved and his capacity to learn new, related tasks is also improved (Katona 1940).

Another important law is the law of closure, which when applied to learning states that the person tends toward bridging the gap between the problem and its solution, toward bringing the parts (means and end) into relation with one another. This tendency toward closure or equilibrium is the Gestalt counterpart of the law of effect: the reaching of the solution to a problem is satisfying to the person and ends the tension that the problem had caused.

The Gestalt approach to learning offers many implications for teaching. The

---

3. More popularly, *pragnanz* (German).

emphasis on problematic situations in learning leads the teacher to stress the essential aspects of a problem and to point out the gaps that need filling. This is both a good motivator because of the tension or disturbance set up and a good beginning toward a solution because of the awareness of the essentials of the problem.

The Gestalt concern with wholes leads to the use of general objectives for a unit or course, e.g., "a knowledge of the main characteristices of urban societies" rather than more specific behavioral objectives. On the one hand, this helps give organization to a course as a whole; on the other hand, such objectives are in keeping with the Gestalt emphasis on understanding rather than on observable behavior.

Similarly, the Gestalt-oriented teacher emphasizes the organization of a topic or a course, for instance through a course outline that shows the structure of the course as a whole including the interrelationship of the various topics. In the same vein, he treats each topic as a whole rather than an assemblage of specific elements. For instance, at the beginning of a unit or topic he gives an overview so that students can get a general idea of the whole topic, and at the end provides a review so that they can see how everything fits together as a whole again.

Finally, the teacher emphasizes understanding and the discovery of meaning; he asks penetrating questions and requires proof for statements. Negatively, he does not use step-by-step recipes, mechanical procedures and drill; he also avoids arbitrary or dogmatic explanations and the expository presentation of solutions. His concern is for the students' grasping relationships and reasons for things, in a word, insight.

Summary of Classical Learning Theorists

A short contrasting summary of what we have seen regarding Thorndike's connectionism and Wertheimer's Gestalt position should be helpful. The two classic theorists differ as follows:

	Thorndike	Wertheimer
Overall emphasis	elements	wholes
Learning process	selecting and connecting	grouping into organized wholes
Result of learning	connections between S and R	insight
Problems solved through	ideas and rules learned in past	present relationships seen
Motivation in learning	reward	tension and closure
Important condition	repetition	orderly explanation

EXERCISE 3-3. Contemporary Learning Theories in Action

Before we get into an analysis of the two leading contemporary representatives of the S-R and cognitive theories of learning, let's consider two strategies for teaching first graders multiple classification that are directly based on their views. The approaches are derived directly from the views of each theorist we will consider: one reflects the position of B. F. Skinner, the other that of Jean Piaget. Analyze the transcripts and try to characterize the approaches by identifying each with some of the statements given below.

In two first-grade classes the following cut-outs are provided to each pupil (figure 3-3). (Teachers have large cardboard cut-outs available.) The objective in each class is to have the pupils classify the forms in different ways. But the approaches used in each class are quite different.

Figure 3-3.

I	II
T. (Holds up large square) This is a square. What is it?	T. You all have different cut-outs in front of you. Remember that we used to put these together to make different things. Now let's do something different. See if you can group them together in different ways. See if some of them belong together in any way.
S. A square.	
T. Again, all together. This is a _____	
S. Square.	
T. (Nods "yes") What color is it?	
S. White.	S. (Move cut-outs around. Some group them according to color dividing them into red and white. Others group them into squares, circles, and triangles. Some have difficulty grouping them in any consistent way. A few group them according to size as well as shape and color.)
T. So it's a white square. What is it?	
S. A white square.	
T. Right (holds up a red square). What is this?	
S. A square.	
T. What color is it?	
S. Red.	
T. So it's a _____	
S. Red square.	T. (Goes around inserting questions and comments to individual students.) Do you know what this is called? This is a square. This is a triangle. How about this one, does that belong? Can you see anything that's the same in any of these? Are there any other ways you can group them?
T. Good (holds up small white square). How about this? What is it?	
S. A white square.	
T. Right. It's a white square. Is it big or small?	
S. Small.	
T. So it's a small white square. What is it?	T. Why did you put these together? Is

S. A small white square.

T. How about this (holds up small red square)?

S. A small red square.

T. Good. OK, we've seen some squares (holds up two in each hand). What do I have in my hand?

S. Squares.

T. What do I have in this hand?

S. White squares.

T. And in this hand?

S. Red squares.

T. Right (changes squares). Now what do I have?

S. Small squares.

T. And in this hand?

S. Big squares.

T. Good. (She then goes through similar sequence with circles and triangles, moving faster.)

T. All right, we've seen some squares, some circles, and some triangles. Now, at your seats, see how many different ways you can put your own figures into groups.

S. (Most group them according to shape first, some according to color. Most succeed in grouping in these two ways. Some also group according to size.)

T. (Goes around checking and inserting questions) Any other ways? How about big and little? (at end) That's great. I'm proud of you. O.K. you've learned to group different shapes in several ways—by shape, by color, and also by size. You all did very well.

this the same or different? (After awhile asks some students) How about size, does that mean anything?

T. (Encourages students who have grouped them in all three ways to work with those who are having trouble) How are your groups different than his? (When he judges they have worked long enough he says the following) All right, how many ways have we grouped these cut-outs? What's one way?

S. By color: red and white.

T. And another way?

S. Into squares, circles, and those with three sides.

T. And another way?

S. Into big and small.

T. So we can group things in different ways depending on what is the same about them. If we group them by color then shape and size are different. It doesn't matter as long as we get every one of the same color in the same group. Right? And when we group them by shape, we have one group of squares, one group of circles, and one group of triangles. Does it matter what color they are?

S. No.

T. Or how big they are?

S. No.

T. And how about when you group them by size?

S. You put them into big and little. It doesn't matter what shape they are, or color either.

T. Good. We've learned a lot about how to group things today, haven't we? We'll do this some other day, only using a lot of different things and pictures of things.

Indicate which of the above approaches is characterized by each of the following statements.

	I	II

1. Teacher leads students step by step to the final objective of forming groupings.   ____ ____

I   II

2. Teacher has students get right to the task of forming groupings more or less by themselves.   ____ ____

3. Lesson was more verbal-oriented, with students encouraged to make responses out loud.   ____ ____

4. Lesson was more thought-oriented, with students encouraged to figure things out themselves.   ____ ____

5. One of the teacher's main functions was to get students to manipulate the objects that were available.   ____ ____

6. One of main functions of the teacher was to give regular approval and praise for correct responses.   ____ ____

7. Considerable repetition is used as students move gradually to the idea of classifying in different ways.   ____ ____

8. Focus seemed to be on the students' forming a basic idea of classifying which will be referred to in the future.   ____ ____

9. The direction of the lesson was from teacher to student and student to teacher, probably best characterized by "back and forth between student and teacher."   ____ ____

10. The direction of the lesson was mainly between student and objects plus sometimes between teacher and student and even student and student, probably best characterized by "an interaction, both physical and social."   ____ ____

In the first case the teacher led the pupils step by step to the objective (1), having them make correct responses verbally (5), giving regular rewards in the form of approval and praise (4), and using a liberal amount of repetition in her teaching (7). The direction was clearly between student and teacher (9).

In the second case the teacher had the students form the grouping by themselves (2) through their manipulation of the forms that were made available (3); the focus of the lesson was on the students' forming the basic idea of classifying (8) by thinking things out by themselves (6). The direction was one of interaction among students, objects, and teacher (10).

The first sequence was a direct application of B. F. Skinner's theory of learning;[4] the second was a typical lesson based on Piaget's view of learning.[5] We will now consider each of these theorists in turn.

Contemporary Learning Theorists

For each of the main contemporary representatives of the S-R and cognitive learning theories we will (1) examine the meaning of the basic concepts that go to make up his theory, (2) analyze how these basic concepts are incorporated into an explanation of the learning process, (3) suggest several applications to

4. Cf. Bereiter and Englemann 1966.
5. Cf. Silberman 1970.

classroom learning that are implicit in the theory, and finally (4) briefly compare each theory with its classical counterpart.

B. F. Skinner

Following in the tradition of Thorndike with the emphasis on reward as the main factor affecting learning, is B. F. Skinner, professor of psychology at Harvard University, and by far the most influential of the contemporary behaviorists. Although his extensive laboratory experimentation has been conducted on subhuman organisms, he has continually shown interest in applying his findings to man's life in society, to psychotherapy and especially to education. His particular concern is not just to understand human behavior but also to control it, to modify it toward desirable ends.

Skinnerian learning involves the acquisition or change of behavior. The most important single principle of the learning process is *reinforcement*. We learn a response if it is immediately followed by some reward. Regarding his position Skinner states:

> The student is more than a receiver of information. He must take some kind of action. . . . But the action demanded of the student is not some sort of mental association of contiguous experiences. It is more objective and, fortunately, more controllable than that. To acquire behavior, *the student must engage in behavior.* (Skinner 1961)

And further,

> Special techniques have been designed to arrange the relations that prevail between behavior on the one hand and the consequences of that behavior on the other—with the result that a much more effective control of behavior has been achieved. . . . We have made sure that effects (rewards) *do* occur and that they occur under conditions which are optimal for producing the changes called learning. Once we have arranged the particular type of consequence called reinforcement, our techniques permit us to shape up the behavior of an organism almost at will. . . . [In fact] a significant change in behavior is often obvious as the result of a single reinforcement. (Skinner 1954)

There are several main concepts in Skinner's view of learning: operant, reinforcement, and shaping.

An *operant* is a response or type of behavior of a student: an action he performs, a word he says, or a statement he makes. It is not elicited by a specific stimulus as in reflex behavior; it is rather emitted by the organism, often in the presence of certain stimulus-type conditions (e.g., a door to be opened, a question to be answered) that perhaps encourage but do not necessarily evoke the response. It is called operant because it is behavior that "*operates* upon our environment to generate consequences" (Skinner 1953). It is distinguished from respondent behavior which is determined by a specific stimulus.

In the act of learning, it is important that the individual perform the behavior to be acquired. For instance, in the above teaching sequence the teacher asked questions and offered incomplete statements that called for the pupils to emit a response verbally. In Skinner and Holland's programmed psychology course a typical unit is:

A technical term for "reward" is reinforcement.

To "reward" an organism with food is to _____ it with food.

reinforce

If the response is followed immediately by a reward—a nod or a smile, "That's good," money, a privilege—then the probability of the individual's making a similar response in the future is increased. But the *reinforcement* or receipt of the reward must be immediate; a delay of over a few seconds will diminish its effectiveness. For one thing, other responses may occur in the meantime which will be reinforced instead of the desired behavior. What can be used as a reinforcer? Anything that works. Skinner does not stress various distinctions among reinforcers; nor does he attempt to explain reinforcement by such constructs as need, drive, or even incentive. He considers it more important to observe what reinforcers give the best results and then use them to control behavior. It should be noted that Skinner and others have found that for the initial acquisition of behavior small rewards given regularly are more effective than large rewards given only once in a while.

Learning occurs when, usually given a set of conditions that encourage some behavior, the individual behaves in a certain way and is immediately given a reward for that behavior. On the one hand the reward is contingent on his behaving in the desired way; on the other hand the individual will probably behave in a similar way again because of the consequences that have followed this type of behavior in the past.

Learning a response or way of behaving can be summarized as follows:

Set of conditions	$\longrightarrow$	Response: overt behavior	$\longleftarrow$	Reinforcement given immediately

Most of what we learn in school consists of, not simple responses, but more complex sequences of behavior such as psychomotor skills, the learning of a language, and the acquisition of information allowing us to solve problems. This more complex behavior can be taught through a process which Skinner terms *shaping.* First, the steps in the sequence are identified, from the initial stage to the end result. Then the teacher, aware of both the final objective and the sequence of steps required to arrive at it, leads the student through each step in the sequence rewarding each response until he arrives at the final stage, the desired behavior. Often, particularly in the learning of skills, the teacher will reinforce responses that only partly approximate the correct behavior. Gradually, however, by rewarding one successive approximation after another, he will lead the student to the correct way of performing the skill.

The sequence of more complex learning can be viewed as follows:

Set of Conditions	$\longrightarrow$	Response$_1$ $\uparrow$ reinforcement	$\longrightarrow$	Response$_2$ $\uparrow$ reinforcement	$\longrightarrow$	Response$_3$ $\uparrow$ reinforcement	$\cdots \longrightarrow$	Desired Behavior

There are other important points in Skinner's view of learning—or more exactly operant conditioning—that deserve mention here. For instance:

Punishment is to be avoided as basically ineffective and as having adverse side effects.

Undesirable behavior can be extinguished by making sure it gets no reinforcement of any kind.

Behavior once learned can be maintained most effectively by intermittent reinforcement given at irregular intervals.

Finally, Skinner long attempted, without success, to identify a workable "unit of behavior" which could serve as a basis for a scientific system of behavior.

There are several current approaches in education that come directly from Skinner's view of learning. For instance, his emphasis on specific observable behavior results in the widespread concern for stating *behavioral objectives* at the beginning of a lesson or unit, objectives that can be phrased in terms of specific tasks to be mastered and that can be measured in terms of observable behavior. An example of such a behavioral objective is: "The student will be able to write the definitions of circumference, radius, diameter and tangent."

In general, the Skinnerian teacher is concerned with changing the students' behavior so that they all meet a certain level of performance related to a topic. He is convinced that the knowledge or skills necessary to meet a desirable performance level can be taught to anyone; and he teaches this knowledge and these skills as well as he can giving immediate reinforcement as often as possible. If students do not meet the criteria right away, it is not because they are not able to, but because they lack the requisite knowledge or skill. The teacher will have them try again, perhaps filling in the required information or skill, and he will make sure the students have mastered the behavior before they go on to further topics.

The most notable application of Skinner's theory to education, the one that he himself has pioneered, is programmed instruction. In Skinner's version of programmed instruction, a topic (or whole course) is carefully analyzed as to its component parts, with each part further broken down into small units which the students go through one after the other, filling in a word to complete a statement and then immediately finding out what the correct answer is. Since the program is designed so that the student gets the vast majority of the units correct, there is immediate reinforcement of the correct response. This general technique can be used in classroom teaching as well. It would involve: (1) analyzing what is to be taught into very specific tasks, actions or concepts; (2) presenting these specific tasks step by step, each one separate from the next; and finally (3) measuring the students' performance regularly to see if they have mastered the tasks they have been taught; if not, they repeat them until mastered. This application of Skinner's view is currently termed "Mastery Learning."

How are the S-R reinforcement theories of Skinner and Thorndike the same; how do they differ? The views of Thorndike and Skinner are similar in that they both consider reward or reinforcement to be the most important principle of learning. Also, they both emphasize smaller units or the elements of what is to be learned, plus some degree of repetition in learning.

However, they differ in several important ways. For Thorndike the prototype of learning is trial and error plus selection of the correct response and its connection with the situation. For Skinner one of the most essential learning requirements is for the learner to emit the correct response; since we learn what we say or do, erroneous responses should be avoided. In Thorndike's view we learn connections or bonds between situations and responses. Skinner, however, is against positing unobservable bonds or habits and stresses that we learn responses. Thorndike explains the law of effect by stating that a reward strengthens an S-R bond. Skinner, on the other hand, says that such a backward influence is impossible: the response has already occurred. What really happens in the law of effect is that reinforcement increases the probability of a similar response reoccurring in the future.

Piaget

Ironically, none of the outstanding cognitive learning theorists was primarily interested in learning. The Gestaltists worked mainly in the area of perception, Lewin was first interested in personality and then in social psychology. The same is true of Jean Piaget, who has probably contributed more to a cognitive view of learning than anyone else. His main area of research has been the development of the thought processes, a field in which he has constructed the only significant theory that currently exists. But at the same time, through his analysis of the processes involved in the acquisition of knowledge, he has contributed significantly to a cognitive theory of learning as well.

Learning, for Piaget, is the active search for and acquisition of knowledge. It is characterized by a process of interaction between the person and his environment, and it is epitomized by the formation and development of cognitive structures. He states:

> Knowledge is not at all the same thing as making a figurative copy of reality for oneself; it invariably consists in operative processes leading to a transformation of reality, either in actions or in thought, in order to grasp the mechanisms of those transformations and thus assimilate the events and the objects into systems of operations (or structures of transformations).
>
> Physical experiments on reality, in which knowledge is abstracted from objects, consist in acting upon those objects in order to transform them, in order to dissociate and vary the factors they present, and not in simply extracting a figurative copy of them. (Piaget 1970, p. 72)

The key concepts of Piaget's view of learning are (1) *structure,* an ordered and interrelated system of knowledge; and (2) *assimilation—accommodation,* the process of interaction between intelligence and reality.

Number, city, evolution, tragedy, and—in the above teaching sequence—the very general structure of classification are all examples of structures.[6] A struc-

---

6. The difference between the general type of structures and the common type of structures illustrated here will be further explained in chapter 8.

ture is a general, basic idea to which many things can be related. We organize the things in our environment into an ordered and interrelated system in our minds; in addition, we can incorporate further things into the structure so as to give them—and the structure—greater meaning.

A structure, then, is simply how things are related, or more exactly, how we group or organize things in our minds. Piaget distinguishes among several types of structures: those involving classification, those involving order, and those based simply on continuity.

The first type of structure is illustrated by such classification systems as the following.

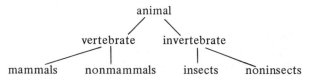

It consists of a series of distinctions or divisions into classes from most general to most specific. This type of structure is called *hierarchical.*

A second type of structure is illustrated by the basic concept of evolution:

$$\text{invertebrate} \rightarrow \text{primitive fish} \rightarrow \text{amphibians} \rightarrow \text{reptiles} \begin{smallmatrix} \nearrow \text{ birds} \\ \searrow \text{ mammals} \end{smallmatrix}$$

It is formed by relating the elements into an order or series according to some basis—in this case simpler to more complex with the latter evolving from the former. This type of structure is called a structure of *order.*

The third type of structure is illustrated by "city" together with its requirements (figure 3-4). This type of structure consists of several aspects, qualities or parts of something that are connected to a central idea. In this example, several characteristics are related as necessary requirements for a city; another basis might be parts of a whole, e.g. anatomy of the cardiovascular system. This type of structure is more flexible than the other two types in that the elements can vary in amount or degree and still not destroy the basic pattern. For this reason Piaget terms it *topological.*

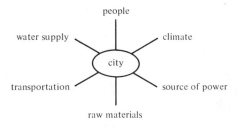

Figure 3-4. *A Structure of City*

According to Piaget, then, we can organize things in our minds in several ways: (1) by classifying and distinguishing, (2) by relating into an order or series, and (3) by grouping the elements around a core idea.

How do we form structures? How is the process of knowledge acquisition best explained? In a word, how do we learn? For Piaget, learning always involves an interaction between mind and reality. For instance, in learning what is involved in the basic concept of city, the student both becomes aware of what actual cities are like (reality), and combines and organizes these facts into a mental grouping or structure (mind). Or in the above teaching example, the underlying structure of classification was formed by the learners' realizing what the several characteristics of the geometric forms were and then grouping them in several ways.

The aspect of learning or structure formation that involves the recognition of how things actually exist in our environment, Piaget calls *accommodation.* The aspect that involves incorporating the objects of our environment into a structure in the mind, Piaget terms *assimilation.* We assimilate the objects of our environment into a mental grouping or structure while at the same time accommodating that structure to the facts of the real world.

Once a structure has been formed, we can learn more about it and add further insights and data to it. Again, we do this through a process of assimilation–accommodation. We incorporate our new data into the existing structure in our minds (assimilation) and in so doing we modify that structure to some degree so that it is in accord with the new data from environment (accommodation).

The interaction view of learning held by Piaget can be schematized as follows:

assimilation: grouping into

Objects in ———————————————————————→ Structures in
environment ←——————————————————————— intellect
accommodation: in accord with

For Piaget, the learner is very active in the learning process. Learning, as we have seen, is the process by which we acquire knowledge, which in turn is derived from the active assimilation of reality into structures. In other words, to know something is to act on it. The learner is active in two ways: on the one hand, he manipulates and transforms the data of environment as he groups them into a cognitive structure; on the other hand, he creates or expands the cognitive structure by actively incorporating the data into it.

Although Piaget has been interested mainly in analyzing man's cognitive behavior, he does claim that the affective side of man is inseparable from his cognitive activity and specifically that it forms an integral part of the learning process. The motivational aspect of Piaget's learning process is not unlike that of the Gestaltists. A person's need for self-actualization, the need to know, to assert himself provide the energetics for our intellectual behavior patterns, including learning. In addition, the conflict or disturbance to one's ordinary way of thinking about things that results from a problematic situation is itself a motivating factor. There is in the person an inbuilt tendency to "right" the situation, to seek a solution, to achieve structure and understanding. When the new insight is achieved, there is satisfaction and equilibrium. The whole process from conflict to equilibrium, Piaget terms *equilibration.*

Piaget has suggested some applications of his analysis of the learning process for teaching. For one thing, teachers should encourage students to be as active as possible in the learning process, having them inquire into problems and manipulate, at least mentally but also physically when appropriate, the things in the environment that they are studying. Role playing, discussions, projects, creative productions, and games are all ways in which a teacher can encourage students to interact with their environment. (You may note the similarity between this application and the "open classroom," which is largely based on Piaget's views.)

Second, teachers should emphasize grouping and organizing facts rather than learning facts for their own sake. They should encourage the student to manipulate and transform the facts of his environment by grouping them into a structure which stresses their essential characteristics and relationships. In a word, the teacher should teach on a level of abstraction higher than the factual level, namely the level of structure.

Finally, teachers must be aware of the type of structures that students can form at different developmental levels (cf. chapter 2) and what structures his students have actually formed in the past, and then teach accordingly. In fact, since cognitive structures are quite individual, a teacher should try to identify the structures possessed by individual students and then relate the course material to those structures.

How are the Gestalt psychologists and Piaget similar; how do they differ? They both stress understanding of relationships and grouping into organized wholes as the most essential aspects of the learning process. They both explain motivation for learning through a state of tension or conflict that results from seeing a problem.

But they differ to some extent. Wertheimer, for instance, explains organized wholes in terms of the relation between parts and whole, or between means and end. Piaget delineates the idea of organized wholes more fully through his concept of structure. Structures are basic types of groupings that consist of a core idea and many other things related to it. Piaget explains both the specific types of structures—a major advance—and also how further ideas can be incorporated into a structure. In a similar way, while both Wertheimer and Piaget explain the learning process as consisting of the learner's grouping and organizing what is to be learned, Piaget adds the concept of learning through the interaction between mind and reality, in which the person transforms the objects of environment into a mental grouping which still reflects the reality of those objects.

EXERCISE 3-4.　Applying Contemporary Learning Theories in the Classroom

How are Skinner's and Piaget's theories applied to teaching? Several approaches employed by teachers are given below. Indicate whether each is an application of Skinner's or Piaget's theory of learning.

Skinner   Piaget

1. An entirely new topic is taught first by identifying its component concepts, and then by gradually leading the students step by step through an orderly sequence to a full understanding of the topic. ____ ____

2. An entirely new topic is taught—when possible—first by pointing out some conflict or contrast between the new topic and what the students had learned previously, and then by having the students examine the new topic and particularly how it compares with what they have previously learned. ____ ____

3. Essential pattern of teaching is:

Teacher presents material or asks a question	→	Student makes a response	→	Teacher rewards response

____ ____

4. Essential pattern of teaching is:

Teacher makes objects available or presents examples, ideas	→	Students manipulate, organize materials and ideas	→	Students form structure or incorporate material into existing structure

____ ____

5. Students are encouraged to try the skills they are to learn, to answer questions orally or in writing, to repeat rules together out loud. ____ ____

6. With students working at seats teacher goes around room asking questions: "Which one is heaviest, which one lightest; can you put them in order?" "Can you group these in any other way?" "What about this one, it seems to be different?" "What would happen if you did it the other way around?" ____ ____

7. With students working at seats teacher goes around room saying: "That's good," "I'm proud of you," "I knew you could do it," "That's right," etc. ____ ____

8. When learning something new, students are encouraged to perform some action on an object themselves rather than simply watch a demonstration or look at pictures. ____ ____

9. Sample objective on a teaching plan: "To have students understand the relationship between the subject of an action and the action that is predicated of the subject." ____ ____

10. Sample objective on a teaching plan: "The students will be able to write a complete sentence." ____ ____

11. Teaching machines are advocated because they give immediate knowledge of results and constant success. ____ ____

12. Problems are fully delineated in order to perplex the students and thus stimulate their desire to solve them. ____ ____

13. If student does not understand something, it is the teacher's fault not the student's; the student should be able to understand anything if it is presented in small enough units. ____ ____

Skinner   Piaget

14. If the student does not understand something, it may be that it was not taught in keeping with his way of looking at things, the way he organizes the world around him.

                                                                    ____ ____

    A teacher who follows Skinner's analysis of learning will: break a topic down into its specific elements and teach one element at a time in an orderly sequence (1); teach by presenting a unit of material, having the students respond and immediately give a reward (verbal or otherwise) for the correct response (3); have students perform actions and say out loud what they are to learn (since we learn behavior by behaving) (5); and give continual reinforcement to students working individually (7). He will also state his objectives in terms of overt, observable behavior (10), and will tend to use teaching machines or programmed texts largely because of the immediate reinforcement they provide (11). He is not concerned about individual differences in aptitude, but concentrates on teaching so that all of the students will grasp the material (13), through teaching in small units and using enough repetition so students are able to master what they learn.

    A teacher who follows Piaget's approach to learning will: emphasize conflict at the beginning and then relate the material to what they already know (2); use a pattern that proceeds from objects provided or ideas suggested, to student manipulation and organization of the objects or ideas, to the students' incorporating the newly organized material into their cognitive structures (4); as much as possible have students do some relevent physical action on an object (since we learn best through action) (8); and also ask thought questions liberally in his teaching, questions relating to the ultimate structure or point to be understood (6). He states his objectives in terms of understanding and grouping into structures (9), and motivates students by emphasizing problems and trying to disturb their ordinary way of looking at things (12). Finally he is very conscious of the developmental level of his students, realizing that—according to Piaget's findings (chapter 2)—children think inductively and organize what they learn mainly by classifying or relating it into some order; only in junior high do students begin to think and organize things in a way similar to the way he (the teacher) is able to (14).

EXERCISE 3-5. Critique of Learning Theories

    Of the two contemporary theories of learning we have examined, which do you prefer—that of Skinner or that of Piaget? Some criticisms of each theory gleaned from several sources (Hill 1971, Flavell 1963, Hilgard and Bower 1966) are offered. First identify each criticism as pertaining to either Skinner or Piaget. Then evaluate the cogency of the criticisms, add this to your positive impressions on the value of each theory for explaining classroom learning, and on this basis decide which position you prefer.

Skinner   Piaget

1. In his insistence on including only what is based on observed behavior he ends up studying an "empty organism"; he makes no statement about the learner, only about his behavior.   ____ ____

2. In his desire to explain the thought processes he does not hesitate to "fill up the little black box" with theories and hypotheses that are yet unproven.   ____ ____

✓ 3. There is a large—and unfilled—gap between pigeons in the laboratory and a student learning about equations in math and significant themes in literature.   ____ ____

4. His explanation of learning has little basis in observable behavior and cannot easily be verified on an observable level.   ____ ____

5. Explanation of learning in terms of internal processes, especially interaction, is too general and vague. A more precise description is necessary for a viable theory.   ____ ____

6. He stresses only a few principles of learning rather than concentrating on a broader understanding of learning.   ____ ____

7. His approach to classroom learning is more verbal-oriented than thought-oriented; as such he stays more on the surface rather than arrives at a basic explanation of the higher types of learning.   ____ ____

8. Problems are solved mainly through a background of concepts and factual knowledge plus relevant skills. Therefore, it is knowledge more than broad cognitive structures that should be stressed in classroom learning.   ____ ____

9. To attempt to explain complex human learning by equally complex constructs such as cognitive structure is not really to explain it; simpler concepts are needed.   ____ ____

−10. His approach to learning is more mechanistic than human, more concerned with control of what students learn than with developing students' minds.   ____ ____

−11. Response learning is one of the simpler forms of learning and should be considered as such, not made the prototype of all learning, including the more complex types.   ____ ____

12. The formation of structures is one of the most complex types of learning; it is not parsimonious enough to explain the simpler forms of learning such as skills and verbal learning.   ____ ____

13. He does not explain *how* reinforcement takes place, or offer any real explanation regarding motivation for learning.   ____ ____

Skinner has been criticized for studying an "empty organism" (1), for staying on the verbal or surface level (7), for including only a limited number of principles in his explanation of learning (6), and for refusing to offer any real explanation of how reinforcement takes place (13). To Skinner these are not criticisms but compliments. They indicate how the "nonessentials" of learning can be stripped away and a theory built on a few basic principles.

Skinner has also been taken to task for applying the results of his laboratory research on a few subhuman species to man's life in society and to the more complex forms of classroom learning (3, 11). Although this does seem to be a rather overgenerous extrapolation from his research, it must be admitted that Skinner is a scientist who has come out of his laboratory and tried to apply his scientific findings to some of the more practical problems of man's life and education. His recommendations may seem mechanistic to some, and his prime concern is the control of behavior (10), but his motives are very humanitarian. He is interested in applying the findings of science to achieve a better life and education for man.

Piaget has been criticized for being too free to propose an explanation that has a limited empirical basis (2) and to phrase his explanations in very general terms (5), too general for easy experimental verification (4).

There is certainly a generous element of truth in these allegations. However, it should also be noted that (a) his views on learning are the compliment of his theory of cognitive development which is based on extensive research with thousands of children and adolescents, and (b) that the complex types of learning that he attempts to explain are themselves not made the easy objects of experimentation. This latter fact goes a long way to explain both why the cognitive learning theories in general do not have a broad experimental base, and why most of the research in the psychology of learning has been concerned with the simpler, more manageable types of learning.

Piaget has also been criticized for using complex rather than simple constructs to explain complex learning processes (9), not only because the simpler principles would offer easier understanding but also because they will make the theory more widely applicable to simpler forms of learning (12). Piaget, of course, answers that complex forms of learning demand complex constructs if they are to be adequately explained; second, he is mainly interested in the higher forms of man's cognitive life and is content to leave the study of the simpler forms of learning to others (he is impressed, for instance, with Hull's S-R theory for explaining some of these other types of learning).

Whether information or developed cognitive structures are more important for problem solving (8) is a point to be determined by experiment. Piaget himself has been more interested in other research questions, but others have begun to consider this problem. Smedslund, for instance, in one of his famous experiments, compared two approaches in the teaching of the concept of conservation of weight through change in shape: learning through repetition and reinforcement versus learning through cognitive conflict plus realization. When a piece was secretly "stolen" from the material being used with the result that the weight was no longer the same when shape was changed, the whole group that had acquired the concept of conservation through reinforced practice showed no resistance to extinction through nonreinforcement and quickly reverted back to a perceptual, nonconserving explanation. On the other hand, almost half of those who had learned conservation of weight by conflict and realization resisted and claimed that a piece of the material must be missing. Since the number of children used in the study was small, and since only verbal reinforcement was used, this study can only be considered suggestive of the fact that it is not information but the possession of basic cognitive structures that contributes more to a person's ability to solve related problems (Smedslund 1961).

Reactions to Theories

There are three possible reactions to the many different explanations of the learning process: (1) treat them as different approaches to learning whose analyses are so diverse as to be irreconcilable; (2) admit that there are several different types of learning and that each theory has something to offer for at least some types of learning; or perhaps (3) try to combine them in some way using elements from each explanation that best contribute to an overall explanation of learning.

If you are convinced that they are quite diverse, and you prefer to follow one position and attempt to explain the various types of learning using the principles suggested by that position, or even if you try to combine the positions into a more comprehensive theory of learning (which I would consider very difficult to do), the schematic review of the theories we have been treating in this chapter should be of some help (table 3-1).

Finally, if you admit there are many types of learning and feel that each theory contains valuable insights for at least some types, the outline given in table 3-2 might be helpful. It is suggested by the approach of Robert Gagné, who, rather than select one principle to explain all learning, has been interested in identifying the laws and conditions of learning relevant to various kinds of learning.

In the schema in table 3-2, a continuum of the basic types of learning is given together with an indication of just what is learned in each case.[7] The types of learning that the S-R and cognitive theorists are mainly interested in are also indicated.

The types of learning that the S-R theorists have researched most and are mainly interested in explaining are the following: the learning of simple responses or S-R bonds, a chain or sequence of those responses (e.g. *skill*), verbal associations (*verbal factual learning*), *concept learning*, and, to a lesser extent, relations.

The cognitive theorists are mainly interested in explaining the following types of learning: *concept formation* and the learning of *relations* and *structures*.

With regard to learning processes, both positions have offered explanations for problem solving, but cognitive-oriented theorists have contributed more to an analysis of comprehension and creativity than have S-R theorists.

---

7. Gagné's original listing has been somewhat modified to reflect the types of learning treated in this volume.

Table 3-1. Theories of Learning

Family	Stimulus-Response	Cognitive
Background	Associationism, Empiricism	Aristotelian tradition
Mind of man	Somewhat active, somewhat passive: acts and also reacts to stimuli in environment	Active: interacts with object in environment
Nature of learning	Behavior change: we learn responses	Acquisition of knowledge: we learn ideas, relationships
Main emphasis in learning	Connections between stimulus and response	Processes between object and our knowledge of it

Theories	Connectionism	Operant Conditioning	Gestalt	Operationalism
Theorists	Thorndike	Skinner	Wertheimer, etc.	Piaget
Learning	Selection and connection	Strengthening responses	Understanding relationships	Formation and development of structures
Prototype of learning	Trial and error	Operant conditioning	Insight	Assimilation-accommodation
Motivation	Reward (law of effect)	Reinforcement	Tension	Needs, Equilibration

Table 3-2. *Basic Types of Learning*

Type of Learning	What Is Learned	Theories
Stimulus-response	Bond or response	
Chaining	Sequence of two or more S-R connections as in a complex skill	S-R
Verbal association	Connection between words, facts; e.g. French-English vocabulary	
Concept formation	Classes	
Relations	Principles, relationships	Cognitive
Structures	Systems, ordered knowledge	

EXERCISE 3-6. Observation of Teacher Strategies

Arrange to observe a class on your level of interest—elementary, junior or senior high—preferably in your subject field. Analyze the approaches or techniques used by the teacher. Are they more S-R-based or cognitive-based? Often a teacher will use several different techniques within a class period; try to decide what the underlying learning theory is in each case and indicate why you think so.

EXERCISE 3-7. Learning Theories in Practice

Select a topic in your field. Draw up two plans for teaching it, one reflecting the S-R approach of Skinner or Thorndike, the other based on the cognitive view of Piaget or Wertheimer. In each case state your objective and then indicate how you would start out the lesson, what specific approaches you would use, what types of questions you would ask, what activities your students would engage in, etc.

Suggested Readings

Primary Sources

Henry, N. B., ed. *The Psycholgy of Learning.* 41st Yearbook, Part II, National Society for the Study of Education. Chicago: University of Chicago Press, 1942.

Piaget, J. *The Science of Education and the Psychology of the Child.* New York: Orion Press, 1970.

Skinner, B. F. *The Technology of Teaching.* New York: Appleton-Century-Crofts, 1968.

Thorndike, E. L. *Educational Psychology: Briefer Course.* New York: Teachers College, Columbia University, 1913.

Wertheimer, M. *Productive Thinking.* New York: Harper, 1959.

Secondary Sources

Bigge, M. L. *Learning Theories for Teachers*. New York: Harper and Row, 1964.

Craig, R. C. *The Psychology of Learning in the Classroom*. New York: Macmillan, 1966.

Hilgard, E. R. and Bower, G. H. *Theories of Learning*. New York: Appleton-Century-Crofts, 1966.

Hilgard, E. R., ed. *Theories of Learning and Instruction*. 63rd Yearbook, Part I, National Society for the Study of Education. Chicago: University of Chicago Press, 1964.

Hill, W. F. *Learning: A Survey of Psychological Interpretations*. San Francisco: Chandler, 1971.

4

Current Issues
in Learning

Of the many issues relating to the different views of learning we have just examined, two of the most current in educational psychology are discovery learning and the use of programmed instruction in the classroom. On one hand, they can be considered approaches to classroom learning that are largely derived from different theories of learning: discovery learning from cognitive theory, programmed instruction from S-R theory. On the other hand, within each approach there are different positions as to whether discovery learning and programmed instruction are advisable in the first place, and whether discovery learning is preferable to reception learning or one type of programmed instruction is better than another. Hence they constitute genuine issues as well as approaches to learning. We will consider each of them in turn.

Discovery Versus Exposition

Is learning more effective when students put things together for themselves or when they have a topic explained to them? Are we able to retain what we learn better and apply it to other situations more readily if we learned it more or less on our own or if the material is presented to us in an orderly way? Which is preferable, discovery or reception learning? We will examine this question in the first part of this chapter. We will consider the nature of discovery learning and how it differs from expository teaching, the pros and cons of discovery and reception learning, what the research offers regarding their relative effectiveness, and finally, how teachers can help students learn by discovery and reception learning.

The Nature of Discovery and Reception Learning

Before we get into the question of which is preferable, it is important to clarify what we mean by discovery learning and reception learning plus its correlative, expository teaching; through a few pertinent examples and later through a more formal analysis. For some examples do exercise 4-1.

EXERCISE 4-1.   Types of Discovery Learning and Expository Teaching

Analyze the several ways of teaching drama given below and see if you can determine the main characteristics of each approach.

1. After a brief background lecture on some main characteristics of Greek drama, the teacher suggests that the students write their own "Greek" play. For homework, each student works up a plot; in class students discuss the various plots and choose the best. Then as a group they fill in the details of the plot, keeping the criteria of unity, nobility, etc., in mind. Finally, doing ground work at home and final work in class, they write the dialogue and stage directions. If interest and time warrant, they produce the play. (7th grade)

2. Students read *The Miracle Worker* and *Inherit the Wind,* and also attend a local production of *No Time for Sergeants.* Discussions are then held on the nature and types of drama, the different patterns and other characteristics of drama, always basing the generalizations or conclusions on the plays the class has read and seen. (9th grade)

3. During a unit on the drama, in which students have read Aristotle's *Poetics,* Shakespeare's *Julius Caesar,* and Ionesco's *Rhinoceros,* plus a modern play of their choice, a discussion is held on the essence of drama and which type offers the best portrayal of human nature: classical drama, modern drama, or the theatre of the absurd. (11th grade)

4. The teacher defines drama, distinguishes among several types of drama, and then explains the basic patterns and other characteristics of drama. He uses examples from Greek drama, Shakespeare, and modern drama to illustrate his main points. Finally, he has the students read *Romeo and Juliet* and *Teahouse of the August Moon.* (10th grade)

5. During a unit on the drama, the teacher states that the theatre of the absurd portrays the characteristics of contemporary man much better than either classical or modern drama. In support of his proposition, he cites quotations from such plays as *Waiting for Godot* (aimlessness), *Rhinoceros* (conformity), and other plays. (12th grade)

How would you characterize each of these strategies for teaching the drama? Some general characteristics are given below; match each of the strategies with one of the characteristics.

_____ Ideas and generalizations are derived from particular instances experienced.

_____ Different views are compared and the most tenable conclusions drawn from them.

_____ Knowledge is gained through being involved in the creation of something.

_____ Ideas and generalizations are given and then illustrated by particular instances.

_____ An assertion is presented and then is supported by proof or data.

Deriving generalizations from particular instances is illustrated by the approach of having students read and attend plays and then drawing out from them ideas on the nature and characteristics of drama (2).

Comparing different views and drawing conclusions from them is illustrated by the discussion of classical drama, modern drama, and the theatre of the absurd (3).

Gaining knowledge from creating something is clearly at work where the students wrote their own Greek drama (1).

Presenting generalizations and then illustrating them by examples is the approach used where the teacher first explained the basic ideas about drama, then gave examples, and finally had the students read two plays (4).

Making an assertion and then supporting it with proof is illustrated by the teacher's stating that the theatre of the absurd portrays contemporary man best and then citing various plays to prove his point (5).

Characteristics of Discovery and Exposition.   Discovery learning has many forms. It can involve any one of the following activities:

1. drawing a generalization from particular instances—the inductive approach;
2. comparing several positions or views on an issue or problem and then arriving at the most tenable conclusion—a dialectical[1] approach;
3. setting up hypotheses, collecting data, and then drawing a conclusion—the experimental approach;
4. doing or making something and learning about it in the process—an experiential approach.

Expository teaching is usually characterized by the following procedures:

1. defining a concept or stating a principle or rule, and then examining some particular instances, examples or implications of it—the deductive approach;[2]
2. presenting an assertion or conclusion and then supporting it with reasons, facts, or other evidence—a didactic[3] approach.

---

1. From the Greek _dialektike:_ debate, particularly in the sense of comparing opinions and drawing truth from them.

2. Sometimes referred to as the "ruleg" method in which first a rule is given and then examples of it are provided.

3. From the Greek _didaskein:_ to teach, particularly in the sense of giving systematic instruction.

Just as in expository teaching students can be given instructions both in *what* to learn (information) and in *how* to learn (procedure), so in discovery learning we can make a distinction between learning *by* discovery and learning *to* discover. Both involve the discovery method as outlined above and can include the inductive, dialectical, experimental, and experiential approaches. In learning by discovery the focus is on what is to be learned. The purpose is to have the student acquire a product of learning—a skill, some information, a concept, relation or structure. In learning to discover the focus is on training in the method. The purpose is to improve the student's capacity for using various inquiry techniques in forming hypotheses, searching for information, evaluating conclusions, or the like.

EXERCISE 4-2. The Discovery-Expository Continuum in Teaching

Given below are several ways of teaching the mathematical value of π. Compare them with a view to determining whether they are more student- or teacher-centered, more inductive or deductive, more problem- or conclusion-oriented.

1. Teacher makes protractors, rulers and tape measures available to students and asks, "What things can you find out about circles?" They draw different sized circles, draw lines and squares inside the circles, etc. Someone suggests that they see what relationships there are among the lines they have drawn. While some compare radius to circumference, others compare circumference to the perimeter of a square, still others compare circumference to diameter. One of their findings is that the ratio between circumference and diameter is always 3.14+.

2. Teacher has three students go to the board and each draw a circle, one small, one medium, and one large. Then she asks them what the mathematical relationship is between the circumference and the diameter. The students measure the circumference and the diameter of their circles with a tape measure, and find that in each case the ratio of circumference to diameter is 3.14+.

3. Teacher reminds students that the circumference of a circle is the curved line indicating the outer boundary of that circle and that the diameter is a straight line extending from two points of the circumference and passing through the middle of the circle. He then asks what the relation would be between the two. He draws a circle on the board, measures the circumference and diameter, and then asks the students to find the ratio of circumference to diameter. They compute it and find that it is 3.14+. The teacher states that this value is a constant and is called π.

4. Teacher defines π as the ratio between circumference and the diameter of a circle, and states that the value of π is 3.14+. He does one example on the board and then has the students work some problems at their seats, e.g. a circle has a diameter of 11 inches; what is its circumference?

Check which of the approaches seem to possess the following characteristics. Usually each characteristic will be found to be present in two of the four approaches.

	1	2	3	4
a. Students are more active than teacher in learning sequence.	___	___	___	___
b. Teacher is dominant and does most of the explaining.	___	___	___	___
c. Teacher provides definite guidance in learning.	___	___	___	___
d. Inductive: a generalization is derived from particular instances.	___	___	___	___
e. Deductive: a generalization is given and then particulars derived from it.	___	___	___	___
f. Problem-oriented: learning sequence either starts with or keys on a problem or question.	___	___	___	___
g. Conclusion-oriented: learning sequence either starts with or focuses on a conclusion.	___	___	___	___

Students are more active than the teacher in the first two approaches, which are more discovery-oriented. The teacher is more dominant in the second two approaches, which are more exposition-oriented.

Teacher guidance in this context is thought of in terms of help that a teacher gives in the learning process. It is a mean between the two extremes of leaving students on their own after offering a problem (1) and giving them the conclusion or concept to be learned (4). It is clearly used to different degrees in the second and third approaches. In the first approach the teacher offers very little help; in the fourth he offers more than help, he explains everything.

The first two approaches follow a more inductive pattern, from particular instances to generalization; the fourth approach follows a deductive pattern, from generalization to specific examples. The third approach cannot neatly be characterized as inductive or deductive; it is more "directive," going from past learning to a new idea based on it.

Finally, the first two approaches are more problem-oriented: the first starting with a general question, the second keying on a specific question. The third and fourth approaches are more conclusion-oriented: the fourth beginning with a statement of a conclusion, the third focusing on the conclusion throughout.

Many of these distinctions are matters more of degree than of exclusive categories, so much so that the four approaches illustrated are better thought of as being on a continuum rather than as forming distinct classifications. The continuum, with the commonly used terms for each approach, is as follows:

1	2	3	4
Discovery	Guided discovery	Guided learning	Expository teaching

The Discovery-Exposition Continuum. Although discovery learning is often contrasted with expository teaching and its correlative, reception learning, they are better thought of, not as exclusive categories, but as points on a continuum that includes pure discovery, guided discovery, guided learning and reception learning. The obvious variable on which the continuum is based is the degree to which the teacher is dominant in the learning process, and conversely, the extent to which the learners manipulate the relevant materials and ideas themselves. Let's consider each point on the continuum in turn.

1. Pure discovery. Students are given (or can themselves suggest) a topic or problem to work on and are then free to explore the topic with a minimum of guidelines or suggestions by the teacher. They not only arrive at conclusions themselves but also plan strategies for acquiring information or solving the problem.

2. Guided discovery. Students are not only given a topic or problem but are also provided with materials to work with and suggestions on procedures to follow; but they arrive at any conclusions themselves.

3. Guided learning. The teacher leads the students through a carefully planned sequence of activities to arrive at the learning objective, using either statements or questions or both.

4. Reception learning. The teacher presents the material or conclusions to be learned in a well-ordered way; students attempt to assimilate and remember the information.

Some further comparisons are in order. The most central difference between discovery learning and expository teaching is the direction or pattern that the learning process takes. In discovery learning, (1) the process begins with either a problem or particular instances, (2) proceeds through some manipulation of ideas or data on the part of the learner, and (3) ends with some conclusion or mental grouping that the learner arrives at himself. In reception learning, the process (1) begins with the presentation of logically organized material, (2) continues with an effort by the learner to either remember it or incorporate it into his existing knowledge, and (3) usually ends with the learner identifying examples or doing specific problems by way of applying what he has learned. In a word, discovery and reception learning follow opposite directions: in the one the problem is emphasized first and the product of learning comes at the end; in the other the product comes at the beginning more or less in its final form and then some problems are given at the end.

Within discovery learning we can also discern some differences, again depending on the degree to which the teacher is involved. In pure discovery learning, the teacher stresses the problem to be solved and perhaps suggests some materials or activities in which the students might engage. Then the students are more or less left on their own to collect and manipulate information and to derive from it what is to be learned. In guided discovery learning the teacher both stresses the problem and provides materials for the learners to manipulate plus suggestions to guide their manipulation of them. At the same time, the students are very active in manipulating and organizing the data, and finally they derive an induction or conclusion from the data.

Similarly in the more expository type of teaching, there are some differences between pure reception learning and guided learning. In pure reception learning, a summary of what is to be learned is often presented to the student first; then the topic is examined more fully, always in a very logical way. In other words, the students are told right away the essentials of what they are expected to learn, and then they become involved in the actual learning of it. In guided learning, the teacher (or programmer) is very conscious of what the student is to learn, and then through a series of statements or leading questions brings him through a step by step sequence that leads to the final conclusion or behavioral outcome. In one approach both teacher and student are aware of the end result at the beginning; in the other, the teacher is aware of what the student is to learn and uses this awareness as a basis for directing the learner to it.

Either approach—discovery or exposition—can be used in the acquisition of skills, knowledge of a language, factual information, concepts, relations or structures. With regard to structures, for instance, Jerome Bruner, a leading proponent of the discovery method, suggests that basic ideas that form the core of a structure be learned by the discovery technique. David Ausubel, the leading advocate of reception learning, claims that ordered and interrelated knowledge is best learned when explained by a teacher and assimilated by the student.

Most cognitive psychologists tend to favor learning through discovery or guided discovery, whereas most behaviorists prefer guided learning or expository teaching. However, there are a few cognitive theorists, especially Ausubel and his colleagues, who favor expository teaching and its correlative, reception learning. So there are a few neo-behaviorists who admit of the value of discovery learning, even though in practice they seem to favor more directed or guided learning.

Finally, we should note that reception learning can emphasize either rote memorization of information or understanding and active assimilation of ideas into one's existing cognitive structure. Often it will involve some of each. Discovery learning always aims at the students' understanding of what they are learning.

Discovery Learning Versus Expository Teaching

Which will you use more in your own teaching, techniques that are more on the discovery or expository end of the continuum? There are two ways of determining your position on the issue: (1) decide which is preferable on the basis of reason, and (2) find out which is more effective on the basis of research. In this section we will present some of the arguments that have been offered for each approach in order to help you decide which emphasis has the weight of reason in its favor. In the next section we will examine some of the experimental evidence which bears on the relative effectiveness of the two approaches.

Arguments Favoring Discovery Learning

1. It makes what one learns more personal, more his own. If he grapples with data, he will better understand what he derives from it. It will be more a part of him rather than something imposed from without.
2. It conveys the true impression of what knowledge really is, namely a product of inquiry rather than a given body of insights and information.
3. It is more in keeping with our natural way of learning, i.e. how we learn when we learn without the help of a teacher. Since teaching is a cooperative art, an art

that cooperates with nature (like counseling, medicine and agriculture), it should follow the natural order of learning, not go against it.

4. It is the better way to teach the scientific method and other techniques of inquiry and problem solving, for it is only through use and practice that students really learn these skills.

5. It is especially necessary for younger students who are on the level of concrete operational thought, since understanding comes only from concrete, inductive approaches and (negatively) since verbal, abstract explanations are of little value at this level. However, even for students on the level of formal operations it is also better—at least at the beginning—in a new or difficult topic or a subject field they have never studied before. It will provide them with a concrete experiential foundation for the more abstract explanations of the subject later on.

6. It has the effect of motivating students through involvement and through the excitement of finding things out for themselves.

7. Finally, it increases the students' self-confidence and reliance on their own intelligence and capacity to learn. It makes them less docile and authority conscious as well as more inquiry-centered and competence-oriented.

Arguments in Favor of Expository Teaching

1. It saves time and therefore reduces the cost required for learning. Students can learn much more and cover more topics when taught in an expository way.

2. It permits a better organized and more exact statement of what is to be learned, and allows students to avoid the pitfalls and errors that they could otherwise fall into.

3. It respects the nature of culture, through which younger members of society can have the discoveries of the past transmitted to them by more experienced members and do not have to rediscover everything by themselves.

4. It is not only adequate for teaching on the level of formal operational thought when students can handle purely verbal exposition, but it also permits topics to be treated on a higher level of abstraction than is possible with discovery learning.

It might also be of interest to hear first hand what the leading proponents of discovery and reception learning say in behalf of their positions. Although not the originator of discovery learning (which is actually many centuries old), Jerome Bruner is the current leading exponent of it. In his now famous "The Act of Discovery" he states:

> It is a conjecture much like that of Maimonides—that a man's intellectual functions are exclusively his own: "no one else owns any part of it"—that leads me to examine the act of discovery in man's intellectual life. For if man's intellectual excellence is the most his own among his perfections, it is also the case that the most uniquely personal of all that he knows is that which he has discovered for himself. What difference does it make, then, that we encourage discovery in the learning of the young? Does it, as Maimonides would say, create a special and unique relation

between knowledge possessed and the possessor? And what may such a unique relation do for a man—or for a child, if you will, for our concern is with the education of the young?

I would urge in the spirit of an hypothesis that emphasis upon discovery in learning has precisely the effect upon the learner of leading him to organize what he is encountering in a manner not only designed to discover regularity and relatedness, but also to avoid the kind of information drift that fails to keep account of the uses to which information might have to be put. It is, if you will, a necessary condition for learning the variety of techniques of problem solving, of transforming information for better use, indeed for learning how to go about the very task of learning.

I would also propose that to the degree that one is able to approach learning as a task of discovering something rather than "learning about" it, to that degree will there be a tendency for the child to carry out his learning activities with the autonomy of self-reward or, more properly by reward that is discovery itself. (Bruner 1961, pp. 22, 26)

In a similar way, although meaningful reception learning has also been used for centuries, the chief contemporary proponent of it is David Ausubel. In his *The Psychology of Meaningful Verbal Learning* he argues:

The art and science of presenting ideas and information meaningfully and effectively—so that clear, stable and unambiguous meanings emerge and are retained over a long period of time as an organized body of knowledge—is really the principal function of pedagogy. This is a demanding and creative rather than a routine and mechanical task. The job of selecting, organizing, presenting and translating subject-matter content in a developmentally appropriate manner requires more than the rote listing of facts. If it is done properly it is the work of the master teacher and is hardly a task to be disdained.

Beginning in the junior high school period, students acquire most new concepts and learn most new propositions by *directly* grasping higher-order relationships between abstractions. To do so meaningfully, they need no longer depend on current or recently prior concrete-empirical experience, and hence are able to bypass completely the intuitive type of understanding reflective of such dependence. Through proper expository teaching they can proceed directly to a level of abstract understanding that is qualitatively superior to the intuitive level in terms of generality, clarity, precision, and explicitness. At this state of development, therefore, it seems pointless to enhance intuitive understanding by using discovery techniques. (Ausubel 1963, p. 19)

Research on Discovery and Reception Learning

According to the research studies that have been conducted, which is more effective, discovery learning or expository teaching? The earlier studies (1930–50) contrasted discovery learning with rote learning; more recent studies (1955–present) have compared different types of discovery and reception learning. Few studies have examined any variables that pertain to either type of learning.

Discovery Versus Exposition.   Discovery learning of rules and principles has been found to be superior to authoritative teaching and rote learning of rules and principles (McConnell 1934, Katona 1940, Anderson 1949). The guided discovery approach has generally been found to be more effective than either pure discovery or reception learning. It usually makes for more effective initial learning of topics and also results in an improvement in the ability to apply what is learned to further instances. A few studies have found no differences among the various approaches (Kittell 1957, Gagné and Brown 1961, Ray 1961, Worthen 1968, Kornreich 1969).

Long-Term Effects.   Students taught by the discovery method tend to get more involved in what they are learning and will tend to continue to inquire and work on their own more than will students taught by an expository or even guided discovery method. The result of this further activity is that even though they might not do as well on tests given immediately after learning, they perform better on tests given a month or so after the learning period (Kersh 1958, 1962).

Individual Differences.   The limited amount of research on individual differences and discovery learning seems to indicate that brighter students profit more from the discovery method than from a more expository approach. For average and slower students the evidence is ambiguous (probably discovery and reception learning are equally effective for them) (Herman 1971, Tanner 1969).

Problem-solving and inductive reasoning abilities seem to be particularly important for successful discovery learning. Students who score high on these abilities do better with discovery than with reception learning; students low on these abilities do better with reception learning (Egan and Greeno 1973).

Teaching by Discovery and Exposition

What suggestions for teaching can we derive from the above analysis? Here are a few implications; perhaps you can think of more.

Selection of Approach.   Decide on which proportion of discovery learning and expository teaching you prefer on the basis of the evidence of both reason and research, then try to reflect that proportion in your teaching. For discovery learning, emphasize an atmosphere of student inquiry and manipulation of data with the students themselves arriving at conclusions. For reception learning, emphasize an orderly presentation of ideas and information, using the order in which students are expected to remember them.

Keep in mind that whatever emphasis you prefer, all of the approaches—pure discovery, guided discovery, guided learning, and reception learning—have been found to be effective to some degree, so you can feel assured in using any one of them when you deem it most appropriate.

Facets of Discovery.   When you decide to use discovery learning, realize that it has many facets and select the particular one that best fits your topic: the inductive or experiential approach for the learning of language, concepts, relations and skills; a dialectical approach for the examination of issues and in the learning of structures; the experimental approach in many problems in the sciences and practical subjects.

Practice.   Help students learn how to discover by providing experience and practice in inquiry techniques, formulation of hypotheses, deriving generalizations from particular instances, collection and organization of data, and use of the scientific method.

Materials.   In using the discovery approach, not only make use of discovery based textbooks and discovery materials available from publishers,[4] but also collect and construct your own materials and exercises plus encourage students to bring in materials that can be used in discovery-based classes.

Expository Approaches.   When you decide to use a more expository method, select the particular approach that is appropriate to the learning outcome: the deductive (ruleg) approach for the teaching of concepts; the didactic (assertion and proof) approach in the teaching of factual information, issues, and structures. Either approach can be used for teaching language, relations, and skills.

EXERCISE 4-3.   Guided Discovery Learning in the Classroom

A good example of the guided discovery approach in the teaching of mathematics is seen in the following sequence in which students are helped to discover the commutative law in arithmetic. The basic material is taken from a University of Illinois Committee on School Mathematics Unit. Analyze the learning sequence and try to see what aspect of the guided discovery technique is at work at each point.

Students are provided with the following multiplication table with the instructions: "Fill in the empty spaces."

$\times$	$\frac{2}{3}$	1200	$\frac{3}{4}$	87	21
21	14		$\frac{63}{4}$	1827	441
87	58	104,400		7569	
$\frac{2}{3}$	$\frac{4}{9}$		$\frac{1}{2}$		
$\frac{3}{4}$		900	$\frac{9}{16}$	$\frac{261}{4}$	
1200	800	1,440,000			25,200

---

4. E.g. American Science and Engineering, Science Research Associates.

2 {
     After noticing that several students seem to be finished, the teacher asks:
     T.   How many computations did you have to do to fill in the table?
     S_1.   None. They were all figured out for you.

3 {
     T.   What do you mean?
     S_1.   Well, the first box that needed filling in was 21 × 1200. But if you look down at the bottom, you'll find 1200 and going across the top you'll find 21. The answer is there where they intersect: 25,200. It's the same with the others.

     T.   Does everyone see that?
     Ss.   Yes (some who were doing computation show surprise).

4 {
     T.   How about another space. John?
     S_2.   87 × 3/4. If you go down and find 3/4 and then go across to under 87, you'll find the answer, 261/4.

5 {
     T.   OK. Now, is there any difference between multiplying 87 by 3/4 and multiplying 3/4 by 87?
     S_2.   No. It's the same thing.
     T.   How about 21 × 1200 and 1200 × 21?
     S_1.   It's the same too.

6 {
     T.   Can anyone suggest a general rule from what we've seen here?
     S_3.   It doesn't matter what order you multiply numbers in; you get the same answer.

7 {
     T.   Everyone agree? So, you can change the order and still get the same answer. What you're doing is interchanging one number with the other. Right? In Latin, change is *mutare* and with is *cum*. So this interchanging one number with the other is called the commutative principle of multiplication.

8 {
     T.   Let's take a look at some other examples. Are these sentences true?
             8 × 12 = 12 × 8
             45 × 2/3 = 2/3 × 45
     S_4.   Yes.

     T.   You don't have to simplify or do any computation in order to know that these sentences are true.

9 {
            How do you know they're true?
     S_4.   By the commutative principle we just saw.

10 {
     T.   Does this work in addition?
            (Pause while students do some figuring)

     S_5.   Yes. You can add 9 + 5 or 5 + 9 and get the same answer.
     S_6.   Or if you're adding numbers like 8 + 6 + 2, you can add the 8 and the 2 first and then the 6. It's easier.
     T.   And you get the same?
     S_6.   Yes.

11 {
     T.   Can you make a general rule about this then?
     S_6.   In addition too, it doesn't matter what order you add the numbers in. You get the same answer.

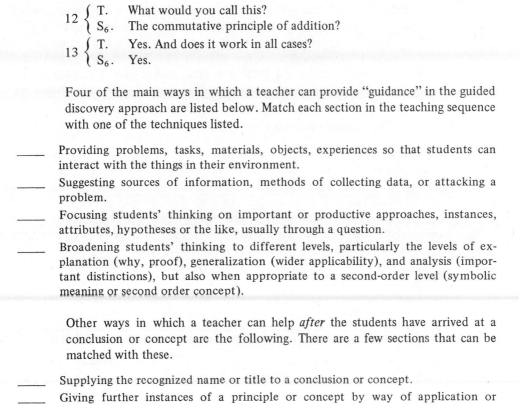

$$12 \begin{cases} \text{T.} & \text{What would you call this?} \\ \text{S}_6. & \text{The commutative principle of addition?} \end{cases}$$

$$13 \begin{cases} \text{T.} & \text{Yes. And does it work in all cases?} \\ \text{S}_6. & \text{Yes.} \end{cases}$$

Four of the main ways in which a teacher can provide "guidance" in the guided discovery approach are listed below. Match each section in the teaching sequence with one of the techniques listed.

_____ Providing problems, tasks, materials, objects, experiences so that students can interact with the things in their environment.

_____ Suggesting sources of information, methods of collecting data, or attacking a problem.

_____ Focusing students' thinking on important or productive approaches, instances, attributes, hypotheses or the like, usually through a question.

_____ Broadening students' thinking to different levels, particularly the levels of explanation (why, proof), generalization (wider applicability), and analysis (important distinctions), but also when appropriate to a second-order level (symbolic meaning or second order concept).

Other ways in which a teacher can help *after* the students have arrived at a conclusion or concept are the following. There are a few sections that can be matched with these.

_____ Supplying the recognized name or title to a conclusion or concept.

_____ Giving further instances of a principle or concept by way of application or evaluation.

In the above example the teacher provided the multiplication table (1) for the students to interact with and in so doing to discover the basic idea behind the commutative principle of multiplication. Later on he presented a problem (10) that called for further manipulation of numbers by the students to see whether the principle also applied to addition.

Although suggesting sources of information and methods of approach is often a way for teachers to give some guidance in discovery learning, it was not used in this sequence since all of the necessary data was supplied and the methods were quite familiar to the students.

The teacher focused the students' attention on some key aspects of the problem at hand, particularly in the earlier part of the session; e.g. through questions on how many computations were necessary to complete the table (2), on a specific instance (4), and on the main idea of the principle (5).

There were several instances of the teacher's encouraging the students to broaden their thinking: (a) to emphasize further explanations by asking what a student meant by the fact that no computations were necessary (3), and by asking how students knew that something was a true statement (9); and (b) to draw generalizations by asking about a general rule (6, 11) and by asking about the universality of the principle (13).

After the students had grasped the essence of the commutative principle of multiplication, the teacher explained the conventional term used for it (7); after they had arrived at the similar principle for addition, he had a student supply the correct term (12). Finally, once the students had derived the commutative principle of multiplication on their own, the teacher gave further examples illustrating the principle by way of application in a slightly different context (8).

EXERCISE 4-4. The Discovery Approach in Teaching

Discovery learning can be used in all fields. For example, in home economics students can learn how to bake a cake with proper moistness and texture by baking several cakes using different proportions of flour and different oven times and temperatures for each (experiential–and somewhat experimental– approach). In social studies students can learn about ancient culture from actual or simulated artifacts plus maps, charts, and reports of an archeological excavation, or about an important battle in history from facsimiles of front pages of newspapers of the time, physical maps of the terrain, records of manpower and weaponry, background information on generals, etc. (inductive approach). In language arts and literature, the relation or difference between two types of stories or periods of literature plus their relative quality can be learned through a discussion of different stories or works of literature plus varying opinions concerning them (dialectical approach).

Although it is much more difficult to plan a discovery-oriented approach to a topic than an expository approach, the possibilities are almost endless. In your own field, select a topic and plan either a straight discovery or a guided discovery lesson for that topic. Use any of the specific strategies, inductive, dialectical, experimental or experiential, which seems to be most promising for your topic. State the topic and the specific strategy you have selected. Then list the materials and activities that you will have your students interact with in order to arrive at the skill, information, concept, or principle that you wish to have them learn.

Although the examples given above are all of learning *by* discovery, you may want to try to plan a lesson aimed at having students learn *to* discover. For instance in science, you might use a demonstration or film clip that mystifies the students, and then have them try to find an explanation by asking you questions answerable by "yes" or "no." For a fuller explanation of this technique see one of the articles by Suchman listed in the bibliography. This technique gives the students practice and training in thinking up hypotheses regarding a problem. In social science, you might give your students a poem which has some historical references and have them figure out as much about the time (or place) in which it was written as they can (cf. Fenton 1967).

Programmed Instruction

If discovery learning is championed by the cognitive theorists, teaching machines and programmed instruction is one of the main approaches to learning advocated by the stimulus-response theorists. In fact, B. F. Skinner himself is the major proponent of the use of teaching machines in the classroom. What exactly is programmed instruction? How effective is it as compared to traditional instruction? In the second half of this chapter we will consider the following points concerning the issue of programmed instruction:

The nature of programmed instruction
Basic types of programs
The pros and cons of programmed instruction
What research offers regarding its effectiveness
The use of programmed instruction in the classroom.

EXERCISE 4-5. The Nature of Programmed Materials

What are the basic characteristics of programmed materials? Given below are frames or sections from several different types of programs. See if you can discern some of their common characteristics.

From a first grade reading program:

a. A bee can sting. Jan was stung by a _____.   bee

From a college psychology text, Holland and Skinner, *The Analysis of Behavior:*

b. In a reflex, the stimulus and the response occur in a given order;
first the (1) _____, then the (2) _____.   stimulus,   response

From a high school mathematics text, Crowder and Martin, *Trigonometry:*

c. You should know that an angle is a geometric figure formed by
two line segments drawn from the same point or vertex. Thus

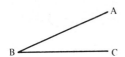

An angle usually is designated by capital letters placed at the
vertex and sides of the angle, as shown above. In this case, we
might speak of the diagram as showing angle ABC (with the
vertex letter in the middle), or as ∠ABC, or just as ∠B.
    Angles, as you know, are measured in degrees.
A circle contains 360 degrees (360°).
    You should remember the answer to this question:
How many degrees are there in a right angle?
    45° (page 29)   90° (page 38)   100° (page 42)

From an elementary school science program:

d. Knowing that (1) jars can be opened easily after running the

metal top under hot water and that (2) railroad track laid in
cooler weather is placed with a space in between sections would
lead you to conclude that heat _____ metal.   expands

From a college developmental psychology program:

e. See if you can discern what intellectual operation is at work in
the following example. Problem: "Are there more boys or girls
in your class?"

Ann, age 5. "There are more boys than girls."
Ben, age 7. "There are more children; there are both boys and
girls."
What was Ben able to do that Ann was not?
A. Distinguish between boys and girls.
B. Combine parts into a whole.
C. Perceive the obvious fact that there were more children.
(Explanations are provided for each option)

From a high school problems of democracy program:

f. "No bill of attainder or ex post facto law shall be passed." U. S.
Constitution (Sec. 9.3)
    An American citizen, sympathetic to the Castro government
in Cuba, unsuccessfully attempts to hijack an American airplane
and fly it to Cuba. A group of patriotic citizens demands that a
law be passed making this a crime punishable by death and that
this man be given the death penalty.
What the group advocates is
a. unconstitutional
b. constitutional
c. legal for the states but not for the federal government.
    What the group advocates is unconstitutional. The group in
its zealousness to prevent hijackings has forgotten an important
right guaranteed all citizens, even those committing such an
unpopular crime. A law passed prohibiting an act after the act is
committed would be an ex post facto law and therefore unconstitutional.

Check the characteristics that are found in each of the above sample frames.

_____ 1. Some material is presented to the student.
_____ 2. The learner discovers solutions through inquiry.
_____ 3. The learner is active, engaged.
_____ 4. The learner is passive, receptive.
_____ 5. Immediate knowledge of results is provided.
_____ 6. Delayed feedback is given regarding answers.

    In programmed instruction, first some material is presented to the student
(1), sometimes in very small units, sometimes in moderate size units. The learner
is forced to become active and engaged in the learning process (3) by answering a

question that is posed, whether it be fill-in or multiple choice. Then immediately after the student answers the question, he is informed whether or not he is correct (5).

Other important characteristics of programmed learning will become apparent as we continue this section.

The Nature of Programmed Instruction

First of all, note that we are using the term "programmed instruction" rather than "teaching machines." This is a more appropriate term for two reasons. First, the essence of any teaching machine is the "program" that is put into it. It is what is contained in the program (sometimes called "software") that we learn from; a machine is only a means of presenting the program to the learner. The second reason is that teaching machines are only one among several means used to present a program. The programmed textbook is another, simpler means; the computer terminal is another, more complex means that can account for much more individual variation among learners. In each case, the program that is fed into the book, the machine, or the computer is much more important than the hardware itself. We should probably also mention that by teaching machine we mean a special type of machine that handles instructional programs; we do not mean machines such as movie and filmstrip projectors, overhead projectors, tape recorders and similar audio-visual apparatus.

What is programmed instruction? It is a way of presenting a topic or some information in a carefully planned sequence with the learner actively responding in some way at each step in the sequence. In addition there is immediate knowledge of results or *feedback* provided after each response. Thus it differs from an ordinary book in that there is a planned interaction between student and program: the student answers questions or fills in blanks and the program gives him feedback. It differs from a regular class session in that each student can proceed at his own rate and sometimes according to his own ability or background knowledge, and also in that immediate knowledge of results is provided to each student.

Programmed instruction is thus a self-instructional technique that is somewhat like a private tutor in the Socratic tradition, i.e. one that uses some explanation but mainly questioning to teach. In addition, most programmed instruction is very much like the guided learning approach that we considered earlier in this chapter.

EXERCISE 4-6.   Two Major Types of Programs

All types of programs have some common characteristics, but they also differ in some important ways as well. The following sequences in the teaching of adjectives represent the two most basic types of programs. Examine them carefully, trying to discern some of the specific characteristics of each and how they differ from one another. (Note: usually in the first type, the student uses a piece of cardboard to shield the answers until after he fills in the blank; in the second type, the commentary for each option is usually on a different page from the question itself.)

I

1. Adjectives are words that describe nouns and pronouns. In the sentence, "Sam is wearing a yellow shirt," the word yellow describes the noun shirt and is therefore an _____.   adjective

2. An adjective is a part of speech that is used to tell something about or _____ another word.   describe

3. In the sentence "Look at the beautiful house," beautiful describes the noun house and is called a(n) _____.   adjective

4. In the sentence "He played a good game," the word _____ describes the noun game. Therefore the word good good
   is an _____.   adjective

5. In the sentence "She is beautiful," beautiful is an adjective that describes she. She is not a noun but a _____.   pronoun

6. The two parts of speech that an adjective is used to describe are _____ and _____.   noun, pronoun

7. An adjective then is a word that _____.   describes
                                                                      nouns and
                                                                      pronouns

II

Besides nouns and verbs in a sentence, we also use words that tell something about these words, for instance yellow shirt, beautiful house, badly burned. Would you say these words are:
a. action words
b. replacing words
c. describing words

_____

A. They're not really action words. Remember that we define verbs such as wear, go, eat, as action words. The words yellow, beautiful and badly don't indicate action but tell something further about a noun or verb. Again what are they:
b. replacing words
c. describing words
B. You've jumped the gun. We haven't come to replacing words yet. Beautiful doesn't replace house; what does it do?
a. shows action
c. describes it
C. Right. They tell more about and therefore describe a shirt, a house or how one was burned.
There are two main kinds of describing words: those that describe nouns are called

adjectives; those that describe verbs are called adverbs. Let's consider adjectives first. In the sentence "Her father is tired," what is the word tired?

a. an adjective

b. a verb

A. Correct. Tired describes her father, so it is an adjective. Whether the descriptive word is right next to the noun or is the other side of the verb, as long as it describes a noun, it is called an adjective.

But an adjective can describe something else. Consider the sentence "She is beautiful." What part of speech does beautiful describe?

a. verb

b. pronoun

B. You probably think tired is part of the overall verb "is tired." Not really. Tired doesn't involve action, but describes someone. Is it then a verb or adjective?

_____

A. Beautiful is next to the verb is but it doesn't say anything about it. Who is beautiful, she or is?

B. Right. So adjectives can describe not only nouns but also pronouns.

Indicate which of the two programs each of the following statements applies to.

	I	II
1. The sequence of items is ordered in a linear way: all students go through the same steps.	___	___
2. The sequence in which the student proceeds depends on his response: the program goes forward or branches back depending on the student's needs.	___	___
3. Explanation is fairly extensive.	___	___
4. Prompts (answer contained in frame) and cues (hints) are provided.	___	___
5. Steps between items are small; programming is "dense."	___	___
6. Steps between items are moderate; each item covers a new aspect of a topic.	___	___
7. Learner makes very few errors; constant success is almost guaranteed.	___	___
8. Learner errors are allowed for; they receive some remedial instruction.	___	___
9. Repetition and review are emphasized.	___	___
10. Multiple choice format is necessary.	___	___
11. Completion (fill in) format is employed.	___	___

You have probably discerned the following important characteristics of either type of program. By juxtaposing them, the differences will be clear.

I	II
The order of items is such that everyone goes through the same sequence; in other words, the steps are arranged in a linear order. Individuals will vary	The sequence that a student follows depends on whether he gets an item correct or not. If he is correct he goes on to the next item; if he is wrong he

I	II
in their rate but not in the order in which they respond to items. Because of the order used, this type of program is called *linear*.	goes back and tries again. Individual differences among students are accounted for not only by rate but also by allowing for those who do not grasp something right away. Because the specific order a student follows is contingent upon the answer he chooses, this type of program is most often called *contingent*.
Prompts, such as "adjectives are" and cues such as "tells something about or" and "not a noun but" are used freely to help students get the correct answer.	Explanation is fairly extensive, either before the question is phrased or certainly afterwards. In the present instance the explanation is only a sentence or two; in other programs it can run up to a paragraph or almost a page.
The steps between one "frame" and another are very small; the items are very close together or—in the official jargon—the programming is "dense."	The steps between frames are moderate, with each item usually treating a different aspect of the topic.
As a result of the prompts and cues plus the dense programming, the student gets practically all of the items correct and therefore constantly experiences success.	Questions are not made intentionally difficult, but errors are not avoided either. In fact, wrong answers receive extra instruction—anywhere from a sentence or two in the present example to a series of special frames in some more complex programs.
Considerable repetition is emphasized throughout the frames and a final review is provided at the end of each section.	
Although it is not absolutely necessary, most programs of this type use a fill in or completion format.	A multiple choice format is called for since the sequence the student follows depends on his choice of a right or wrong answer.

Basic Types of Programs

Although the vast majority of available programs are of one type, it is important to realize that there is more than one type of program, and that even within the basic types there are distinct variations. What are these types and how do they differ from one another?

The most common type of program is one in which the material to be learned is broken down into very small units which each student goes through in sequence, and in which the student is required to fill in blanks at each step in order to complete a statement. Since everyone follows the same order of units, this program is called *linear*. It was devised by Skinner as a direct application of his theory of learning and has been expounded by him in a number of articles (Skinner 1958, 1961).

Another popular type of program is that in which the material is divided into larger chunks that include some explanation plus a question phrased in multiple choice form. Depending on whether the student's answer is right or wrong, he is sent on to the next frame or is referred elsewhere for further explanation. Since the student's every move depends on his last response, this type of program is often called *contingent*. It is the creation of Norman A. Crowder and forms the chief competitor to linear programming (Crowder 1963).

How do the two types of programs differ? Primarily they differ in terms of how and when learning takes place. Skinner claims that we learn behavior by behaving in a certain way. The programmer outlines the behavioral objectives that he wishes the student to achieve, and then writes the program so that the student will have to engage in the appropriate behavior, e.g. stating the correct word, definition, or rule. According to Skinner, the learning occurs as the student responds by filling in the blanks. Crowder, on the other hand, believes that the learning takes place while the student reads the explanation of new material on each page. The programmer decides how big a chunk of material to present at a time, explains it as clearly as he can, and then asks a question to see if the student has understood it. If he has, the student goes on to learn the next section; if he hasn't, he is given further explanation to clear up his misunderstanding.

The other main difference between the two basic forms of programmed instruction is the relative importance placed on correct answers. Skinner considers it essential that the student make the correct response since he learns the response that he makes. The programmer insures that students make correct responses in several ways: (1) by planning the program so that the student progresses easily from one frame to another, with the steps in between made very small; (2) by providing prompts or cues within each frame that contains new material; and (3) by field testing and revising the program until students are able to get the vast majority of items correct. In the program's final form, if the student makes an error, it is considered the fault of the program, not of the student. The program always should allow students to make the correct response.

Crowder is not nearly as intent on the student's getting each item correct. In contingent programming, the program writer does not try to make the multiple choice questions difficult, but designs them so that they will determine whether the student has understood the material presented in the first part of each frame. He uses the "distractors" or wrong answers to provide for individual differences in either background knowledge or comprehension ability. If a student fails to grasp the material and chooses an incorrect option, he is given further instruction that either supplies the necessary background information or further clarifies the expository material. Wrong answers are not avoided but are used to provide for individual differences among students.

Programmed materials are not limited to the purely linear or purely contingent formats that we have just analyzed. Within each basic format we can discern further subtypes, distinguishable either by their design or purpose. Within linear programs, for instance, there are at least two types: basic and adjunct programs. The basic type of program is the one we have analyzed above. It employs a completion format, prompts, cues, repetition, etc., and is used mainly for basic teaching purposes. An adjunct program is one that employs either a completion or multiple choice format and consists of items that reflect material that is treated in a textbook. Prompts and cues are not used, nor is the programming at all dense. Repetition is used in some cases, e.g. grammar and arithmetic, but for most subjects it is not emphasized. Adjunct programs are used for review, drill or self-evaluation purposes, usually concurrent with or immediately following each chapter or section of a text.

Within the basic contingent type of programming, in which explanatory material is presented and then a multiple choice question is given, we can also distinguish two subcategories: intrinsic and extrinsic. Intrinsic programs are those in which the branching that occurs depends only on the student's answers to the multiple choice question. Extrinsic programs are those in which the branching depends not only on the student's immediate answers but on other data as well, such as intelligence or achievement test scores or patterns of earlier responses. In the first case, the branching can consist either of an explanation for each answer plus the instruction to go back and try the question again, or it can consist of an extra series of frames or other material for those who need specific background information or further explanation of a topic. In the case of extrinsic programs, usually there will be extra frames or even whole subprograms available for students who evidence a need for them (remedial frames for slower students, enrichment subprograms for the brightest students). For the most part a computer is necessary to analyze all of the data and to determine what branches a student works on at various points in an extrinsic program.

Another type of program that most often uses the contingent format is one that has been termed a "discovery program." A case, a capsule experiment, an illustration, an example or the like is presented in the first part of each frame, and then a multiple choice item is given that calls for the student to derive a generalization, a conclusion or an element of theory from the data. The discovery type of program, which is not generally available but shows much promise for teaching for understanding, problem solving and critical thinking, is illustrated by several examples given in exercise 4-5 (d, e, and f).

Finally, we should mention that recently a few programmers have been using some linear and some branching techniques in the same program, depending on which best fits a particular subtopic. Also, there have been some creative combinations of the two formats, such as in example f of exercise 4-5, which is largely contingent but with all students following the same linear order.

Which do you prefer, linear or contingent programming? To help you decide, here are some relevant passages from the main proponents of each, B. F. Skinner and Norman Crowder. Skinner objects to the multiple choice format of contingent programming and argues:

Teaching machines based on the principle of "multiple choice" often show a misunderstanding of the learning process. When multiple-choice apparatuses were first used, the organism was left to proceed by "trial and error." The term does not refer to a behavioral process but simply to the fact that contingencies of reinforcement were left to chance: some responses happened to be successful and others not. Learning was not facilitated or accelerated by procedures which increased the probability of successful responses. The results, like those of much classroom instruction, suggested that errors were essential to the learning process. But when material is carefully programmed, both subhuman and human subjects can learn while making few errors or even none at all. . . . Of course we learn something from our mistakes—for one thing, we learn not to make them again—but we *acquire* behavior in other ways. . . .

In the first place, the student should *construct* rather than *select* a response, since this is the behavior he will later find useful. Secondly, he should advance to the level of being able to emit a response rather than merely recognize a given response as correct. This represents a much more considerable achievement, as the difference between the sizes of reading and writing vocabularies in a foreign language demonstrates. Thirdly, and more important, multiple choice material violates a basic principle of good programming by inducing the student to engage in erroneous behavior. . . . In a multiple choice *test,* wrong answers may do no harm, since a student who has already learned the right answer may reject wrong answers with ease and possibly with no undesirable side-effects. The student who is *learning,* however, can scarely avoid trouble. Traces of erroneous responses survive in spite of the correction of errors or the confirmation of a right answer. . . .

Multiple-choice techniques are appropriate when the student is to learn to compare and choose . . ., but not in the simple acquisition of knowledge. . . . In solving an equation, reporting a fact of history, restating the meaning of a sentence, or engaging in almost any of the other behavior which is the main concern of education, the student is to *generate* responses. He may generate and reject, but only rarely will he generate a set of responses from which he must then make a choice. (Skinner 1961, pp. 392-95)

Crowder defends the use of the multiple choice format even though it allows for some errors.

The rationale of intrinsic programming postulates that the basic learning takes place during the student's exposure to the new material on each page. . . . The direct purpose served by the multiple choice questions in intrinsically programmed material is to determine whether the student has understood the material he has just read. Our reason for wanting to make this determination is that we know that the process of symbolic communication is fraught with the possibility of error, and if there has been an error, or failure of communication, we wish to detect and correct the error before proceeding. By letting the student choose the next material he will see (by his act of selecting an answer to a multiple-choice question), we have the possibility of detecting and thereby taking direct automatic action to correct any errors that occur.

We have based our technique on the possibility of detecting and correcting errors because we think it both impractical and undesirable to attempt to eliminate errors. We think it is impractical to eliminate errors because of the inevitable individual differences, both in ability and information, that will occur among our students. We think it is undesirable to eliminate errors because to do so we would have to present material in such small steps and ask such easy questions that we would not be serving the educational objectives we desire to serve.

On the question of individual differences alone it seems self-evident that a program written in such tiny steps as to allow the dullest student to succeed almost all the time must inevitably waste the time of the brighter student. It is also unrealistic to believe that in any practical situation all students come to the beginning of a program with the same amount of information. The alternatives available are (1) to make the most pessimistic possible assumptions about the background of the student and teach all of the information to all of the students or (2) to provide diagnostic questions and remedial material as an integral part of the program for those who demonstrate a need for such material. We chose the latter course. (Crowder 1963, pp. 186-87)

The Pros and Cons of Programmed Instruction

Will you use programmed instruction in your teaching? As in the issue of discovery learning, the two bases for reaching a decision as to its value and effectiveness are reason and research. Some of the arguments for and against programmed instruction are presented in this section. Rather than simply offer a summary of the main arguments on either side, it might be more interesting to consider some actual statements by some chief proponents and critics of programmed learning.

Main Arguments Favoring Programmed Instruction

1. "With teaching machines each student is free to proceed at his own rate. Holding students together for instructional purposes in a class (or through TV instruction) is probably the greatest source of inefficiency in education" (Skinner 1961).

2. "A member of a (regular) class . . . cannot always make up for absences. Working on a machine, a student can always take up where he left off or, if he wishes, review earlier work after a longer absence" (Skinner 1961).

3. "The coherence of the program helps to maximize the student's success, for by thoroughly mastering one step he is optimally prepared for the next" (Skinner 1961).

4. "Immediate and frequent reinforcement sustains a lively interest" (Skinner 1961).

5. "The effect upon each student is surprisingly like that of a private tutor: (1) There is a constant interaction between program and student. The student is always alert and busy. (2) The machine insists that a given point be thoroughly

understood before the student moves on. (3) The machine presents just that material for which the student is ready. (4) It also helps him come up with the right answer" (Skinner 1958).

6. "By relieving the teacher of much that is routine, the teaching machine and program permit other activities greater play: creative thinking, participating in group processes, searching out facts and solving problems" (Hilgard 1961, adapted).

Main Criticisms of Programmed Instruction

1. "Most programs teach by conditioning rather than discovery and insight. However, in schools we should maximize insight learning and minimize conditioned learning as much as possible" (Thelen 1963).

2. "The single answer approach to education . . . assumes that our knowledge of the world is a fixed and orderly body of facts and conclusions. But . . . education is also inquiry, insight, emergence, the development of a critical faculty, and . . . the structure of abstractions about the seen and the unseen that comprises our understanding of the physical world" (Fitzgerald 1962).

3. "Programmed learning by its nature requires plodding, step by minute step, across the expanse of a subject or sub-subject. The machines do not readily lend themselves to skimming for over-all view, to dipping into a future chapter to anticipate development or returning to an earlier chapter to check points already made to weigh and compare information" (Fitzgerald 1962).

4. "Teaching machines lead to the slow spread of . . . authoritarian thinking" (Fitzgerald 1962).

5. "Some students will find a deeper, more personal distaste for learning from a machine, from interacting with it. . . . Interaction with is not the same as using a machine, but involves being somehow part of the machine or being subjected to it" (Fitzgerald 1962).

Research on Programmed Instruction

How effective are programmed books and other self-instructional devices? Do students learn from them? Do they save time? How do they affect students' motivation? The following conclusions seem to be warranted on the basis of the research.

Effectiveness. Programmed materials are effective in teaching both factual and meaningful material. In some studies they seem to be equally as effective as regular classroom instruction; in other studies they have proven more effective, as measured by achievement tests, reduced failure rates, etc. (Gropper and Lumsdaine 1960, Klaus 1960, Porter 1959).

Efficiency. In terms of time spent on a course taught through programmed instruction, some studies indicate substantial savings. However, there are wide individual differences. Brighter students complete a program in a relatively short time and so save time; students of lesser ability sometimes take even more time than they ordinarily would have spent in a regular classroom group (Boroff 1960, TEMAC 1961).

Attitudes.   For the most part, students seem to have favorable attitudes toward the use of teaching machines and programmed texts. Interest in the course material has been found to range from adequate to high, with students sometimes devoting considerable free time to the programmed materials. However, some students consider programmed instruction to be too easy, and to reflect on their intelligence or their "dignity as human beings" (Clark 1961, Porter 1959, Mager 1959).

Types.   Linear and contingent programs are equally effective for accomplishing learning outcomes. Comparative studies regularly show no significant differences between them (Silberman 1961).

Adjunct Materials.   When used as adjunct materials in connection with a regular course, programmed texts and teaching machines have been found to be particularly valuable in terms of more thorough coverage and increased comprehension of course material. Substantial savings in class time because of a common knowledge of basic ideas have also been reported (Blyth 1960, Klaus 1960, McCullough 1960).

Responses.   Whether requiring written (overt) or purely mental (covert) responses to the question in each frame is more effective is an open question. Studies sometimes favor one, sometimes neither. However, overt responses have been found to be more effective for technical, unfamiliar or difficult material (Cummings and Goldstein 1962).

Feedback.   Similarly, supplying the correct answer (feedback) after students have filled in completion items has not always been found to be necessary. In dense programming, students seem to do equally well whether the correct answer is supplied for each frame or for only some of the frames. In other programming, students learn more when feedback is given than when there is no feedback or when answers are given with the frames. In other words, giving feedback is less important when prompts and cues are supplied, and more important for difficult material or later in a program when prompts are often withdrawn (Krumboltz and Weisman 1962, Moore and Smith 1964, Anderson, Kulhavy and Andre 1971, 1972).

Classroom Use of Programmed Instruction

If you decide to use programmed instruction in your own teaching, there are several points that you would do well to keep in mind.

Functions.   Be aware of the many ways that programmed materials—either programmed books or teaching machines—can be utilized: (1) as means for the students to learn whole subjects (spelling, advanced math in a small high school), certain aspects of subjects (grammar rules in language arts), or specific units within a course (probability in mathematics); (2) as adjunct material to be used in conjunction with a regular text; (3) as make-up material for a student who has been absent for a week or more; and (4) as an enrichment program on advanced topics for the brighter students and as a remedial program on basic topics for slower students.

Selection. Be alert to the several types of programs that you might use and choose the best for your purpose. Although the linear type is more prevalent, if you search you should be able to find contingent programs in your field and maybe even a program designed to promote discovery learning, problem solving, or critical thinking.

Examine several programs in your subject field carefully before you buy a program, just as you would in selecting a textbook. You should consider not just the topics covered but also the general quality of the program and how you think your students will react to it.

Suggested Readings

Discovery Learning

Keislar, E. and Shulman, L. M., eds. *Learning by Discovery.* Chicago: Rand McNally, 1966.

Programmed Instruction

Glaser, R., ed. *Teaching Machines and Programmed Learning II: Data and Directions.* Washington, D.C.: National Education Association, 1965.

Lumsdaine, A. A. and Glaser, R., eds. *Teaching Machines and Programmed Learning: A Source Book.* Washington, D.C.: National Education Association, 1960.

Lysaught, J. P. and Williams, C. M. *A Guide to Programmed Instruction.* New York: John Wiley, 1963.

Pipe, P. *Practical Programming.* New York: Holt, Rinehart & Winston, 1966.

5

Motivation

Ask an experienced teacher what his major concern is regarding his students' learning. The overwhelming probability is that he will answer that it is how to get his students involved in learning and how to keep them interested—in a word, *motivation.*

Motivation is what initiates and sustains a student's involvement in the act of learning. To a large extent it determines the direction and efficiency of his learning. It can also offset fatigue and even some lack of ability for learning.

Of the many problems that you will face as a teacher, your main one will be how to motivate your students. To approach this very real problem constructively, you will want to be aware of several things. On a practical level, what are some techniques for motivating students? On a more psychological plane, to what psychological needs and other motives do these techniques appeal; which type of motivating techniques should you emphasize in your teaching (and why)? On the level of theory, how is the relation between motivation and learning best explained? And returning to a practical concern, what applications for teaching can be drawn from the available research data regarding motivation for learning? These are some of the questions that we will try to answer in this chapter.

EXERCISE 5-1. Motivating Factors in Practice

Consider the following attempts of teachers to motivate their students. In each instance try to determine to what motivating factor in his students the teacher has appealed.

1. An English teacher, teaching grammar to a slower class of ninth graders, sets up role-playing situations in which students act as applicants and employers. After several

"interviews" the class comments on the grammar of the applicants; a discussion is then held on the importance of good usage in applying for a job.

_____ Emotions

_____ Incentives

_____ Goal

2. The manual arts teacher informs the English teacher of the projects that his students have chosen to work on, e.g. water skis, rifle holders, coats-of-arms. The English teacher suggests books in the school library on water skiing, hunting, heraldry, etc. for the students to read.

_____ Interests

_____ Goal

_____ Need for self-esteem

3. A general science teacher, introducing a unit on electricity, connects the two ends of a large coil of insulated wire to a galvanometer. He takes a bar magnet, first puts it inside the coil of wire one way and then pulls it out the other. He asks the class: "Why did the galvanometer act the way it did?"

_____ Activity drive

_____ Curiosity need

_____ Goal

4. A fifth-grade teacher divides the class into two groups and holds a "college bowl" as a review for a social studies unit; the winning team is excused from homework for two days.

_____ Emotions

_____ Interests

_____ Incentives

5. A history teacher, trying to impress upon his students the extreme working conditions imposed on children in factories during the early days of the Industrial Revolution in England, turns the lights out, closes the blinds and for twenty minutes has the students put screws and washers on bolts according to a diagram sketched on the board.

_____ Curiosity need

_____ Emotions

_____ Values

Answers:

1. Goal
2. Interests
3. Curiosity need
4. Incentives
5. Emotions

Motivating Factors

There are many human needs, motives, and emotions that you as a teacher can appeal to in attempts to motivate your students. What are these needs, motives, and emotions, and how would you appeal to each one?

First, for purposes of clarification it will be helpful to distinguish among these basic motivating factors that are an integral part of a person's life, and that in turn form the basis for his becoming involved in the learning process. Consider the schema in figure 5-1.

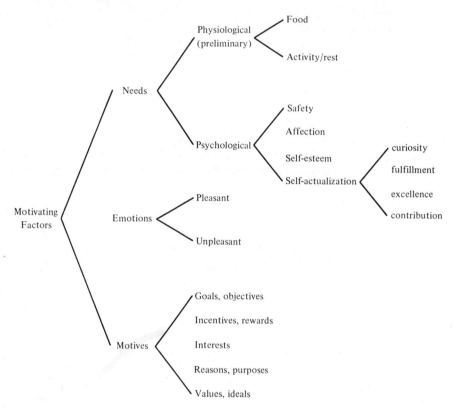

Figure 5-1. *Motivating Factors in Relation to Learning*

All men possess basic psychological needs that underly much of their behavior. Among them are the needs for:

Safety—the need to be free from danger, from harmful influences in the environment

Affection—the need for loving and being loved; the need to belong to a group

Self-esteem—the need for self-respect, a sense of worth or accomplishment, the need for the approval and recognition of others

Self-actualization—the need for actualizing one's potential, developing one's abilities; it includes the needs for:
curiosity—the desire to know and understand
excellence—the need to achieve a high standard
fulfillment—the need to reach a stated goal
contribution—the need to contribute to society, to help others.

Every man has an emotional substructure that is an integral part of his personality. An emotion is a conscious tendency toward or away from an object, accompanied by certain physical feelings.

> Pleasant emotions—those that involve an attraction to the emotionally toned object, include love, joy, desire, and happiness
>
> Unpleasant emotions—those that involve a tendency away from the object, include fear, anger, hate, sadness, and antipathy.

Finally, a person often acts for a conscious motive, which can take any one of the following specific forms:

> The goals and objectives that a person sets up and attempts to achieve
>
> Incentives or rewards that are offered to the person for certain behavior
>
> The interests and curiosity that the person has developed regarding various fields or activities
>
> Specific reasons or purposes that a person has for acting
>
> The system of values and ideals that he is committed to and that in turn influences his actions.

A teacher can appeal to any of these motivating factors as he teaches a class; or often he will appeal to several factors during a class session. The question is *how*. The following suggestions should indicate how this appeal to a person's needs, emotions, and motives can work out in practice. In turn the examples may suggest further applications in your own field.

Needs

Food	The need for food is usually considered to be a prerequisite that should be satisfied before further activity takes place in the classroom, not as a need to appeal to in motivating students for learning (although some behaviorists direct reinforcement, e.g. M & M's, to this need).
Activity/rest	Have pupils—especially in primary grades—stand up or sing a song after a period of intensive seat work.
Safety	Suggest ways in which a lesson or topic will help prepare students to make a living and be economically secure.
Affection	Have a warm and accepting attitude toward all students; don't be afraid to show genuine interest by a hand on the shoulder as you help an individual student, or by a literal pat on the back when he expends a little more effort than usual.
Self-esteem	Give praise for accomplishments, no matter how small; display students' artistic productions; read better compositions of all students aloud sometime during a course.
Self-actualization	Stress what students can do with what they learn: how reading skill opens books to them, how mathematics lets them understand science, etc.; mystify students, disturb their ordinary way of thinking, offer challenges to them, suggest that they have the potential to do a little better; suggest how they can use their knowledge and skill to help others and contribute to society, have them engage in pupil-team learning (one student explaining something to another with each quizzing the other).

Emotions

Pleasant emotions | Play appropriate music on occasion as you read poetry; set up simulated situations and games such as a pre-Civil War game with students representing various sections of the country and making decisions on the major problems facing the country at the time. In other words, make learning fun.

Unpleasant emotions | Set up situation in which dark-haired students are objects of prejudice for seven days; then light-haired students are objects of prejudice for several days.

Motives

Goals, Objectives | Plan with the student how many tasks or objectives he would like to master in a given portion of a course; try to relate at least some topics to the occupations that students are tentatively interested in.

Incentives, Rewards | Indicate what grade can be expected for a certain level of performance; and divide the class into several teams, set up a prize, and award points for a certain amount of work, a number of correct answers, etc.

Interests | Assign outside reading according to main interests of students, e.g. *National Velvet* or *The Old Man and the Sea* for those with strong outdoor interests; allow science students to work up their own experiments or problems that interest them rather than always doing uniform experiments.

Reasons, Purposes | Emphasize why a student should study your subject field, what practical value it has; for instance, one can study foreign language in order to communicate with people, to increase his business opportunities, to enjoy opera and works of literature.

Values, Ideals | Have students work on projects, reports, oral presentations that are in keeping with their leading values: humanitarian, scientific, religious, economic, etc. Have them read biographies that exemplify important ideals that students have mentioned in discussions.

EXERCISE 5-2. Specific Motivating Techniques—Intrinsic and Extrinsic

Given below are motivating techniques grouped into categories that emphasize: (1) student involvement, (2) curiosity, (3) something that is of current or immediate interest to students, (4) concrete experiences, (5) specific incentives, or (6) some type of verbal reinforcement.

First, add your own suggestions to the appropriate categories.

Then classify the types in terms of their relation to learning as:

A. Naturally related to learning or inherent in the act of learning itself
B. Artificially related to learning, i.e. depending on some authority for its connection with the learning act.

	Naturally related	Artificially related
Involvement		
Creative activities, e.g. students writing their own play as a class	___	___

Discovery learning   N   A
Dramatization, e.g. an event in history
Debate, discussion
Games, simulation
Contrived experience, e.g. brown-eyed students as objects of
     prejudice
Curiosity   —   —
Thought questions, problem-centered teaching
Doubt, perplexity, e.g. an instance that doesn't fit a supposed
     universal
Bafflement, contradiction
Divergent thinking questions
Immediate to Students   —   —
Current event
Local or school issue, event, situation
Application to practical use, student needs, e.g. getting a job,
     cooking
Contrived experience, e.g. brown-eyed students as objects of
     prejudice
Concrete   —   —
Pictures, records, films
Field trips
Demonstrations
Personal experience of teacher
Incentives   —   —
Marks, honor roll
Group, individual competition
Prize, privilege
Display of exemplary work
Reinforcement   —   —
Praise, compliment
Encouragement
Knowledge of results

What percentage of the techniques listed (plus those you thought of) are natural and intrinsically related to learning, what percentage are artificial and dependent on someone else (a teacher)?

The first four categories involve motivating techniques that are naturally and intrinsically related to the act of learning. The last two categories include techniques that are more extrinsic to learning itself. They involve an artificial connection between the motivating technique and the learning act.

It seems that in terms of quantity of motivating techniques available, most are intrinsic and natural rather than extrinsic and artificial. What techniques are actually used more often is another question—one that really doesn't concern us here. What motivating techniques *should* be used more is an important question which will be examined in exercise 5-3.

Motivating Techniques: Intrinsic and Extrinsic

The motivating techniques used in the classroom can be thought of as being on a continuum from intrinsic to extrinsic. Intrinsic motivating techniques are those that are naturally related to learning; they are inherent either in the learning process itself or in the knowledge or behavior acquired. Extrinsic motivating techniques have an artificial connection with learning; they are not part of the learning process itself, but are imposed from outside by some authority, usually a teacher. Each motivating technique can also be thought of as appealing to a certain need or other motivating force within the person. The intrinsic–extrinsic continuum of motivating techniques, together with the motivating force to which they appeal, is as follows:

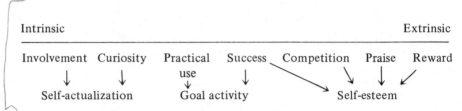

Intrinsic   Extrinsic

Involvement   Curiosity   Practical use   Success   Competition   Praise   Reward

Self-actualization   Goal activity   Self-esteem

Student involvement is obviously an integral part of the learning process. Curiosity regarding a topic is also very closely (and naturally) related to learning about that topic. Similarly, the practical use of what we learn is an important and intrinsic aspect of that subject or skill.

On the other end of the continuum, tangible rewards such as marks, privileges and the like, given for good performance, are extrinsic to the act of learning. Any connection between these rewards and what is learned must be established by a teacher or other authority; this is true whether the reward is given as a result of some competition or after a successfully completed learning sequence. Similarly with verbal praise there is only an artificial—not natural—relation between learning something and being praised for doing so.

The feeling of success in learning is at the center of the continuum because it can be either an intrinsic or extrinsic motivating force: intrinsic if it involves the satisfaction that often comes towards the end of a successful learning sequence; extrinsic when the feeling of accomplishment becomes the student's main concern regardless of what is learned.

Each motivating technique appeals to a certain need or other motivating force within the person. Involvement in learning subject matter or skills and curiosity for learning about them are closely related to a person's need for self-actualization. Learning something for its practical use is related to one's purpose or goal-oriented motivation: we learn something as a means to a goal. Tangible rewards and verbal praise given for good performance as well as competition among students are all directed to the individual's need for self-esteem. The emphasis on success in learning activities can be directed either to the student's goal-oriented activity if satisfaction with the outcomes is stressed, or to his need for self-esteem if satisfaction with self is emphasized.

EXERCISE 5-3.   Intrinsic and Extrinsic Motivation: Evaluation

Which type of motivating techniques will you use in your teaching, intrinsic or extrinsic? Some of the arguments for each type are given below. Indicate which type of motivation each argument applies to. On the basis of the arguments, which emphasis do you prefer, intrinsic or extrinsic?

	Intrinsic	Extrinsic
1. They appeal to the need for self-actualization, a higher need (in terms of greater satisfaction and nobility) than the need for self-esteem.	____	____
2. They appeal to the need for self-esteem, which is still seeking satisfaction during the school years—especially elementary school.	____	____
3. The need for self-actualization—including the curiosity need—ordinarily begins to emerge by age 5 or 6, at about the time the child enters school; unless it is appealed to, it will be stunted and therefore will be difficult to satisfy later.	____	____
4. They are especially necessary for students who have not had their need for self-esteem sufficiently satisfied at home.	____	____
5. They are needed for many students to overcome inertia and procrastination connected with the sustained work and the study involved in learning.	____	____
6. They help a person develop greater independence in learning; he will tend to learn on his own more when he is not in school.	____	____
7. They are more immediate and therefore more effective, especially for younger children who are not influenced by delayed rewards and distant goals.	____	____
8. They tend to be permanent and have a more lasting effect, even after a course is completed.	____	____
9. They are especially helpful when students are disinterested or find a particular subject unpleasant.	____	____
10. They have informative value, i.e. they indicate correct or accurate information to the student.	____	____
11. They respect the proper relationship between motivation and learning: motivation as a means to learning rather than learning as a means to obtain a reward.	____	____

Intrinsic motivation appeals to the need for self-actualization (1), extrinsic motivation to the need for self-esteem (2). Those who have had all of their psychological needs satisfied to an adequate degree usually claim that self-actualization is more important to them and gives them more of a sense of human satisfaction and nobility than does self-esteem. According to Abraham Maslow (1954, p. 197), the chief proponent of the theory of psychological needs, the needs for safety, affection, self-esteem and self-actualization are arranged in a temporal order as well as in a hierarchy of mobility. If the more basic needs are satisfied to a certain degree, then the higher needs emerge in the order indicated. Ordinarily, the need for self-esteem is satisfied by attentive parents in the first few years of life to the extent necessary for the need for self-actualization (plus the curiosity need that is a part of it) to begin to emerge, at least by the time the child enters school. The best time to satisfy a need is when it first emerges; the longer you wait the more difficult it will be to satisfy it. Therefore, intrinsic motivation with its appeal to self-actualization is called for even in the primary grades (3). However, the need for self-esteem does not cease to require more satisfaction, and so some extrinsic incentives are also called for in the elementary school for all pupils, but especially for the pupils whose need for self-esteem was satisfied only to a minimal degree at home (4).

Intrinsic motivation, with its emphasis on interest and excitement in learning itself, has the advantage of fostering greater independence in learning (6), whereas extrinsic incentives, regulated as they are by an authority, tend to foster dependence and docility. Because of the development of greater independence in learning, intrinsic motivation has a greater chance of being permanent in its effect. When a person is genuinely interested in a topic he will tend to learn more about it even when a course is over (8). On the other hand, if he is conditioned to expect a reward when he learns, it is questionable whether he will continue to study a topic once the structure of rewards is removed. The hope in extrinsic motivation is that gradually students will be weaned away from rewards and be stimulated by an interest in the subject itself. This transfer has yet to be demonstrated satisfactorily; those who favor intrinsic motivation say that it is much safer to begin with intrinsic motives from the start.

Extrinsic incentives, because they are immediate and concrete, have the advantage of being more effective with children who need such motivation. Although younger children can become excited about learning something, they are not impressed with the long-term value and practical use of the subject they study (7). Short-term incentives and rewards are particularly effective with economically disadvantaged students and students who simply are not interested in a subject for its own sake (9), at least not sufficiently to overcome the inertia associated with the sustained effort necessary for learning (5).

Regarding the relationship between motivation and learning, the natural relationship is one of means to end: we are motivated in order to learn. Intrinsic motivation conforms to this pattern: the students' focus is always on what is to be learned (11). There is a danger in extrinsic motivation—particularly competition and tangible rewards—that the natural relationship will be inverted: students will learn in order to get a reward. (Competition also runs the risk of producing anxiety and unsocial attitudes; in addition, the reward is effective only for the students who win—most are disappointed.) Extrinsic motivation in the form of encouragement, praise, and knowledge of results has an important informative value which is lacking in intrinsic motivation. It indicates to the student the correct information or answer to a problem (10).

On the basis of the arguments, again, which do you think is preferable, and, more important, which will you emphasize in your teaching—intrinsic or extrinsic motivation?

Theories of Motivation

Up to this point we have been treating only types of motivating factors and motivating techniques. Now we get into the more important and involved questions of why students put forth the effort required to learn something and how the motivational factors that influence learning are related to one another.

There are two leading contemporary theories that attempt to explain the relation between motivation and learning. One is the drive theory originally devised by Clark Hull which stresses basic needs and extrinsic incentives, particularly rewards. The other is the theory of achievement motivation developed by John Atkinson and David McClelland which emphasizes the motive of achieving success. Before we analyze them systematically, consider how each theory would work out in practice.

EXERCISE 5-4. Theories of Motivation in Action

Given below are different approaches that two foreign language teachers used to motivate their students, with each approach based on a different theory of motivation as it relates to learning. Analyze the approaches and then indicate what you think the general characteristics of each approach are.

I

Teacher stresses the importance of learning the language if students want to take advantage of the excellent business opportunities with countries in which the language is spoken.

Teacher mentions the good grades that will come if students learn the language well. In addition he promises to take the class to an appropriate restaurant (French, Spanish, etc.) if the students learn to speak the language well enough.

Teacher constantly uses the equivalent of "very good," "that's right," etc., in the foreign language when students respond correctly and especially when they use the correct pronunciation and idiom.

II

Teacher conducts a brief conversation in the language, but students do not understand it. He asks, "Wouldn't it be great to be able to speak the language and converse with others?"

Teacher tells students that they can learn the language: many others have learned it; they have learned their own language, and learning a second one is easier.

Teacher examines counselors' files on aptitude and achievement of students, trying to determine how motivated they are, whether they are under- or over-achievers or about average. He holds conferences with the students early in the course to discuss the importance of motivation for learning and suggests several reasons for studying a foreign language.

Indicate which approach to the motivation of students is characterized by each statement below.

_____ Challenge is provided to students; an indication of how satisfying it would be to be able to perform the activity is given.

_____ Students are encouraged to anticipate success in learning; emphasis is given to the moderate—not extreme—degree of difficulty of the learning task.

_____ An attempt is made to arouse a need for what is to be learned, so as to provide a desire for learning.

_____ Attractive incentives are offered and students expect to be rewarded for their efforts.

_____ Individual differences in motivation are analyzed; students are encouraged to increase their achievement motivation.

_____ Reinforcement is given for correct responses as students attempt to learn the language.

I

The teacher who stresses the importance of what is to be learned (business opportunities) is trying to arouse a need for learning in the student. The need gives rise to a desire or *drive* for learning, which is a necessary prerequisite if learning is to take place. The mention of good grades and the promise of eating in a restaurant where the language is used are both designed to have the students look forward to a reward for their efforts. This anticipation of reward is called *incentive motivation*.

The continual *reinforcement* of correct responses is simply the law of effect in action. The verbal reinforcement after each correct response increases the probability that that response will be repeated in the future.

II

The teacher who has students experience what it is like not to understand a conversation is trying to provide a challenge to them. At the same time he suggests that learning the language well would be satisfying. The attractiveness of succeeding at a challenging task is termed the *incentive value of success*.

By reminding the students that they have mastered a similar task before, the teacher leads them to anticipate that they will be successful in this learning task also. The awareness that the task is not too difficult and that the person will probably be successful is called *expectancy* of success.

The teacher who tries to determine how motivated for learning his students are—and also tries to make them more motivated—realizes that each student has a certain degree of need for achievement which is a basic part of his personality, but which can be increased to some extent. This need to achieve success is termed *achievement motive*.

In your own teaching, which will you tend to do more: offer incentives that encourage students to learn or point out to a student the challenge that a learning task presents? With individual students, which approach will you prefer: instill in them a need for what is to be learned or stress the satisfaction which comes from achieving a worthwhile goal? In the case of students who don't seem to be motivated at all, what means will you take to try to shake them out of their lethargy?

To help you answer these questions with some degree of satisfaction, it will be worth examining more formally the major theories of motivation in relation to learning.

Drive Theory

The first theory we will consider is the drive theory of Hull, on which the first teacher in exercise 5-4 based his approach to the motivation of his students. Hull explains the basic nature of his theory as follows:

> The needs of organisms operate both in the formation of habits and in their subsequent functioning. Because of the sensitizing or energizing action of needs . . ., they are called *drives*.
>
> If the central afferent receptor discharge (s) of a stimulus (S) is active in the central nervous system at the time that a reaction (R) is evoked, and if at about this time there occurs a "reinforcing state of affairs," there will result from this conjunction of events an increment to a habit (sHr).
>
> Ordinarily at least, a habit must be conjoined with a motivation or drive (D) before action will follow recurrence of conditioned stimulation (S). A recent experiment suggests rather strongly that the relationship of habit strength (sHr) and drive (D) to the evocation of conditioned reaction is a multiplicative one. (Hull 1942, pp. 65, 73)

In Hull's theory, a drive that results either from a need for food, safety, etc., or from other needs associated with those primary needs, e.g., a career, money, etc., is necessary both for a person to learn something and for him to be expected to perform what he has learned subsequently. A drive must be present for a connection between a stimulus and a response to form in the first place. This connection or "habit" is formed and strengthened by reason of the response reducing the drive, i.e. providing reinforcement; in fact, the strength of a habit depends on the number of reinforced trials. Drive is also necessary if an individual is to use the habit he has formed. If he has no need or drive to perform an action, he will not perform it. On the other hand, if he has an intense drive, he will probably perform the action even though his habit is not very strong; the drive makes up for the weak habit. As Hull says, the relation between drive and habit strength is multiplicative: strength of a connection between S–R (sHr) $\times$ Drive (D) = probability of response (sEr).[1] For instance (if we can suppose quantitative values for a moment), moderate sHr but no D results in

---

1. Literally, sEr means: exitatory potential; it is also called potential for response or simply reaction potential.

zero reaction potential (4 × 0 = 0), whereas some sHr and strong D results in rather high sEr (2 × 8 = 16). Note that the latter is the equivalent of moderate amounts of each (4 × 4 = 16).

More recently other factors have been identified as contributing to reaction potential, particularly the factor of incentive motivation (K) or the anticipation of a reward. The degree of incentive motivation is determined directly by the amount and kind of reward offered in the reinforcement of learning. Incentive motivation (K) also enters into a multiplicative relationship with habit strength (sHr) in determining the strength of reaction potential, so that the full formulation of Hull's motivational theory is: sHr × D × K = sEr. In other words, if either habit, drive or expectation of reward is very strong, it can make up for a weakness in another factor (e.g. 2 × 8 × 4 = 4 × 4 × 4). If any one is lacking, the person will probably not respond (4 × 4 × 0 = 0). It is important to note that on the basis of further experimental evidence, Kenneth Spence, a disciple of Hull, revised the pattern to sEr = sHr (D + K), where drive and incentive motivation are additive so that if either one is present, the individual very probably will perform the relevant behavior. It is quite possible that if Hull had lived he would have agreed with Spence that the lack of one motivating factor does not cancel out the effect of the other.

In the classroom, the teacher who follows Hull's theory will stress felt needs, making each student aware of how important a skill or information is for him. This will set up the necessary motivational condition (drive) for learning to take place, and it will also provide the basic motivation for the student to perform what he has learned.

A teacher will also emphasize rewards ("That's good," "That's correct") as an integral part of the learning act, so that the students will learn the skills or information well (reinforcement). He will also offer specific rewards (a good report, an A, a privilege) as incentives for students to perform well in review sessions or on tests (incentive motivation).

Finally, the teacher will be aware of the relationship among felt needs, rewards offered, and the degree of skill or knowledge. The best situation is when all are present to a maximum degree; but if one is weaker, a teacher can either work on that factor or try to increase one of the other factors. Finally, if one factor is not present (zero), he will understand why a student will not perform at all.

Theory of Achievement Motivation

The second explanation of learning motivation that we will examine is the theory of achievement motivation developed by Atkinson, McClelland and others. It is the theory on which the second teacher above based his approach to the motivating of students. Atkinson explains the main thrust of the theory as follows:

> The strength of the tendency in an individual to achieve success (T_s) in a task is a multiplicative function of three variables: motive to achieve success (M_s), conceived as a relatively general and relatively stable disposi-

tion of personality; and two other variables which represent the effect of the immediate environment—the strength of *expectancy* (or subjective probability) that performance of a task will be followed by success (P_s), and the relative attractiveness of success at that particular activity, which we call the incentive value of success (I_s). In other words, $T_s = M_s \times P_s \times I_s$.

According to his kind of Expectancy $\times$ Value Theory, one can influence motivation by manipulating cues which define an individual's expectations concerning the consequences of his actions and/or the incentive value of the consequences (or goals) produced by action.

It is assumed that the incentive value or attractiveness of success is greater the more difficult the task. Similarly the estimated probability of success decreases as the difficulty of the task increases. This can be stated as a relationship between the incentive value of success (I_s) and the strength of expectancy or subjective probability of success (P_s): viz., $I_s = 1 - P_s$. (Atkinson 1965, p. 29)

In the theory of achievement motivation, whether or not a person will strive to reach a goal depends on several variables: (1) one's basic need for achieving a degree of excellence or for becoming involved in a worthwhile goal activity; (2) how certain (or probable) a person is that he will be successful; and (3) how attractive reaching the goal is, i.e. the degree of satisfaction one will experience in achieving a goal.

The person's need for achievement is a basic factor of his personality. Some students by temperament are aggressive and achievement-oriented; others are more adaptive and easy-going; and still others are more pensive and submissive. But all of them will have some degree of achievement need.

The extent to which a person expects to be successful depends either on his degree of skill in the activity or on the relative ease of the task itself. The more skillful he is or the easier the task, the more likely it is that he will succeed.

The incentive value of success depends on how attractive the goal is, how difficult or challenging it is, and therefore how satisfied the person will be in attaining it. The relative attractiveness of success becomes greater as the difficulty of the task increases.

The relation between the attractiveness or incentive value of success and the expectancy or subjective probability of success is important for the theory. Note that as the difficulty of a task increases the incentive value goes up, but the expectation (probability) of success goes down. Hence, the probability of success is inversely related to the incentive value of success (I_s), or, $I_s = 1 - P_s$.

Whether or not a person strives to achieve success in a task depends on all of the factors, his achievement motive (M_s), his expectancy of success (P_s), and the incentive value of success (I_s); they are related in a multiplicative way, i.e. strength of tendency to achieve success (T_s) = $M_s \times P_s \times I_s$.

If a task is very easy or very difficult, the tendency to achieve success will be considerably less than if the task is of moderate difficulty but still somewhat of a challenge. For instance, if there is a 50/50 chance of success, the task is not too difficult but challenging, so that the person figures that he has a good chance of success (P_s) and that the success will bring considerable satisfaction (I_s). Therefore, his tendency to achieve success will be relatively strong. If there is only a 1 in 10 chance of success and hence a low expectancy of success, or if it is a "sure thing" and hence offers very little satisfaction, the person will figure "why bother?"

Putting it quantitatively, for the person of moderate achievement need, say a score of 8, given the 50/50 chance of success the equation would be $T_s = 8 \times 0.50 \times 0.50$ or 2. For a very difficult task, e.g. one with only 10 percent probability of success and therefore an incentive value of 0.90 $(1 - 0.10)$, the equation is $T_s = 8 \times 0.10 \times 0.90$ or 0.72. Similarly for a fairly easy task with a 70 percent probability of success and an incentive value of 0.30: $T_s = 8 \times 0.70 \times 0.30$ or 1.68. A person with a higher need for achievement, say a score of 16, would have a proportionately stronger tendency to achieve success at the same tasks, viz. 4, 1.44, and 3.36 respectively. The curves of the two persons (M_s of 8 and M_s of 16) would appear as shown in figure 5-2. Note that the tendency to achieve success is greatest when the task difficulty is moderate, and that the difference in the tendency to achieve success among individuals is greater for moderately challenging tasks but relatively small for tasks of extreme ease or difficulty.

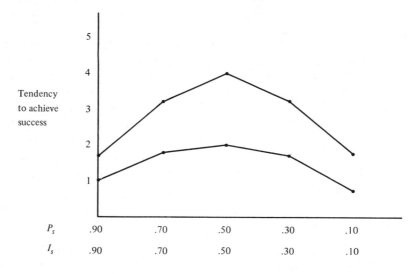

Figure 5-2. *Theoretical Implications of $T_s = M_s \times P_s \times I_s$ and $I_s = 1 - P_s$*

Applying the theory of achievement motivation in the classroom, a teacher will try to involve the students in subject matter or skills that are not too difficult but are sufficiently challenging to them so as to keep both probability of success and incentive value at the most effective level. Although the basic need for achievement is difficult to assess, a teacher will realize that his students vary in their degree of achievement motivation; in turn, they also differ in their tendency to achieve success in specific tasks. In other words, he will expect some to work harder on projects and problems than others. He will not blame the less motivated but will try to counsel them and get them to increase the degree of their achievement motivation. Since it is a relatively stable aspect of personality, a teacher will not expect to increase his students' need for achievement too markedly.

A final application has to do with the contract system in which a student signs an agreement as to the amount of work he will do for a course or a unit, in return for an appropriate grade. In using any form of the contract system, the teacher will make the students aware of both the amount and difficulty of the various achievement levels and their respective abilities for the different levels. He will encourage them to choose a reasonable level, one that is in keeping with their need for achievement as well as one that will offer good probability of success and give sufficient satisfaction once achieved.

EXERCISE 5-5. Evaluation of Theories of Motivation

Which theory do you prefer and why? Given below are some criticisms (pro and con) of the two theories we have examined. They may help you in your evaluation of the theories. Check the statements with which you agree.

Hull's Drive Theory

_____ + Emphasis on drive as a prerequisite to learning is valuable; it points up the importance of having students feel a need before getting into the actual business of learning itself.

_____ + Including incentives and rewards in the theory explains the relation of extrinsic motivation and learning.

_____ + The multiplicative relationship between what a person has learned previously and his present need or drive plus his anticipation of a reward is a reasonable one.

_____ − Emphasis on reduction of a need is only part of the story; it does not explain curiosity, success, and interest in learning.

_____ − There is an overemphasis on extrinsic motives to the detriment of intrinsic motivation.

The Theory of Achievement Motivation

_____ + The emphasis on challenge and the value of success takes into account an important aspect of motivation in relation to learning.

_____ + The emphasis on aiming at a difficult but reasonable goal, one that the person will be able to achieve, is an important point to include in an explanation of motivation for learning.

_____ + The inverse relationship between the incentive value and the probability of success is sound.

_____ + The multiplicative relationship among a person's basic achievement motivation plus the environmental variables of expectancy and incentive value of success seems to be reasonable.

_____ — Including a construct such as "motive to achieve" gives the theory less of an empirical basis than it should have.

_____ — The emphasis on success is important but is only part of the whole picture; interest, curiosity, and extrinsic motives must also be taken into account for a complete theory.

Both of the main theories of motivation as it relates to learning have strengths and deficiencies. Positively, both stress a multiplicative or interactive relationship rather than a purely additive one. Both include elements that are important for any adequate explanation of how motivation and learning are related.

They are both limited as well. They include only a few of the many variables that enter into a full explanation of motivation for learning. However, to date, a more comprehensive theory that attempts to interrelate more of the variables that enter into a person's motivation for learning is not available. The more comprehensive motivational theories (Maslow, Freud) pertain to personality rather than learning. The recent explorations of cognitive conflict and the curiosity motive (Berlyne, cf. next section) have contributed an important dimension to any attempt to explain motivation for learning. But for the present a comprehensive theory of motivation for learning is more a need than an actuality.

Research on Classroom Learning Motivation

What does research offer to the teacher in this most important problem of motivating students? Are intrinsic or extrinsic motives more effective? What kinds of intrinsic motives have proven successful? What kinds of extrinsic incentives are preferred over others? What can be said about goal setting, feedback, etc. that a teacher can incorporate in his classes?

Much of the research on motivation in relation to learning has been done in laboratories with animals. Much of the motivation research conducted with humans refers more to personality than to learning; hence it is of limited relevance to our main interest here. The conclusions given below are derived only from studies done with human subjects in the context of classroom learning. First, some findings related to intrinsic motives and achievement motivation will be given; then some of the main results of studies dealing with feedback and extrinsic incentives will be presented.

Intrinsic Versus Extrinsic Motives

Instruction and involvement in ways of producing new ideas (intrinsic motivation) results in more and better ideas than does offering prizes for the best performance (extrinsic incentive) (Torrance 1962).

Curiosity and creative drive (intrinsic need) result in higher motivation and performance in reading than does competition among individuals (extrinsic incentive) (Roberts 1960).

Conflict and Curiosity

Arousing a degree of conflict in students before a task results in superior performance rather than simply presenting the task with no element of conflict (Mittman and Terrell 1964).

Provoking curiosity through a pre-test results in greater retention of information than simply presenting the information without any pre-test (Berlyne 1960).

Arousal of attention and curiosity to a moderate degree results in the most efficient learning. Moderate arousal is the mean between too little (lethargy) and too intense (panic) (Berlyne 1960). The following factors have been shown to activate the arousal function: intense sensations, such as bright color, dynamic sound, and stimulus patterns that are complex, mildly ambiguous or somewhat incongruous, arouse students' attention; novel, surprising, changing or conflicting aspects of the environment arouse students' curiosity (Berlyne 1957).

Achievement Motivation

Students who succeed in learning tasks tend to set somewhat higher levels of aspiration and have a realistic expectancy of success in future learning tasks. Students who get low and failing grades tend to be erratic in their levels of aspiration, setting goals either too low (overly cautious) or unrealistically high ("at least I *aim* high"), and sometimes withdrawing from setting any goals (Child and Whiting 1949, Sears 1940).

A concerted effort at increasing the achievement motivation of students (through counseling, contracts, awareness of characteristics of highly motivated persons, etc.) can result in an improvement in school achievement, particularly with above-average socioeconomic class students (Kolb 1965).

Knowledge of Results

Feedback or knowledge of results helps to improve a student's performance, with immediate feedback usually more effective than delayed. Students learn better if they are given positive feedback for correct answers ("That's right") than if they are given negative feedback ("No, that's wrong") for incorrect answers. Those with high achievement need perform more effectively when given feedback which emphasizes the task they have performed. Those who are more socially oriented perform better if the feedback includes compliments for cooperation, acceptance of others' ideas, etc. (French 1958, Angell 1949, Van Wagenen and Travers 1963).

Praise

Praise is more effective than blame as an incentive; blame is more effective than no incentive at all, although repeated blame results in a decrease in performance. Praise is particularly effective for girls, introverts, and those of average ability and below—although it does not seem to help severe underachievers. Reproof is safer to use with boys, extroverts, and very bright students than with girls, introverts, and those of average or below ability. Although praise is generally more effective for all groups, it is definitely preferable for the latter groups (Hurlock 1925, Thompson and Hunnicutt 1944).

Students who receive a personal comment on a test paper, or one that relates to how well they expected to do, perform somewhat better on subsequent tests than those who receive a stereotyped comment; both groups improve more than those who simply receive a grade (Page 1958, Hammer 1972).

Competition

Competition and cooperation are probably equally effective as incentives. Some studies favor one, some the other, while many studies show no difference. A decision as to which to use has to be made on grounds other than research (Stendler et al. 1951).

Socioeconomic Differences

In comparing verbal praise ("That's good") with verbal feedback ("That's correct") when used with lower and middle socioeconomic class children, it seems that verbal praise is more effective for improving performance for lower class children and verbal feedback more effective for middle class children (Zigler and Kanzer 1962).

In comparing tangible (e.g. paper star, token) and intangible (e.g. word, smile) rewards used with children of different socioeconomic classes, it is found that those from lower class homes respond most favorably to tangible, material rewards, whereas students from middle class homes respond more favorably to intangible rewards (Hoffman et al. 1958).

There are other areas of research on motivation in relation to learning that we have not touched on, especially anxiety and punishment, for two reasons: they are negative and inhibitory and so are to be avoided by teachers; and they are more related to personality than to learning.

Motivating Students

On the basis of the research and other ideas presented so far in this chapter, what are the best motivational techniques for a teacher to use in his classroom? Here are some suggested applications from what we have seen. Perhaps you can think of others.

General

Use a variety of motivating techniques: personal goals, practical value of a subject, individual interests, felt needs, and praise. Motivating students is often difficult; having a repertoire of techniques will prove valuable. Emphasize intrinsic motives such as curiosity, involvement, and discovery as much as possible. When necessary use extrinsic incentives to a lesser extent.

Curiosity

Provoke curiosity in students before starting a topic by pointing up a problem or conflict, or giving a pre-test to make them realize what they don't know about the topic. Arouse surprise and a feeling of contradiction in students by presenting a phenomenon that violates their expectations or runs counter to their experience and former training, e.g. plants that live without sunlight or chlorophyll (fungi). Arouse doubt, uncertainty, bafflement by giving students a problem with no indications for its solution, e.g. how to find one's position (latitude and longitude) in the middle of the desert.

Attention

Arouse attention in students by starting a class with something novel, different, unusual, e.g., a brainstorming demonstration or a copy of an old newspaper in history. Maintain attention and interest through variety and change: never start a class the same way three times in a row.

Level of Aspiration

Provide for different levels of aspiration among students by encouraging them to strive for levels of performance in keeping with their abilities and by having differentiated materials, activities, and projects available for students of different ability and aspiration levels. This is as important for the student's involvement as it is difficult for a teacher. The contract system and the task-oriented nongraded programs can be of help here.

   With individual ability levels in mind, set standards and provide tasks of intermediate difficulty that are within the reach of students but still offer some challenge. Provide easier tasks for students who are discouraged because of low or failing grades. Mastering easier tasks will help them set realistic—and gradually higher—levels of aspiration for their work.

Achievement Motivation

On occasion, try to increase the basic achievement motivation of some students through talking with them, having them read about highly motivated persons, putting them in with a group of highly motivated students, etc. Chances of an increase in achievement motivation are greater with above average socioeconomic class students. Make students aware of their successes and the satisfaction they bring through comments such as: "You really did well in that," "Didn't it feel good to get so many right?" etc. Try to divert students' attention away from their failures by not threatening or punishing them or dwelling on their errors.

Reinforcement

Use praise and encouragement often, particularly for average and slower students and those who are more introverted and lack self-assurance. Give personal, encouraging comments on tests and other work rather than just a grade. Inform students regularly on how they are doing in a course, the sooner after a test or assignment the better. Use positive comments as much as possible.

Competition

Use group cooperation and team competition as incentives rather than have individuals compete against each other through such methods as group murals and "spelling baseball" (with correct words getting "on base" and misspelled words as "outs").

Socioeconomic Differences

Provide for socioeconomic class differences in motivational techniques: praise is more effective with lower class, feedback with middle class children; tangible rewards are more effective with lower class, intangible with middle class students.

Measuring Motivation

How can a teacher evaluate the motivation of his students? It is difficult to assess such an elusive variable as motivation. To get some idea of their students' motivation, teachers often use informal methods such as observation, a comparison of ability and achievement, or a friendly chat or interview. There are other more systematic techniques available such as check lists and course interest scales. But most of the measuring instruments used in the research studies demand considerable training and sophistication in measurement, more than a teacher is expected to possess. Here we will consider a few of the available techniques.

Informal Assessment Techniques

Teachers often use informal observation of students as a means of judging their degree of motivation: how attentive they are in class, whether they complete assignments, how active they are in discussions and projects, and how many books they seem to read. Even though this method is open to the grave limitations of subjective judgment and lack of systematic measurement, it does have the advantage of assessing how students actually behave rather than how motivated teachers think they behave (action is the real test of motivation).

Another common method of assessing student motivation is to analyze any discrepancy between his ability and achievement levels. The difference between a student's ability and how well he achieves is due to many factors, a major one usually being motivation. If he is not achieving up to his ability, it is often a sign that his achievement motivation is low. Conversely, if he is an "over-achiever," he is most probably highly motivated. Again, this is a rather global and subjective type of assessment, and it must be tempered with the realization that other factors may be playing the dominant role in the underachievement of some students, but it is a convenient technique that has some basis in research.

An informal interview is often the best way to assess a student's goals, both short-term goals connected with a specific course and long-term career goals. Since goals are both individualized and on the conscious level, the personal interview is a more appropriate method of inquiry than a systematic inventory. A teacher with a knowledge of course objectives and possible applications of a subject area plus an awareness of the various occupations available to young people will provide enough "structure" to such an interview to make it productive.

Systematic Techniques

Some teachers, concerned about forming a more definite judgment about their students' motivation and degree of interest, may wish to use a more systematic measurement instrument such as a rating or interest scale. A teacher himself can construct a simple rating scale such as the following.

Student Rating Scale

For each of the following adjectives put a check under the category that you feel best applies to you in relation to your life at school.

	very much so	quite	moderately	not very
studious				
cooperative				
industrious				
friendly				
intellectually curious				
respectful				
interested				

Only every other word is counted, i.e. the motivation-related words. A score can be obtained by assigning numerical values to the categories: "very much so" = 4, "quite" = 3, etc., and totaling them. Note that such a checklist is dependent upon individual student judgment and self-awareness, and so will not be entirely accurate—but then even the more sophisticated measures of motivation are somewhat deficient in accuracy.

Also, for teachers who wish to assess their students' motivation for a subject field more systematically than they usually do, the following interest-in-a-subject scale may be of help.

Interest in Subject Scale

Check the statements with which you agree.

_____ This is a fascinating subject covering very interesting topics (10).

_____ This is a very dull subject; I wouldn't recommend it to anyone (2).

_____   This subject is quite stimulating at times, but at other times only mildly interesting (7).

_____   I find this subject fairly interesting (6).

_____   Of all the subjects I have studied, this is the most interesting (11).

_____   This is the least interesting subject I have ever studied (1).

_____   I have little or no interest in this subject (3).

_____   This subject is interesting most of the time (8).

_____   I find this subject rather typical: not terribly interesting but not dull either (5).

_____   I find this subject quite interesting, in fact at times very interesting (9).

_____   Only now and then is this subject interesting, usually it is quite boring (4).

The numbers in the parentheses are not shown to the students but are used to score the inventory. Each value represents a point on a scale from 11 to 1. The values of the items that a student checks are averaged, and that average becomes his score. Although ordinarily such inventories are two or three times longer, this one can be used to obtain a relatively systematic evaluation of student interest in a subject.

To determine individual interest areas so as to provide for different interests in such subjects as reading and literature, you might obtain the Kuder Preference Record scores from the school counselor if he has given it to your students, or, almost as good, you can use the following checklist based on the Kuder listing of interest areas.

Interest Checklist

Rank the following areas of interest from 1 to 10 according to your preferences.

_____   Outdoor: outside activities usually having to do with animals and growing things.

_____   Mechanical: activities involving tools and machines.

_____   Computational: working with numbers.

_____   Scientific: discovering new facts and solving problems, particularly in the sciences.

_____   Persuasive: dealing with people, promoting projects, selling things.

_____   Artistic: doing creative work with the hands.

_____   Literary: reading and writing.

_____   Musical: playing instruments, singing, going to concerts.

_____   Social Service: helping people.

_____   Clerical: doing office work that requires precision and accuracy.

There are other more standardized measures of motivation that could well be used in the classroom, but they would take special training for their scoring and interpretation. An example of such an instrument is the need for achievement measure that is used to identify the basic achievement motive in Atkinson's and

McClelland's theory (cf. above). It consists of four pictures for which students tell a story. The content of each story is analyzed for achievement-oriented phrases and theme, and a total need for achievement score is obtained.

The above measures are offered as examples of assessment instruments that a teacher can use in his classroom. He should always keep in mind, however, that even the best instruments are only moderately accurate and are thus more serviceable for assessing groups rather than individual students. Also, the supposition that they really measure motivation or interest is based on their obvious content more than any empirical data. With these cautions in mind a teacher may use them to assess this elusive quality of motivation that is so essential for learning.

EXERCISE 5-6. Observation of Motivational Techniques

Observe a class on the grade level that you are interested in teaching, looking for motivational techniques the teacher employs. Is the teacher using intrinsic or extrinsic motivation? Does he try to motivate the students at the beginning of a lesson, does he use motivational techniques throughout the class session, or does his whole approach have a motivational aspect to it?

How would you attempt to motivate the students if you were teaching the same lesson?

EXERCISE 5-7. Using Motivational Techniques in Teaching

Select a topic in your field. Decide how you will attempt to motivate your students to learn it. In one paragraph describe the motivational technique that you will use for one class session in which you teach the topic.

Indicate to which motivating factor (need, emotion, motive) you are appealing. Also, describe the technique in terms of the intrinsic-extrinsic continuum, the theory to which it is more related, etc.

Suggested Readings

Fowler, H. *Curiosity and Exploratory Behavior.* New York: Macmillan, 1965.

Krumboltz, J. D., ed. *Learning and the Educational Process.* Chicago: Rand McNally, 1965. (Chapters by Atkinson and Berlyne)

Marx, M. H. and Tombaugh, T. N. *Motivation: Psychological Principles and Educational Implications.* San Francisco: Chandler, 1967.

Russell, I. L. *Motivation.* Dubuque: Wm. C. Brown, 1971.

Seagoe, May V. *The Learning Process and School Practice.* San Francisco: Chandler, 1970. (First half)

part three

Learning:
Products

We now come to the heart of the book, an analysis of the various types of learning that take place in the classroom. In this section we will be treating the main objects of our learning or *what* we learn: facts, language, concepts, relations, and structures. In a word, these are the *products* of our learning as distinct from our thought processes or operations. Taken together they represent the major portion of all the learning that will go on in your classroom when you begin to teach. Needless to say, there are no more important three chapters in the entire book.

You will probably notice a degree of continuity with regard to the order used in these chapters. For the most part, they are structured around six aspects of each type of learning: its nature, the learning process, the intellectual abilities involved, the conditions favoring learning, applications for teaching, and the evaluation of learning. The treatment of language learning is sufficiently complex for an additional section on the different types of language learning in the classroom.

Before we begin the analysis of the several products of our learning, do the following exercise which should prove to be of value and interest to you, particularly if you have wondered how the various types of learning are related to Guilford's model of intellect or even to "Bloom's Taxonomy."

EXERCISE A: Types of Learning, Intellectual Abilities and Educational Objectives

How does Guilford's structure of intellect model relate to the types of learning that we will be treating? How do they in turn compare to the objectives that you are concerned with in your teaching?

The leading analysis of educational objectives is the Taxonomy of Educational Objectives developed by Benjamin Bloom and his associates.[1] The taxonomy is based on no

---

1. If you are not familiar with the taxonomy, read through the summary provided in appendix B.

one philosophy of education; in fact it can be assimilated into several varying philosophies (pragmatism, Thomism, Whitehead's view, etc). Yet the taxonomy, with its objectives phrased in terms of knowledge and intellectual skills, can be used by a cognitive-oriented teacher in its present, general form; or it can be used by a more behaviorist-oriented teacher as a basic classification system for the many specific, behavioral objectives that he prefers to construct.

Both the basic types of classroom learning that we are about to consider, the product and process dimensions of the Structure of Intellect model, and the Taxonomy of Educational Objectives—Cognitive Domain are given below. Try to relate them by drawing a line from each category under types of learning first to the equivalent category in the Structure of Intellect and from there to the similar category in the Taxonomy. There are one or two categories in each list that will not match up with the other lists, but for the most part the correspondence is substantial.

Types of Learning	*Structure of Intellect*	*Taxonomy of Objectives*
Products	Products	Knowledge of:
verbal-factual	units	terminology, facts
concepts	classes	classification
		trends, methodology, etc.
relation	relations	principle, generalizations
structures	systems	theories, structures
	transformations	
	implications	
Processes	Processes	Intellectual Skills and Abilities
Comprehension	Cognition	Comprehension
	Memory	Application
Creativity	Divergent thinking	Analysis
Problem solving	Convergent thinking	Synthesis
Critical thinking	Evaluation	Evaluation
Retention		
Transfer		

There are many one-to-one correspondences particularly in the Product-Knowledge categories.

Product	Product	Knowledge
verbal-factual	units	terminology, facts
concepts	classes	classifications
relations	relations	generalizations
structures	systems	theories, structures

The two other obviously equivalent categories are:

critical thinking	evaluation	evaluation
transfer	implications	application

There are other similarities among the different categories, for instance:

comprehension	cognition	comprehension
creativity	divergent thinking	synthesis
problem solving	convergent thinking	analysis

Comprehension or understanding of a communication as a type of learning and an educational objective are the same. The cognition process involves comprehending and understanding, so it is partly coterminous with comprehension; but it also includes discovering and realizing groupings and relationships that are involved in the learning of concepts, relations, and the like.

Creativity mainly involves divergent thinking, but a few other specific intellectual abilities can be active in the creative process as well. The educational objective termed synthesis is defined in terms of the production of something new, which is what creativity essentially is.

Problem solving most often involves convergent thinking; in fact some problems call almost exclusively for this type of thinking. But problem solving can also involve divergent thinking and evaluation as well, so it is not coterminous with convergent thinking. The educational objective analysis is distinct from problem solving, but it is related to convergent thinking; in the latter we start with data and then either analyze it into categories or draw further conclusions from it. The relationship among them, then, can be thought of as a continuum from broad to specific, in order: problem solving, convergent thinking, and analysis.

In one area there is only a partial parallel, viz. memory. The *retention* of learning involves the process of *memory,* which together with cognition is only implied in the various knowledge objectives of the taxonomy.

Finally, there are some categories that do not have counterparts in other listings, e.g. skills, which are accounted for in another taxonomy of objectives and in a special matrix of psychomotor abilities; transformations, a comparatively new concept and thus far unique to Guilford's schema; and knowledge of trends, criteria, conventions and methodology, which are specified in the taxonomy of objectives but not in the other listings.

For the most part there is a basic correspondence among Guilford's Structure of Intellect, the Taxonomy of Educational Objectives—Cognitive Domain and the types of learning that we will be considering in the following chapters. Since we are mainly concerned with classroom learning, we will emphasize the types of learning more than the other listings; but we will continually refer to Guilford's structure of intellect in our analysis of the types of learning. Also, in the context of evaluation (final chapter), where objectives usually play a major role, we will treat types of learning and the corresponding objectives interchangeably.

In any event, when you teach it is important that you have a specific objective in mind as you plan a class session, that you keep that objective in mind as the most important thing for your students to achieve during the lesson, and finally, that you evaluate the learning outcomes of the class session in terms of that objective. Whether or not you use "objective," "type of learning," or "intellectual product and process" in your teaching is for the most part immaterial: they are all basically the same.

6

Verbal and
Factual Learning

A large portion of classroom learning is concerned with words and factual information. Reading, grammar, and foreign language involves words, their meaning, and their combinations; history, science, and social studies require the student to learn much factual information: dates, events, names, functions, etc. In fact, every subject area includes terminology or a symbol system as well as basic information that must be learned if a student is to obtain any kind of an adequate background in that field. It is this type of learning, the learning of language and factual information, that we will treat in this chapter.

Whereas the nature of factual information is relatively simple, the nature of language is quite complex. Before we try to understand the processes involved in the learning of a language, we should have some idea of its nature and structure; hence a fairly extensive treatment of the nature of language is in order.

Of great importance to the teacher is an analysis of how we learn language and information as well as how we learn them most effectively. In other words, the teacher should know what the available theory and research offer toward an understanding of verbal and factual learning. In addition, we will also consider some specific suggestions for teaching and evaluating verbal and factual material. We will inquire into these specific questions:

What is the nature and structure of language?
How is the verbal-factual learning process best explained?
What are some of the types of language learning that take place in the classroom?
What are the intellectual abilities involved in verbal and factual learning?
What are some important conditions that foster the efficient learning of language and factual information?

What applications can be drawn from research and theory for the effective teaching of verbal and factual material?

What are some ways of evaluating how well verbal and factual material has been learned?

The Nature and Structure of Language

The nature of factual information needs little further explanation, except to note that we are here referring to facts such as 1492, The Battle of Thermopolae, and sodium, rather than "facts" in the popular sense such as "heat expands metal" and "Leif Ericson was the first to discover America." These latter are more properly relations or conclusions from data whereas facts in the strict sense are simply units of information.

While the nature of factual information needs little explanation, the nature of language is something else. It is sufficiently complex to warrant scientific study in its own right, in linguistics, semantics, and related fields. Certainly it deserves some further treatment before we attempt to examine the process by which verbal material is learned.

During the past two decades a considerable number of psychologists have begun to study language learning and the factors connected with its use. A few of them have attempted to construct an analysis of language behavior that is based on an S-R theory of learning; many more have used the behavioral science of language (linguistics) as a base on which to build their analysis of how language is learned and what processes are involved in its use. We will consider the latter, psycholinguistic approach to the nature of language here. In the subsequent section we will take a brief look at both the S-R and psycholinguistic explanations of the processes involved in language learning.

The Nature of Language

Language is a conventional system of communication. It consists of a set of sounds, or signs, that stand for objects or ideas. Originally the signs were arbitrary, but gradually they were agreed upon by a certain speech community and thus became conventional. Signs, things that stand for something else, can be of two types: (1) those, such as smoke or a cough, which are *natural* signs of fire and a cold respectively; and (2) those, such as the words (and numbers) you are now reading, which are the *conventional* signs that make up the English language.

The once arbitrary, now conventional, sign system that we call a language serves two functions: (1) it is the means by which individuals communicate with one another (interindividual communication), and (2) it helps us to think clearly and more easily by providing labels for our concepts and experiences (intraindividual communication). Language is not absolutely necessary for either type of communication. For instance, we can share experiences with others through pictures and facial expressions; also, deaf persons form basic intellectual structures even though their language experience is very limited. However, language is certainly a great help to clarity and exactness of thought just as it is an obvious boon to communication among people.

The Structure of Language

The most essential aspect of a language is its structure. The basic elements from which a language is built are the *sounds* of that language (selected from the total range of speech sounds). English, for instance, has forty-four basic sounds or *phonemes.* Although it uses basically a phonetic alphabet, it is not as phonetic as Spanish or Turkish, for instance, in which there is a simple correspondence between phoneme and letter (*grapheme*). In English, there are forty-four phonemes to only twenty-three usable graphemes (*q, x,* and *k* are extras); the vowels and a few consonants (*s, g, c, t*) do yeoman duty and represent two or more sounds.

Sounds are combined into the basic functional signs of the language, commonly called words. Linguists term these units *forms* and distinguish among four main form classes: nominals, verbals, adjectivals, and adverbials, plus two additional form classes, prepositionals and conjunctives. The classes include the traditional parts of speech plus the corresponding types of phrases: nominal = nouns, pronouns, and noun phrases.

Words or forms are combined into clauses and sentences, called *constructions* by linguists. The constructions that are of primary interest to linguists as well as teachers are complete utterances or expressions, whether they be simple expressions such as greetings, exclamations, and responses to a speaker, or full sentences, both statements about the existence of something and statements that tell or "predicate" something about a subject.

EXERCISE 6-1. Forming a Grammar

Below is an informal plan for the teaching of basic sentence types that form a major part of a linguistic analysis of the language. Analyze *what* is to be taught as well as *how* it will be taught.

1. Distribute the following mimeographed passage to the students.

Baseball fans stated their approval recently when such players as Early Wynn, Sandy Koufax and Yogi Berra were elected to the Hall of Fame. *But there was considerable question* why the superb Warren Spahn has not yet made it to Cooperstown. *Spahn, whose 363 victories are* the most ever for a lefthander, *won 20 games or more in a season 13 times,* more often even than Walter Johnson. *He last pitched in the major leagues in 1965,* which means that *he has been retired more than the five seasons* a player must be before he becomes eligible for election. Where, then, is Warren's plaque?

The rule says a player must not only be out of the majors for five years, he must be out of all baseball. In 1966 *Spahn served as pitching coach* for the Mexico City Tigers and one day agreed to pitch to help draw a crowd. That brief outing was duly entered in his official playing record. In 1967, when he was managing Tulsa, *he did the same thing.* Again *the appearance went into his record,* and again the earliest date he would be eligible for election was set back, this time to 1973.

"I didn't know such things would affect my eligibility," Spahn says now, "but *I'd do it again. Baseball has been good to me. It's been my whole life.* If I can put something back, *I'm going to do it. I owe baseball everything.*"

2. Have students analyze and classify sentences into similar kinds; let them figure out classifications.

Subject + transitive verb + object

fans	stated	approval
Spahn	won	games
rule	says	player
he	did	same thing
I	do	it
I	owe	everything

Subject + intransitive verb

He	pitched
be	retired
appearance	went

Subject + linking verb + noun

Spahn	served as	coach
it	has been	everything

Subject + linking verb + adjectival

Baseball	has been	good

There + verb phrase

there was question

3. Ask: What do some types have in common?
   action (first two) vs. existence (last three)
   subject–predicate (first four) vs. existence assertion (fifth)

4. Mention about the omitted sentences: various transformations—which will be considered in a few days.

5. Have students make up their own sentences; have rest of class try to classify them into one of the basic types identified.

6. Review basic sentence types.

Check which of the following statements describe the planned teaching sequence.

_____ Students induce a classification system for sentences.

_____ Classification scheme is set up for students to put various types into.

_____ Students figure out broad categories or divisions of basic types.

_____ Teacher is aware of basic linguistics and uses it to help students structure a grammar themselves.

_____ Teacher presents basic sentence types which form a structure of grammar.

The teacher, who himself knows what the basic sentence types are, plans the class session so that the students will induce these sentence types themselves and thereby form a structure of the language, in other words, a grammar. This structure includes not just the main sentence types but also their grouping into, for example, predications and existence assertions.

Although a grammar is often presented in a more expository way, e.g. with sentence types outlined and then sentences identified as belonging to one class or another, in the present case the teacher used a discovery approach to the forming of the grammar structure.

Both grammatical forms and constructions can undergo changes or *transformations*. For instance, verbs can be changed to past tense (sit–sat), nouns made adjectival (wood–wooden) and adjectives nominal (honest–honesty); actions can be reversed (connect–disconnect), and qualities can be negated (covered–uncovered). Similarly, a construction such as a declarative sentence (You said that) can be transformed into a negative (You didn't say that), an interrogative (Did you say that?), a transposition (*That* you said), a deletion with part of the utterance understood from the context (That). In addition there are other transformations such as an imperative, an exclamation, passive voice, etc.

In sum, language is structured in somewhat of a hierarchical part-whole manner in which:

phonemes (sounds) are the elements which make up
↓
forms (words), which are the functional units or signs of a
    language and in turn are combined into
↓
constructions (phrases and sentences) which are the expression
    units of a language and which in turn can undergo
↑
transformations (changes of various kinds)

Meaning in Language

The previous analysis of the structure of language was concerned more with form and construction than with content and meaning. Linguists for the most part prescind from content when they analyze language, somewhat in the same way that logicians ignore specific content as they analyze the form of thought.

But content and meaning are important both to the users of a language and to the teachers who guide those users. In fact, much of the teacher's work consists in conveying the proper meaning of words to students. Therefore, a brief analysis of the types of meanings involved in a communication system and of their relation to the signs of that system is important here.

EXERCISE 6-2. Words and Their Meanings

A teacher plans a portion of a class session on the various kinds of words and their meanings. Given below are a sentence plus the questions that he plans to ask concerning it.

In the *light* of recent research, it is apparent that *porpoises communicate* with each other through a *language* distinctly their own.

1. Light here means mental illumination, i.e. in terms of what research has found. Does light have one or many meanings? (several) How do you tell which meaning it has here? (context)
2. What is a porpoise? (use dictionary)—a fairly small (7 foot) sea mammal (dolphin) having a blunt snout. How many meanings does porpoise have? (one)
3. What does communicate mean?—to share something in common, specifically to convey information (or disease). Does it have basically the same or different meanings when used in the contexts of language and disease? (basically the same, with just a little different flavor)
4. What is a language?—a means of communicating thought or feeling. How many meanings does it have? (one with differences) Does it mean the same in the context of men and animals? (partly the same, partly different)
   > human language—a set of conventional signs to express thought or feelings
   > animal "language"—sounds used to express feelings

The teacher obviously is trying to get his students to become aware of the various kinds of words and their meanings. What are these basic types of words? Match each type with a specific word.

_____	Word with one meaning (univocal)	A. light
_____	Word with basically one meaning (univocal) but with different connotations depending on context	B. porpoise
_____	Word with several meanings (equivocal); specific meaning depending on context	C. communicate
_____	Word with the same general meaning but a different particular meaning depending on its specific referent (analogical)	D. language

Words are obviously of several types, depending on their meaning(s). Most words, for instance, porpoise, recent, communicate, have one meaning—they are *univocal.* Some univocal words, such as porpoise, will have the same meaning for everyone no matter what the context; other univocal words, such as communicate, recent, have the same basic meaning in all contexts, but gain a slightly different connotation or flavor from their specific context.

Some words have two or more meanings—they are *equivocal.* Their exact meaning has to be determined from the context. Light is obviously an example of an equivocal word; quarters (money and lodging) and vital (life giving and important) are other examples.

Still other words, such as language and intelligence, will have meanings that are partly the same and partly different when used in different contexts. For instance, animal "language" is a communication system that is simple, natural, and determined by heredity, whereas human language is a communication system that is complex, conventional, and constructed by men. Since they involve somewhat of an analogy, these words are called *analogical.*

Words have meaning in themselves and in addition often derive meaning from the context in which they are used. The meaning that a word has in itself apart from any context, for instance its dictionary definition, is what the word itself denotes or its *denotative* meaning. It is the conventional meaning of the word and does not (or should not) vary from person to person. The meaning that a word derives from its context, i.e. the meaning or flavor its context connotes, is called its *connotative* meaning. Some words such as "light" even depend on the context for their specific meaning—light breakfast, bright light, light a lamp, etc. Other words such as "problem" gain specific flavor among individuals depending on whether they—either the word or the individual—happen to be in a context of (for example) science or art, the classroom or the counselor's office, the city commission meeting or the end-of-month bout with the checking account.

Taking into account both types of meaning, Guilford has formulated a core-context theory of meaning. According to this view, a verbal sign both stands for an object or idea (the core) and also points to something beyond that is implied by the core (the context). The core consists of semantic content and is the equivalent of a word's denotative meaning. The context can consist of images and feelings as well as other words and so can involve any kind of content (figural, semantic, behavioral); from the context is derived a word's connotative meaning (see figure 6-1).

What are some basic relationships between words and their meanings? Since meanings are often coterminous with concepts which in turn use words for labels, what is the relation among words, concepts and meanings? John B. Carroll, a leading analyst of the nature and acquisition of language, distinguishes and relates them as follows:

> Perhaps it is useful to think of words, meanings, and concepts as forming *three* somewhat independent series. The words in a language can be thought of as a series of physical entities—either spoken or written. Next, there exists a set of "meanings" which stand in complex relationships to the set of words. These relationships may be described by the

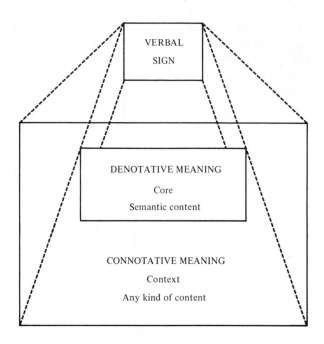

Figure 6-1. *The Core-Context Theory of Meaning (Guilford 1967, p. 230)*

rules of usage that have developed by the processes of socialization and communication. A "meaning" can be thought of as a standard of communicative behavior that is shared by those who speak a language. Finally, there exist "concepts"; the classes of experience formed in individuals either independently of language processes or in close dependence on language processes.

The interrelations found among these three series are complex: almost anyone can give instances where a word may have many "meanings," or in which a given "meaning" corresponds to several different words. The relationships between societally-standardized "meanings" and individually-formed "concepts" are likewise complex, but of a somewhat different nature. It is a question of how well each individual has learned these relationships, and at least in the sphere of language and concepts, education is largely a process whereby the individual learns either to attach societally-standardized words and meanings to the concepts he has already formed, or to form new concepts that properly correspond to societally-standardized words and meanings. A "meaning" of a word is, therefore, a societally-standardized concept, and when we say that a word stands for or names a concept it is understood that we are speaking of concepts that are shared among the members of a speech community. (Carroll 1964b, p. 185)

The Process of Verbal-Factual Learning

How are language and factual information learned? What are the essential elements in the process by which they are acquired? First consider an example of factual learning.

EXERCISE 6-3.   Factual Learning in the Classroom

Analyze the following lesson plan for the teaching of factual information.

Objective: students should be able to recite the names of the presidents and their dates of office.

1. Write on board
   5th—James Monroe (1817–1825)
   6th—John Quincy Adams (1825–1829)
   7th—Andrew Jackson (1829–1837)
2. Distinguish between John Quincy Adams and his uncle John Adams; between Andrew Jackson and Andrew Johnson (after Lincoln). Dates overlap because of early spring inaugurations.
3. Suggest ways of relating presidents through important intervening facts.
   James Monroe (two terms)—Monroe Doctrine, early 1820s (2nd term)
   Election of 1824: (1) Jackson, (2) Adams, (3) Crawford, (4) Clay

   threw his
   support to

   John Quincy Adams (one term)
   Next election (1828): Jackson in landslide
   Andrew Jackson (two terms)
4. Pupils pair off, with one reciting names and dates to the other, then the second reciting names, dates and intervening events to the first. Instruct students to indicate to each other whether the name-date combination is correct or not.

Indicate which of the following approaches are provided for in the plan.

_____ 1. Discrimination among items to be learned is made.
_____ 2. Clarification is made between items and other information with which students are familiar.
_____ 3. Intervening facts or mediators are provided.
_____ 4. Attempt is made to relate specific associations into an organized pattern.
_____ 5. Opportunity for practice in forming the factual associations is provided.

_____ 6. Immediate feedback for correct associations is provided.

_____ 7. Reward in the form of teacher praise and encouragement is given to each student.

The teacher first makes it clear what is to be learned and how the items are distinct from one another by putting the names and dates on the board (1). He provides additional clarifications that will help students keep the material to be learned distinct from other facts that they probably know (2). Rather than just have students try to associate presidents and dates, the teacher suggests intervening facts that will serve as mediators (Monroe Doctrine) (3) and will help to relate the material into an organized pattern (Election of 1824) (4).

Practice and feedback are also provided, in this case through the students' pairing off and reciting the name-date associations (5), with the students informing each other whether or not they are correct (6). Although it is often helpful, in this instance reward in the form of praise for correct responses is not given.

Factual Learning

Factual information is learned through a process of association in which the fact and its referent are experienced together, e.g. Declaration of Independence and 1776, Hemingway and *The Old Man and the Sea,* Albany and capital of New York.

To help the student learn an association more easily, a mediator, either verbal or pictorial, is often useful, e.g. Declaration of Independence–(Philadelphia 76'ers)–1776; Hemingway–(beard)–Old Man and the Sea.

Similarly, learning has been found to be particularly facilitated if the learner relates factual material into an order or organized whole: bones of the leg put in order from hip to ankle–femur, patella, tibia and fibula; state-capital associations grouped according to section of the country–New England, Mid-Atlantic, etc. In some instances, where a logical order or grouping is not possible, an artificial order can be effective in the learning of factual information: thirty days hath September, etc.

Ordinarily the factual learning process entails the following phases:

Discrimination ⟶ Practice ⟶ Learning ⟶ Overlearning
      ↑   ↑   ↑
   Mediation,   Feedback   Reward
   Organization

With more than one item to be learned, the person must first *discriminate* among the stimulus items before he attempts to learn any connections; unless the items are distinct, errors will tend to occur. Often verbal or pictorial *mediators* or some *organization* of the items into an order or pattern is employed to make learning easier. One or more "trials" or *practice* periods during which the person attempts to learn the material are necessary. Some *feedback* after each trial as to the correctness of the person's responses is extremely valuable. Either the person himself can compare his responses with a model, or a teacher can supply the required information.

Learning has occurred when the person is able to recite the material correctly. This involves one or more of the following:

1. Learning *responses,* being able to give the correct response when presented with the stimulus;
2. Forming associations or *connections* between items of information, words, i.e., between stimulus and response;
3. Learning an *order,* either a sequence of events, an order of words, or an organized pattern of material.

Although verbal-factual learning can take place without it, some *reward*—most often given in the form of mild, intermittent praise—can be an effective part of the learning process. Finally, *over-learning* is the additional practice the person devotes to the material after he has learned it.

Language Learning

How is a language learned? How is the process best explained? There are two leading contemporary explanations, the analysis of verbal behavior proposed by B. F. Skinner and the psycholinguistic analysis enunciated by Noam Chomsky. We will consider each briefly. But before we get into treatment of the theories themselves, take a look at how they work in practice in an English class.

EXERCISE 6-4. Language Learning: Two Approaches

Given below are two ways of teaching *lie* and *lay.* Analyze the two approaches and then try to identify some of their main characteristics.

I

(Teacher lies down on his desk)
T. What am I doing?
S_1. You're laying on your desk.
T. No, I'm not *laying* on the desk; what am I doing?
S_2. You're lying on the desk.
T. Right. I'm *lying on the desk.* (Gets up) How about this book; what is it doing?
S_2. It's lying on the desk, too.
T. Right. If someone or something is just resting in a place, we say he or it is *lying* there.
T. What am I doing now? Takes a book and lays it on a table.

II

(Teacher lies down on his desk)
T. I am lying on my desk, taking a brief rest. (Gets up) This book is also lying on the floor. How about that pad over there on the table, what is it doing?
S_1. It's lying on the table.
T. And that pen?
S_1 It's also lying on the table.
T. So if someone or something is just resting in a place, we say he or it is *lying* there.
T. All right. Watch. (Takes a book and lays it on a table.) I just laid this book down on the table.

S₃. You're laying the book on the table.

T. *Laying* it. Right. I'm *laying* the book on the table. (Takes his glasses off and lays them on his desk.)

T. What did I do then?

S₄. You put your glasses on your desk.

T. Put or _____.

S₄. Laid.

T. Right. I laid my glasses on the desk. All right, everyone lay their books on their desks. Jim, what did you just do?

S₅. Laid my book on my desk.

T. Right. You put or *lay* something down. You yourself *lie* down to rest. Lay takes an object; lie doesn't. Joe, would you come up here? (Explains to Joe) Joe will do what you tell him to do with himself, the book and the table if you use lie or lay correctly.

S₁. Lay down on the table. (Joe does nothing.)

S₂. Lie down on the table. (Joe lies on the table.)

S₃. Lay the book on the table. (Joe lays the book on the table.)

T. Good.

(Takes his glasses off and lays them on his desk.) I am laying my glasses on my desk. Now everyone lay their books on their desks. Sam, what did you just do?

S₂. I laid my book on my desk.

T. (Takes off his coat and puts it on the table.) Ann, what I just do?

S₃. You laid your coat on the table.

T. So if we put something down somewhere, we say we lay it down. What's the difference then between lie and lay?

S₄. Lie means rest and lay means put something down.

T. Any other difference?

S₄. Lay has an object, lie doesn't.

T. OK. Now everyone think of a sentence that uses either lie or lay in it. Jim?

S₅. She was lying on the beach getting a sun tan.

T. Good, Kathy?

S₆. She layed the keys on the table.

T. Good.

How would you characterize each approach? Check whether each statement best fits I or II.

	I	II
1. Students first respond to a question regarding a situation by naming the action that is taking place.	____	____
2. Students induce the use of two verbs from several examples that they hear.	____	____
3. Once they have induced the correct usage, students use the verb themselves spontaneously.	____	____
4. Teacher gives immediate reinforcement of students' correct responses to each question.	____	____
5. Students figure out the difference between two verbs—both their meaning and whether they take an object or not—on the basis of the many examples that they have seen.	____	____
6. Students' correct usage is reinforced by an action that indicates that their statements were correct.	____	____

In the first approach above, the students respond to a situation, and specifically to a question, by naming the action of *lying* on the desk (1). All through the lesson, the teacher uses "right" to reinforce correct usage (4). In addition, the teacher sets up the situation in which a student (a "member of the speech community") reinforces correct usage by doing what is commanded by another student (6).

In the second approach, the students first experience several statements containing the verb "lie" and then induce the correct usage from the examples (similarly for "lay") (2); once they have induced the correct usage they use the verbs first in sentences that are answers to questions and then in sentences that they think up (3). On the basis of the examples of both verbs given, the students also induce the difference between the verbs (5). This awareness of the difference—according to one theory—is part of a "grammar" that allows the student to make further correct utterances.

B. F. Skinner.   Skinner describes the process of language learning as follows:

> Verbal behavior is behavior reinforced through the mediation of other persons.
>
> Any operant, verbal or otherwise, acquires strength and continues to be maintained in strength when responses are frequently followed by the event called "reinforcement." The process of "operant conditioning" is most conspicuous when verbal behavior is first acquired. The parent sets up a repertoire of responses in the child by reinforcing many instances of a response. Obviously, a response must appear at least once before it is strengthened by reinforcement. It does not follow, however, that all the complex forms of adult behavior are in the child's unconditioned vocal repertoire. The parent need not wait for the emergence of the final form. Any response which vaguely resembles the standard behavior of the community is reinforced. When these begin to appear frequently, a closer approximation is insisted upon. In this manner very complex verbal forms may be reached.
>
> Operant reinforcement, then, is simply a way of controlling the probability of occurrence of a certain class of verbal responses. If we wish to make a response of given form highly probable, we arrange for the effective reinforcement of many instances. If we wish to eliminate it from a verbal repertoire, we arrange that reinforcement shall no longer follow. Any information regarding the relative frequency of reinforcement characteristic of a given verbal community is obviously valuable in predicting such behavior. (Skinner 1957, pp. 14, 29, 30)

For Skinner, speech sounds are emitted and reinforced—just as any other behavior—through a process of operant conditioning. In this process there are three important events: a stimulus, a response, and a reinforcement, each depending on the other.

> The stimulus, acting prior to the emission of the response, sets the occasion upon which the response is likely to be reinforced. . . . (Once it

has been reinforced), the stimulus becomes the occasion upon which the response is likely to be omitted. (Skinner 1957, p. 81)

Verbal behavior is reinforced initially by others (parents) and eventually both by others and by the individual himself. Requests and commands are reinforced by the hearer complying with the request. Naming things is reinforced either by the explicit approval of others or by the implicit approval involved in the fact that others respond to an utterance in a way that indicates it was clear and correct. In other words, an individual's verbal behavior is shaped by the reinforcements of his speech community. The ordinary paradigm for the learning of verbal behavior (language) according to Skinner's view is as follows:

Stimulus:	Response is emitted:	If reinforcement is provided,
$\longrightarrow$	$\longrightarrow$	
Object perceived	an utterance that names the object	the response is strengthened and is likely to occur again

Noam Chomsky.   Chomsky, while admitting that the process by which we learn a language is a virtual unknown, hypothesizes:

> As far as acquisition of language is concerned, it seems clear that reinforcement, casual observation, and natural inquisitiveness (coupled with a strong tendency to imitate) are important factors, as is the remarkable capacity of the child to generalize, hypothesize, and "process information" in a variety of very special and apparently highly complex ways which we cannot yet describe or begin to understand, and which may be largely innate, or may develop through some sort of learning or through maturation of the nervous system. . . .
>
> It is quite possible that given an input of observed English sentences, the brain produces (by an "induction" of apparently fantastic complexity and suddenness) the "rules" of English grammar. . . . It seems that the child is capable of constructing an extremely complex mechanism for generating and understanding a set of sentences, only some of which he has heard. . . .
>
> The child who learns a language has in some sense constructed the grammar for himself on the basis of his observation of sentences and nonsentences (i.e. corrections by the verbal community). Study of the actual observed ability of a speaker to distinguish sentences from nonsentences, detect ambiguities, etc., apparently forces us to the conclusion that this grammar is of an extremely complex and abstract character, and that the young child has succeeded in carrying out what from the formal point of view, at least, seems to be a remarkable type of theory construction.
>
> The fact that all normal children acquire essentially comparable grammars of great complexity with remarkable rapidity suggests that human beings are somehow specially designed to do this, with data-handling or "hypothesis-formulating" ability of unknown character and complexity. (Chomsky 1959, pp. 43, 44, 57)

For Chomsky, language learning involves mainly the internal construction of a set of rules and patterns (a grammar) that is induced from the utterances that a person hears. In turn, this structure of rules and patterns allows the person not only to understand further utterances of others but also to generate utterances that are distinctly his own. Chomsky's explanation of this inductive-deductive process can be schematized as follows:

$$
\begin{array}{ccc}
\text{Utterances} & \text{Induction} & \left\{ \begin{array}{c} \text{Set of rules} \\ \text{and patterns} \\ \text{(grammar)} \end{array} \right\} & \begin{array}{l} \text{Allowing} \\ \text{the person} \\ \text{to} \end{array} & \begin{array}{l} \text{Understand} \\ \text{new sentences} \\ \text{of others} \\ \\ \text{Generate new} \\ \text{sentences of} \\ \text{his own} \end{array}
\end{array}
$$

EXERCISE 6-5. Critique of Theories of Language Learning

What do you think of these two points of view? Which offers more for a genuine explanation of the language learning process? Admittedly we have been able to present only one or two essential points of each theory here; they are much more extensive in their full form. Nevertheless, you should be able to grasp at least the general emphasis of each explanation, and decide which you think is worth examining more fully.

It might be interesting to see what Skinner and Chomsky say about each others' explanations of language learning. Given below are some quotations from each writer; indicate to which approach each criticism is aimed.

Skinner   Chomsky

1. "Linguistics has recorded and analyzed speech sounds and semantic and syntactical practices, but comparisons of different languages and the tracing of historical changes have taken precedence over the study of the individual speaker."   ____   ____

2. "Prediction of the behavior of a complex organism (or machine) would require, in addition to information about external stimulation, knowledge of the internal structure of the organism, the ways in which it processes input information and organizes its own behavior."   ____   ____

3. Meanings and ideas do not have an observable, experimentally based referent; they appeal to something supposedly taking place inside the organism and which is therefore unobservable; finally they do not really explain the functional relations which govern verbal behavior (paraphrased from several pages).   ____   ____

4. "What happens when a man speaks or responds in speech is clearly a question about human behavior and hence a question to be answered with the concepts and techniques of psychology as an experimental science of behavior."   ____   ____

5. "The insights that have been achieved in the laboratories with lower organisms, though quite genuine, can be applied to complex human behavior only in the most gross and superficial way. . . . What is necessary is research, not dogmatic and perfectly arbitrary claims; based on analogies to a small part of experimental literature."

____   ____

6. "Invoking terms (from the laboratory) has no explanatory force. The only effect is to obscure the important differences among the notions being paraphrased. . . . The terms borrowed from experimental psychology simply lose their objective meaning with this extention, and take over the full vagueness of ordinary language."

____   ____

The quotations are taken from Skinner's *Verbal Behavior* and Chomsky's famous review of Skinner's book.

Skinner considers the linguistic approach to the analysis of language to be too concerned with language in general and not sufficiently concerned about the individual speaker (1). More specifically, he is very much against an attempt to explain language in terms of "meanings" or the older "ideas" on several bases: (a) they depend on some unobservable process within the person; (b) only some of them have a concrete objective basis or referent, others do not; and (c) they actually restate the behavior in vague terms rather than explain any causal or functional relationships (3). Such a causal explanation of man's language is more the province of experimental psychology, which attempts to explain and control human behavior, including verbal behavior (4).

Whereas Skinner was referring to the linguistic approach in general, Chomsky was speaking specifically to Skinner's analysis of verbal behavior. Even judging from the few quotes above, his evaluation was not very friendly (in other sections he is even more scathing). Chomsky claims that any satisfactory study of human language must take into account the human being, and specifically what goes on in the person as an organizer of information. Chomsky claims that we only have a vague notion of this at present, but that is no reason to exclude the internal processes from an explanation (2). He further states that the extrapolation of laboratory work with lower organisms can hardly be meaningful when applied to the complex human behavior of learning and using a language (5). Similarly, the use of terms based on such laboratory experimentation out of their proper context offers no real explanation of the language processes; instead the terms become vague and as lacking in objectivity as any of those used in previous attempts to explain language behavior (6).

Which offers the better explanation of language learning? Most probably they both have something to contribute toward an understanding of this complex process.

A full explanation should contain the following elements or phases (probably in this temporal order, with each phase continuing after the emergence of the later phases).

Learning to Understand the Language

1. *Exposure* to one or more models or users of the language.
2. Forming *associations* between verbal signs and their referents: objects, actions, persons that the child has perceived.
3. *Induction* of the basic types of utterances and grammatical constructions from the utterances that have been observed.
4. *Formation* of an internal grammatical system which allows the child to understand further specific utterances, and later to generate specific utterances himself.

Learning to Speak the Language

5. *Imitation* of the models or language users with whom he has come in contact.
6. *Reinforcement* of correct utterances; this serves both a feedback and a reward function.

Developmentally there are two important considerations that should be added. First, as a prerequisite to understanding the language, the awareness that one thing can stand for another must have emerged, e.g. that a group of sounds (a word) can represent an object or action. This *symbolic function* (as Piaget calls it) begins to develop toward the end of the first year and is fairly well established by age two. Second, throughout the early years of language learning there is a gradual differentiation among phonemes, and among words and their transformations, particularly with regard to the child's speaking the language but also as part of his understanding it.

Language Learning in the Classroom

Before the child enters first grade, he has learned at least one language fairly well. He already possesses a workable vocabulary of 10,000 words or more, and has used almost every basic grammatical construction of the language. So what verbal learning is left to the classroom? The answer is "a great deal," specifically:

Learning to decipher written language (reading)
Learning to write language
Vocabulary development and clarification
Analysis and specification of grammatical constructions
Improved use of language in speaking and writing
Learning a second (or third) language.

Each of these areas deserves some further analysis plus some suggestions by way of application of what we have seen so far.

Reading.   Reading is the activity in which we reconstruct a spoken message from a printed text. This obviously requires that the learner have a fairly good knowledge of the spoken language before he attempts to learn how to read. (Witness the difficulty a bilingual child whose native language is not English has in learning to read his second language.) A major part of learning to read is learning to form associations between spoken sounds (phonemes) and written symbols (graphemes). If, as in some languages, the correspondence between phoneme and grapheme is regular and direct, the associations are rather simply made. If, as in English, the correspondence is somewhat irregular, learning the associations is apt to be quite difficult. Much discussion and considerable research has been devoted to the question of teaching children how to read. For the most part the problem results from this partly regular, partly irregular correspondence between sounds and letters in the English language. Several solutions have been offered through the years, only a few of which we can consider here.

Based on a stimulus-response theory of learning, the whole word, "sight vocabulary" approach has children form associations between words and objects from the beginning, with no analysis given to the sounds of the letters involved. Although some sight vocabulary (*the, to*) is necessary, the whole word approach actually tries to solve the problem by getting around it more than attacking it directly. It is generally found to be less effective than the more phonetic approaches that emphasize the sounds of letters.

A solution that has support in both reason and research—to say nothing of teacher satisfaction—is one that resolves the inconsistencies between phonemes and graphemes by augmenting the twenty-six letter alphabet with additional symbols (shown in figure 6-2) so that each of the forty-four basic phonemes has a corresponding grapheme. The associations between sound and symbol are made quickly, and many studies show that children who learn how to read using the initial teaching alphabet are considerably more advanced after a year or two than those who have learned via the traditional orthography. The transition from i.t.a. to t.o. is made quickly and easily with the gains in both speed, accuracy and comprehension lasting even after the transfer (Downing 1968).

The problem of irregular phoneme–grapheme correspondence in English is accentuated by the fact that such a situation requires that the pupil be able to *conserve* the basic letter through changes in its sound, e.g., A through $\bar{a}, \breve{a}, \ddot{a}, \hat{a}$, and a. This means that unless he is in the stage of concrete operational thought and hence able to conserve, he will have great difficulty with vowels and with the several consonants that have more than one sound. You may recall (chapter 2) that typically about half of those in a first grade class are not able to do operational thinking or conservation; hence the problem is magnified. Whereas most other methods of teaching reading require perceptual abilities plus conservation ability, the i.t.a. approach requires only the perceptual abilities, particularly auditory and visual discrimination. For this reason, learning to read through the i.t.a. can be mastered with relative ease even by younger pupils.

The method of teaching beginning reading that involves having children read whole stories that they have made up themselves, the "language experience" approach, has considerable support in initial research, in the experience of teachers, especially teachers of low income pupils, and in developmental psychology.

Figure 6-2. *The Initial Teaching Alphabet*

(Piaget notes that the thinking of the preoperational child is marked by a "syncretism" or wholistic approach in which the child is more concerned about whole sentences and stories than in specific words; if he doesn't know what a word means, he will fill in a meaning so as to get to an overall meaning of a sentence.) Whereas the phonetic approach first stresses sounds of letters and the sight word approach first stresses the word as a unit, and only then do they move on to sentences, the language experience approach starts with whole sentences and short stories and lets the elements (letters and words) be clarified in due time or when the need arises.

The problem of initial reading instruction is one of the thorniest of all educational problems and cannot be solved satisfactorily here. You may want to consult further sources on the question, some of which are listed at the end of the chapter. Whatever method you decide is the best will depend on many things: what the recent extensive research studies have found on the question (cf. pp. 172-74), your convictions on theories of learning, the insights of developmental psychology, and an analysis of the nature of the language that the child is attempting to read.

Traditionally reading teachers have not been partial to any one theory of learning and certainly not to any single method of teaching reading. We can, however, note certain relationships between teaching methods and learning theories. For instance, a cognitive-oriented teacher would prefer the language experience approach with its holistic emphasis and would tend toward using the i.t.a. orthography. Most stimulus-response—oriented teachers would use a combination phonetic and sight-word approach with either traditional orthography or perhaps i.t.a.

Since reading is primarily a process of comprehending the meaning from the printed text, we will treat it more at length under the topic of comprehension (chapter 9).

Learning to Write Language.   Writing involves both making associations, imitation of a model, and acquiring a psychomotor skill. Since printing and writing ordinarily come after a pupil has mastered the initial stages of reading, they do not usually entail the problems of irregularity and conservation that reading does.

Vocabulary Development.   Vocabulary development involves exposure to new words and their meanings together with the associative and differentiation processes entailed in their learning. It also involves becoming aware of both the denotative and connotative meanings of words, and the ability to arrive at the probable core meaning from the context. In addition, it includes the knowledge (and concomitant skill) of word analysis as to etymology, root and variations, transformations, etc.

Analysis and Specification of Grammatical Constructions.   The study of grammar in elementary school basically involves a reflection on the patterns and rules that the child has induced and has used for several years. In other words, if the pupil studies the modern linguistic-based grammar, he is not learning anything new as much as he is analyzing and becoming conscious of the constructions that he has long since learned. On the other hand, if he studies the traditional Latin-type grammar, he *will* be learning a considerable amount of new information.

Just as in the learning of factual information, specific grammar rules can either be learned more or less in isolation, or they can be combined into a structure or interrelated system. The linguistic-based analysis of the structure of language presented above is one possible system. A system based on the functions of grammatical forms and construction is another. The basic idea of this latter system is that all words, phrases, and clauses perform either a main, a modifying, or a replacing function in a sentence. The functions are related in this way:

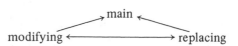

It should be noted that since the study of any type of grammar, whether transformational or traditional, involves classifying words, phrases and sentences, plus relating these words and phrases into a certain order (or more exactly orders), it requires only the concrete operational stage of intellectual development with its structures of classifying and ordering. The stable or equilibrium stage of concrete operations around age 9 or 10 is more appropriate for grammar study than the initial stage, age 7 or 8.

Improved Use of Language in Speaking and Writing. Although much of this advanced type of language learning involves creative expression and the application of logical reasoning and critical thinking, there is some verbal learning involved as well; e.g. differentiation and forming of associations in learning the criteria and rules of clarity and style, and often some learning through imitation of others in the attempt to improve one's style.

Learning a Second Language. Traditionally a foreign language was taught inversely from the way that children learned their first language. Students were taught grammar rules and how to read the language before they learned to converse in it. Recently, however, several approaches more in keeping with the natural way of learning a language have been developed. In these techniques, the student first hears the language used and then learns to speak it; later he learns to read and then to write it; finally he analyzes its grammatical constructions.

This latter approach seems preferable for two reasons. On the basis of research, it has been found to be more effective than the traditional approach at least for learning to speak a language (Scherer and Wertheimer 1964). Second, on the basis of the nature of things both the nature of first language learning and the nature of teaching, which is a cooperative art that should imitate and foster the natural way of learning, not go against it.

In the newer approach, modeled after first language learning, words and expressions are associated directly with the objects and actions themselves rather than through the first language, unless an explanation of meaning or usage is necessary. It has been found that if the student learns a second language through his first, he will not only be less fluent in it, but he will also reflect traces of the structure of the first language in his speech (Carroll 1964a).

The learning processes involved in the newer experiential–inductive approach to second language learning are similar to those mentioned above for first language learning:

1. Observation and imitation of a model
2. Forming associations with the help of repetition, feedback and reinforcement
3. Induction of basic grammatical constructions
4. The formation of an internal grammatical system which allows one to both understand and generate new utterances in that language.

Intellectual Abilities Involved in Verbal-Factual Learning

In terms of the structure of intellect model, verbal-factual learning is really learning *units* of information, specifically:

1. Units involving perceptible or figural content (things, events)
2. Units of symbolic content (words, names, symbols)
3. Units of semantic content (meanings of words and symbols).

It involves mainly the cognition of units: verbal comprehension, recognition of symbols, and experience with things and events. Secondarily it can involve other processes as well: evaluation of units whenever there is learning by differentiation, cognition of relations or systems whenever facts are related or grammatical structures are formed (respectively), and often divergent thinking when a person expresses himself in a language. Of course retention of language and factual information involves the corresponding memory abilities as well.

If we refer to Guilford's structure of intellect model, we can see specifically what abilities are involved in verbal-factual learning (table 6-1).

Table 6-1. *Abilities Involved in Verbal-Factual Learning*

	Units	Classes	Relations	Systems	Transformations	Implications
Cognition	*		*	*		
Memory	*		*	*		
Divergent Thinking	*					
Convergent Thinking						
Evaluation	*					

Conditions Favoring Verbal and Factual Learning

What conclusions can be drawn from the extensive research on verbal learning that have relevance for classroom learning? Specifically, how can verbal-factual learning be made as effective as possible? First we will consider some general factors that apply to all verbal and factual learning, and then we will present some particular findings regarding the area of reading.[1]

Preliminary

Students learn better when they intend to learn and are given instructions on what to learn (intentional learning) than if they are simply exposed to the material (incidental learning). Specifically, they do better on a follow-up test if they are told beforehand to study for details of content than simply for a general comprehension of the material (Postman 1964).

Material of Learning

Learning of verbal-factual material is much more effective when the material is organized and put into an appropriate type of order—organized around basic

---

1. The three short experiments in exercises 6-8, 6-9 and 6-10 can be done in conjunction with this section.

concepts or put into a hierarchical order. For example, lists of words are recalled two or three times better when they are presented in a hierarchical order than when they are in a random order (Bower et al. 1969, Frase 1969, Cohen 1973).

Although students tend to organize material by names or titles most easily, organization by categories or attributes (fish by color, behavior, diet rather than by specific names), even though requiring more experience and acquired only gradually, is more effective for both initial learning and later recall (Friedman and Greitzer 1972, Schultz and DiVesta 1972).

The more familiar individuals are with a certain type of verbal material, the more easily and rapidly they will learn it and the longer they will retain it (Underwood 1964). As the amount of verbal-factual material increases, it takes much more time to learn it, i.e., the time spent per unit of information increases considerably (not quite geometrically, but certainly more than additively) as the amount of material increases (Ebbinghaus 1885).

Aids to Learning

Verbal mediators are usually helpful in forming verbal associations; easily recallable mediators that the individual himself devises are particularly effective (Montague et al. 1966).

A general topic sentence which gives context to several facts is helpful in learning factual material in prose form (Gagné 1969, Gagné and Wiegand 1970, Bruning 1970). When students form vivid mental images of events described in sentences or prose passages, they tend to learn and retain more than when they simply read them (Anderson and Hidde 1971, Anderson and Kulhany 1972).

Methods of Learning

Whether a person learns verbal material through the whole method, the part method, or the successive parts method, depends more on the material itself than on the method, since none has been found to be consistently superior. The whole method is often best for shorter and easier meaningful material. For longer, more difficult material, the whole-part-whole method is very effective (Postman and Goggin 1966, Jung 1964).

> Whole: the material is practiced as a whole over and over.
> Part: the material is broken into logical or convenient parts, each of which is practiced separately.
> Successive part: the convenient parts are learned one at a time, but prior ones are repeated as a new section is attacked.
> Whole-part-whole: the whole is gone through first, then broken into logical parts which are learned one at a time; finally the material is reviewed as a whole.

Ordinarily, spaced or distributed practice, with rest periods between sessions, results in greater retention of verbal-factual material than does massed practice, being almost twice as effective in terms of recall of factual data. Spaced practice is of particular value if other material tends to interfere with the learning and retention of the original material. However, if the learner tends to make a large number of errors, or if he forgets the material easily, the intervals between practice sessions should be shortened. The length of the practice sessions depends on the pupil, the material, and the method used. Other things being equal, the younger the pupils, the shorter the periods usually have to be; the more difficult the material and the more teacher-centered the methods used, the shorter the periods usually have to be. If the students are involved and interested, they will be attentive longer and the periods can be lengthened accordingly (Underwood 1961, 1964).

Overlearning

At least in rote learning, some continued practice or "drill" (overlearning) is very effective for the retention of verbal material. It has been found that about 50 percent additional practice after one has learned the material results in a substantial increase in retention; 100 percent additional practice brings only slight improvement over the 50 percent level and results in boredom. Hence some overlearning is worthwhile, but the law of diminishing returns soon sets in (Kreuger 1929, Postman 1962).

Reading

In the mid-1960s an extensive research program on the most commonly used methods of teaching reading was sponsored by the United States Office of Education. From these studies, several conclusions seem warranted.

The quality of the teaching seems to be more important than the method used; in the research studies there was greater variation among teachers within a method than there was among the various methods themselves.

Each method examined was found to be superior to at least one or two other methods. The basic reading, language experience, phonetic, linguistic and individualized reading approaches received some support in the twenty-seven studies conducted. At the same time some studies found no significant differences among methods.

With regard to orthography, the i.t.a. was usually shown to be superior to traditional orthography. (Kerfoot 1967)

EXERCISE 6-6. Application of Verbal-Factual Learning

Analyze the following audio-lingual sequence in the teaching of beginning German. What kinds of learning are involved? What conditions favoring efficient learning are employed?

With several books, a boy and a girl in the front of the class, the teacher conducts the following lesson.

   1. Teacher says the following:
   2. Das ist ein Buch.   (points to book on table)

3. Ich habe ein Buch.   (holds book up)
4. Er hat ein Buch.   (points to boy with book)
5. Sie hat ein Buch.   (points to girl with book)
6. Wir haben Bucher.   (points in circle to include all three with books)
7. Teacher has class repeat the sentences twice;
8. he says the sentence or word if they do not pronounce it correctly.
9. T.   Das ist gut!   (smiles approvingly)
10. T.   Was ist das?   (holds up book)
11. Ss. Das ist ein Buch.
12. T.   Haben-sie ein Buch?   (T. asks three students individually)
13. S.   Ja. Ich habe ein Buch.   (each replies)
14. T.   Gut!
15. T.   Er hat ein Buch. (points to boy; gives class sign to repeat)
16. Ss. Er hat ein Buch.
17. T.   Sie hat ein Buch. (points to girl; gives sign to repeat)
18. Ss. Sie hat ein Buch.
19. T.   Haben-sie Bucher?
20. Ss. Ja. Wir haben Bucher.
21. T.   Das is gut.   (smiles approvingly)
22. In all of the above instances, teacher repeats sentence if a student or the class is not pronouncing it correctly.
23. Teacher has class repeat original sentences all the way through.
24. T.   Gut!
25. The next day, teacher holds up book and asks:
26. Was is das?   (to class as a whole)
27. Ss. Das ist ein Buch.
28. T.   Haben sie ein Buch?   (to a few students)
29. S.   Ja.   Ich habe ein Buch.
30. Teacher asks further questions, pointing to a boy, then a girl.
31. Students respond with the appropriate sentences.
32. T.   Das ist gut!

Check each of the types of learning that are in evidence in the above sequence. Also check any of the conditions that make for more effective learning that the teacher used. Better still, match each section (line number) of the instructional sequence with one of the conditions listed.

Types of learning

_____ Association between verbal sign and its object

_____ Imitation learning with model provided

_____ Induction of subject-predicate pattern

Conditions of learning

_____ An intention or "set" to learn is emphasized

_____ Whole presented first

_____ Group practice provided on the whole
_____ Group practice provided on main parts
_____ Individual practice given
_____ Feedback given
_____ Reinforcement (reward) provided
_____ Distributed practice is provided for
_____ Verbal mediators are encouraged

It would seem that each of the types of learning listed are evidenced in this audio-lingual sequence in the learning of beginning German. Association is made between *Buch* and an actual book; a model is provided which the students imitate; and finally, the students most probably induce a subject-predicate pattern from the sentences given.

Most of the conditions of learning listed are employed in the instructional sequence as well, in fact all but the first and last. The whole sequence is presented initially (1–6); then group practice is provided, first on the whole (7) and then on the parts (11, 16, 18, 20). The practice session is varied by including some individual practice where appropriate (13, 29). Feedback is given regularly (8, 14, 22, 24) as is praise or reward (9, 14, 21, 24, 32)—frequently both at the same time. The whole-part-whole approach is completed with the whole sequence reviewed at the end (23). Distributed practice is provided for by repeating much of the sequence the following day (25–31).

The teacher may well have emphasized the objective of the sequence and tried to set up an intention to learn in the students previously, but it is not reflected in the transcript. In the audio-lingual method, in which associations are made directly between words and objects, verbal mediators are not encouraged— in fact they are strongly discouraged.

Teaching Verbal and Factual Material

Now to draw several applications for teaching from what we have seen on the nature and conditions of the verbal-factual learning process: first, some general points that apply to most verbal-factual learning that takes place in the classroom, then a few points that apply to language learning in particular.

Preliminary

State the objectives for each topic clearly before you begin to involve students in learning about it. Even mention what the students are expected to have learned for a test or other evaluative technique that is to be used. In this way, they will have the proper intention or "set" for effective learning.

Material to be Learned

When appropriate, have students organize or relate the verbal-factual material to be learned in some way; into categories or a hierarchy, into a temporal or spatial sequence or order, or perhaps even into some verse or other mnemonic device.

Where appropriate, encourage students to use verbal mediators as a help in learning verbal or factual material:

French		English
dormir	(dormitory)	sleep

Methods of Learning

As a general rule, use and encourage a whole-part-whole approach in student learning of verbal-factual material: first have them go over the material as a whole, then break it into logical parts to study it, and finally review it as a whole after they have learned the several parts.

Plan your classes so that verbal-factual material is learned in moderate-sized chunks, some each day, rather than large amounts all at once. Similarly, encourage your students to distribute their study over several weeks rather than cram it all into one or two days, for example, through giving more frequent, shorter tests rather than one major exam.

Reinforcement

Provide frequent feedback or knowledge of results, particularly in the early stages of the verbal-factual learning process. Whether this is in the form of verbal comment in class, written comments on seat work, home work or on quizzes, the feedback will help to decrease erroneous associations and also serve as a motivater for further effort.

Provide encouragement, approval, and praise in generous amounts, not constantly but intermittently and as naturally as possible.

Overlearning

For subjects such as spelling, foreign language and arithmetic, provide some, though not extensive, drill or overlearning for the students in the form of games, workbook exercises, objective-type items, etc.

Language Learning

Respect the natural way of learning a language and employ the methods that are most in keeping with the psychological analysis of the child's capacities and the learning process: the audio-lingual method in foreign language, i.t.a. in beginning reading, etc. In grammar, have students induce the various types of sentences plus their transformations and then use them in their own sentences.

Make students aware of both the essential or core meaning of words plus their meanings and connotations in different contexts. Give them practice at determining the core meaning from the context. Also alert them to the various kinds of words and their meanings, not only univocal, but also equivocal and analogical. The latter two types usually cause the students to get involved in semantic arguments which are not genuine problems and should be avoided if discussions are to be worthwhile.

EXERCISE 6-7.   Teaching Verbal-Factual Material

Select some verbal or factual material in your field. Plan an instructional
sequence that includes activities which reflect the process and conditions of
verbal-factual learning as analyzed in this chapter. State what topic you wish to
teach and then list the learning activities that you would use in one class session.
In the margin of your teaching plan, specify which aspect of the learning process
or which condition of learning each activity is supposed to reflect.

Evaluation of Verbal-Factual Material

How can a teacher evaluate verbal and factual learning? Among the many ways
to evaluate how well students have learned verbal-factual material are:

> Test items
>> objective items: matching, multiple choice, true–false
>> short answer questions
>> identification or definition of items
>
> Other techniques
>> oral questioning
>> game-type activities

We will give some suggestions and an example or two for each.

Test Items

Matching.   The matching item is a convenient and compact way of evaluating
a large amount of homogeneous factual material, e.g., title-author, event-date,
event-name, thing-characteristic. For instance:

Identify the author of each by putting the appropriate number in the blank.

___	Gulliver's Travels	1. Sir Walter Scott
___	Vanity Fair	2. George Eliot
___	Ivanhoe	3. Charles Dickens
___	Robinson Crusoe	4. Victor Hugo
___	Tale of Two Cities	5. Jonathan Swift
___	The Three Musketeers	6. Emily Bronte
___	Silas Marner	7. Daniel Defoe
___	Wuthering Heights	8. William Thackeray
		9. Henry Fielding
		10. Alexander Dumas

Multiple Choice.   The versatile multiple choice format is commonly used to
measure verbal-factual learning as well as other types of learning. For example:

John Quincy Adams won the presidential election of 1824; who was his vice-president?

    ___ Calhoun

    ___ Clay

    ___ Crawford

    ___ Jackson

What is the name of the group of complex organic compounds that are present in small quantities in natural foods and are essential to normal nutrition?

    ___ Minerals

    ___ Vitamins

    ___ Calories

    ___ Nutrients

Definition items can also be phrased in an alternate way, with the name on the stem and the correct definition plus three distractor definitions as options. The first approach (cf. example) is easier and takes less reading; it is usually better for the junior high level but is appropriate for senior high also. The second approach is usually more demanding and is probably better for senior high students.

True-False. A final objective-type item that you may want to use occasionally is the true-false item. It is a little more versatile than you might have supposed.

1. Regular true-false

    The volume of a mass of gas tends to increase as the temperature increases.   T   F

2. Right-wrong (particularly useful in grammar or usage)

    If I was older, I couldn't do all of the things I enjoy now.   R   W

3. True-false or right-wrong with "Correct the underlined portion if false" (this is more demanding and reduces guessing, which is a real problem with true-false items)

    In 1824, John Quincy Adams was elected president when Henry Clay threw his support to him in the Senate.   T   F

4. A true-false cluster of items about the same topic (this is half-way between a true-false and multiple choice item)

    Czechoslovakia has a common border with:

Poland on the north	T	F
Yugoslavia on the south	T	F
Germany on the west	T	F
Rumania on the east	T	F

5. The true-false-sometimes type of item, i.e., either absolutely true, absolutely false, or sometimes true and sometimes false (this does away with the rigidity of the ordinary true-false item that must be absolutely true or false)

If a person is living at a latitude of 20°, he is living north of the equator.   T   F   TF

Short Answer.   The short answer question is more demanding than the objective item since it measures recall rather than recognition and since it does not allow for guessing. Samples of the three types of short answer or "fill in" items are:

What is 24 multiplied by 3? _____	(question)
The author of *Twelfth Night* was _____.	(completion)
North Dakota _____ (capital)	(association)

Identification.   A little further along on the objective-essay continuum is the identification or definition item such as the following:

Who was Elias Howe?
Define photosynthesis.
List the important bones in the leg.

Finally, factual information can be tested for within an essay question designed mainly to measure some other type of learning. For instance in a major essay question you might include the statement: "Support your position by giving relevant factual data" or the like.

Other Techniques

Oral Questioning.   Factual questions similar to the short answer or identification questions given above can be asked in class either to the group or to individual students.

Game-Type Activities.   Activities such as a college bowl, "spelling baseball," and informal crossword puzzles that you construct are further ways of evaluating verbal and factual learning. They usually take a little time and imagination to prepare, but they can be very engaging for students and provide a pleasant change from the ordinary variety of evaluation techniques.

EXERCISE 6-8:   Discrimination among Stimuli

Given below are two lists of memorable dates in American history. Flip a coin to determine which list you will read first: heads—I, tails—II. Read through the list once with a view to being quizzed on the events later. Then read through the other list once with the same purpose.

I

1607   First permanent settlement in the New World, Jamestown, Va.
1783   Treaty of Paris formally ending the Revolutionary War
1869   Transcontinental railroad completed
1932   Franklin D. Roosevelt elected president

II

1820   Missouri Compromise bill passed Congress
1823   Monroe Doctrine promulgated
1825   Erie Canal opened
1828   Andrew Jackson elected president

When you have read through both lists, cover the lists and fill in the blanks.

Give the memorable event for each of the following dates.

1607   _____
1783   _____
1820   _____
1823   _____
1825   _____
1828   _____
1869   _____
1932   _____

Which group did you learn better, I or II? If you got more of the 1-2-7-8 group
of items correct than the 3-4-5-6 group, it was probably because you were able
to discriminate more sharply between the dates since they were in different
centuries as opposed to being in the same decade. This illustrates the importance
of stimulus discrimination, differentiating among the several stimuli, particularly
those that are similar or close together, before one begins to learn associations.
(If you got more of the 3-4-5-6 group right, this little experiment failed.)

EXERCISE 6-9. The Role of Organization in Verbal-Factual Learning

Given below are two lists of minerals, each list arranged differently: one in an
organized pattern, the other in random order. Flip a coin for which one to learn
first: heads—I, tails—II. Spend 45 seconds learning the first list, then cover the
list and fill in the blanks under the proper column. Take a rest—a minute or so.
Then spend 45 seconds learning the second list and fill in the other blanks. Note
that any additional data is included as an aid and is not to be memorized—only
the minerals.

List I

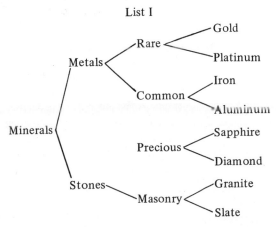

List II

Ruby
Lead
Uranium
Marble
Copper
Emerald
Limestone
Silver

I   II

——————————   ——————————
——————————   ——————————
——————————   ——————————
——————————   ——————————
——————————   ——————————
——————————   ——————————
——————————   ——————————
——————————   ——————————

How many in each list could you give?

A similar study reported in the research literature (Bower et al. 1969) showed that learning a list of minerals was much more effective—at least the list was recalled more than twice as easily—when it was organized in a hierarchical way than when it was just presented in random order. Do your results square with theirs?

For a follow-up, you might retest yourself after half an hour or so.

EXERCISE 6-10. Familiarity with Type of Material to be Learned

Which half of the following list of province-capital associations is easier to learn, those of Australia or those of China? Read through the list three times and then cover it and complete the pairs (which will not be in the same order as in the list below).

New South Wales   Sidney
Victoria   Melbourne
Queensland   Brisbane
South Australia   Adelaide
Kansu   Lanchow
Yunnan   Kunming
Shansi   Taiynan
Kwangsi   Nanning

Queensland	_____
New South Wales	_____
Victoria	_____
South Australia	_____
Shansi	_____
Kansu	_____
Yunnan	_____
Kwangsi	_____

Most students will find the Australian province-capital associations easier to learn, and will get more of them right because the names are more familiar to them than the Chinese names are. Several research studies on the variable of familiarity support the fact that the more familiar one is with a certain kind of material, the more quickly and easily he will learn it.

How do your findings compare with these studies?

Suggested Readings

General

DeCecco, J. P., ed. *The Psychology of Language, Thought and Instruction.* New York: Holt, Rinehart & Winston, 1967.

Jung, J. *Verbal Learning.* New York: Holt, Rinehart & Winston, 1968.

Language

Carroll, J. B. *Language and Thought.* Englewood Cliffs, N. J.: Prentice-Hall, 1964.

Marchwardt, A. H., ed. *Linguistics in the Schools.* National Society for the Study of Education, 69th Yearbook, Part 2. Chicago: University of Chicago Press, 1970.

Foreign Language

Lado, R. *Language Teaching: A Scientific Approach.* New York: McGraw-Hill, 1964.

Scherer, G. A. and Wertheimer, M. *A Psycholinguistic Experiment in Foreign Language Teaching.* New York: McGraw-Hill, 1964.

Reading

Aukerman, R. C. *Approaches to Beginning Reading.* New York: Wiley, 1971.

Downing, J. *Evaluating the Initial Teaching Alphabet.* London: Cassell, 1968.

7

Concept
Formation

Concepts are basic to any significant interchange in the classroom. Without concepts teachers and students would be limited to talking about facts, events, and individual objects in the environment. Concepts allow us to group the multiplicity of specific things that we experience into classes or categories so that we can identify and recall them easily and talk about them intelligently by relating them into statements that give them some meaning. As a teacher you must have a thorough knowledge of concepts and how they are formed if you are to be effective.

What is a concept? How do students form concepts? What intellectual abilities are active in the concept formation process? What approaches help students to form concepts more effectively? What are the implications of all this for the teaching of concepts? How can the teacher best evaluate to what extent concepts have been learned? These are the important questions that we will try to answer in this chapter.

The Nature of Concepts

First of all, what are concepts? Consider the following:

B.   apple, banana, pear, peach = fruit

A is an example of particular concrete objects being grouped into a concept. B is an example of several concepts being classified into a more general concept. In each case the objects or concepts have certain similarities that provide a basis for the grouping or classification. Concepts, then, are either groupings or classes of objects, persons, events, or other concepts that are formed on the basis of some common feature or characteristic.

The distinctive features or characteristics that serve as the basis for the grouping or classification into a concept are called *attributes;* e.g., the distinguishing features or attributes of banana are its shape, color, texture and taste.[1] The specific objects, events, or persons that are grouped together are called *instances.* A positive instance is a specific thing that contains the essential features of the concept or class. A negative instance is one that does not illustrate the concept.

What is the value of a concept? Concepts are the basic elements that we use in our higher thought processes. They allow us to reduce the complexity of the many specific experiences we have of our environment by grouping them according to their common characteristics. We use these concepts or groupings of experiences to form relations and structures as well as to solve problems and produce new creative combinations of ideas.

Types of Concepts

There are many types of concepts, some more difficult for students to form than others. What are these various types of concepts and how should you provide for their relative difficulty in your teaching of them?

We can divide concepts into several different types according to the bases we use to distinguish among them. Some of the main bases are: (1) the type of rule by which the attributes are joined, (2) how a concept is best defined, and (3) the degree of complexity of a concept. Let's consider each in turn.

First, according to how the distinctive features of things are combined to form a concept, there are several types.

1. In boy or "young male human being" there are several attributes present together (conjointly); this most common type of concept is termed *conjunctive.* Other examples are noun, autobiography, etc.
2. Such concepts as distance or "the space between one object and another" are defined by a relationship between attributes and are termed *relational* concepts. Superior, younger, and similar concepts are also relational.
3. Other concepts such as adverb or "a qualifier of a verb or of another adverb, adjective, etc." call for the presence of either one attribute or

---

1. The particular variations that these attributes have, viz. long and somewhat curved shape, yellow color, smooth peel and relatively soft texture inside plus delicious taste, are termed the "value" of an attribute.

the other (or sometimes both); this often arbitrary type of concept is called *disjunctive.* A strike in baseball, a pitch thrown in the strike zone or swung at and missed or both, is another example of such a concept.

EXERCISE 7-1. Degree of Difficulty in Concept Learning (1)

Some concepts are relatively easy to form, others are more difficult. It will take much more planning, effort, and imagination to teach the more difficult concepts well. Which of the above types are easier, which more difficult to learn: conjunctive, disjunctive, or relational? Try the following experiment which uses figures typical of those used in concept attainment research.

From the array of instances with three attributes (number, color, figure) in figure 7-1, form as many concepts (groupings) as you can ("as many squares as borders," "two squares," "two squares or two borders or both" etc.). List them on a separate sheet of paper.

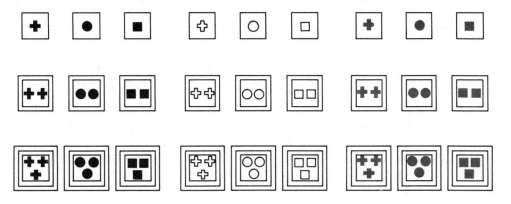

Figure 7-1.

There are 33 possible conjunctive concepts (e.g., one black figure), 18 possible disjunctive concepts (e.g., black or/and white cross[es]), and 8 possible relational concepts (e.g., as many circles as borders). The proportion if each were of equal difficulty to construct would be about 4-2-1. There are two criteria that can be used to determine the relative difficulty in attaining the several types of concepts: (1) the proportionate number of each in your total list, or (2) the proportion of each in the early part of the list versus the proportion in the last part.

Although this experiment involves material that is not very similar to that used in the typical classroom, we can make at least a tentative application to teaching. The formation of more difficult types of concept will call for more guidance, explanation, and often a greater number of examples provided by the teacher.

Another way of distinguishing among concepts is according to the direct basis for the concept. Thus they can be divided in the following way.

1. Some types of concepts are based directly on experience or observation. Most of our concepts, particularly our conjunctive concepts, are of this simpler, experience-based kind, e.g. house, honesty.
2. Other types of concepts are based directly on a definition or an agreed upon combination of attributes. Technical and disjunctive concepts plus many relational concepts are of this kind, e.g. standard deviation, tort. Whereas students can usually derive experienced-based concepts from a number of instances more or less on their own, they will usually require more guidance or even pure explanation in their attempts to form concepts that are based on a given definition.

Concepts can also be distinguished according to how they are best defined.

1. Some concepts are best defined in terms of use, e.g., "automobile is a vehicle that is used for transportation of people"; they are called *functional* concepts.
2. Other concepts are defined in terms of their intrinsic make-up, e.g., "a square is a four-sided figure with all sides and angles equal"; these are called *structural* concepts.
3. Still others are defined in terms of observable characteristics or behavior, e.g., "electrician is a person who installs or repairs electrical equipment"; these concepts can be termed *descriptive* or *behavioral.*

Other popular ways of defining concepts are by using synonyms or by giving examples.

All of the above, functional, structural, and descriptive, are common types of concepts that involve valid kinds of definitions; some concepts are best defined in terms of use, others in terms of make-up, and still others by way of description.

Teachers can expect first and second graders to define something through its use (a coat is something you wear) or to a lesser extent by way of illustrations or examples (fruit is like oranges, apples, etc.). In the middle grades and even in junior high, synonyms become an increasingly popular way of defining concepts (an infant is a baby). During these same years also, but to a lesser extent, students will define concepts by explaining them in terms of their intrinsic attributes (cf. structural concepts above).

A final basis for distinguishing among types of concepts is the degree of complexity and/or abstractness involved. For instance, story or "a narrative of events" is simpler than autobiography or "a narrative of one's life as written by oneself," which is more complex because it is composed of more attributes, viz. narrative, one's life, and by oneself.

EXERCISE 7-2.   Degree of Difficulty in Concept Learning (2)

An important basis for the relative ease or difficulty in forming different concepts can be illustrated in this simple exercise. Given below are words with their definitions. Read each word and definition through *once* trying to understand each concept.

hot: having a high temperature

heat: a form of energy which is the product of mass times temperature

temperature: the degree of hotness measured on a definite scale

ratio: the relationship of quantity or size between two things

number: a sum of units

proportion: a relation of equality between two ratios

story: an account of incidents or events

tragedy: a serious drama involving a main character in conflict and having a sorrowful or disastrous conclusion

allegory: the expression of abstract meaning or truth through concrete or symbolic fictional figures or actions

transposition: a change in the relative position of words in a sentence

noun: a word in a sentence that is the subject of discourse

house: a building in which people live

Now define each word as well as you can.

hot   temperature   heat

number   ratio   proportion

story   tragedy   allegory

house   noun   transposition

Compare your definitions with those above. How many did you get correct in each column? Which column of words proved easiest, which most difficult?

The three columns (types of words) can be thought of as being on a continuum from concrete to abstract. The words in the first column are related to sensory characteristics of things; those in the second column are first order operational concepts derived from perceptible reality; those in the third column are second order operational concepts derived from first order operational concepts and therefore most abstract, most removed from concrete reality.

Whatever type of concept proved to be most difficult (the hypothesis is that the abstract, second order concepts are most difficult) will require more extensive explanation on the part of the teacher and more work on the part of the students.

On a continuum of complexity and abstractness, first order concepts such as "story" or "temperature" are more basic and simple than their related second order concepts "allegory" and "heat" (mass X temperature). While first order or regular concepts are derived from particular, concrete instances, second order concepts are derived from one or more first order concepts; they are thus more abstract or removed from the concrete than first order concepts, are more difficult to grasp, and hence require more explanation and effort than first order concepts. Recall from chapter 2 that they also require formal operational thinking.

Also, a concept can *become* more complex with the accumulation of further knowledge or experience. For instance, a person's concept of size is a basic and absolute concept. It soon develops into the relational concepts of expansion and contraction; with additional knowledge it takes on even more complexity, in the concept of relativity or "size as related to velocity and the system in which it is measured."

You will teach thousands of concepts each year during your career, some of them simple, others complex, some of them easy, others difficult, some experience-based, others depending on a definition. To teach them knowledgeably, you should be aware of not only the various types of concepts but also their relative difficulty and the amount of explanation required for students to learn them adequately.

Since our analysis of the several types of concepts has been fairly comprehensive although necessarily brief, a schematic review of the main types is in order here.

Basis for Distinction	Type of Concept
how attributes are combined	conjunctive
	relational
	disjunctive
direct basis for concept	experience
	definition

how concept is defined	functional
	structural
	descriptive
degree of complexity	simple
	complex
degree of abstractness	concrete
	first order
	second order

The Concept Formation Process

How do students learn concepts? How is the concept formation process best explained? In this section we will consider (1) two general approaches in concept learning and (2) two divergent theories that attempt to explain how concepts are formed.

EXERCISE 7-3. Concept Learning in the Classroom

Analyze the following brief transcript and attempt to identify the essential elements in the formation of a concept.

A teacher supplies the following material to the students:

Deep sea divers who carry aqualungs on their backs are called scuba divers. They can go down into the ocean about 400 feet and can stay down for long periods of time because they carry their own supply of air. They frequently study the ocean bottom and bring back samples of life and other items from there.

The English language as spoken in America is a real melting pot of words borrowed from many languages. Most English words are derived from either Latin or Anglo-Saxon languages. But some are taken from German, such as waltz and zinc, and some are from Indian, like moccasin and moose. Then there are words that are taken directly from French or Spanish such as menu and chili.

There are basically two types of trees. One type has leaves that drop off at some season of each year. This group of trees is called "deciduous." The other type does not shed its leaves at all, even during winter. These are called "evergreens" or—because they are cone-bearing—conifers.
The following exchange takes place:

T. What do you notice about these?
S. They're made up of sentences.
T. Anything else?
S. They all start with the first word put in a little.
T. Anything else? (No reaction) All right, here is another group of sentences.

The earth is about 93 million miles from the sun. Mules are animals that are half donkey and half horse. The ocean breeze makes our house comfortable even on the hottest days. The earliest settlers in the "new world" were people who objected to the strict laws concerning religious beliefs in their old countries.

T. Is this the same?

S. No. The first three had to do with one idea. This one is made up of sentences that have nothing to do with each other.

T. Good. We have found several things about the first three groups we saw. (1) They are groups of sentences; (2) each of them tells about one idea; and (3) they seem to have a certain form, that is, the first word is set in a little. We call this a paragraph. Now, who can tell me in his own words what a paragraph is?

S. It's a group of sentences that have something to do with each other.

T. Anything else?

S. Oh yes. The first word is set in a little.

T. Very good. Now I'm going to give you some more groups of sentences and I want you to tell me whether they are paragraphs or not.

The teacher then gives them half a dozen groups of sentences, four with a common theme, two unrelated. The pupils indicate whether they are paragraphs or not.

Analyze what took place in this interchange in which the students learned the concept of paragraph. Check which of the following steps or activities were involved in the above sequence.

_____ 1. A series of examples or instances, in one or more ways similar, are experienced.

_____ 2. Students use past knowledge or concepts already known.

_____ 3. Students grasp the common elements or attributes of the positive instances provided.

_____ 4. The concept is further clarified through comparing and seeing the difference between positive and negative instances.

_____ 5. The teacher first defines the concept and then gives the students examples of it.

_____ 6. The teacher supplies a name for the concept.

_____ 7. Students express the concept in their own words.

_____ 8. The teacher evaluates whether the students understand the concept by having them identify further examples of the concept.

_____ 9. The teacher has the students recite *the* definition of the concept.

The above steps are in the approximate order in which they actually occur in the concept formation process, with the exception of numbers 5 and 9 which are "distracters."

The two most important elements in the process are (3) grasping the essential or common attributes in the specific instances (generalization) and (4) differentiating between positive instances of the concept and objects that are not instances (discrimination). Also integrally related to the process are: (6) naming the concept, (7) defining the concept to both clarify it and secure it in the person's mind, (8) evaluation in which the learner shows he has grasped the concept by applying it to further instances, and frequently (2) the use of past experiences and previously acquired concepts ("sentence" in learning the concept of paragraph).

The steps from 1 to 8 (excluding 5) in the sequence follow an inductive order. If the teacher first defined and explained "paragraph," then gave some examples (as in 5), and finally had the students repeat the definition (9), he would be using the expository or deductive approach.

Patterns of Concept Learning

In school, concepts are learned both through discovery and through exposition. The discovery approach to concept learning most often follows an inductive pattern. For instance in learning the concept "island," children will be shown pictures of different islands. The teacher will ask them what these things have in common, and the students will probably realize that they are all bodies of land surrounded by water. Supplying them with further pictures, the teacher will then have them distinguish between an island and a peninsula and perhaps a small continent (Australia). Once the students have grasped the essential attributes of an island, the teacher will indicate what it is called. As a way of evaluating how well they have learned the concept, the teacher might ask them again what an island is, or he might have them identify the islands from among pictures of islands, peninsulas, and lakes.

In this inductive or discovery approach the following elements are involved: (1) *experiences* with positive instances of the concept, (2) grasping what the common or essential attributes of the particular instances are, i.e. *generalization,* (3) distinguishing between positive instances of the concept and things that are somewhat similar but are not positive instances (*discrimination*), (4) giving a label or *name* to the concept, and (5) finding out how well the concept has been learned (*evaluation*).

In the expository approach to concept learning the pattern is almost reversed. A teacher will first state that an island is "a body of land surrounded by water"; then he will provide some examples (pictures) of islands. Often the teacher will explain how an island differs from a peninsula and a small continent. Finally, he will evaluate his students' knowledge of island by asking for its definition or by having them identify islands from among islands, peninsulas, etc. In other words, the pattern is largely deductive.

The expository or deductive approach entails the following steps: (1) *naming* the concept, (2) *defining* it, emphasizing its essential attributes, and then (3) giving some *examples* (positive instances) of the concept; frequently it will also include (4) *distinguishing* between the concept and similar but different things (negative instances), and finally (5) *evaluating* the learning of the concept.

Somewhere in between the discovery and expository approaches to concept learning lies the guided learning approach which follows a planned and ordered sequence with the teacher presenting instances, naming and defining the concept, and the student verbalizing the name and the essential attributes plus identifying positive instances of the concept.

EXERCISE 7-4.   Learning Relational Concepts

An example of a relational concept taught in school is that of "weight." Analyze the following lesson plan for the teaching of the concept of weight. How does the teacher provide for the essential elements of the concept formation process in his plan?

Objective: To have the students arrive at an understanding of the concept of
weight.

Procedures:
1. Weigh a rock with a spring balance.
   Q. What makes the platform of the scale go down rather than stay even?
   A. The pull of gravity on the stone.
   Q. Would the scale go down more or less: at sea level, 10,000 feet above sea level, in orbital flight around the earth, on the moon? Why?
   A. More to less: sea level, 10,000 feet above, moon, orbital flight. Because weight differs according to the gravitational pull.
2. Using a large magnet to represent the gravitational pull of the earth and a small magnet to represent that of the moon, put magnets under a balance which holds up a metal object.
   Q. What happens? Why?
   A. The large magnet makes the balance go down more because of the greater ability to attract or pull.
   Q. How would the weight of a small stone on earth compare to that of a large stone on the moon?
   A. They could be about equal because of the difference in gravitational pull.
3. Ask: How then would we define or describe the idea of weight so far?
   Ans: (1) A measurable property of objects
        (2) that depends on the gravitational force exerted on the object.
4. Ask: How does it differ from the concept of "mass" (studied previously)?
   Ans: Mass is constant, weight is variable.

5. Ask: By way of review, what are the main elements in the concept of
      weight?

   Ans: (1) a property of objects
        (2) variable
        (3) depends on degree of gravitional force

Match the procedures of the teacher with the elements of the concept
formation process (one or more procedures are possible for each element—or
perhaps none).

Procedures	*Elements*
A. Initial definition of weight (#3)	_____ Experience(s)
B. Review definition of weight (#5)	_____ Generalization
C. Weighing of rock with balance	_____ Discrimination
D. Questions and answers concerning pull	_____ Relating to past knowl-
of gravity (#1)	edge and experience
E. Demonstration of comparative pull of	_____ Naming
large and small magnets	
F. Comparison with mass	_____ Evaluation
G. Question and answer involving weight	
in orbital flight and on moon (#1)	

The experiences provided by the teacher in this guided discovery approach in
the teaching of the relational concept of weight are *C* and *E*. The generalization
phase of the process takes place gradually as the learner comes to grasp the
relation between the weight of an object and gravitational pull, and culminates
in *A,* the initial expression of the generalization. Further clarification of the
concept, i.e. the aspect of variability, comes with discrimination, exemplified in
F. As is true in most concepts learned in school, the learner draws from past
experience and from concepts formed previously in acquiring a new concept; in
this instance he uses the concept of gravitational pull (*D*) and the information he
has gained about orbital flight and the moon (*G*). Finally, the teacher evaluates
whether the class has understood the concept of weight by asking them for the
basic elements in a definition (*B*). In this case the naming of the concept was not
a separate and conscious phase of the process because the word "weight" was
familiar in a general way to the learners; the objective of the lesson was to have
them clearly understand the real meaning of the concept.[2]

Theories of Concept Learning

What goes on in the person's mind when he forms a concept? In other words,
how is the concept formation process best explained? Of the several theories
that psychologists have offered to explain concept formation, two seem most
relevant here: the neo-behaviorist form of S-R theory and the more cognitive
abstraction theory. They are illustrated in exercise 7-5.

---

2. This lesson plan was adapted from an example given in Carroll 1964.

EXERCISE 7-5. Two Approaches to Concept Learning

Given below are two somewhat different approaches to the teaching of the concept "simile." Analyze the two sequences, and see if you can identify some of the basic aspects of each approach.

I

T. Look at this sentence: "Clouds are like puffs of smoke."

T. What are we comparing clouds to?

S. Puffs of smoke.

T. Yes. We're saying that clouds are similar to puffs of smoke. This is called a simile.
What is "clouds are like puffs of smoke"?

S. A simile.

T. How about this sentence: "That house is like a fortress." What are we doing here?

S. Comparing the house to a fortress.

T. Right. We're saying the house is similar to a fortress. So what is "That house is like a fortress" called?

S. A simile.

T. Right. So a simile is a description of something in which one thing is compared to another thing; usually in a simile you use "like" or "as" to compare the two things.

T. How about this, "He's like an elephant."

S. It's a simile.

T. Why?

S. Because you're comparing someone to an elephant.

II

T. See how many things you can think of that are like clouds. Just complete this sentence, "Clouds are like _____."

S. (Write ideas on their papers).

T. What are clouds like?

S. Puffs of smoke; floating cotton; a soft white mattress.

T. How about this.
"That house is like _____."

S. A jewel box; a fortress; a castle.

T. What are we doing in these examples?

S. Comparing one thing with another.

T. We're saying that one thing is similar to another, right? Similar, so it's called a simile. How about: "The tree is huge." Is this a simile?

S. No, it's an adjective.

T. So "Clouds are like puffs of smoke" or "That house is like a castle" are similes but "The tree is huge" is not. Yet they all describe something. What's the difference?

S. "Huge" just describes the tree, there's no comparison.

T. And how about "castle"?

S. It describes "house" but it also involves a comparison, so it's a simile. Also it uses like!

T. What is a simile then, by way of review?

S. A description of something that uses a comparison with something else.

Indicate which approach illustrates each of the following statements.

I   II

1. The name of the concept is brought in early in the learning process, before the concept is really formed.

____   ____

	I	II

2. The name of the concept is injected after a generalization has been drawn from the instances.

3. The teacher suggests the key aspect of "comparison," and then the students mention "comparing" as the essential element.

4. The teacher has the students experience several examples before they derive the essential element of the concept, comparison.

5. The students draw the common attribute from the examples experienced.

6. Students respond in the same way—"simile"—to two different short statements.

7. The students distinguish between simple describing (adjective) and describing involving a comparison (simile).

8. Process can be described as follows: instances → awareness of key feature of instances → knowing what the class name is → saying the name.

9. Process can be described as follows: instances → drawing out common attribute → distinguishing between positive and negative instances → knowing the concept.

10. Sequence is more toward the discovery end of the discovery–expository continuum, probably best characterized as guided discovery.

11. Sequence is more toward the expository end of the discovery–expository continuum, probably best characterized as guided or directed learning.

In the first sequence the teacher supplies the name (1) and the essential feature of the concept (3) early in the process, before the students actually form the concept. The conceptual behavior consists in the students responding to two similar but different instances with the same word (6). The learning process goes from instances to awareness of the key feature, to knowing the class name, to responding with the name (8). The sequence used in the teaching of the concept is more one of guided learning. This approach to concept formation is of the stimulus-response type but includes some intervening steps between the instances (S) and the common response (R).

In the second sequence the teacher first has the students experience several instances (4) and then draw out what is common to them (5). At some point after the essential element is grasped, the concept is given a name (actually naming often comes at the very end of the process) (2). An integral part of the process is distinguishing between positive and negative instances or between the concept and a previously known concept (7).[3] The learning process goes from

---

3. Although the S-R theorists allow for discriminating between positive and negative instances, for them it comes either at the beginning when instances are presented or at the end of the process when the conceptual behavior is evaluated. It is not included in their basic model, whereas it is in the present explanation.

instances to drawing out the common attribute, to distinguishing positive and negative instances, to knowing the concept (9). The teaching sequence is more toward the discovery end of the continuum; it uses an inductive approach. This approach to concept formation, based on what is most commonly referred to as an abstraction theory,[4] is one suggested by many educational psychologists of a cognitive persuasion.

The S-R Internal Mediator Theory.   The first theory is a contemporary S-R theory that stresses intervening variables. Behaviorists traditionally have defined concept formation as the acquisition of a common response to dissimilar stimuli $\left(\begin{smallmatrix}S_1\\S_2\end{smallmatrix}\nearrow R\right)$. The process is said to involve *stimulus generalization* in which the organism makes the same response to a range of partly similar, partly dissimilar stimuli, as though they were equivalent. What many contemporary behaviorists have added to this explanation are some internal activities or variables within the person that intervene between the external stimuli and the overt response and affect the overt response. These intervening variables or internal mediators are usually symbolized as r–s, making the overall paradigm: $\begin{smallmatrix}S_1\\S_2\end{smallmatrix}\nearrow \boxed{r\text{-}s} \longrightarrow R$, where:

S$_1$ and S$_2$ (or S$_3$, etc.) are partly similar stimuli;
r represents an internal response, for instance the awareness of the important features of the stimuli and/or an internal verbalization of the class or concept;
s is the internal stimulus or specifically the cue that is provided by the internal verbalization (r); and
R is the overt response elicited by the cue (s).

Hence, the internal mediator theory of the contemporary behaviorists explains the concept formation process in the following way: We experience stimuli that are at least partly similar (S$_1$, S$_2$, etc.) and become aware of their common attributes (r); we internally verbalize the class name (s) for these stimuli and this gives rise to the overt response (R), i.e. the class name stated orally (Bourne 1966).

The Abstraction Theory.   The second theory that we will examine is that held by some cognitive-oriented psychologists who emphasize the cognitive processes involved in the various types of learning. They define concept formation as the process by which we abstract the common and essential attributes from similar instances and disregard the dissimilar, particular characteristics.

A schema of the abstraction explanation of the concept formation process is as follows:

---

4. Abstraction: literally meaning "the act of drawing out of."

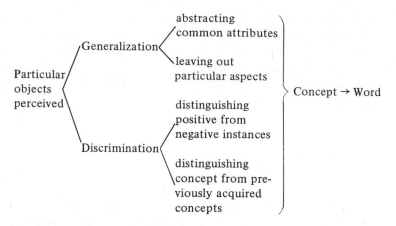

First, we experience particular objects that are partly similar, partly dissimilar, both in the present and in the past (memory is often involved here). Then we become aware of and draw out the essential and common attributes from among the objects we have experienced; at the same time we ignore or leave out of our consideration the nonessential, dissimilar aspects of the objects. On the basis of their common attributes we group the objects together into a general class or concept. Almost at the same time we discriminate positive from negative instances of the concept and distinguish the newly acquired concept from those that we have already acquired. In this way our awareness of the essential features that form the basis for the grouping of the positive instances into a concept is sharpened. The result of this whole process is the knowledge of a class of things based on common attributes or, in other words, an awareness of what a thing basically is. This internal knowledge is expressed overtly in a word or symbol, i.e. a class name (Pikas 1966).

There are other theories of concept learning, notably the information processing model of Hunt and Hovland but they are more theories of concept attainment than of concept formation and so will not be treated here.

How do the two theories of concept learning work out in practice? On the basis of both the theories themselves and the sample teaching sequence on similes above, we can discern the following differences in teaching a concept in a classroom.

	S-R Internal Mediator Theory	*Cognitive Abstraction Theory*
Objective	"Given a group of objects the student will be able to respond by giving the class name."	"A knowledge of the concept."
Instances	Supplied by teacher together with name and essential attribute.	Several experienced as first step—either supplied by teacher or created or recalled by students.

	S-R Internal Mediator Theory	Cognitive Abstraction Theory
Essential attribute	Supplied by teacher with an early instance.	Derived by students after they experience several instances.
Name	Given by teacher early in process.	Indicated by teacher toward end of process.
Pattern	Guided learning (directed) or perhaps expository teaching; deductive.	Guided discovery or even pure discovery; inductive.
Emphasis	Student giving class name on the basis of common attribute among instances.	Student deriving common attribute from instances.
Negative instances	Can be brought in early or after concept is learned.	An integral part of the concept formation process; sharpens awareness of essential feature among positive instances.
Definition of concept	Supplied by teacher somewhere during learning process.	Either expressed by student or given by teacher toward the end of the process.
Evaluation	Students identify positive instances of concept; perhaps define concept.	Students identify positive instances of concept; perhaps define concept.

EXERCISE 7-6. Critique of Theories of Concept Learning

Which explanation of the concept formation process do you prefer? First check
which points of criticism apply to which theory. Then, using these points plus
others you may think of, try to decide on which theory you will base your own
teaching of concepts.

	S-R	Cognitive
1. More explicit and comprehensive.	___	___
2. More concise and simpler.	___	___
3. Teacher is more in control of the process.	___	___
4. Student is more actively involved in the process.	___	___
5. Insures that all students see the essential feature of the concept.	___	___
6. Emphasizes main element in concept formation: grasp of basis for the grouping.	___	___
7. Should prove more helpful in teaching a concept.	___	___

The S-R theory seems to be more concise and simpler, the cognitive theory
more explicit and comprehensive. In the S-R approach the teacher is more in

control; in the cognitive approach the student is more actively involved. While the S-R approach insures that all students see the essential feature of the concept since the teacher states it, the cognitive approach emphasizes the essential feature more by centering the whole process around it. Which should prove more helpful in your own teaching? What do *you* think?

Intellectual Abilities Involved in Concept Learning

What intellectual processes are active in learning a concept? It is important that a teacher realize what abilities are involved as he guides his students in learning a concept.

In terms of Guilford's structure of intellect, concept learning basically involves the cognition of classes: concept formation is simply a process of grouping into classes on the basis of common properties. Memory for units and classes that have been known previously is also active: memory for units in supplying positive instances experienced previously for the generalization phase plus negative instances for the discrimination phase of the process; memory for classes in distinguishing the new concept from previously acquired ones. In the same way the evaluation of units and classes is also involved in concept formation, not only in the final evaluation phase but even in the generalization and discrimination phases: evaluation of units to see if they are the same or different, i.e., positive or negative instances; evaluation of classes in distinguishing between the new concept and other similar but different concepts.

Once a concept has been acquired and named, convergent thinking about it is possible, particularly the ability to name abstractions and the ability to classify data. Similarly, the divergent thinking abilities of fluency in producing ideas (ideational fluency) and the ability to classify things in various ways (spontaneous flexibility) also become possible.

A summary of the intellectual abilities involved in concept formation appears in table 7-1.[5] The *most* essential ability is indicated by a double asterisk.

Table 7-1. *Abilities Involved in Concept Formation*

	Units	Classes	Relations	Systems	Transformations	Implications
Cognition	*	**				
Memory	*	*				
Divergent Thinking						
Convergent Thinking						
Evaluation	*	*				

---

5. Cf. P. R. Merrifield 1966, Hoepfner 1969.

Conditions Favoring Concept Learning

What approaches help students learn concepts more effectively? We can gain some suggestions from the extensive research on the conditions that favor efficient concept learning; however, a degree of caution is in order. The vast majority of laboratory studies on concept learning have been concerned with concept attainment, in which instances are presented to a subject and he must "guess" what the class is that the experimenter has in mind, rather than concept formation in the sense in which it takes place in the classroom. Also, research has been more concerned with the ease of concept attainment rather than with the effectiveness of learning procedures. Hence many of the studies conducted have little relevance for classroom learning, and those that are related must be applied with reservation. With this enjoinder in mind, we can draw the following conclusions from the laboratory research on concept learning.[6]

Presentation of Instances.   Subjects learn concepts most easily when they are presented with all positive instances; a mixture of positive and negative instances is intermediate in difficulty; finally, it is very difficult to learn a concept from all negative instances (Hovland and Weiss 1953, Fryatt and Tulving 1963, Haygood and Stevenson 1967). Concepts are learned much more efficiently when all of the positive instances are available for a student to examine than when the instances are presented one at a time and removed. In a typical experiment concerned with this question, the instances of the concept are either presented singly and left in view (simultaneous presentation) or presented singly and then removed (successive presentation). The superior performance of subjects using the simultaneous presentation procedure is due mainly to the fact that they do not need to use memory in forming the concept. Memory errors are frequent in successive presentation, particularly when the concept is somewhat complex (Cahill and Hovland 1960, Bourne, Goldstein and Link 1964, Schwartz 1966).

Providing positive instances that are widely different (that share few irrelevant attributes) helps concept learning more than providing positive instances that share the same irrelevant attributes (Houtz, Moore and Davis 1973, Tennyson, Woolley and Merrill 1972). Negative instances are an integral part of concept acquisition (they make individuals concentrate on critical attributes). Most effective are negative instances that are missing only one relevant attribute when compared to positive instances (Tennyson 1973, Houtz, Moore and Davis 1973).

Learning Several Concepts.   Concepts are best learned one at a time rather than many at the same time. If several related concepts are to be learned together, it is better to present all instances of one concept first, then all instances of the second concept, and so forth. Mixing the instances of several concepts—even to show similarities and differences among them—only leads to confusion and interference of one with the other. Compound concepts are best

---

6. Exercises 7-7 and 7-8 provide two interesting experiments that you can do in conjunction with this section.

learned when the component concepts have been completely learned first (Kurtz and Hovland 1956, Kendler and Vineberg 1954, Bourne and Jennings 1963, Sanders, DiVesta and Gray 1972).

Verbalization of Concepts.   Concepts are more easily learned and retained better if students verbalize the essential attributes plus the name of the concept. Also, when students are called on to identify concepts, they are given feedback for both correct and incorrect responses which helps retention, especially in cases of more complex concepts (Buss and Buss 1956, Meyer and Seidman 1961).

Order of Difficulty.   Concrete concepts, based on perceivable characteristics, are easier to form than abstract concepts, those that are somewhat removed from the perceptual realm (Heidreder 1946, Grant 1951). The order of difficulty seems to be the following:

   a. concepts based on concrete objects, e.g. house, tree
   b. concepts based on qualities of objects, e.g. circular, living
   c. concepts based on the quantity of objects, e.g. ten, many
   d. concepts based on the relation between objects, e.g. distance, compensation
   e. concepts formed from other concepts, e.g. allegory, mass

When concepts are distinguished according to the rules that underly them, it is found that conjunctive concepts are easiest to form, closely followed by relational concepts. Disjunctive concepts are definitely more difficult to form than either of the others. One reason for the difficulty of disjunctive concepts is that they are much less common than conjunctive and relational ones and hence students have less experience in forming them (Bruner et al. 1956, Hunt and Hovland 1960, Youness and Furth 1967).

Finally, the number of dimensions, and number of values per dimension, that a concept has will in part determine its difficulty. As the number of relevant dimensions increases so does difficulty in forming the concept. Also, as the number of irrelevant or noncritical dimensions increases, the difficulty increases proportionately. By way of explanation, the more dimensions a concept has the more complex it is. The more irrelevant dimensions that are included in the instances, the more likely one will be distracted from the essential characteristics (Bulgarella and Archer 1962, Schvaneveldt 1966, Haygood and Stevenson 1967).

Teaching Techniques.   Classroom experimentation on concept learning is rather meager. However, one helpful study showed that employing a combination of approaches in teaching a concept is better than using just one method. For instance, the techniques of providing synonyms to convey the meaning of the concept, providing sentences containing the concept, having students construct definitions, and having them relate short descriptions of objects (examples) to the concept were found to be more effective when they were all used together than when only one technique was used (Johnson and Stratton 1966).

Teaching Concepts

What are the implications of what we have seen for teaching concepts? Putting together what we have analyzed regarding the process of concept formation (theory) plus what we have examined regarding the conditions that favor concept learning (research), we can offer the following suggestions for guiding concept learning in the classroom.

Experience with Instances

Provide experience with positive instances of the concept. These can take the forms of direct experience, for instance field trips, visual aids or creative sessions in which students actually experience what the concept is; or they can be indirect experiences, for instance verbal examples, illustrations of the attributes of the concept, or vicarious experience through stories. In addition, students' relevant past experiences can be recalled and added as positive instances.

  a. Use only positive instances initially.
  b. If possible leave the instances in view once they are presented.
  c. Select simpler examples that illustrate the concept clearly, i.e., examples in which the common attributes are as obvious as possible and which do not possess any irrelevant characteristics that will confuse or distract students from the common characteristics.

Identification of Common Attributes

Encourage the students to identify the characteristics that are common among the examples or experiences provided. Since this generalization phase is the most central and essential part of the concept formation process, sufficient time and emphasis should be devoted to it.

  a. As much as possible students should be encouraged to be actively engaged in discovering the common characteristics of the positive instances provided.
  b. Having students give a tentative definition or an initial expression of what is common to the positive instances is helpful.
  c. Guidance in the form of pointed questions or explanation that focuses on the essential attributes of the instances is helpful, particularly for the more complex, technical or disjunctive concepts.
  d. A variety of approaches should be used. In addition to the above, for example, a teacher might have the students write out the definition, he might provide synonyms, background and context for the concept, etc.

Discrimination

Supply negative instances of the concept, examples that are somewhat similar though different from it. Allow students to discriminate between the concept learned and these negative instances and have them explain the differences.

Again, pointed questions or explanation may be in order in the more difficult types of concepts.

Naming the Concept

Once the concept has been understood, indicate the conventional term that is used to identify it and have the students use the term when they speak about the concept. Although naming a concept sometimes comes earlier, in the inductive approach it comes toward the end of the concept formation process. If students are already familiar with the name but do not have a clear idea of what it means, then the name is used even in the initial stages; but ordinarily naming comes after the concept has been formed.

Evaluation

Evaluate how well the concept has been learned by (1) having students identify further examples of the concept from among a group of new positive and negative instances, or (2) having students define the concept in their own words, or (3) both. Further illustrations of evaluation procedures are presented in the following section.

Several Concepts

If you are teaching several related concepts together, keep them distinct by presenting examples of one and having the students grasp the common features from them, then presenting examples of another with students drawing the common features from those, etc. If you are teaching a compound concept, make sure the students have learned the component concepts well first.

Difficult Concepts

For concepts that are more difficult to form, e.g. complex, abstract, disjunctive, use more examples and more thorough explanation than you would for easier concepts.

Evaluation of Concept Learning

There are many ways of evaluating how well your students have learned a concept; for instance oral questioning in class, short essay test item, multiple choice test item, varied group techniques.

Oral questions and short essay test items can be of several types and can involve several intellectual processes. Here are some examples:

1. What is a paragraph?
2. In your own words define totalitarianism.
3. Which of the following are examples of the subjunctive mood? Tell why or why not.
   If I were to go
   I might attend

If I am seen

If I were recognized

4. What are the main characteristics of a republic? How does it differ from an oligarchy, a democracy?

5. Give as many examples of the concept of compensation as you can.

6. Explain Shakespeare's concept of tragedy and show how it is exemplified in two plays that we have read.

Questions 1 and 2 call for a basic knowledge of the concept and involve the process of cognition. Questions 3 and 4 call for a more thorough knowledge of a concept and require the student to discriminate between positive and negative instances or between the concept and related concepts. Question 5 requires divergent production as well as a knowledge of what the concept is. Question 6 calls for both an understanding of the concept and the ability to apply it to specific instances.

Among the several types of objective test items, the best for measuring concept learning is the multiple choice item. For instance:

1. What is an indictment?
   a. an official statement accusing someone of a crime[*]
   b. a notarized testimony given by a witness
   c. the verdict of the jury in a criminal case
   d. a formal notice of insufficient evidence in a criminal case
2. Which of the following is an example of a chemical change?
   a. mixing of flour and sugar
   b. freezing of water
   c. burning of oil[*]
   d. evaporation of alcohol

The first question requires simple knowledge of the essential attributes of an indictment. Another, often simpler, version of the same item would be to give the definition in the stem and then list indictment plus several related concepts such as deposition, verdict and sentence as distractors. The second question represents a convenient way of evaluating concept learning through finding out whether students can identify an example of a concept. Alternative forms of this same kind of item would either list several positive instances plus one negative instance with the instructions calling for the student to check which is *not* an example of the concept, or list half a dozen or more positive and negative instances with the instructions to check all of those that are examples of the concept.

Other evaluation techniques besides oral questioning, essay and multiple choice items that can be used for variety are: students pairing off with each testing the other on certain concepts, small groups of students taking turns defining concepts listed by the teacher, a "college bowl" session with some students serving as contestants, others as sources of questions, and one as master of ceremonies.

EXERCISE 7-7. Conditions of Concept Learning—Successive Versus Simultaneous Presentation

Which is more effective in teaching a concept: presenting all the instances simultaneously or each in succession? In this experiment:

1. Flip a coin to determine which sequence you will follow: heads, sequence 1 below; tails, sequence 2 on page 207.
2. Time yourself to the second.
3. Turn to the proper page and begin reading over the instances that make up a class concept.
4. When you think you have grasped the class concept, first check your time and then look at the answer on page 208.

Sequence 1

What is the general class of measures to which each of these statistics belongs?

Mean: the arithmetic average of a group of scores:

e.g. 2, 4, 5, 6, 6, 7, 7, 7, 7, 8, 9, 9, 11

$$\frac{\Sigma X}{N} = \frac{88}{13} = 6.77$$

Median: the midpoint in a distribution of scores:

e.g. 2, 4, 5, 6, 6, 7, 7, 7, 7, 8, 9, 9, 11

Median = 7

Mode: the score which occurs most frequently in a distribution of scores:

e.g. 2, 4, 5, 6, 6, 7, 7, 7, 7, 8, 9, 9, 11

Mode = 7

Answer on page 208.

What is the general class of measures to which each of the following statistics belongs? (Follow fold instructions)

Mean: the arithmetic average of a group of scores:

      e.g. 2, 4, 5, 6, 6, 7, 7, 7, 7, 8, 9, 9, 11

$$\frac{\Sigma X}{N} = \frac{88}{13} = 6.77$$

Once you have spent a sufficient amount of time on this, fold this page in half (toward you) so that you are looking at only half of the next page.

Median: the midpoint in a distribution of scores

e.g.

2 4 5 6 6 7 7 7 7 8 9 9 11

Median = 7

Mode: the score which occurs most
frequently in a dis-
tribution of scores

e.g.

2 4 5 6 6 7 7 7 8 9 9 11

Mode = 7

Once you have grasped what the
median is, keep the page folded and
turn it over so that only the other
half of it is showing.

Without looking back at the other
two statistics, what is the general
class to which the three measures
belong?

Answer below.

The class concept is "measure of central tendency" or the like.

In class: (1) compare the number of those who followed sequence 1 and achieved the concept correctly with those who followed sequence 2 successfully; and (2) compare the average time of each group of successful concept achievers (subtract 20 seconds from the average of the sequence 2 group to allow for reading additional directions).

The application is simple: the procedure found to be more effective as determined by the greater number of successful concept attainers and the lesser average time should be used in teaching concepts in the classroom.[7]

EXERCISE 7-8. Conditions of Concept Learning—Positive and Negative Instances

How is a class concept best learned (and taught): through all positive instances or through some positive plus some negative instances?

In the following experiment the task is to discover the class or grouping that can be derived given certain instances, in this case statistical concepts. One grouping includes all positive instances, one mostly positive, and one half positive and half negative instances.

For this experiment:

1. Pick a number from one to three.
2. Turn to the combination you chose. Do not look at combinations other than the one you chose.
3. Time yourself to the second.

---

7. If you wish to check on whether the difference in the number of successful concept attainers was due to a real difference in method of presentation, do a chi-square on the data; similarly, to test for real versus chance difference in average times do a t-test (cf. appendix C).

Combination 1: three positive instances, one negative instance

Percentile rank: the percent of the group that an individual scores above (e.g. 70th %ile: 30% above, 70% below)

Standard Score: the number of standard deviations times 10 that an individual is from the Mean (50) (e.g. 55: ½SD above the Mean)

Age Score: the average age of those achieving the score that an individual attained (e.g. 10.6: score is that of the average 10½ year old)

Mean: the average or balancing point of a group (sum of scores divided by the number)

What is the class concept?

Answer on page 210.

Combination 2: all positive instances

Percentile rank: the percent of the group that an individual scores above (e.g. 70th %ile: 30% above, 70% below)

Standard Score: the number of standard deviations times 10 that an individual is from the Mean (50) (e.g. 55: ½SD above the Mean)

Age Score: the average age of those achieving the score that an individual attained (e.g. 10.6: score is that of the average 10½ year old)

Grade Score: the average grade level of those achieving the score that an individual attained (e.g. 5.4: score is the same as the average fifth grader, fourth month)

What is the class concept?

Answer on page 210.

Combination 3: half positive instances, half negative instances

Percentile rank: the percent of the group that an individual scores above (e.g. 70th %ile: 30% above, 70% below)

Age Score: the average age of those achieving the score that an individual attained (e.g., 10.6: score is that of the average 10½ year old)

Mean: the average or balancing point of a group (sum of scores divided by the number)

Correlation: a mathematical index of the relationship or "going togetherness" of two variables (e.g. 0.90: a high correlation)

What is the class concept?

Answer below.

The class concept is "scores of an individual" or the like.

In class: (1) compare the number[8] of students in each group who attained the concept, and (2) compare the average time of each group of successful concept attainers. The highest number and the lowest time will indicate which proportion of positive and negative instances was most effective: (1) three-fourths positive instances, (2) all positive instances, or (3) half positive, half negative instances.[9]

EXERCISE 7-9.   Teaching a Concept

Select a concept in your area of interest that you would like to teach. Prepare a list of activities that you and your students will engage in so that they will learn the concept effectively. Your procedures should reflect one of the approaches analyzed in the chapter: either an inductive approach based on the abstraction theory or a more guided learning approach based on an S-R internal mediator theory. You might also bring in some of the research findings and the related suggestions for teaching offered in the chapter.

Suggested Readings

Bourne, L. E. *Human Conceptual Behavior.* Boston: Allyn and Bacon, 1966.

Bruner, J. A., Goodnow, J. U. and Austin, G. A. *A Study of Thinking.* New York: John Wiley, 1956.

Klausmeier, H. J. and Harris, C. W., eds. *Analyses of Concept Learning.* New York: Academic Press, 1966.

Pikas, A. *Abstraction and Concept Formation.* Cambridge, Mass.: Harvard University Press, 1966.

---

8. Or proportion if the total number in each group is too unequal.

9. Chi-squares and t-tests (respectively) can be done on any differences that seem sizable.

8

Relations and
Structures

In every field there are a number of abstractions that summarize the findings of scholars and researchers in that field. These are the structures and relations that give meaning and order to the many facts and concepts of a field and that allow a person to solve relevant problems and to deal creatively with his environment. Relations and structures constitute knowledge in the strict sense. Facts and words comprise information and language respectively; concepts are groupings or classes of experiences. It is only by being incorporated into a relation or a structure that the facts, words, and concepts that we have learned attain their full meaning and the status of genuine knowledge.

Ironically, even though most of the learning that goes on in the classroom involves learning relations, and even though the most important concept underlying the widespread curriculum reform of the past decade or two is that of structure, these two types of learning have received the least attention from educational psychologists both in terms of research and theory. Although we will try to indicate here some of the conclusions from the limited research as to how relations and structures are learned most effectively, much of our analysis will of necessity be general or theoretical and will be concerned with the nature of relations and structures plus the nature of the process by which we acquire them. Specifically, we will treat the following questions in this chapter.

> What is the nature of relations and structures?
>
> How are relations and structures learned, or more specifically, how is the learning process best explained?
>
> What intellectual abilities are involved in learning relations and structures?
>
> What does the limited research offer regarding the conditions that help in learning relations and structures?

How do we teach relations and structures?

And finally, how can we evaluate how well students have learned relations and structures?

Nature and Types of Relations

What is the nature of a relation? Below you will find some examples of relations in several subject fields; what do they have in common?

The pressure of a given quantity of gas increases with an increase in temperature. Basis: many experiments.

A truly democratic spirit developed out of the conditions of frontier life in the United States. Basis: many events, facts.

Plural nouns are followed by the plural form of a compound verb. Basis: convention (the way language developed).

All men should respect the lives of their fellow men. Basis: the nature of man, especially his right to life.

If you analyze these relations, you will see that they are all combinations of two or more concepts that have some basis in fact or reason. For instance on the basis of many experiments, the concepts "pressure of gas" and "increase in temperature" have been found to be related by the connective "increases." Similarly, after analyzing many facts historians have concluded that the concepts "democratic spirit" and "frontier life" are related by the connective "developed out of."

There are many possible ways in which concepts can be related. The basic ways plus some typical connectives used in each are as follows.

Types of Relations	*Typical Connectives*
cause-effect	_____ causes _____
agent-action	_____ expands, moves, etc. _____
action-consequence	_____ results in _____
whole-part	_____ is a part of _____
substance-attribute	_____ is a quality (or aspect) of _____
genus-species	_____ is a _____ *(general class)*
identity	_____ is the same as _____
equality	_____ is equal to _____
analogy	_____ is to _____ as _____ is to _____
similarity	_____ is like _____
opposite	_____ is the opposite of _____
inequality	_____ is not equal to _____
contrast	_____ is contrasted with _____
difference	_____ is unlike _____
correlation	_____ goes together with _____
reciprocity	_____ compensates for _____
negation	_____ cancels out _____
order:	
lesser-greater	_____ is greater than _____
sequence	_____ comes after _____

trend   _____ is tending toward _____
prerequisite   _____ is necessary for _____

The basis for any of these types of relations can be either experience, fact, scientific research, convincing reasons, or even authority.

Different relations enjoy different degrees of certitude depending on how convincing the evidence supporting them is. The various kinds of evidence or bases for a relation plus their characteristics and the degree of certitude they provide are given in table 8-1, pp. 214-15.

As a final clarification regarding the nature of relations we should note that several terms are used as the equivalent of a relation, each one having a different emphasis or connotation, e.g. principle, generalization, rule. Brief definitions will help to distinguish among each of these terms.

Relation: connection between classes or concepts.

Generalization: relation that summarizes a body of information and has an element of universality.

Rule: relation that has an element of constancy.

Conclusion: relation which is the end product of problem solving or reasoning.

Principle: relation which represents a basic truth which in turn can be the source of action or further conclusions.

Proposition: relation expressed in the form of a statement (often to be proven).

Nature and Types of Structures

Nature

What do we mean by structure? Given below are some examples of structures in one subject, biology. From an examination of them, see if you can discern what is meant by structure.

The whole of biology can be structured around *life,* with the main aspects of life, unity, diversity, continuity and interaction, having further elements or aspects related to them (figure 8-1).

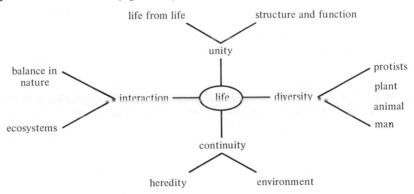

Figure 8-1. *A Structure of the Field of Biology*

Table 8-1. *The Continuum*

Example	Specific Basis
Man is unique among the animal kingdom	He can create his own language, can manufacture, etc.
A broken home is the primary cause of juvenile delinquency	Research supports the connection, but further research shows that it also causes mental illness, etc.
Heat expands metal	It always happens; the molecular theory is a plausible explanation
Intelligence correlates moderately with achievement	Correlational studies indicate that they are found to go together; causal connection can be reasonably inferred
Blue-eyed parents will have blue-eyed children	This happens so often that it very probably is not due to chance
More complex species evolved from simpler species	This explains many facts of paleontology, comparative anatomy, geology
A democratic system is the most effective form of government	Arguments of human dignity and freedom support it; arguments of economic welfare of all citizens could support another system.
Industry is responsible for the pollution of rivers	For instance, Hudson River, Mohawk River
Slavery was a cause of the Civil War	The massacre of proslavery men at Pottawatamie Creek
Jealousy results in a man's ruin	Othello
"Shakespeare's plays were the work of several authors"	Teacher's statement

The animal kingdom can be structured in terms of the order in which the more complex animals evolved from the simpler ones (figure 8-2).

Protists → simple multicellular animals → worms → insects → fish → amphibians →
reptiles ⟨ birds
lower mammals → lower primates → man

Figure 8-2. *A Structure of the Animal Kingdom*

of Certitude

Type of Basis	Characteristic	Degree of Certitude
Proper cause, precise reason	Causal connection established, necessity seen	Certain
Common cause	One thing is the cause of something else, but also the cause of other things as well	Certain
Constancy	Things are always found together; we don't know why for sure, we can only theorize	Quite certain
Correlation	Variables go together to a degree; causal relation may be inferred	Most probable
Statistical probability	Results or relationship is most probable; little chance for error	Most probable
Theory	An explanation that is based on fact or research	Probable
Argument	Statement offered to support an opinion	Probable
Examples	Instances used (e.g. in speeches) to support a statement	Possible
Fact	Historical event (although we can be certain of a fact, it takes more than one fact to establish a generalization)	Possible
Case, instance	Literary portrayal	Possible
Authority	Only extrinsic evidence provided, credibility of person (no intrinsic connection seen)	Possible (often indoctrination rather than certitude)

The animal kingdom can also be structured by way of the basic classifications and subclassifications that are made by biologists (figure 8-3, p. 216).

From the examples given you will probably conclude that a structure is simply a way of organizing our concepts and relations. It represents the interrelatedness of parts within an organized whole. Whereas concepts are ways of classifying the multiplicity of things in the environment, and relations are ways of combining two or more concepts, a structure is our way of organizing and interrelating the concepts and relations that we have formed. Ultimately it is our

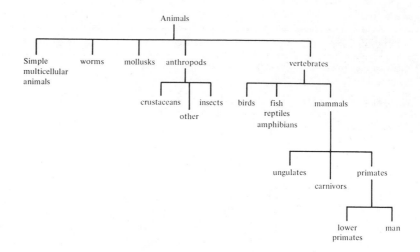

Figure 8-3. *A Structure of the Animal Kingdom*

way of organizing the multiplicity of our environment from which our concepts are abstracted.

A cognitive structure is our organized knowledge about a topic; it consists of an organized conceptual system or network with one or more basic ideas at the core and then other relations, concepts, and facts related to it/them. For instance, in the above examples our knowledge of some or all of biology is structured around the core ideas of life, evolution, and basic categories respectively. As Jerome Bruner says in a classic definition of structure: "Grasping the structure of a subject is understanding it in a way that permits many other things to be related to it meaningfully. To learn structure, in short, is to learn how things are related" (Bruner 1960, p. 7).

In Guilford's structure of intellect model, structure for all practical purposes is the equivalent of system. For him there are two types of systems: (1) cognitive or input systems such as patterns, models, theories (the biological structures above), and (2) executive or output systems such as plans, strategies, programs, that are designed to direct some activity. In our analysis of structure in this chapter we will be concerned with cognitive systems rather than executive systems.

Cognitive structures have many important characteristics.

1. They are comprehensive, broad, and inclusive of many various subideas; for instance, more abstract concepts such as number, life, man can serve as the core of a structure, whereas more concrete concepts such as chair, foot, fern are too narrow.
2. They are composed of one or more basic concepts or relations at the core or most general level, and then many more concepts and/or relations related to the basic idea(s).
3. They provide a framework for much of the information regarding a

topic, and also a frame of reference for inquiring further into that topic.

4. While they themselves are learned, they also make further learning about a topic more intelligible and meaningful; understanding is increased by relating new knowledge to one's cognitive structure.

5. They are individual: (a) a person forms his own unique cognitive structures, similar to those of other persons, but still unique; (b) he relates new knowledge to his own cognitive structures. Therefore a teacher must be aware of his students' individual cognitive structures and whether they are sufficiently developed to incorporate new knowledge adequately.

EXERCISE 8-1. The Nature of Structures

Earlier in this chapter we saw how much of biology can be structured in several different ways: a hierarchy, an evolutionary order, and a cluster of topics around a central theme. But how about other subjects? Can certain material in your subject field be organized into different types or structures? Undoubtedly yes. Take for example the area of literature. Given below in alphabetical order are some works of literature together with author, type, and theme. See if you can organize them in at least two different types of structures, using a different basis for each structure.

Death Be Not Proud. John Gunther. Biography. Courage.
Dr. Schweitzer of Lambaréné. Norman Cousins. Biography. Nobility of man.
How Do I Love Thee. Helen Elmire Waite. Biography. Love.
"If Thou Must Love Me." Elizabeth Barrett Browning. Poem. Love.
Jane Eyre. Charlotte Bronte. Novel. Love.
"Lee." Stephen Vincent Benet. Poem. Nobility of man.
A Man for All Seasons. Robert Bolt. Drama. Nobility of man.
The Miracle Worker. William Gibson. Drama. Courage.
"The Night Has a Thousand Eyes." Francis William Bourdillon. Poem. Love.
The Old Man and the Sea. Ernest Hemingway. Novel. Courage.
"Paul Revere's Ride." Henry Wadsworth Longfellow. Poem. Courage.
Romeo and Juliet. William Shakespeare. Drama. Love.
The Wall. John Hersey. Novel. Nobility of man.

As you have probably figured out, the two ways of structuring these works of literature are shown in figure 8-4 (p. 218).

Obviously the bases for the groupings are (1) types of literature and (2) main human experiences or themes. Both groupings are comprehensive; and contain a basic idea at the core and can include many subtopics within them. They provide a framework for organizing much of the literature we have read or will read in the future. In addition, we can incorporate further subtopics into them: the short story, the epic, and the essay can easily be added to the types structure;

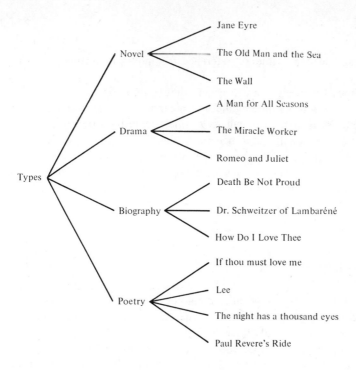

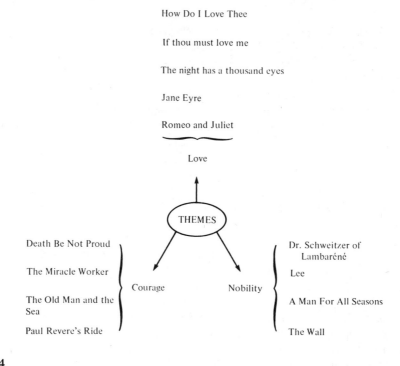

Figure 8-4

similarly, other human experiences such as loneliness, alienation, conflict with society, adventure, and integrity can be added to the thematic structure together with the works depicting them.

The value of these structures, particularly for making literature more meaningful, can be better appreciated if you realize that only a decade or two ago the main way of organizing literature was the chronological order in which it was written plus the nationality of the author. During the 1960s, however, the curricula in all fields were reorganized to bring out the interrelationships among the topics within each subject. Scholars and teachers of mathematics and the sciences were the first to restructure their content to emphasize basic ideas and how everything else relates to them; they were soon followed by similar attempts in English and the social sciences.

For ways in which your own field can be structured, examine several up-to-date elementary or secondary textbooks, looking at the tables of contents, skimming the introductory chapter(s) and perhaps some of the other chapters to see how the content is organized. Again, look for several basic ideas around which the material seems to be structured or simply the overall basis for ordering the topics that are treated.

Types

There are many ways in which concepts and relations can be organized and interrelated into a structure; the following types of structures or models represent the more popular ways. Rather than give further examples for each type, we will simply refer to the examples that have already been used or will be used in this and in other chapters of the book.

1. Structures based on classification, with classes within broader classes distinguished: the hierarchical structures illustrated by the classificational model of the animal kingdom above, and also by the British hierarchical model of intelligence in chapter 2.

2. Structures based on an order or a dimension with each point larger or more complex, etc. than the last: often termed a dimensional model; a typical example is the evolutionary continuum above.

3. Structures based on continuity or neighborhood, consisting of a cluster of ideas or areas around a core idea or area, for example the main aspects of biology that are structured around life above: we might call this a topological model, as it is called in mathematics, or simply a cluster.

4. Structures based on cross classification of data with interacting categories or dimensions: termed a morphological model and exemplified by the matrix of psychomotor abilities in chapter 13 (two dimensional) and the structure of intellect model in chapter 2 (three dimensional).

5. Structures based on interconnected series of events or transmissions of information: the operational models illustrated by the information

processing model of skill acquisition (chapter 13), Skinner's theory of learning (chapter 3) and—a more complex model—Guilford's problem-solving model (chapter 11).

Piaget makes the further distinction between (1) ordinary structures that are derived from our experience with the objects of our environment (physical structures) and (2) the underlying types of groupings or structures that are derived from our actions upon those objects (logico-mathematical structures). Physical structures are illustrated by the five types of structures or models specified above; logico-mathematical structures are any of the basic manipulations or groupings that we perform on the objects of reality, for instance classification, ordering, and number. In forming physical structures, we abstract and relate the qualities of the objects themselves; in forming logico-mathematical structures, we abstract the properties of the actions that we perform on the objects.

For example, in biology we order animals into an evolutionary continuum; in history we order important events into the correct temporal sequence; we can order paints into different shades and hues in art and can order measures into various sizes in home economics. In each of these cases we are acting on physical objects (or events), grouping or structuring them into an order (a physical structure).

If we consider what there is in common to each of the above groupings it is clear that each involves an ordering. The mental action that was performed in each instance was an ordering, which is one of the basic ways of grouping things in our environment. Ordering, then, can be said to be an underlying or logico-mathematical type of structure (specifically a logical structure, number being an example of a mathematical structure).

The two types of structures are themselves related in that the logico-mathematical structures serve an organizing function for the physical structures. Physical structures are actually specific instances of logico-mathematical structures and can be coordinated into these more general, underlying structures as parts into a whole. For instance, the classification of the animal kingdom above and of the intellectual abilities in chapter 2 (both the hierarchical view and the S-I model) plus any general concept (class) are subsumed under the general structure of classification. The continuum of evolution, the information processing model of skill acquisition and other structures of temporal or spatial order can all be coordinated into the underlying structure of order.

Developmentally, the two types of structures are related in that the underlying logico-mathematical structures must develop before the child can form the many physical structures that he acquires throughout the school years (recall from chapter 2 that these develop around the age of 7).

The Learning Process

How are relations and structures learned? What is involved in the process of acquiring knowledge, both ordinary and ordered? The two theories that seem to have most relevance for classroom learning are the cognitive approach of Piaget and other cognitive psychologists, and the learning hierarchy approach developed recently by Robert Gagné.

Before we get into a systematic treatment of the two theories, examine how they might work in practice.

EXERCISE 8-2. Two Approaches to Teaching a Relation

Given below are two plans for teaching the relation between factor and product and grouping factors into a set. Compare the two approaches and try to discern the differences between them.

I	II
Objective: an understanding of factors and sets of factors (in terms of relation: $x \cdot y = n$).	Objective: students will be able to specify the set of factors for any given two-digit number.
Procedure:	Procedure:
Have students make as many true statements as they can from $n \times m = 12$, using only natural numbers.	Tell students that at the end of the lesson they should be able to identify the set of factors for any given two-digit number.
Ask students whether 5 or 8 will satisfy either unknown value.	Have students recall the definition of natural number.
Identify the numbers which when multiplied by another number form a given product as a "factor."	Define factor: any number which when multiplied by another number forms a product.
Ask students whether 4 is a factor of 12 and why.	Give examples of factors: 2 and 6 are factors of 12, so are 3 and 4, 12 and 1.
Ask students to list the factors of 12.	
Have students make as many true statements as they can from $n \times m = 25$ and $n \times m = 42$. If they miss any, ask whether they have tried all possibilities starting with 1, 2, 3, 4, etc.	Have students make as many true statements as they can from $n \times m = 25$ and $n \times m = 42$.
Have students list factors of 25 and then of 42 in order.	Have students recall the definition of set.
Ask students to suggest a mathematical name for each list; if necessary, identify it as a set of all the factors of a certain product.	Define set of factors: a group of natural numbers each of which is a factor of a given product. Suggest that for a given product they start with 1, then try 2, 3, etc. until all factors are identified.
Evaluation:	Evaluation:
Ask students to state the relation between a factor and its product.	Ask students to give all factors of 12, of 32.
Ask students whether 1, 2, 3, 4, 5 and 6 are factors of 32.	Ask students to define "set of factors."
Have students give the set of all the factors of 32.	

Although these two approaches to teaching factors and sets of factors may seem at first glance to be somewhat similar, they are actually quite different. See if you can identify these differences.

	I	II
Objective is more specific, behavioral.	___	___
Objective is more general, to be inferred from behavior.	___	___
Starts with a problem.	___	___
Starts with a statement.	___	___
Has students recall past knowledge.	___	___
Gets students active and involved, manipulating symbols.	___	___
Provides cues to learning in the form of explicit statements regarding key concepts, relations—so as to make sure students form correct connections.	___	___
Has students induce the essential idea through their own mental activity.	___	___
Provides terms and clarification *after* students have grasped the essential idea involved more or less on their own.	___	___
Gives examples of the relation to illustrate the essential idea after it has been stated by the instructor.	___	___
Gives thought questions encouraging students to arrive at relation together with its basis (why).	___	___
Gives students practice in applying the concept or rule that they have learned.	___	___
Has students demonstrate that they have grasped the idea or relation.	___	___

The differences between the first and second approaches seem to be these.

I	II
Objectives are more general, emphasizing such aims as knowledge, understanding.	Objectives are phrased in behavioral terms, e.g. "will be able to . . ."
Begins with a problem to be solved.	Begins with a statement of what students will be expected to do when they have learned the topic.
Gets students involved in manipulating ideas early in the learning session.	Has students recall past knowledge that pertains to the relation to be learned.
Encourages students to induce the main ideas as much as possible on their own, i.e. through their mental activity regarding examples suggested by the teacher.	Provides explicit statement of the relation or rule so that students will learn it in its correct form, i.e. with each term or concept in its right position.
Provides correct terms and needed clarification after the students have grasped the essential idea or relation.	Gives examples to illustrate the relation that the teacher has stated.

I	II
Provides thought questions regarding the relation, emphasizing its basis or proof.	Gives students practice in applying the relation by providing specific problems for them to work on.
Has students indicate whether they have grasped the essence of what they have learned.	Has students demonstrate whether they have learned (and understood) the relation.

The first approach, in which students grasp an idea or relation through their own manipulation of objects or ideas, is that recommended by most cognitive psychologists. The second approach, in which the teacher specifies the relation to be learned, is that of Robert Gagné who has formulated a learning hierarchy theory that is an outgrowth of a stimulus-response view of learning.

In the cognitive approach students first get involved with examples from which they derive the relation or general idea and only then become concerned about stating the relation using the recognized terminology. In Gagné's approach, early emphasis is placed on component concepts and terms and especially on the explicit statement of the relation by the teacher; this is followed by examples or problems to be worked by the students.

There are other differences as well, especially in the beginning of the learning sequence. The main similarity is at the end where both approaches include evaluation of learning. Gagné is very explicit about the student's demonstrating that he has learned the relation; the cognitive theorists also admit that this is an integral part of the learning sequence.

The Cognitive Approach

Piaget believes knowledge is acquired "through the medium of action." He states:

> Knowledge is not at all the same thing as making a figurative copy of reality for oneself, but it invariably consists in operative processes leading to a transformation of reality either in action or thought, in order to grasp the mechanisms of these transformations and thus assimilate the events and the objects into systems of operations (or structures of transformations). (Piaget 1970, pp. 71-72)

For Piaget, the process of acquiring knowledge is characterized by an interaction between mind and object that he summarizes as follows:

> It is possible to say that thought is well adapted to a particular reality when it has been successful in assimilating that reality into its own framework while also accommodating that framework to the new circumstances presented by the reality. Intellectual adaptation is thus a process of achieving a state of balance between the assimilation of experience into the deductive structures and the accommodation of those structures to the data of experience. Generally speaking, adaptation presupposes an interaction between subject and object, such that the first can incorporate the

second into itself while also taking account of its particularities; and the more differentiated and the more complementary that assimilation and that accommodation are, the more thorough the adaptation. (Piaget 1970, pp. 153-54)

The cognitive explanation of how we learn relations and structures is not new. For instance, George Katona, a leading disciple of Wertheimer, gives the following account of how knowledge is acquired.

Learning by understanding involves substantially the same process as does problem solving—the discovery of a principle. . . . Both problem solving and meaningful learning consist primarily in changing or organizing the material. The role of organization is to establish or to discover or to understand an intrinsic relationship. . . . Learning by understanding consists essentially of grouping (organizing) a material so as to make an inner relationship apparent. (Katona 1940, pp. 53-54)

According to the cognitive view, we acquire knowledge through interaction with our environment, both physical, ideational, and social. We interact with the objects, ideas, and persons that are part of our psychological world, manipulating them, experimenting with them, organizing them, discovering relationships and interrelationships among them.

The process by which relations and structures are learned is quite similar to the problem-solving process which we will examine more explicitly in chapter 11. First, the question arises: "What is the relation between . . . ?" or "What is the interrelationship among . . . ?" To answer the question and acquire a relation or structure, the person must actively manipulate the objects (physical manipulation) or the ideas (abstract manipulation) that are relevant to the question. He can do this in one or more of the following ways, depending on the specific subject area or topic:

1. experimentation, using either a trial and error method (child) or the strict hypothetico-experimental approach (adolescent) to arrive at a conclusion;
2. induction of a generalization from several instances or examples, including present instances perceived, past experiences recalled, and further examples thought up through divergent production;
3. comparison of ideas and possibilities dialectically or analytically with a view to arriving at a new conclusion or synthesis;
4. deduction of a new conclusion from data or relations already known;
5. combination of ideas in a "playful" way with a view to arriving at a new relation or to integrating the ideas into a new structure.

Through one or more of these types of active manipulation, our concepts are organized in such a way that there is a coherent relational arrangement (1) between two or more concepts that form the relation or structure and (2) between the relation or structure and its basis, proof, or explanation. In other words, concepts are not merely related by connectives such as the verbs "is," "causes," "equals," etc., but relationship is also supported by convincing evidence, whether fact or reason.

The criteria of the relation or structure and of the evidence are:

1. For the relation or structure itself: generality and necessity, i.e., it must apply to many instances and it must occur with regularity or some degree of necessity;
2. For the evidence supporting the relation or structure; truth and logic, i.e., it must have a basis in fact or in the nature of things and also have a logical connection with the relation or structure it supports.

For the relation or structure to be considered genuine knowledge rather than just factual information, it must have a fairly general applicability, and it must be either necessary or at least highly probable. The necessity is established by the evidence which must not only consist of established fact or convincing reasons, but must also be clearly supportive of the relation or structure.

The end result of this organization of concepts then is (1) an understanding of the relation or structure and (2) the realization that it is supported by evidence and is therefore necessary or at least constant or probable. The result is genuine knowledge.

The process of learning relations and structures can be schematized as follows.

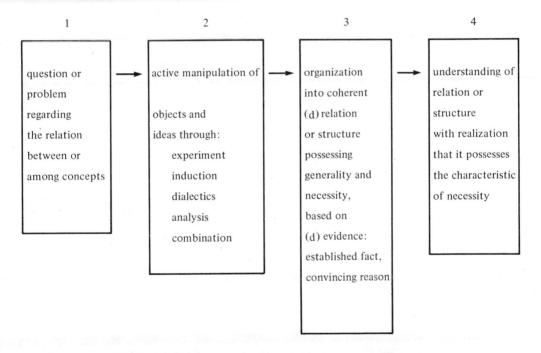

1	2	3	4
question or problem regarding the relation between or among concepts	active manipulation of objects and ideas through: experiment induction dialectics analysis combination	organization into coherent (d) relation or structure possessing generality and necessity, based on (d) evidence: established fact, convincing reason	understanding of relation or structure with realization that it possesses the characteristic of necessity

Understanding of a relation or structure (4) results when the learner organizes the relevant concepts into that relation or structure plus the facts or reasons (evidence) in such a way that they clearly support that relation or structure (3). This organization in turn results from the active manipulation of objects and ideas (2) which most often was stimulated by a question or problem (1).

Note that the process by which we learn relations and structures follows the order:

question ⟶ manipulation of ⟶ organization of ⟶ understanding of
                    data and reasons   data and reasons   relation or structure

We might call this the *order of learning,* since it is the order we follow when we acquire knowledge. It is just the inverse of the *order of knowledge* or the way in which relations and structures exist in our minds once we have learned them:

relation or structure ⟶ based on data ⟶ resulting from experiment,
understood   and reasons   induction, dialectic, etc.

Although schools have traditionally taught relations by "packaging" and presenting them according to the order of knowledge, e.g. relation→ proof→some examples, the cognitive theorists have long stressed that the acquisition of relations and structures should follow the order of learning, i.e. examples → manipulation and organization → relation (or structure). As Katona states, although this order is indirect, it often proves to be "simpler, more natural and more efficient."

The order of learning is simpler for the student to follow (although much more difficult for the teacher to arrange) because it proceeds from the concrete and particular to the more abstract and general. It is more natural because it follows the order by which we discover things on our own, namely an inductive or dialectical order. Finally, the order of learning is more efficient since as Katona showed years ago and the discovery learning experiments have supported more recently, a principle or generalization is retained more permanently when it is discovered by the student himself than when it is simply presented to him.

The Learning Hierarchy Approach

The other major contemporary theory of the formation of relations and structures is that of Robert Gagné, who explains his approach as follows, using the term "rule" in place of relation.

> Typically, a rule is composed of several concepts. . . . The individual must have learned these component concepts as prerequisites to learning the rule. Assuming he has acquired these concepts, learning a rule becomes a matter of learning a correct sequence for them. When the individual possesses the rule as a capability, one observes that he is able to identify these component concepts and also to demonstrate that they relate to one another in the particular manner of the rule. . . .
>
> Although it is useful to discuss the learning of a single rule, most rules are not learned in isolation, except perhaps by the young child. Instead, the school student or the adult typically learns related sets of rules pertaining to a larger topic. What he learns is an *organized set of intellectual skills.* The individual rules that compose such a set may have demonstrable relations to each other in a logical sense. They are also related to each other in the *psychological* sense that the learning of some are prerequisite to the learning of others, just as concepts are prerequisite to the learning of rules. Here the interest centers on the psychological

organization of intellectual skills and not on the logical organization of verbal information which may be involved in their learning.

The psychological organization of intellectual skills may be represented as a *learning hierarchy,* often composed largely of rules. As previously shown, two or more concepts may be prerequisite to (and in this sense subordinate to) the learning of a single rule. Similarly, two or more rules may be prerequisite to the learning of a superordinate rule. Once the latter is learned, it may combine with another rule to support the learning of still another higher-order rule, and so on. The entire set of rules, organized in this way, forms a learning hierarchy that describes an *on the average* efficient route to the attainment of an organized set of intellectual skills that represent "understanding" of a topic. (Gagné 1970, pp. 192-93, 203-4)

Gagné's learning hierarchy approach to learning relations and structures is an outgrowth of the S-R theory of learning. For Gagné, learning relations and structures is called rule or principle learning. A rule is a group of concepts that are related in a chain or sequence; a structure is simply a higher order rule. The two essential elements in learning a rule are: (1) the learner's possession of the concepts that constitute the rule or are prerequisite to it, and (2) the instructional sequence consisting of the verbal instructions of the teacher plus the appropriate responses of the learner.

The first step in learning a rule or principle is for the teacher to determine the knowledge and skills (rules, concepts, S-R chains, etc.) that are necessary for learning the rule, and also to determine to what extent the learner possesses these prerequisites. In the first place this entails a structural analysis of the rule, its components and prerequisites, the results of which can be ordered in a hierarchical way. Figure 8-5 shows one of Gagné's simple examples: the rule that "round things roll."

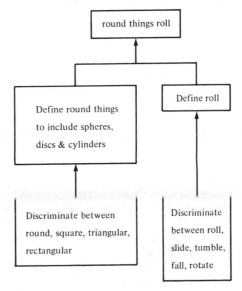

Figure 8-5. *A Simple Learning Hierarchy*

In the second place, it must be determined whether the learner possesses the requisite concepts or other types of learning essential for acquiring the new rule. If some students do not already have the required knowledge, they should either learn it before proceeding, or it should be made an integral part of the overall instructional sequence.

Once the analysis of the prerequisites has been made and it has been determined that the students possess them, the learning itself can begin. It follows the sequence given below, with a decided emphasis placed on verbal instructions.

1. The teacher states what kind of performance is expected of the student once the learning is complete. For example, "I want you to answer the question of. . . ." or "You should be able to. . . ." The instructor does not explicitly state the rule itself, but only the type of performance that will show that the student has learned the rule.
2. The learner recalls the component concepts that make up the rule. The teacher either verbally encourages him to recall the previously learned concepts ("You remember. . . .") or he provides objects or pictures and has the student identify instances of the concepts.
3. The teacher then states the rule, that is, puts the concepts together in the proper sequence. This serves as a "cue" for the learner to put the rule together with each element in its proper order.
4. Finally, the instructor has the student demonstrate the rule by using or applying it in a specific situation. In addition, he may ask the student to state the rule verbally. The demonstration, however, is much more important than the verbal statement because it proves that the student has actually understood the rule; a verbal statement alone could mean that he has only learned a verbal chain, not the rule itself.

The process of learning a relation, then, goes as follows:

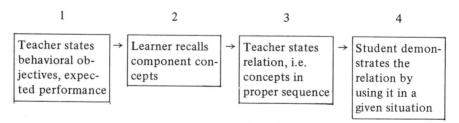

1		2		3		4
Teacher states behavioral objectives, expected performance	→	Learner recalls component concepts	→	Teacher states relation, i.e. concepts in proper sequence	→	Student demonstrates the relation by using it in a given situation

In the same way, more organized sets of rules can be identified and learned in all subject fields. In fact, our knowledge of a certain topic consists of the organized set of intellectual skills that form the learning hierarchy relating to that topic.

The cognitive theory and Gagné's approach to learning relations and structures are decidedly more different than they are similar. The major points of difference are summarized below.

Aspect of Theory	Cognitive	Gagné
Objective in the learning of relations, structures	Understanding of a relation or a structure in terms of its evidence or basis	Understanding of a rule to be used, a capability or intellectual skill
Emphasis in a statement of objective	Knowledge, understanding	Performance, behavior
Procedure	Discovery: students manipulate objects, ideas, arrive at conclusion	Guided learning: teacher gives instruction, supplies cues for students
Prerequisites to learning	Capacity for operational thinking, either concrete (child) or formal (adolescent)	Component concepts of rule, further concepts, skills, etc. needed for these component concepts
Sequence of learning	Problem solving is means to acquire relations, structures	Relations (and concepts) are used as means in problem solving
Pattern of knowledge	Relations: statement plus evidence Structures: hierarchical, dimensions, cluster, etc.	Hierarchical order with highest level rule at top and subordinate or prerequisite rules and concepts below

Whether you settle for the fact that they are basically different explanations or whether you try to make at least a partial rapprochement between them is up to you. If you decide on the first alternative, you can either choose between the two approaches or use the cognitive in some cases and Gagné's in other cases, depending on which you judge is more appropriate for the specific topic or situation.

If you decide on the second alternative, you might wish to consider some of the possible points of compromise suggested below.

1. Objectives: understanding relations is worthwhile in itself but it can also serve the practical purpose of giving us the capability of using a relation in solving problems.
2. Procedure: the guided discovery approach has fared well in the research, both for short-term retention and long-term transfer to related instances. If the student manipulation of ideas (cognitive) is given considerable guidance by a teacher (Gagné), the result is the rather effective guided discovery approach to learning.
3. Prerequisites: you will probably find as a teacher that both the ability for operational thinking and some basic, relevant concepts are necessary for forming relations and structures.
4. Sequence of learning: you can make a case for both sequences. The one you use more often in your own teaching will no doubt depend on

both your psychological and philosophical persuasions, e.g. cognitive and Aristotelian: problem solving used to acquire relations, structures; S-R and pragmatist: relations used in problem solving.

5. Pattern of knowledge: further clarification should come at the end of the next section when a type of structure specified by Piaget is compared to a structure of Gagné's. In the meantime, there are two differences to note: (1) the cognitive theorists allow for several types of structures, Gagné only one; and (2) while Gagné's structure of a topic is more functional in purpose than structural, the cognitive theorists structure a topic mainly to give it organization and meaning but are also aware that the structure is very functional in teaching.

EXERCISE 8-3. Teaching a Structure

How is a structure learned? There are several ways: teacher explanation of the structure, student induction of the structure from instances provided by the teacher, and more creative approaches that involve the students' divergent thinking plus the induction of the structure from their own ideas. The following description of the learning of the basic idea or structure of "city" is an example of a more creative approach. Analyze it and try to identify what is taking place in each section.

1 { Early in the fall term of the fifth-grade geography class, a physical map of the United States showing rivers, lakes, relative distance above sea level, and main natural resources is provided to each student. The teacher asks the question: "Where do you think the largest cities are located?"

2 { Students work at their desks for twenty minutes. Then the teacher asks for ideas. A lively discussion follows on where the large cities are probably located and why.

3 { Rivers and large lakes are key items in the discussion. Students say that they are necessary for transportation and that there is probably drinking water there. Land closer to sea level is favored over the West (except the coast) because the people came mainly from Europe. Raw materials are also considered to be important so that people can make a living.

4 { After a while the teacher asks the students to state what they feel is necessary for a city to grow. The students mention: people, water, transportation, food, good climate, plus raw materials and some kind of power supply (water, coal, etc.).

5 { The teacher then pulls down a large political map of the United States showing the large cities. After a flurry of excitement at the realization that some of their hypotheses matched reality, the teacher has the students consider several of the major cities and why they grew as large as they did.

6 { The following day, the class considers other cities, discussing why they grew and for what they are noted.

7 { They also discuss why some of them, e.g. Denver, Phoenix, grew in places nobody chose.

8 { Subsequently, when students are studying various sections of the United States, the teacher reminds the students—usually with a question or two—of how specific cities are related to the general idea of city they induced at the beginning of the year.

Indicate which section(s) of the above description illustrates each of the following statements.

_____ Materials with which to interact are provided for students.
_____ Students manipulate facts and ideas.
_____ The class organizes the main ideas into a structured whole.
_____ Specific examples are incorporated into the structure.
_____ The structure is changed to some extent to allow some near exceptions to fit into it.
_____ Further instances of the structure are given more meaning by being related to it.

1. In learning the structure "city," the learners are provided with material with which to *interact,* specifically maps with key information on them.

2 and 3. Students *manipulate* this information by themselves for a while and then exchange ideas with one another in a discussion of why cities are probably located in certain places.

4. The main requirements for a city are identified and *organized* into a structure, namely the basic idea of "city."

5 and 6. Specific cities are then considered in light of the basic characteristics of a city; in other words they are *incorporated* into the structure "city."

7. When it becomes clear that some cities flourish with only some of the ordinary requirements for a city, the students' basic idea of "city" is *modified* somewhat and becomes a little more flexible.

8. The students' cognitive structure of "city" is used throughout the year with further cities studied more in relation to the basic requirements of a city than as separate entities. On the one hand, relating to cognitive structure provides the students with a greater understanding of the specific cities and why they developed; on the other hand, it enriches the students' cognitive structure of "city" itself by incorporating further supportive instances into it.

It should be noted that the students' basic idea or structure of the nature of city in turn can be incorporated into a larger structure that will include other aspects of city such as the inner life: politics, culture, education, business, industry, religion, media, etc., and the network of cities: communication, suburbs, interdependence, etc. This larger structure of city (nature-life-network) is usually one of several structures that form a course in social studies; other basic ideas or structures that might be treated in the course are manufacturing, natural resources, agriculture, and the like.

Further Development of Structures

A structure is usually a dynamic rather than a static kind of knowledge. Once a cognitive structure has been learned it can be further developed in several ways: (1) by incorporating new facts, concepts, and relations into it, (2) by giving it further support through adding additional evidence to it, (3) by making further distinctions among concepts that are related to the core idea and then further differentiating among the elements of the structure, and (4) by comparing the structure with other structures and grasping the similarities and differences among them.

Since it is both comprehensive and fundamental in a subject field, a structure is open to the incorporation of new data and ideas into it. In fact, one of the main values of a cognitive structure is that many facts, concepts, and relations can be related to it in a way that gives them more meaning and makes them more understandable to the person.

Just as being aware of the supporting evidence plays an integral part in the original learning of a structure, so additional data or reasons can increase the extent of our certitude regarding the structure. Also, a structure may consist of a general idea at its core which can be further differentiated and its aspects subdivided so as to form a more extensive structure. For example, the child's basic idea of man is gradually subdivided into "man: mind, body, will, and emotions," and man's body even further subdivided into its basic organs and systems plus their functions and interrelationships. Finally, a structure can often be further clarified by comparing it with related structures and discerning their points of similarity and particularly how they are different.

EXERCISE 8-4. Further Development of Structures

Once a structure has been formed, it can be further enriched and expanded upon. But how? Take, for example, the basic concept of number in mathematics; it develops from a simple awareness of "discontinuous quantity that stays the same through changes in arrangement" in the first grade to the complex structure that includes algebraic values in high school. Try to follow the sequence of the development of the structure of number given below.

1. Number: discontinuous quantity of something

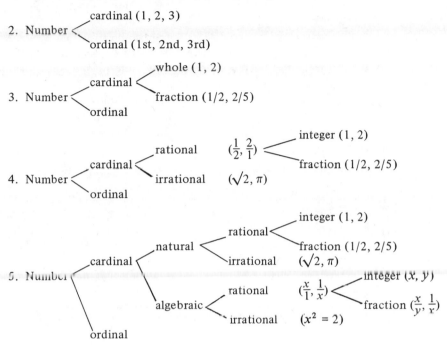

2. Number ⟨ cardinal (1, 2, 3)
              ordinal (1st, 2nd, 3rd)

3. Number ⟨ cardinal ⟨ whole (1, 2)
                        fraction (1/2, 2/5)
            ordinal

4. Number ⟨ cardinal ⟨ rational $(\frac{1}{2}, \frac{2}{1})$ ⟨ integer (1, 2)
                                                               fraction (1/2, 2/5)
                        irrational $(\sqrt{2}, \pi)$
            ordinal

5. Number ⟨ cardinal ⟨ natural ⟨ rational ⟨ integer (1, 2)
                                            fraction (1/2, 2/5)
                                  irrational $(\sqrt{2}, \pi)$
                       algebraic ⟨ rational $(\frac{x}{1}, \frac{1}{x})$ ⟨ integer (x, y)
                                                                            fraction $(\frac{x}{y}, \frac{1}{x})$
                                   irrational $(x^2 = 2)$
            ordinal

Definitions of interest:

Integer, whole number and *natural number* are coterminous. A *rational number* is the ratio of two whole numbers, the denominator not equal to zero; an *irrational number* is one that is not the ratio of any pair of whole numbers—it will never come out evenly if divided. An *algebraic number* is one that is variable, unknown.

Try to characterize the several stages in the development of the concept number. Each statement may be appropriate to one or two stages.

_____ Incorporating a new kind of number into the structure resulting only in the simple modification of further differentiation.

_____ Incorporating new kinds of numbers into the structure resulting in some modification of the structure.

_____ Incorporating basically new kinds of numbers into the structure resulting in a dramatic modification of the structure.

Stages 2 and 3 represent the simple incorporation of new distinctions into the structure; the only modification is the further differentiation of the structure. With the addition of the rational-irrational distinction in stage 4 there is both incorporation of the new distinction plus some basic modification of the structure. Finally, branching the structure into algebraic numbers in stage 5 results in a change that can only be called "dramatic" since the concept of number changes from something definite (1, 2, 3) to something either definite *or* variable (*x, y*).

In all these cases, first note that it is the same structure of number that is being further differentiated or changed to a degree. Second, note that in each instance there is both incorporation of new concepts into the structure and a modification of the structure to some degree.

Finally, a point of application: in teaching for structure, a teacher will continually relate new concepts and distinctions to the existing cognitive structure of his students, indicating how it either enriches or modifies (or both) that structure.

According to Piaget, further development of a cognitive structure can be characterized as a process of interaction between the structure (mind) and further data (reality). Ordinarily in this process there are two aspects: the incorporation of new data into the existing structure, which Piaget terms "assimilation," and a resulting modification of that structure, which he calls "accommodation." The new facts, concepts, and relations that we learn gain more meaning by being assimilated into a cognitive structure; at the same time, the structure is given further clarification and support—or perhaps even changed to a degree—by accommodating itself to the new data.

At times, if it is a question of simply adding one or two facts or distinctions, the structure develops mainly through assimilation. At other times if the structure is changed markedly in the face of new concepts or relations (or other structures), accommodation mainly is at work. Most often, however, assimilation and accommodation occur together as two aspects of the interactive process by which we further develop our cognitive structures.

There are some important differences between the structures of the cognitive theorists and "structure" according to Gagné that we should mention at this point. First, the cognitive theorists admit of several types of structures: hierarchical structures, structures involving order or dimensions, topological structures. Gagné, on the other hand, speaks only of a hierarchical structure. Second, "hierarchical" structure is explained quite differently in the two approaches. Consider, for example, the structures in figure 8-6 that underly the relation between factor and product and the grouping of factors into a set (cf. exercise 8-2).

The hierarchical structure used by the cognitive theorists (I) is based on classes and distinctions among classes, with the most general concept given at the top and the brackets indicating the several subdivisions. Its purpose is to give greater clarity and understanding by showing how a specific concept or relation fits into a larger whole. The most general idea at the top is learned first, then the first main distinction, followed by the further, more specific distinctions at the bottom. The hierarchical structure used by Gagné and his associates is based on the concepts and skills that are prerequisite to learning a relation. Its purpose is to clarify what must be learned prior to learning a specific relation. The highest

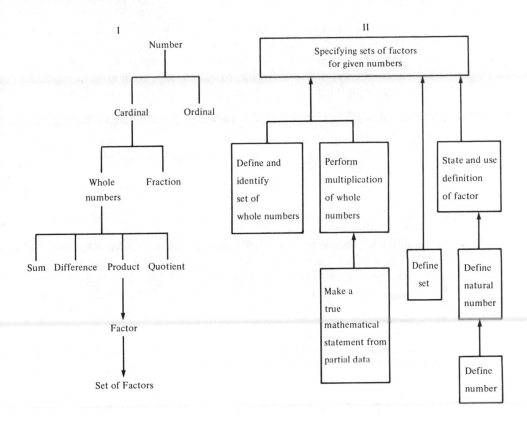

Figure 8-6. *Two Types of Hierarchical Structures*

level rule or relation is placed at the top with subordinate or prerequisite rules and concepts given below. The more basic concepts or skills at the bottom are learned first, then those above, ending with the relation given at the top.

Intellectual Abilities Involved in Learning Relations and Structures

What intellectual abilities are active in learning relations and structures? Primarily, their learning involves the cognition process, specifically the cognition of relations and systems respectively—grasping the relationship or order among ideas.

But in the overall process of learning relations and structures, several other factors are often involved as well: cognition and memory of the classes and perhaps units that go to make up the relation or structure, and divergent production of relations or systems (fluency). Since relations and structures are ultimately composed of concepts and experiences, the learner must first understand and remember the component concepts as well as the facts and events on which they are based. Hence cognition and memory of the classes (and units) that go to make up the relation or structure are integrally involved in the learning process. Also, since the learner sometimes reorganizes the component concepts and constructs a new (to him) relation or way of structuring those concepts, the divergent production of relations or systems (fluency) can also be active.

Also involved in the problem-centered learning of relations and structures are specifically: evaluation of the cogency and validity of the evidence, and convergent production of relations and structures relating and ordering ideas on the basis of the evidence.

Sometimes other abilities will be active in learning relations and structures. For instance:

> convergent production of implications—deductive reasoning;
> evaluation of semantic or symbolic units and classes (in learning relations);
> divergent and/or convergent transformation abilities, i.e. originality and/or redefinition abilities (in forming structures); but for the most part the cognition, memory and divergent production factors mentioned above are the main abilities involved.

The many abilities that may be active in the learning of relations and structures can be seen graphically in table 8-2. The most important abilities are indicated by double asterisks.

Table 8-2. *Abilities Involved in Learning Relations and Structures*

	Units	Classes	Relations	Systems	Transformations	Implications
Cognition	*	*	**	**		
Memory	*	*				
Divergent Thinking			*	*	*	
Convergent Thinking			*	*	*	*
Evaluation*	*	*	*	*		

Conditions Favoring Learning Relations and Structures

As was mentioned earlier, the amount of research done on relations and structures is not proportionate to their importance in classroom learning. The following conclusions are suggested by the limited number of studies conducted to date.

Learning Relations

Relations are learned more effectively and retained longer in proportion to the degree of certitude the learner has regarding their truth and the degree of background knowledge he possesses relating to the subject area (Poulton 1957).

When students discover a principle themselves, or at least discover it under the guidance of a teacher, they retain it longer and are able to apply it more widely than when they are simply told the principle by a teacher (Kittell 1957, Worthen 1968).

In learning a principle by induction, a higher proportion of positive instances results in superior learning than a lower proportion of positive instances. Similarly, the more that relevant attributes of the principle are stressed, the more that learning is facilitated; irrelevant attributes tend to delay learning a principle (Dervin and Deffenbacher 1970, Scandura and Voorhies 1971).

Most types of relations can be learned by elementary school children, specifically those pupils who are on the level of operational thinking. The order of difficulty in learning at least some kinds or relations is (from easiest to hardest): agent–action, substance–attribute, genus–species, whole–part (Schooley and Hartmann 1937).

The degree to which a person's cognitive structure of a topic is clearly understood and deep-rooted determines to a large extent how efficiently he will learn related material. This clarity and stability of cognitive structure particularly helps the learner to discriminate between what he already knows and any new material to be learned (Ausubel and Fitzgerald 1961).

The Importance of Structure

Students learn related concepts better when their interrelationships are emphasized than when they are learned in isolation from one another. For example, in elementary science multiple concept instruction, presenting simple descriptions of several related concepts first, then gradually introducing increasingly complex material pertaining to all these concepts, has been found to be superior to single concept instruction, presenting one concept at a time, proceeding from a simple description of the concept to a more complex treatment, and then going on to another concept (Short and Haughey 1967).

In this connection, the newer curricula that structure material around several basic ideas have usually been found to be more effective in learning concepts and principles than the older curricula that do not stress structure. For instance, SMSG math students[1] do much better than traditional math students on measures requiring understanding and application of concepts and principles; however, it should be added that on measures of computation they show no such superiority (Hungerman 1967, Grafft and Ruddel 1968).

Advance Organizers

The use of introductory general summaries emphasizing the main ideas of material to be learned is a very effective preparation for learning meaningful material. These "advance organizers" provide basic ideas to which the student can relate the material to be learned. Specifically, expository organizers that emphasize main ideas, similarities, and differences plus the main evidence regard-

---

1. School Mathematics Study Group centered at Yale University.

ing a topic are more effective for learning that topic than are historical, biographical, and descriptive introductions. Such organized summaries have been found to be more effective before a topic or question is studied than after it has been studied (Ausubel 1960, Merrill and Stolurow 1966).

Teaching Relations and Structures

How can we teach relations and structures? Applying the analysis of the process by which we learn them plus the conclusions of the research on how they are learned most effectively, we can offer the following suggestions for teaching relations and structures.

Assess Student Background

Assess the current knowledge of the student regarding the topic, specifically his cognitive structure of the topic so far, e.g. that acquired in previous grades or courses, plus the quality of his concepts and skills that are prerequisite to the learning of the topic. This can be done through a pretest that measures not so much the student's present knowledge of the material to be studied, but his grasp of the more basic and general concepts regarding the topic plus the intellectual skills that are essential for learning it. Frequently in a sequential curriculum in which one topic builds on the next, the results of the measures that were used previously to evaluate relations and structures that have already been studied will serve as a sufficient indication of the student's background for the new learning.

Whether you prefer a cognitive or an S-R approach to learning the specific relation or structure under consideration, this is a very important step. For the cognitive theorist, relations are best learned when the student incorporates them into their existing cognitive structure; for the S-R hierarchical theorist, relations are best learned by bringing the requisite concepts and skills to bear in the process of learning. In either event, the teacher will be most effective in helping his students learn a relation if he is aware of their current knowledge regarding it and so is able to design the best strategy for their learning of it.

Prepare Students for Learning

Make your students aware of the problem or objective with which they are to be concerned. Depending on the instructional approach employed, ask a question such as: "What is the relation between (or interrelationship among). . . . ?" perhaps giving a little background on the problem; or state what the students should be able to do once they have learned the topic to be treated.

(At this point if you are generally of a cognitive persuasion but are more teacher-centered in your outlook, you will find that giving students an overview of what is to be learned stressing its essential ideas and organization will be quite effective. If you are more student-centered, you will do better to get right into the next step, which is student manipulation of ideas and objects.)

Employ Appropriate Strategy

Select the most appropriate strategy for the specific relation or structure to be learned:

1. experimentation
2. induction from examples, instances
3. recall of past experience (concepts, instances, intellectual skills)
4. analysis of the component concepts—clarifying, distinguishing
5. comparison of ideas and possible relationships in a dialectical way
6. explicit statement of the relation or explanation of the structure by the teacher
7. deduction from previously acquired relations or structures
8. combining ideas in either a logical or "playful" way to come up with new relations or interrelationships among them.

Your choice of strategy will depend basically on two things: the subject area and specific relation or structure to be learned, and your theoretical persuasion regarding the kind and degree of student and teacher involvement in the learning process. For instance, experimentation is obviously appropriate for the sciences, while induction can be used in almost any subject: science, language, literature, history, math, and the practical subjects. Analysis of concepts and comparison of ideas and possibilities are most appropriate in the social sciences and literature but can be used in the sciences and other subjects as well. Combining ideas in various ways is a main way of forming structures, whereas deduction from previous knowledge usually results in a new relation.

Most of the strategies listed are of the student involvement type advocated by the cognitive theorists (1, 2, 4, 5, 7, 8). A statement of the relation by the teacher is called for by Gagné's theory (6). Recall of past experience (3) is an essential step in Gagné's approach but is also commonly used in the cognitive approach.

Evaluate Learning

Make sure your students have achieved the end result of the learning process, viz. the acquisition of the new relation or structure. This can be done: (1) by a question at the end of the learning session regarding what the relation or structure is and what its basis is (the students should be able to state the relation or structure and summarize the evidence for it); or (2) by asking the students to demonstrate that they have learned the relation or structure by applying it to a specific situation or problem that you give them.

The cognitive-oriented teacher will certainly use (1) and perhaps in addition use (2). The teacher using Gagné's approach will certainly use (2) and sometimes (1).

Keep Students' Knowledge Active

As a follow-up, have your students compare the relation or structure that they have acquired with the relations and structures they have learned previously, stressing similarities and differences, how the new relation fits into their existing cognitive structure or how the new structure enriches or changes the cognitive structures they already possess.

In subsequent classes, relate new facts, concepts, relations, and even smaller structures to the cognitive structures that students have already acquired. Incorporating these new learning products into the students' cognitive structures will both give the learning products more meaning and develop the cognitive structures more fully.

Evaluating Relations and Structures

How is learning relations and structures evaluated? Since relations form the bulk of what is taught in schools and since structures are becoming increasingly more important in the curriculum, the teacher should be aware of the several types of measures available to him for evaluating relations and structures.

The most commonly used techniques are: (1) essay type questions used either on tests or as oral questions in class, and (2) objective items, particularly multiple choice and more complex items.

Evaluating Relations

Knowledge of principles and generalizations can be measured by an essay or problem type question that calls for either explaining a relationship, proving a relationship, or both. For example, in English and mathematics:

1. A work of literature can be considered either in itself or as the product of its time and milieu. Select one novel written in nineteenth-century England and show how it reflects the values and customs of the author's social environment.
2. The length of a diagonal of a square is $x + y$. Find its area.
3. Traditionally a hero in literature is a person of noble character. Explain why Willie in *Death of a Salesman* can be considered a hero.
4. Prove by induction that $\sum_{k=1}^{n} k = \frac{n(n-1)}{2}$

Questions 1 and 2 call for the student to state or delineate a relation; questions 3 and 4 state a relation and then ask the student to give reasons or proof for the relation.

Relations can also be conveniently measured by a multiple choice item that calls either for choosing one side of a relation or choosing a basis for a stated relation. Several examples follow; in the first, the student must complete the relation "wise consumer is. . . ."; in the second he must complete the relation "fog is caused by. . . ."; in the third the relation is given and the student must support it with the best reason.

5. Which of the following is the chief characteristic of a wise consumer?
   a. He knows that the least expensive goods are the best buys.
   b. He knows that the more expensive something is the higher its quality.

    c. He realizes that he must plan his spending.

    d. He realizes that advertising is generally misleading.

6. Which of the following would be most likely to cause fog?

    a. A layer of warm dry air meeting a layer of cool moist air.

    b. One layer of warm moist air meeting another layer of warm moist air.

    c. Cool air meeting a layer of warm moist air.

    d. Cool air meeting a layer of cooler moist air.

7. Plains states usually produce more crops than hilly states because:

    a. plains get more rain which is a main requirement for agriculture.

    b. plains are warmer and hence have a longer growing season.

    c. plains hold topsoil much more easily, whereas it erodes from hills.

    d. plains allow crops to take firmer root than is possible on hills.

Finally, a more complex objective item is often a very convenient way to measure knowledge of a relation. For example, in the following extension of the multiple choice format, the students are instructed to check as many reasons as apply.

8. If a person is planning to bathe in the sun, he is most likely to receive a severe sunburn in the middle of the day (11 A.M.–1 P.M.) because:

    _____ We are slightly closer to the sun at noon than in the morning or afternoon.

    _____ The noon sun will produce more "burn" than the morning or afternoon sun.

    _____ When the sun's rays fall directly (straight down) on a surface, more energy is received by that surface than when the sun's rays fall obliquely on that surface.

    _____ When the sun is directly overhead the sun's rays pass through less absorbing atmosphere than when the sun is lower in the sky.

    _____ The air is usually warmer at noon than at other times of the day.

    _____ The ultraviolet rays of the sunlight are mainly responsible for sunburn.

Evaluating Structures

Structures are not easy to evaluate, but they are not as difficult as you might imagine either. An essay question, either on a test, as a take home question, or even as an oral question in class, is probably the best technique since it allows the student the freedom to explain the structure as he understands it. An essay question such as the following can be used to measure the students' knowledge of a structure.

9. Explain the theory of evolution as it is commonly held today, indicating some of the more important evidence from paleontology and comparative anatomy.

Objective items can also be used to evaluate structures, as witness the following examples, first a multiple choice and then a more complex item.

10. Natural selection, as described in Darwin's scheme of evolution, assumed
    a. a stable nonchanging population of organisms.
    b. changes from generation to generation based upon mutation.
    c. environmental stimuli that resulted in changes of body structure in successive generations of offspring.
    d. differential survival value of random differences in offspring.

11. Two theories are used at the present time to explain the nature of light and other electromagnetic radiation. The first of these theories is the wave theory which proposes that all electromagnetic radiation consists of waves whose period and frequency coincide with the period and frequency of the source which gives rise to the waves. The second of the theories is the corpuscular or quantum theory of radiation which proposes that all electromagnetic radiation consists of corpuscles or packets of energy, the energy content of any one packet being dependent upon the energy difference between two stationary energy states of an atom or molecule. Items 1 – 4 are experimental observations of electromagnetic radiation phenomena. Indicate whether the observation can be best explained by:

	A	B	C	D
1. When radiation passes through an aperture or past the edge of an obstacle, it always spreads to some extent into the region which is not directly exposed to the oncoming radiation.	___	___	___	___
2. When a beam of light is incident on certain materials, such as cesium, electrons may be ejected from the material, the maximum speed of the ejected electrons begin independent of the intensity of the incident light.	___	___	___	___
3. When light from a single source is split into two beams by passing the light through two slits and then allowing it to fall on a screen, a symmetrical pattern of evenly spaced light and dark bands or fringes may be observed.	___	___	___	___
4. The velocity of light (and other electromagnetic radiation) in a vacuum has been accurately determined to be 2.99776 X 10 centimeters per second.	___	___	___	___

Finally, an interesting way to measure a structure in math, viz. the basic laws of computation, is provided by the following series of short answer questions.

12. Fill in the missing numbers. Give the basis or any computation in the margin.
    a. $54 + 38 = 38 + \Box$
    b. $61 \times 27 = \Box \times 61$
    c. $(12 + 9) + 15 = 12 + (\Box + 15)$
    d. $7 \cdot 13 + 7 \cdot 17 = \Box (13 + 17)$
    e. $(7 \cdot 9) 13 = \Box (9 \cdot 13)$

The student should not have to do any computation but should answer the questions on the basis of the distributive, associative, and commutative laws or properties that form one structure in mathematics.

EXERCISE 8-5. Teaching a Relation or Structure

Select a relation or structure from your major field and plan a class session in which you will teach it. State what the relation or structure is and then list the activities that you would involve your students in so that they will learn it effectively. Since the research on relations and structures is so spotty, you will probably have to depend mostly on the theory you like best for ideas on how to teach it.

Suggested Readings

Bruner, J. S. *The Process of Education.* Cambridge: Harvard University Press, 1960.

Gagné, R. M. *The Conditions of Learning.* New York: Holt, Rinehart & Winston, 1970.

part four

Learning:
Processes

Besides the learning of facts, language, concepts, relations and structures, i.e. the products of learning, the other main type of learning that goes on in the classroom is learning how to think: specifically how to understand a communication, how to solve problems, how to think creatively, and how to think critically. These represent the main intellectual operations that a person is capable of, and one of your major tasks as a teacher will be to help your students learn how to perform them more effectively. This improvement of the thought processes is what we have referred to as the learning of processes as distinct from the learning of products. We will be concerned with the learning of processes in the next four chapters.

Whenever possible, the structure used in the last section on learning products will be followed in this section as well. For each type of learning we will consider: its nature, the learning process, the intellectual abilities involved, the conditions favoring learning, applications for teaching, and the evaluation of learning.

9

Comprehension

The comprehension process is pervasive in classroom learning. In fact, most of what we learn comes from comprehending what we read in books and hear in class. Comprehension is important in all fields:

A scientist and mathematician must comprehend symbols and equations in their work.

A student of art is continually called on to interpret paintings and works of sculpture.

A student of foreign language must translate passages and stories written in that language.

A musician must know how to read notation, and a person who appreciates music fully must first comprehend the pattern and meaning of a composition.

A student of business must know how to interpret graphs and tables.

A social studies student must know how to interpret various kinds of maps.

An industrial arts student must be able to read blueprints and other types of plans.

All students must be able to read the sources important in the field they are studying as well as be able to comprehend what they listen to in class.

Comprehension is both an important means to learning the products that we have been treating in the previous four chapters and an intellectual process that is worth improving in its own right. In this chapter we will be concerned with the nature of the comprehension process and how it can be improved. Specifically, we will treat the following questions:

What is comprehension?

How is the comprehension process best explained?

What intellectual abilities are involved in comprehension?

What variables are related to the comprehension process?

How can a teacher help his students improve their comprehension?

How can the comprehension process be evaluated?

The Nature and Types of Comprehension

Nature

Comprehension is the process of grasping the meaning of a communication, whether that communication is in the form of the printed word, the spoken word, pictures, drawings, music, or whatever. The process begins with perception of an object, or a series of sounds, or of some printed symbols or words. It requires not only knowledge of the words, symbols or figural content and what they stand for, but also knowledge of their combinations and relationships in a sentence, an equation, a pattern, a melody, a picture. Although comprehension essentially involves understanding the meaning of what is communicated by a certain combination of words or other content, it often goes beyond to include understanding the author's purpose, his underlying or symbolic meaning plus the implications of his communication as well.

It should be clear even from what we have seen so far that comprehension is a complex process that is more active than passive and more intellectual than perceptual. On one hand, it requires activity in the forms of concentration, attention, and analysis of parts plus combining them internally into a whole. On the other hand, although it begins with the visual or auditory sensations of color, shape or sound which in turn are synthesized into the perception of an object, symbol or word, the process essentially involves the intelligent activity of grasping the meaning of the communication. For instance, in reading a person directs his eyes and attention to the printed page with his mind intent on the meaning that the author is attempting to convey.

Levels of Comprehension.   We can comprehend the meaning of a communication on several levels:

1. We can grasp the given content, what the author specifically says or depicts; this is the surface or *literal* meaning.
2. We can understand the author's meaning in relation to the context in which he wrote (or painted, etc.), or what the author really means; this is the *interpretive* level of meaning.
3. We can understand the author's underlying or symbolic meaning, what the literal meaning in turn actually stands for or represents; this second order meaning (second order because it is abstracted from the first order or surface level) is called the *symbolic* or analogical level of meaning.

4. We can integrate the author's meaning into our own cognitive structure, relating or juxtaposing his ideas and propositions with our own concepts, relations and structures, reworking his meaning, producing new ideas as a result of relating his ideas with ours, etc; this level of comprehension can be called applied or *integrative*.

EXERCISE 9-1.   Levels of Comprehension

Given below is an informal plan for teaching a painting that stresses the various levels of comprehension. Analyze the different sections with a view to determining what level of comprehension the teacher is attempting to reach.

Pablo Picasso. *Girl Before a Mirror.* 1932. Oil on canvas, 64 × 51 1/4″. Collection, The Museum of Modern Art, New York. Gift of Mrs. Simon Guggenheim.

Plan for teaching Picasso's "Girl Before a Mirror." Show painting on screen. Hold discussion on its interpretation keying on the following questions and points of interpretation.

1. What do you see? What is it?
   After a few interpretations give name of painting and artist.
2. Do you see movement? Simultaneity?
   Movement is relativistic and based on multiple images.
   Simultaneity is indicated by the two views of the girl—profile and full face—at the same time.
3. In what century was it painted? Why?

20th (1932). It reflects our dynamic view of reality, not a static view, but one that sees things as in flux.

4. Is the painting related more to Einstein's or Newton's view of the physical world?

   Einstein's: a relative view of the world in a space-time continuum.

5. How would you characterize it in terms of its form and content?

   Its place on a realistic-abstract continuum?

   More emphasis on form than content; more abstract than realistic.

6. Is the painting expressionist, cubist, or surrealist? Why?

   Cubist. The emphasis is on play of line, shape and color which are manipulated to form a picture that holds together. The subject is structured to suit the picture rather than the other way around.

Indicate which questions are designed to get at which level of comprehension. Put the respective number(s) in the blanks.

_____ Literal: what the artist depicts.
_____ Interpretive: what the artist means by his painting.
_____ Symbolic: the underlying meaning, what the painting actually represents.
_____ Integrative: relating the painting to our cognitive structure.

Asking what the figure is gets at the literal meaning of the painting—a girl before a mirror.

Asking about movement and simultaneity is aimed at the interpretive meaning—what the artist is indicating.

The questions about the century in which it was painted pertain partly to its context—interpretive meaning, and partly to what it represents—symbolic meaning. You can make a case for either.

The question about the view of the physical world is designed to get at the symbolic meaning—the painting as a reflection of a dynamic and relative world view.

Although the question on cubism is designed to bring the students' knowledge of basic periods to bear on the painting so that they can better comprehend it, the question also aims at having the students incorporate the painting of Picasso into their cognitive structure of the main periods of art. This relates to the integrative level of comprehension.

Types

There are several types of comprehension, based mainly on whether the communication is expressed in print, in sound, or in pictorial form. An outline of the various types of comprehension, together with several possible purposes of each, follows.

Type of Comprehension	*Purpose*
Reading—printed verbal communication	
Skimming: reading first sentences of paragraphs, italicized phrases, summaries	To get main idea; to get overview before studying
Ordinary reading: reading at fast rate, concentrating on ideas in sentences plus main ideas in paragraphs and a chapter as a whole	To understand main ideas plus supporting details and evidence; to enjoy and/or evaluate stories, works of literature
Study: intensive reading usually involving (1) an overview to get an idea of the whole and to formulate the main questions the author treats, (2) reading to find answers to the questions, plus outlining and taking notes, and (3) reviewing to see how well one can summarize the main ideas	To gain thorough knowledge, detailed information; to organize the material and integrate it into one's cognitive structure
Special types of reading—printed symbolic or figural communication	
Reading symbols, equations, notation: careful analysis of mathematical and other symbolic content	To understand meaning, to discern problems to be solved
Interpreting graphs, plans, diagrams: careful examination of figural content that indicates information or how to do or make something	To gain data, to get directions
Listening—spoken verbal communication	
Cursory: attending to main ideas	To get general trend of communication
Intensive: concentrating on main ideas, details and line of reasoning; organizing and taking notes on ideas expressed	To gain detailed knowledge, to organize content and integrate it into one's cognitive structure
Special type of listening—musical communication	
Listening to music: following a melody with some awareness of harmony, structure, and other aspects	To enjoy, to analyze, to criticize, etc.
Pictorial—graphic communication	
Looking at drawings, cartoons, photos: examination of characteristics, meaning, story line depicted	To enjoy, to understand meaning
Examining paintings, sculpture: observation and interpretation of artistic productions	To enjoy, to analyze, to criticize, etc.

EXERCISE 9-2. Comprehending a Paragraph

What particular intellectual functions are involved when we attempt to comprehend a communication? What are the basic elements of the comprehension
process that can be identified?

Read the following paragraph, trying to comprehend the main idea presented.
Then we will attempt to analyze the process you used and to identify its
essential elements.

> Educational psychology goes beyond the archaic conceptualization that
> it is "the application of psychological principles to education." It is time
> for us to practice a liberal conceptualization of educational psychology as
> the scientific study of human behavior in educational settings. As scien-
> tists, we should attempt to describe, understand, predict, and control
> behavior in education. That is, educational psychology should invest most
> of its resources into its most important activity—basic research aimed at
> control and understanding of the problems and phenomena of instruction
> in schools. Research explicitly aimed at the production of useful knowl-
> edge is an activity defensible in its own right, with its own important
> *products*—functional relations, generalizations, and theories. (Wittrock
> 1967)

What particular intellectual functions can you identify that were involved as
you read—and comprehended—the paragraph? Check those that you believe are
relevant.

_____   1. Perceiving individual words
_____   2. Memory for words and their meanings
_____   3. Understanding the meaning of words
_____   4. Attention to the main words in a sentence
_____   5. Memory of words from the beginning to the end of a structure
_____   6. Familiarity with the grammatical constructions used
_____   7. Understanding the meaning of sentences
_____   8. Attention to the main ideas contained in the paragraph
_____   9. Memory of main ideas from the beginning to the end of the paragraph
_____ 10. Bringing your knowledge of educational psychology to bear as you attempted
         to understand the paragraph
_____ 11. Understanding the message contained in the paragraph

Actually all the above intellectual functions are active in the act of comprehending a communication. The most essential functions are understanding the
meaning of words (3), sentences (7), and paragraphs (11). The means to this are
many: in order to understand the meaning of words we must first perceive them
(1) and be familiar with their meanings (2); to understand the meaning of a
sentence we must attend to the main words (4), remember the words as we read
(5), plus be familiar with the grammatical constructions used (6); finally, in

order to understand the meaning of the paragraph as a whole, we must attend to the main ideas (8), remember them until the end of the paragraph (9), plus have some background knowledge of the relevant subject area (10).

As we will see presently, these functions can be combined into a model that can serve as a tentative explanation of what goes on in understanding the comprehension process.

The Comprehension Process

What is involved in the process by which we comprehend the meaning of a communication? How is the process best explained? The comprehension process, particularly reading comprehension, has been the subject of considerable research but has not been noted for any fully developed theories that adequately explain it. Instead, a few researchers have suggested tentative models of the reading process that have some basis in research. The model offered in figure 9-1 combines some of the findings of psycholinguistics with an information processing approach to form a functional model of the comprehension process.[1] It applies specifically to both reading and listening comprehension; for comprehension of symbols, patterns, pictures and the like, you can make the appropriate adaptations.[2]

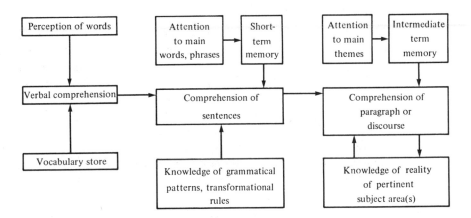

Figure 9-1. *Functional Model of the Comprehension Process*

1. Cf. Singer and Ruddell 1970.
2. Note that we are not concerned here with the whole reading or listening process. For instance in reading, decoding symbols, particularly recognition of grapheme-phoneme correspondences, forms one essential aspect of the reading act; we have already treated this aspect in the chapter on verbal-factual learning. Similarly, some considerations that are important for critical reading and listening and for the more creative activities connected with reading will be gained from the analysis of critical thinking and creativity in the chapters treating these processes.

The central phase of the process, as depicted in the model, is comprehension of the meaning of a communication. The immediate means for this is the perception-attention-memory phase. The long-range means are the background knowledge and vocabulary that allows one to understand what is being communicated. This means-end relationship is indicated by the vertical arrows in the model.

The main flow in the model is indicated by the horizontal arrows from verbal comprehension to comprehension of sentences to comprehension of a longer passage or discourse. The arrows indicate at once a temporal flow plus an increase in the amount of information handled at each point.

Once the person has perceived the printed (or spoken) words in a communication, he understands their meaning (having established a vocabulary store over the years). Attending mainly to the more important words and phrases—and remembering them from the beginning to the end of the sentence—he understands the meaning of the sentence (unconsciously applying his knowledge of grammatical patterns). Concentrating on the main ideas expressed in the sentences—and remembering them from one sentence to the next—the person grasps the theme and the main propositions expressed in the paragraph (often using his relevant knowledge to enhance his understanding as well as adding to that knowledge itself).

Let us consider each of the functional elements in the model separately; note particularly how the immediate and long-range means contribute to each stage of the comprehension process.

Perception of Words.   A case can be made for the word being the basic unit in the act of comprehension. The first step in the process itself is the perception of words. For instance, in reading we perceive one or more words each time our eyes stop along a line of text. Faster reading comes mainly from broadening one's fixations and taking in as many words as possible per stop or glance, conversely making fewer stops along a line. In this regard, "speed of comprehension" or rapid rate but with adequate understanding is the ideal. Several skills are important for the perception of words, particularly phonetic analysis, an awareness of the correct sound of the letters in relation to the specific word, and structural analysis, recognition of the basic root of the word plus any prefixes and/or suffixes attached.

Vocabulary Store.   This consists of the sum total of words and their meanings that one has learned and has stored in long-term memory. It includes both common words that are extremely accessible as well as infrequently used words that are retrieved with more difficulty.

Verbal Comprehension.   Almost at the same instant that the person perceives a commonly used word, he becomes aware of its meaning, both the denotative or basic meaning of the word and the connotative meaning or what it means in the specific context. For more technical words or those not as commonly used, some analysis or search is usually called for before the meaning becomes apparent.

Attention to Main Words, Phrases.   In reading, while our eyes are taking in several words per fixation, our immediate attention is focused on the main words and the ideas they convey. Less important words are not specifically attended to, but are filled in through the context formed by the more important words. Similarly, in listening our attention is focused on the most important words spoken although we do hear the articles, connectives, and other words of lesser import. In both cases, we are also aware of the function of the important words and phrases: whether they are the subject or object of an action, whether they modify a main word, etc.

Short-Term Memory.   The time that elapses is so short that we usually do not advert to the fact that there is some retention of words and phrases from the beginning to the end of a sentence. However, the main words and phrases that are the object of our attention in the reading or listening process plus their functions are retained until the end of the sentence in what is usually called short-term memory.

Knowledge of Grammatical Patterns.   Our background knowledge of grammatical patterns, both basic sentence types and transformational rules (for negatives, passives, etc.), that we have induced and formulated into a system is maintained in long-term memory and in turn makes it possible for us to comprehend further sentences, whether written or oral.

Comprehension of Sentences.   The important words and phrases, with their meaning and functions recognized, are presently related into a sentence and comprehended as the unit of communication. In psycholinguistic terms, the integration of the semantic component (the meaning of words) with the structural component (grammatical pattern) conveys meaning to an utterance. In Guilford's terms, comprehension of sentences involves the cognition of relations.

Attention to Main Themes.   Besides the attention to the main words in a sentence, the person's attention is also focused in a broader way on the main ideas in a paragraph, chapter or period of oral discourse, as well as on the supporting details and line of reasoning offered. Just as was the case in the more narrow type of attention above, so in this broader focusing the person leaves out the unimportant ideas and details (the filler) as he concentrates on the main concepts, propositions, and evidence presented in the communication.

Intermediate Term Memory.   The main ideas are retained from sentence to sentence and the main propositions retained from paragraph to paragraph together with the basis or evidence offered in their support.

Knowledge of a Subject Field.   Our cognitive structures relating to the topic at hand allow us to understand the content of a communication. On one hand, we integrate our background knowledge into the main ideas and evidence contained in the communication and in so doing make them comprehensible to us (by contrast witness the trouble we have understanding a passage in symbolic logic or chemistry if we have not studied these areas previously). On the other hand, a major result of comprehending a communication is the incorporation of new insights and information into existing cognitive structures.

Comprehension of Passage, Discourse.   The sentences that we have comprehended are organized into larger complexes in which we comprehend the main themes and propositions expressed in the communication plus the supporting reasons and details. This is the final stage of the communication process itself; however, as was mentioned above, we can in turn assimilate our new knowledge into our cognitive structure of the topic.

In the main phase of the process, the comprehension of words, sentences and longer passages, we can distinguish between two levels, the grammatical and the psychological, each correlated with the other.

grammatical: words   → sentences → paragraphs, discourse
               ↓   ↓   ↓
psychological: meaning → relations → organization

The grammatical level is that found in the communication itself; the psychological level is what occurs within the person who comprehends the communication.

In most acts of comprehension there is a balance between the two functional phases, the perception-attention phase and the background knowledge phase. However, in comprehending ordinary conversation or light reading material, the perception-attention phase moves at a smooth pace with little or no conscious application of background knowledge. In digesting difficult or dense material there is usually much conscious search into our vocabulary store, application of grammatical structures, and especially integration of previous knowledge of the relevant subject area.

The model in figure 9-1 attempts to explain only the essential aspects of the comprehension process. A more complete model would take into account the levels of meaning (literal, interpretive, etc.) as outlined above as well as allow for comprehension of paintings, music, drawings, and so forth. But on the basis of our current knowledge of the comprehension process, this will have to suffice.

EXERCISE 9-3.   Teaching for Improvement in Comprehension

A junior high social studies teacher decides to emphasize his students' ability to comprehend what they read. One day he uses the following approaches and materials. Analyze them and try to discern what phase of the comprehension process he is attacking at each point.

The teacher has the students read from their textbooks at their seats and then walks around watching their eye movements. He notices that some students are moving their lips slightly and that most of the others are making eight to ten fixations for each line.

The teacher gives an explanation that stresses:

a. the basic difference between oral and regular reading: oral reading is concerned with both ideas and words, regular reading only with ideas;

b. an attitude of respect for the worthwhile ideas contained in a passage, but almost one of contempt for the print as print: print should be considered a means to ideas and not be allowed to become the master of the reader;

c. the importance of concentrating on the main words and ideas in a sentence rather than on every word;

d. the possibility of taking in two or more words each time the eyes stop along a line of print (several words per fixation).

The teacher then shows some transparencies he has prepared on a screen in front of class. Examples are:

The need to
The air is clear
once and for all
from bad to worse

Each group of words is shown for only 1/3 of a second so students will have to take all of the words in at one glance.

two . . . . sides
given . . . . behalf
action . . . . progress
aspirin . . . . headache

Students are told to stare at the dots until they are able to perceive the full line, i.e. both words; It is mentioned that this will help their peripheral vision and hence broaden their fixations.

Sheets are then distributed with the following paragraphs printed on them. Students are told to read the first paragraph quickly, trying to get the main ideas, and not bothering to figure out what goes in the blanks (every fourth word of the original text).

Even law-and- advocates sometimes find sensibilities offended
by most unstable adjunct police work, informer. Trained
from childhood disparage tattletales, Americans hardly a decent for those who information to authorities. glossary
runs to pejorative nouns as , stoolie, rat, canary, . In
some police they are snitches. no major police can operate without of the shady who will go cops seldom
can, to a meeting conspirators, or do cops won't,
for , shoot heroin before cautious pusher will a sale,
Informers long been found every area of , but since
McCarthy era there has been so much concern about
them the U.S. as is now.

Before students read the next paragraph, the teacher asks someone in the class to define or explain the following words: reflector, retina, transparent, carnivorous, primitive.

Students are told to read the paragraph looking for main ideas on which they will be questioned afterwards.

All eyes that shine in the dark do so by means of a reflector behind the retina. The little light that is stirring in the outer world enters the pupil, passes through the transparent retina, which utilizes this light for vision, and on to the reflector, which sends it back to the object from which it came. Here it is joined to fresh original light from the object, and the process is repeated. Thus the Carnivora and some other animals whose vision is very much poorer than ours by day see much better at night. And that is why primitive man lived in terror of the dark. He was eater by day, eaten by night.

Turning their sheets over, the students write their answers to the following questions and then compare their answers with the paragraph.

How do some animals' eyes shine in the dark?

What is the principal effect of the reflector in an animal's eyes?

How do the eyes of some animals compare to human eyes, during the day and at night?

Why did primitive man live in terror of the dark?

Define or explain: transparent, retina.

Students are then told to go back over the paragraph and underline the words that are most important for an understanding of each sentence, but no more than half of the words in any sentence.

Further questions are asked to the class as a whole, e.g. How does the makeup of the animal eye that shines in the dark differ from the makeup of the human eye? How would you characterize the life of primitive man?

Students are told to re-read the paragraph concentrating on the main theme plus the reasons or detail offered in its support. They are asked: In one sentence state the main theme of the paragraph. Then state the basis for this main proposition as given in the paragraph.

Finally, the students are encouraged to offer their answers orally, and a discussion follows on what is actually the main theme and the basis for it.

What phase of the comprehension process is the teacher stressing at each point in the class session? Match each of the approaches used with the respective factor or phase of the process.

Approach Used in Class	*Factor of the Comprehension Process*
1. Watching students' eye movements	_____ Analyzing the students' need for training in comprehension
2. Suggestions about differences between oral and regular reading, print as a means to ideas	_____ Instruction of perception-attention phase of comprehension process
3. Suggestions about taking in several words per fixation, concentrating on main words and ideas	_____ Instruction on some basic aware-nesses and attitudes regarding comprehension
4. Showing words on screen for a fraction of a second, having students work on peripheral vision	_____ Practice in improving the perception phase of comprehension

5. Having students read passage with every fourth word blanked out, plus underline the most essential 50 percent of the words

_____ Activating the students' vocabulary store

6. Having students define some key words of a passage to be read

_____ Practice in attending to main words and ideas in sentences and paragraphs

7. Having students answer questions on a passage they have read, both on (a) the ideas contained in the sentences; and (b) the meaning of some important words

_____ Analysis of the students' degree of comprehension of sentences

8. Having students consider related questions not contained in a passage

_____ Practice in attending to the main idea of a passage together with its supporting evidence

9. Having students re-read a paragraph with a view to grasping the major theme and its basis

_____ Bringing students' relevant background knowledge to bear on comprehension of a passage

10. Having students answer a question on the main proposition of a paragraph

_____ Analysis of the students' degree of comprehension of a passage

11. Holding a general discussion on the students' answers concerning the main proposition of the paragraph

_____ Emphasizing the main goal in reading: comprehension of the main ideas in a communication plus the basis for them

The model of the comprehension process outlined above plus some related considerations are provided below together with the number indicating the approach used in the above classroom illustration.

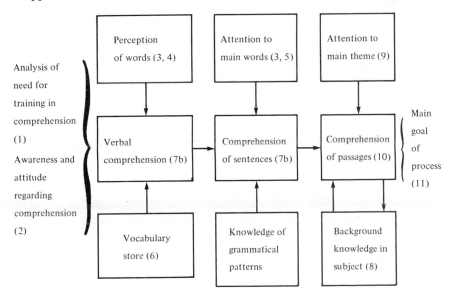

Practically all phases of the comprehension process were given some attention in the class session. The example shows how a model of a process, which has its basis in research findings, can help a teacher approach a type of learning in the classroom. The model indicated the essential elements of the comprehension process, and based on this, the teacher sought specific materials and techniques that would help to improve comprehension among his students.

Intellectual Processes Involved in Comprehension

To understand the comprehension process adequately, we must analyze what intellectual processes and abilities are involved in it.

Comprehension is essentially a process of grasping or recognizing the meaning of something. It is a process of cognition, particularly cognition of meanings (words), relations (sentences), and systems (central thought plus line of reasoning). Comprehension specifically involves the cognition of:

> units: understanding the meaning of words (verbal comprehension)
> relations: grasping the relationships among ideas in sentences
> systems: understanding the main ideas plus the line of reasoning supporting them

plus sometimes the cognition of

> transformations: imagining scenes depicted or suggested by the communication (visualization)
> implications: recognition of the implications of the author's ideas.

Also involved in comprehension is the process of memory for:

> units: recall of words and meanings learned in the past
> classes: short-term memory of concepts to be processed and combined into a sentence
> relations: intermediate term memory for relations from sentence to sentence, necessary for discerning the main theme plus the line of reasoning
> systems: recall of grammatical patterns and of cognitive structures of relevant subject fields
> transformations: recall of transformational rules.

Convergent thinking frequently is active in the comprehension process, regarding:

> classes: when some classification of words or ideas is called for, e.g. into noun, verb, or into fact, possibility, assumption
> relations: if the communication is open to a symbolic interpretation or contains figures of speech, then the ability termed "education of correlates" is active as the person derives the symbolic meaning from the literal meaning by analogy

systems: when the person orders what he is reading or listening to into a logical outline or structure and in turn integrates this into his existing cognitive structure.

Divergent thinking can also be active in the comprehension process:

units: thinking up possible meanings of difficult sections that could be derived from the context
relations: thinking of examples to illustrate ideas conveyed
systems: coming up with one's own way of organizing the ideas presented
implications: amplifying the implications stated, drawing applications to one's own area(s) of interest.

Particularly in critical reading, several abilities related to the evaluation process are very much involved, particularly the evaluation of:

units: comparison of meanings to see which fits the context best (e.g. when words have equivocal meanings)
classes: comparison of concepts used with those already possessed by the person
relations: judgment as to validity or truth of statements, whether they are fact or opinion
systems: judgment as to the logical connection between the main ideas and the bases in fact or reason that are offered for them
implications: judgment about the inferences and applications that the author draws.

It is rather obvious that most of the intellectual abilities can be brought to bear in the complex activity of comprehending a communication, whether the communication is written, spoken, or graphical. By way of review, table 9-1 provides a summary of the abilities that are involved in the comprehension process, with three asterisks indicating the abilities that are essential or always involved, two indicating those that are often active, and one those that are occasionally involved.

Table 9-1. *Abilities Involved in the Comprehension Process*

	Units	Classes	Relations	Systems	Transformations	Implications
Cognition	***		***	***	*	**
Memory	***	***	***	***	**	
Divergent Thinking	*		*	*		**
Convergent Thinking		**	*	**		
Evaluation	*	*	**	**		*

Factors Influencing Comprehension

What procedures are helpful for increasing a person's capacity for comprehending a communication? The research, particularly on reading comprehension, offers some valuable suggestions regarding the factors that influence a student's degree of comprehension.

Vocabulary

The extent of one's vocabulary is highly correlated with the ability to comprehend what one reads. Since mere frequency of words does not seem to help a person's understanding of their meaning (extensive reading does not automatically build vocabulary), it seems that a well-developed vocabulary definitely helps the person to read with greater comprehension (Dunkel 1944, Reed and Pepper 1957, Traxler 1938).

Students' vocabularies can be expanded in several ways, all of which have been found to be effective: direct experience with things in environment, experiences with films and pictures, and conversation with others concerning the meaning of words (Anderson and Dearborn 1952, Reid 1958, McCullough 1959).

Direct instruction in the meaning of words, whether in the context of the student's reading or by themselves, is also very effective. A teacher's supplying a definition, explanation and illustrations, plus perhaps the history or etymology of the word is superior to having the student use the dictionary himself (Serra 1953, Gray and Holmes 1938).

Grammar

There is a high correlation between the ability to see relationships between parts of sentences and the ability to comprehend the content of sentences and paragraphs. In this regard, familiarity and understanding of grammatical patterns more than simply knowledge of grammatical classifications seem to affect reading comprehension. In particular, an emphasis on the relationship between important structural elements in sentences can significantly improve comprehension (Gibbons 1941, Strom 1956, Ruddell 1965, 1968).

Rate

In general, there is a moderate to high correlation between speed of comprehension and level of comprehension, higher for easier material (0.80), moderate for more difficult material (0.51). Particularly among students of above average intelligence, rapid reading is more effective than a slow rate; for students of average and below intelligence, a slower rate seems to be more effective, especially for more difficult material (Carlson 1949, Tinker 1945).

Rate seems to have little effect on listening comprehension. Even rates up to 475 words per minute (compressed speech) result in a degree of comprehension similar to slower rates, at least for normal students. For many handicapped children (mentally retarded, cerebral palsied, etc.) rates of 200 words per minute or less have been found to be most effective (DeHoop 1965, Orr, Friedman and Williams 1965).

Comprehension in reading is greater if the reader adapts his speed to his purpose and the type and difficulty of the material. Poorer readers usually proceed in the same, inflexible way with all kinds of material (Pressey and Pressey 1921, Shores and Husbands 1950).

Questions

Questions placed either before or after a prose passage, or interspersed within the passage, increase learning and retention. Questions which encourage students to focus on the meaning of a passage and questions which require them to apply the concepts and principles contained in the passage help comprehension more than purely factual questions (Frase 1968, Rathkopf and Bisbicos 1967, Borrow and Bower 1969, Watts and Anderson 1971).

Questions placed before a passage not only help students grasp relevant data but they also seem to increase general attentiveness and help students comprehend even what is not specified in the questions (Peeck 1970, McGaw and Grotelueschen 1972).

Individual Differences

Students who tend to be more convergent or more divergent in their thinking show different strengths in their capacities for comprehending the information they read. Convergent thinkers show a good mastery of detail but poorer comprehension of the overall theme and its implications. Divergent thinkers show greater ability to grasp logical connections and to draw inferences from the communication; they are also faster and depend less on word recognition than on context to get the main idea from what they read. (Harootunian 1966)

Instruction

Instruction and practice in reading and study skills (comprehension, outlining, etc.) have been found to result not only in improved performance on measures of reading comprehension and study skills but also in increased knowledge of subject matter. Such training is particularly effective when students seek it voluntarily (Howell 1950, Barbe 1952).

Listening comprehension can be improved by instruction and exercises designed for the purpose. For instance, training in the ability to detect a speaker's purpose and to evaluate his arguments has proven effective, has resulted in permanent gains and even transfer to other situations (Fawcett 1963, Lundsteen 1963, 1965).

Levels of Comprehension

Students find the several levels of comprehension to be of varying degrees of difficulty. For instance, the literal meaning is easier to grasp than the interpretative meaning, which in turn is easier than drawing inferences from the text. Again, when asked about the most important ideas in a passage, students tend to answer on the level of facts and concrete concepts. It usually takes further urging and questioning before they respond on the level of abstract concepts and generalizations (McNaughton 1960).

Especially in symbolic or metaphorical prose passages, comprehension is greater if some help, for instance a short title reflecting the theme or central meaning of the passage, is provided at the beginning of the passage (Dooling and Lackman 1971).

Teaching for Comprehension

How can a teacher help his students improve their ability to comprehend the meaning of what they read or listen to? Based on the research studies and the resulting model of comprehension outlined above, we can offer the following suggestions for improving the comprehension process in students.

Vocabulary

Give students instruction and practice in expanding their vocabularies. Use various techniques: direct experience with objects, pictures, explanation by the teacher, discussion among students as to the meaning of words, etc.

Grammar

Make certain that students are aware of the various grammatical patterns: sentence types, relation between parts of sentences, and transformational rules. Provide particular emphasis on the relation of parts of sentences—whether a phrase or word is the subject or object of an action, a modifier, and so forth.

Rate

Provide instruction and particularly practice in speed of comprehension in reading—going as fast as one can and still understanding. Help students to take more words in per fixation and hence use fewer fixations per line of print; use such techniques as having students time themselves with easy material, the quick flashing of two or more words on a screen or at their seats (tachistoscope), and the like.

Encourage students to adjust their speed of reading to fit their purpose, the type and difficulty of the material, and their degree of familiarity with the topic: fast for fiction and easier material that requires little background knowledge or for material that they are familiar with; slower for more technical and difficult material that calls for integrating their background knowledge with the text if they are to comprehend it.

Attention

Encourage students to concentrate on the important words in a sentence or paragraph rather than on each and every word. Make them realize that this actually helps comprehension since it focuses the attention on the meaning of a passage rather than on the words themselves.

Levels

Emphasize different levels of comprehension: literal and interpretative plus symbolic and integrative where they are appropriate. Explain the nature of each level that is applicable to your field plus the differences among them. Ask students questions that call for them to explain the meaning of a passage, discourse or picture both in itself and in relation to its historical or other context; have them draw inferences from the communication, compare and contrast it with what they have learned previously.

Study Skills

Give students instruction and practice in study skills necessary for your specific field and a general pattern of study. In reading, (1) skim to get a general idea plus the questions to be treated, (2) read looking for the solutions, taking notes and organizing important points, (3) review with the book closed to see how well they have learned the main points, then go back over the points that have not been grasped. In listening, (1) take notes on important points plus supporting reason and detail, (2) work over notes, organizing them, structuring the ideas in an appropriate way.

Testing for Comprehension

How can a teacher evaluate the comprehension process in his students? There are several techniques ranging from more informal questioning to some complex objective formats. We will consider the several most usable techniques in turn.

Informal Techniques

The most frequently used approach for evaluating comprehension is the informal and on-going classroom technique of questioning about the content, main ideas, central theme, or sequence of events of a communication. Similarly, deeper levels of comprehension can be evaluated by oral questions calling for the underlying purpose of the author, the symbolic or allegorical meaning of phrases or of the entire communication, how a communication relates to what the students already know about the topic, or what the implications or possible applications of the communication are for certain situations.

Essay Questions

Either an essay question on a test or a more extended take-home essay question calling for the interpretation of a communication is one of the best ways to measure the comprehension process. The communication can be prose, poetry, a painting, cartoon, a graph, a piece of music, or a speech. For example, an essay question on a prose passage might take the following form.

The following quotation is taken from the second inaugural address of President Thomas Jefferson. As you read it, attempt to discern what Jefferson's concept of the American system of government was and what implications can be derived for several important problems facing America today.

It is proper you should understand what I deem the essential principles of our Government, and consequently those which ought to shape its administration. I will compress them within the narrowest compass they will bear, stating the general principle, but not all its limitations. Equal and exact justice to all men, of whatever state or persuasion, religious or political; peace, commerce, and honest friendship with all nations, entangling alliances with none; the support of the State governments in all their rights, as the most competent administrations for our domestic concerns and the surest bulwarks against anti-republican tendencies; the preservation of the General Government in its whole constitutional vigor, as the sheet anchor of our peace at home and safety abroad; a jealous care of the right of election by the people—a mild and safe corrective of abuses which are lopped by the sword of revolution where peaceable remedies are unprovided; absolute acquiescence in the decisions of the majority, the vital principle of republics, from which is no appeal but to force, the vital principle and immediate parent of despotism.

In your own words, explain Jefferson's view regarding the relation between federal and state government.

What are some of the implications of Jefferson's stated principles for three important current issues that are of concern to the American people?

Objective Items

Since comprehension is an important process, a teacher may want to include an item or two that measures it on an objective test. A multiple choice item measuring comprehension would use a passage in the stem plus a question calling for its interpretation. For example:

In three wealthy northern states the average salary of teachers is three times that in the three poorest southern states of the United States. However, the three poorest states have a higher tax in proportion to their income than do the wealthy states.

For which of the following propositions is this statement the best evidence?

    a. State governments should increase their contributions to local school districts.

    b. The South is not interested in good education.

    c. Education should be controlled by the national government.

    d. Federal financial aid to education is necessary.

The most convenient type of objective item for measuring comprehension is the complex item that gives a passage, poem, cartoon, etc. and then provides a series of multiple choice or true-false items about the communication. An example follows.

    1. When the spent sun throws up its rays on cloud

  2. And goes down burning into the gulf below

  3. No voice in nature is heard to cry aloud

  4. At what has happened. Birds, at least, must know

  5. It is the change to darkness in the sky.

  6. Murmuring something quiet in her breast,

  7. One bird begins to close a faded eye;

  8. Or overtaken too far from his nest,

  9. Hurrying low above the grove, some waif

10. Swoops just in time to his remembered tree.

11. At most he thinks or twitters softly, "Safe!

12. Now let the night be dark for all of me.

13. Let the night be too dark for me to see

14. Into the future. Let what will be, be."

1. The central meaning of the poem is that
   - a. men should not use artificial illumination.
   - b. creatures of the earth accept the processes of nature.
   - c. birds notice the coming of darkness more quickly than do men.
   - d. men should not provide for their old age.

2. The poem implies a conflict between
   - a. birds and nature.
   - b. man and nature.
   - c. night and birds.
   - d. nature and all living things.

3. The poet's attitude toward his subject is
   - a. flippant.
   - b. sarcastic.
   - c. serious.
   - d. humorous.

4. In the poem, what does the female bird do at nightfall?
   - a. Hurries low over the grove.
   - b. Accepts the dark without comment.
   - c. Swoops to a remembered tree.
   - d. Murmurs something quiet.

5. Why is the sun called the "spent" sun (line 1)?
   - a. The sun is setting.
   - b. The sun is going behind the clouds.
   - c. Nothing in nature is paying any attention to the sun.
   - d. The winter sun has little warmth.

6. The phrase "to cry aloud" in line 3 probably means
   - a. to protest.

b. to cry in fear.
c. to shout in anger.
d. to cheer.

Note that in such an item you can ask questions about the main theme, the underlying purpose and mood, plus questions on specific phrases and words, their literal, interpretative or symbolic meanings.

Complex items calling for the interpretation of a communication are more or less self-contained in that the specific questions are answerable on the basis of the passage provided more than on the basis of outside knowledge. Of course, a background in the related subject area helps in the comprehension, but the items are based mainly on the communication itself, i.e. they do not ask for knowledge over and above what is contained in the quoted passage.

It is not as hard to construct such complex items as it might seem. You first select a passage, picture, or something related to the topic you wish to test on and that seems to offer possibilities for the types of questions you wish to ask. Then you construct several questions, e.g. on the main thought, some of the supporting detail, the underlying purpose, or the meaning of specific sections. If it is prose, you can always omit sections that offer no suggestions for questions, or you can even add some material to the passage that can be the basis for further questions.

EXERCISE 9-4. Teaching for Comprehension

Every teacher should teach for comprehension in his field. Select a fairly difficult passage, painting, equation, cartoon, piece of music, or whatever is applicable to your field, and plan a short lesson in which you aim at helping students comprehend it fully. You will probably want to emphasize questions that get students thinking in terms of (1) the main idea plus supporting detail and (2) the various levels of meaning of the communication.

Suggested Reading

Singer, H. and Ruddell, R. B., eds. *Theoretical Models and Processes of Reading.* Newark, Delaware: International Reading Association, 1970.

10

Creativity

Of all man's intellectual processes, the one that has received the most emphasis and scientific study in the past two decades is creativity. Both educational psychologists and teachers have come to realize that students are not merely receivers of information and solvers of problems presented to them; they are also creative human beings whose creative abilities should be developed to the fullest and used to advantage in the teaching-learning process.

What is the nature of the creative process? What intellectual abilities are involved in creativity? What are some characteristics of more creative students? How can creative abilities be improved? What are some ways in which a teacher can teach concepts and relations creatively? How can creativity be measured and evaluated?

All these questions are important for a teacher: he must understand the creative process and all that is involved in it if he is to teach for creativity; he must be aware of the techniques of both creative teaching and how to improve creative abilities if he is to be a genuinely effective teacher. Many students learn better when their creative abilities are involved in the learning process; all students have creative abilities that must be developed if they are to live a rich, full life and be productive in their work or profession.

The Nature and Extent of Creativity

What do we mean by creativity? It is that spontaneous, adventurous, imaginative type of thinking that characterizes artistic productions, scientific discoveries, and mechanical inventions. It involves the production of something new—either absolutely new to the cultural or scientific world, or relatively new to the person himself (even though others have produced it before). A person can be a creative mathematician, philosopher, or scientist as well as a creative writer, artist, or inventor. Similarly a student can involve his creative abilities in learning the sciences as well as the arts; and he can improve his abilities through creative approaches in the more abstract subjects such as mathematics and social studies as well as the more practical subjects such as physical education and home economics.

The Nature of the Creative Process

What is involved in the creative process? There are two major views of what the process essentially consists in, the cognitive and associationist views. For the S-R theorist, creativity involves the formation of stimulus-response associations which are characterized by the fact that the elements linked together are not normally associated. It involves the linking of stimuli with highly unlikely responses. The emphasis in this view is placed on the previously learned associations that are revived and then combined. For the cognitive theorist, creativity involves combining ideas and information in new and different ways; it consists in a "restructuring of our universe of understanding" (Ghiselin). Our ideas are transformed and put into new combinations so that there is actually the production of a novel, original idea which is then expressed through some medium. The emphasis in the cognitive analysis of creativity is not simply on unusual associations but on the generation of new ideas.

However, the research on creativity is not extensive enough as yet for any complete theory to be constructed regarding the internal processes involved. The best insight into the nature of the creative process we have is still one that was formulated by Wallas almost fifty years ago on the basis of an analysis of personal accounts of creative artists, scientists, and mathematicians. Since Wallas based his analysis of creativity on the accounts of some creative persons, you might find it interesting and worthwhile to do your own analysis before we consider Wallas's. If you agree, do exercise 10-1.

EXERCISE 10-1.   Analysis of the Creative Process

What are the essential components of the creative act? Given below are some sample accounts of creative productions of a scientist, a poet, two mathematicians, and two musicians. Analyze them, trying to discern the characteristics of the creative process in each case. After each account, match the sections indicated with one of the possible characteristics listed on page 272.

> In all the creative work that I have done,
> R1 { what comes first is a problem, a puzzle involving discomfort. Then comes concentrated voluntary application entailing great effort.
> R2 { After this a period without conscious thought,
> R3 { and finally a solution bringing with it the complete plan of a book. This stage is usually sudden and seems to be the important moment for subsequent achievement.   (Bertrand Russell)

W1 { Were you to put me into a good mood, I might perhaps show you my heroes, though I had the greatest difficulty with them.

W2 { Although I had been carrying the ideas about with me for a long time,

W3 { the material for their objectification first came to me like a flash of light in the greatest clarity and definiteness, but not altogether in complete detail. (Richard Wagner)

E1 { Taken from a psychological viewpoint, this combinatory play with the signs and images of thought seems to be the essential feature in productive thought—before there is any connection with logical construction in words or other kinds of signs which can be communicated to others . . .

E2 { Conventional words or other signs have to be sought for laboriously only in a secondary stage, when the above mentioned associative play is sufficiently established and can be reproduced at will. (Albert Einstein)

H1 { As I walked along, there would flow into my mind, with sudden and unaccountable emotion, sometimes a line or two of verse, sometimes a whole stanza at once, accompanied, not preceded, by a vague notion of the poem which they were destined to form a part of. . . .

H2 { When I got home, I wrote them down, leaving gaps and hoping that further inspiration might be forthcoming another day. Sometimes it was, . . . but sometimes the poem had to be taken in hand and completed by the brain, which was apt to be a matter of trouble and anxiety, involving trial and disappointment, and sometimes ending in failure. (A. E. Housman)

P1 { For fifteen days I strove to prove that there could not be any functions like those I have since called Fuchsian functions. I was then very ignorant; every day I seated myself at my work table, stayed an hour or two, tried a great number of combinations and reached no results.

P2 { One evening, contrary to my custom, I drank black coffee and could not sleep. Ideas arose in crowds; I felt them collide until pairs interlocked, so to speak, making a stable combination. By the next morning I had established the existence of a class of Fuchsian fuctions, those which come from the hypergeometric series;

P3 { I had only to write out the results, which took but a few hours. (Henri Poincare)

P4 { Most striking at first is this appearance of sudden illumination,

P5 { a manifest sign of long, unconscious prior work. The role of this unconscious work in mathematical invention appears to me incontestable. . . .

P6 { The need for the second period of conscious work, after the inspiration, is still easier to understand. It is necessary to put in shape the results of this inspiration, to deduce from them the immediate consequences, to arrange them, to word the demonstrations, but above all is verification necessary. (Henri Poincare)

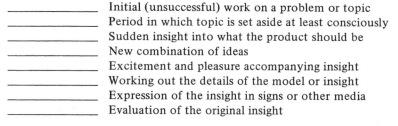

T1 {
Generally speaking, the germ of a future composition comes suddenly and unexpectedly. If the soil is ready—that is to say, if the disposition for work is there—it takes root with extraordinary force and rapidity, shoots up through the earth, puts forth its branches, leaves and, finally, blossoms. . . .

T2 {
It would be vain to try to put into words that immeasurable sense of bliss which comes over me directly a new idea awakens in me and begins to assume a definite form. I forget everything and behave like a madman; hardly have I begun the sketch ere one thought follows another. . . . If that condition of mind and soul, which we call inspiration, lasted long without intermission, no artist could survive it. . . .

T3 {
It is already a great thing if the main ideas and general outline of a work come without any racking of brains, as the result of that supernatural and inexplicable force we call inspiration.

T4 {
But what has been set down in a moment of ardour must now be critically examined, improved, extended, or condensed, as the form requires. Sometimes one must do oneself violence, must sternly and pitilessly take part against oneself, before one can mercilessly erase things thought out with love and enthusiasm. (Peter Ilyich Tchaikovsky)

Match each section above with one of the phrases below.

_____ Initial (unsuccessful) work on a problem or topic
_____ Period in which topic is set aside at least consciously
_____ Sudden insight into what the product should be
_____ New combination of ideas
_____ Excitement and pleasure accompanying insight
_____ Working out the details of the model or insight
_____ Expression of the insight in signs or other media
_____ Evaluation of the original insight

Several of the creative persons claimed that they engaged in some initial work on a problem and were unsuccessful. Poincare (P1) "tried a number of combinations and reached no results." Russell (R1) applied himself to problems with "great effort." Wagner (W1) also at first "had the greatest difficulty" in delineating his heroes.

These same persons claimed that there then followed a period in which they set the topic aside and devoted no conscious effort to it. For instance, Poincare (P5) refers to a long period of "unconscious prior work" which resulted in an illumination. Russell (R2) used to spend "a period without conscious thought," and Wagner (W2) says that he "carried the ideas about with me for a long time."

Practically all of the accounts of creative productions stress the sudden illumination or insight as to what the final product should be. Sometimes this is a complete model, other times it is only partial; but it is always present. For example: Housman (H1) says that a few lines or a whole stanza "would flow into my mind, with sudden and unaccountable emotion." Poincare (P4) speaks of an "appearance of sudden illumination." Russell (R3) claims that he experienced a sudden appearance of "a solution bringing with it the complete plan of a book." Tchaikovsky (T1 and 3) speaks of the "general outline of a work" coming to him "suddenly and unexpectedly." Wagner (W3) tells about ideas coming to him "like a flash of light in the greatest clarity and definiteness."

This illumination often consists of new combinations of ideas. Einstein (E1): "combinatory play" with the elements of thought. Poincare (P2): "ideas interlocked . . . making a stable combination." It also is accompanied by excitement and pleasure. Housman (H1): "with sudden and unaccountable emotion." Tchaikovsky (T2): an "immeasurable sense of bliss" and "I forget everything [else] and behave like a madman."

A final phase of any creative production is bringing the insight into actuality. It involves working out the details of the model. Housman (H2): "I wrote the lines down. . . . Sometimes it was . . . a matter of trouble and anxiety, involving trial and disappointment." Poincare (P6): "a period of conscious work . . . is necessary to put in shape the results of this inspiration." It also involves expressing the insight in signs or other media. Einstein (E2): "conventional words or other signs have to be sought for laboriously . . . when the associative play is sufficiently established." Poincare (P3): "I had only to write out the results." Evaluation of the original insight also occurs. Tchaikovsky (T4): "what has been set down in a moment of ardour must now be critically examined, improved, extended, or condensed, as the form requires."

In his analysis of the creative process, Wallas distinguished four phases: preparation, incubation, illumination, and verification.

> Our mental life is a stream of intermingled psychological events . . . which are extremely hard to distinguish from each other. We can, to some degree, avoid this difficulty if we take a single achievement of thought—the making of a new generalization or invention, or the poetical expression of a new idea—and ask how it was brought about. We can then roughly dissect out a continuous process, with a beginning and a middle and an end of its own. . . . There seem to be three stages in the formation of a new thought.
>
> The first in time I shall call Preparation, the stage during which the problem is investigated; the second is the stage during which one is not consciously thinking about the problem, which I shall call Incubation; the third, consisting of the appearance of an idea together with the psychological events which immediately precede and accompany that appearance, I shall call Illumination. I shall add a fourth stage, of Verification. . . . In the daily stream of thought these four different stages constantly overlap each other as we explore different problems. (Wallas 1926, pp. 80-81)

Preparation.　　The preparation phase is both long-range and immediate. On a long-term basis it involves many things: a searching, inquiring attitude, observation of the world around us, knowledge of a subject field, and facility with the techniques of that field. More immediate preparation can include thinking, reading, observation and other background work regarding the specific topic or problem, plus the initial attempts at producing something.

Incubation.   The incubation stage is characterized by a relaxation of effort, putting the topic out of the consciousness for a time—anywhere from minutes to months—and a seeming lack of activity. However, at the end of this period there is evidence of progress toward a new insight. It may be that a more or less unconscious assimilation or transformation of the information gained in the preparation phase has occurred. Or it may simply be that performance has improved after a period of rest. We do not know for sure.

Inspiration.   The most essential aspect of the creative process, the culmination of the first two stages, is the inspiration, the idea or image that serves as the model for the creative production. In the arts, this is the ideal image that will be brought into reality on canvas or in stone. For a writer, scientist, or philosopher, it is the key idea that provides structure to the story, poem, or theory to be produced. Most often this insight comes suddenly and spontaneously and is accompanied by a feeling of excitement and satisfaction and a degree of certainly that "this is it." Sometimes the complete outline of the work to be produced is grasped; sometimes only a partial idea emerges with the complete model to be worked out later. At times, in the first flush of inspiration, the model is overvalued, but further effort and some revision can correct this situation.

Verification.   In the final phase of the creative process, usually the longest in terms of time, the model that emerged in the inspiration phase is worked out ("elaborated") on paper, canvas, or other material. In other words, the image or insight is expressed in the concrete via words, mathematical symbols, paints, etc. Often further insights or minor inspirations occur as the model unfolds during this elaboration phase. An integral part of this stage is the running evaluation of what is produced. Revisions are made, parts are rearranged, new and better ways of expressing the model are discovered. Particularly self-criticism is employed here, but in addition the judgment of others can sometimes be sought.

Individual variation in the creative process is nowhere more evident than in the elaboration phase. For those whose inspiration is complete and immediate, the expression on paper or canvas is rapid and needs little revision; for those whose insight is only partial, the full model must usually be worked out gradually, step by step, throughout the verification phase. For the former, this fourth phase is characterized mainly by expression of insight or image; for the latter, it is characterized by elaboration (hard work), plus continual evaluation and revision.

Not all creative productions entail all these phases, and certainly not all follow the implied order. Evaluation can come early as well as late in the process. Often the incubation stage is very brief or nonexistent. And finally, the inspiration phase can either be all at once or gradual and extend through most of the verification stage. Nevertheless, even though there may be variation among individual persons and even among specific creative productions by an individual, the four-phase analysis of the creative process is helpful and seems to correspond with the experience of creative persons and with the limited research on creativity.

Intellectual Abilities Involved in Creativity

What intellectual abilities are involved in the creative process? In terms of Guilford's structure of intellect model, creativity involves mainly the process of divergent thinking, particularly: (1) originality, thinking of uncommon, clever, novel ideas and images, (2) the flexibilities, thinking up a variety of ideas and new ways of dealing with situations, (3) the fluencies, coming up with a large quantity of ideas, words, and ways of expressing things, and (4) elaboration, enriching our experiences through filling in details. It often involves as well: (5) many evaluation abilities, (6) memory for ideas, (7) sensitivity to problems (a cognition factor), and (8) redefinition abilities, putting something to use in a new way (a convergent production factor). In the earlier stage of the creative process, sensitivity to problems, the memory abilities, and to some extent ideational fluency are active; at the time of inspiration, originality, fluency for the production of systems, the flexibilities, and perhaps the redefinition abilities are active; during the final stage, elaboration, the evaluation abilities, plus expressional and word or figural fluency are at work.

In terms of the product dimension of the structure of intellect, all the types can be involved in creative activity. In the inspiration phase, restructuring and interrelating ideas into a new combination which forms the model of the creative work entail the production of both transformations and systems. In the elaboration phase, drawing out the implications of this model is mainly involved.

The content dimension of the structure of intellect model offers some interesting insights regarding creativity among individuals. The creative abilities involving figural content are important for the painter (visual), musician (auditory), and the inventor. Similarly, the symbolic abilities are important for creative work in mathematics and such diverse areas as linguistics, symbolic logic, and the physical sciences. Semantic or ideational content is involved in the creative productions of the writer, the poet, the philosopher, and the scientist. (It should be added that in such fields as creative dance and mime both figural and psychomotor abilities are integrally related in a creative production.)

The major abilities most often involved in the creative process are summarized in table 10-1. The numbers indicate when each ability is mainly active (1. early, 2. inspiration, 3. elaboration); the double asterisks indicate which abilities are most essential to the process.

Table 10-1. *Abilities Involved in the Creative Process*

	Units	Classes	Relations	Systems	Transformations	Implications
Cognition						1
Memory	1	1	1			
Divergent Thinking	1, 3	2	3	2**	2**	3
Convergent Thinking					2	
Evaluation	3	3	3	3	3	3

EXERCISE 10-2.   Creative Teaching and Teaching for Creativity

Now that we have analyzed the creative process and the intellectual abilities involved in creativity, let's see how an emphasis on creativity can work in the classroom.

Given below are some examples of (1) creative teaching and (2) teaching for creativity in various subject areas. By creative teaching we mean teaching a concept, relation, or skill through a technique that involves the students' creative thinking abilities. Teaching for creativity refers to giving students experience in creative thinking so as to develop their creative abilities.

Many of the activities will certainly serve both functions, but most of them are examples of creative teaching *or* teaching for creativity. Check which you think each illustrates; if you think some are examples of both, check both. For those that you feel illustrate teaching for creativity, also indicate what creative abilities they are designed to develop: sensitivity to problems, fluency, flexibility, originality, or implications.

Teaching Techniques	*Purpose*		*Creative Abilities*				
	CrT	TCr	S-P	Flu	Flx	Org	Imp
1. Social studies teacher holds a United Nations session in which each student chooses a country to represent, does background reading, and then discusses a current world issue accordingly.	___	___	___	___	___	___	___
2. At several points in a story, teacher asks, "What do you think will happen now?" After she has read about four-fifths of the story she asks how the students would end it.	___	___	___	___	___	___	___
3. In a communication arts class a teacher has two students who are separated by a screen build a tinker-toy model: one student has a picture of the model and as he builds tells the other what to do step by step. At the end, the models are compared and a discussion ensues on clarity in communication.	___	___	___	___	___	___	___
4. Physical education teacher, after teaching several basic gymnastic skills, has each student make up a 15-second program to present to the rest of the class. He en-							

Teaching Techniques	Purpose		Creative Abilities				
	CrT	TCr	S-P	Flu	Flx	Org	Imp
courages them to be as different in their programs as possible.	___	___	___	___	___	___	___
5. Art students bring in old small objects of various kinds: buttons, jar tops, clothes-pins, matches, and put them all together in a pile. Groups of three students each draw a slip of paper with a mood (happy, sad, fearful, triumphant, etc.) and proceed to make a collage reflecting that mood.	___	___	___	___	___	___	___
6. Math teacher has students build geodesic structures of their choice with toothpicks and glue.	___	___	___	___	___	___	___
7. Teacher shows the class a picture of an alligator "licking his chops" and has the pupils ask as many questions as they can think of about the alligator— things they can't tell just by looking at the picture.	___	___	___	___	___	___	___
8. Music teacher gives a summary of the plot of *West Side Story* and has the students select roles; he then plays the record with the students acting out the parts in pantomime.	___	___	___	___	___	___	___
9. Teacher plays a record, Debussey's "La Mer," and has students write a description of what they imagine as they listen to the music.	___	___	___	___	___	___	___
10. Teacher has the students read an essay and think of (1) further problems suggested by the topics treated, (2) missing information that should have been included, (3) other possible conclusions that might be drawn from the findings. Students contribute their ideas in an open discussion.	___	___	___	___	___	___	___
11. English teacher writes the first line of a poem on the board and							

Teaching Techniques	Purpose		Creative Abilities				
	CrT	TCr	S-P	Flu	Flx	Org	Imp
then invites ideas for the remaining lines. After the class has composed the poem, the teacher leads a discussion of imagery in poetry, using the figures of speech contained in the poem for examples.	___	___	___	___	___	___	___
12. Science teacher encourages groups of students to prepare and perform dramatizations of the discoveries of Copernicus, Harvey, Darwin, Einstein, etc.	___	___	___	___	___	___	___
13. Pupils choose what persons they would like to be, the group makes up a story and then all act it out, each playing the role they have chosen (creative drama).	___	___	___	___	___	___	___
14. Teacher has pupils bring a leaf to class. She tells them: "Get to know your leaf as well as possible: feel it, smell it, listen to it, experiment with it (without damaging it), imagine yourself in its place—anything." Afterwards pupils share their "knowledge" in small groups.	___	___	___	___	___	___	___
15. Physical education teacher draws a diagram of a new type of zone defense and has students suggest various offensive plays for attacking it.	___	___	___	___	___	___	___

The United Nations session (1) and the tinker-toy approach (3) are quite clearly creative ways of teaching international affairs and clarity of communication respectively.

Asking questions during a story (2), having pupils make up their own gymnastics program (4), and having them ask questions about the alligator (7) are designed mainly to improve the creative thinking abilities of the students.

Making a collage (5), building a geodesic structure (6), acting out West Side Story (8), and writing a description while listening to a record (9) are creative ways of teaching art, geometry, music and writing, and also ways of developing the creative abilities of students—particularly originality but other abilities as well.

Teaching imagery through the analysis of the students' own poems (11) and having students dramatize famous discoveries in science (12) are mainly creative techniques of teaching (although secondarily they do involve some improvement of students' creative abilities).

Having students suggest additional problems, information, and conclusions for an essay (10) and get to know an object (leaf) as much as possible (14) are aimed at improving the creative thinking abilities or the creative process in students.

The rest of the examples, creative drama (13) and making up plays in sports (15), can be either teaching for creativity or creative teaching, or both.

These are my judgments; you are free to disagree. The important thing is that you become aware of the many possible applications of creativity in teaching and the two major purposes that were distinguished above: teaching something by involving the creative abilities of students and teaching primarily to develop those creative abilities.

As far as the specific abilities that are intended to be developed in the examples above, it is difficult to say exactly which ability is improved by which specific approach; in fact you could make a case for not being overly concerned about the matter. However, since several distinct abilities have been identified through factor analysis, it is important for a teacher to be aware of how to help students develop these abilities. The following abilities are improved through the indicated techniques.

Ability	Examples
Sensitivity to Problems	7, 10
Fluencies	7, 10, 13
Flexibility	13, 15
Originality	4, 5, 6, 8, 9, 11, 13, 15
Implications	2, 8, 9

It might be added that redefinition abilities are activated in example 5. Intensifying the students' experience of nature—an integral part of the creative process—is intended in example 14.

Factors Relating to Creativity

What conclusions can be gained from the research on creativity? Specifically, what are some of the characteristics of creative people, and how is creativity best fostered in students? First we will summarize some of the more important characteristics of creative people; then we will consider some suggestions for improving creativity.[1]

---

1. The main researchers who have stressed creativity are J. P. Guilford, of the University of Southern California, who was the originator of the emphasis on creativity and more than

Personality Characteristics of Creative Individuals

The highly creative person, when compared to the general population, has been found to be more emotionally mature and sensitive, more self-sufficient, independent and self-confident, more dominant, adventurous, and resourceful (Barron 1963, MacKinnon 1961). Similarly it has been found that highly creative children possess greater self-awareness, a greater sense of humor, and tend to give unconventional ("wild") responses more than less creative children (Torrance 1962, Weisberg and Springer 1961, Taft and Gilchrist 1970). They also have a strong curiosity drive, a capacity to be puzzled, and also evidence marked persistence, energy, and effort in their work (Miles 1960, Roe 1960).

Intellectual Interests and Abilities of Creative Persons

Creative persons like ideas rather than people or things, prefer complexity and theoretical concepts, are open to new experiences, and seek for comprehensive and satisfying answers (MacKinnon 1960, 1965).

Highly creative students may or may not be highly intelligent, although they are usually found to be at least above average in general intelligence. The correlation between creativity (divergent thinking) and "intelligence" (mainly cognition) is moderately low, usually found to be around .30. Similarly, when students are measured for both divergent thinking and cognition abilities, about seventy percent of the "highly creative" (upper one-fifth in divergent thinking) will not be in the "high I.Q." (upper one-fifth in cognition) group. In other words, students vary in the relative strength of their intellectual processes: some are considerably stronger in cognition, others in divergent thinking; some are strong in both (Getzels and Jackson 1961).

Creative Students in the Classroom

Some studies show that highly creative students do as well as high I.Q. students on general achievement tests. Even though they may not study class and text material as intensively as the very bright students, they probably read more widely and hence have as much general academic knowledge as the high I.Q. student (at least this is one hypothesis). Other studies, however, fail to support this finding and show that high I.Q. students are superior in both achievement test scores and grade point averages (Getzels and Jackson 1961, Edwards and Tyler 1965).

It has often been noted that many teachers feel threatened by the expressions of creative children; they particularly do not know how to evaluate their work. Similarly it has been found that teachers tend to prefer the more docile,

---

anyone has contributed to an understanding of the nature of man's creative abilities; E. Paul Torrance, formerly at the University of Minnesota and now at the University of Georgia, who has examined the many variables relating to creativity in education; Frank Barron and Donald MacKinnon, of the University of California, Berkeley, who have studied the personalities of creative people. Although there are other centers for the study of creativity at the Universities of Utah, Buffalo, Penn State, etc., a great deal of the significant research has come from the first three mentioned.

predictable bright student to the independent, bothersome creative student (Getzels and Jackson 1961, Torrance 1962).

In classroom groups, the more creative students often experience resentment, rejection, and hostility by their classmates because of their superior ideas. This pressure to reduce creative production can result in either compliance, aggressive persistence or withdrawal to work alone, depending on the individual (Torrance 1962).

Group Techniques for Improving Creativity

Group idea-generating sessions, brainstorming, are effective in improving the divergent thinking abilities of students—originality and the flexibilities much more than the fluencies. Whether it is that the training emphasizes quality more than quantity (fluency) or whether the fluencies are little affected by training is not known (McFee 1964, Parnes 1962).

Brainstorming sessions result in twice as many unique and useful ideas when evaluation is suspended until the end as when individuals evaluate their ideas critically throughout the session (Meadow et al. 1959). On the other hand, when a group is instructed to think of as many "clever" ideas as possible, fewer ideas result, but more clever-rated ideas than when the group is given no such suggestion (Christensen et al. 1957).

Students working in pairs on exercises calling for creative thinking produce higher quality responses in terms of originality, flexibility, and fluency. Such students also report stronger feelings of stimulation, enjoyment, and originality than those working individually (Torrance 1971).

Finally, instruction about the nature of the creative thinking abilities plus exercises in their use are more effective than the exercises alone (Forehand and Libby 1962).

Teacher Attitudes

When teachers treat students' ideas and questions with respect and when they allow them to do some things without threat of evaluation, students seem to improve in originality, fluency, and elaboration abilities (Torrance 1960, Rusch et al. 1965). Too frequent evaluation or overemphasis on evaluation interferes with a student's creative thinking. For instance, divergent thinking practice sessions with no evaluation tend to produce more originality, sensitivity, and elaboration than evaluated sessions (Torrance 1965).

As far as type of evaluation is concerned, the use of both constructive and critical evaluation seems to result in a higher quantity and quality of ideas than does just constructive or just critical evaluation, though constructive criticism is better than critical evaluation (Hyman 1964).

Teaching for Creativity

Creative ability is important for well-rounded intellectual development, success in many occupations and professions, and for significant contributions to society. Hence it is well worth the teacher's effort to try to develop creativity in his students. How can this be done? The following suggestions are drawn from the above analysis of the creative process plus the research on creativity. They concern an atmosphere for creativity, teaching strategies, how to improve creative abilities, and approaches to student productions.

Atmosphere

Establish an atmosphere conducive to creativity, particularly by:

1. being open and accepting of student contributions and suggestions;
2. treating their ideas with respect, even their "wild," nonconforming, or radical ideas;
3. asking open-ended questions and problems, not always convergent ones;
4. promoting free discussion of issues not dominated by yourself as the teacher;
5. using active, discovery, student-centered, and creative methods of teaching.

Encourage creative thinking by providing opportunities for self-expression and independent work, and by giving students freedom to select topics to work on (experiments, essays, problems).

Remove blocks to creativity by:

1. dispelling a sense of awe of masterpieces (emphasize personal creativity instead);
2. not expecting to produce a professional artist or scientist, but rather to develop more creative persons;
3. avoiding constant use of textbooks and an emphasis on the "right" answer;
4. attempting to reduce social pressures against creativity, especially pressure for conforming to peer values and interests and pressure for avoiding characteristics of opposite sex (feminine sensitivity, male independence).

Approaches in Teaching

Encourage students to manipulate ideas and objects in different ways, to "toy" around with various combinations of ideas, to list the parts of an object and then think of different ways to change each part, and similar activities.

Ask questions regularly that call for students' divergent thinking; "How would you end this story?" "What would it be like if Germany had won World War II?" "What would you do in a one-on-one situation in soccer?"

Ask questions that you do not know the answer to, and that call for genuine information from students rather than the "correct" answer that you already know. Allow students to ask questions often, and let the class (you and students) search for the answers. These approaches not only give practice in creative thinking, but they also indicate to the students that learning involves more than always arriving at the one correct answer (convergent thinking).

Vary teaching strategies so as to appeal to students whose creative abilities and interests are stronger than their cognition and convergent thinking abilities and interests, and vice versa. Similarly, in classes for the "gifted," allow for both those gifted in "intelligence" and those gifted in "creativity."

Training for Creativity

Give your students instruction on the nature of the creative process and particularly on the nature of the creative thinking abilities (originality, the flexibilities, etc.). Give students practice and training in creative thinking:

1. brainstorming: have students give suggestions on a topic or problem with no critical evaluation imposed, except for perhaps a hint that they should come up with clever ideas;
2. inquiry training: given a problem or baffling demonstration, students ask questions (answerable by yes or no) in an attempt to discover a solution;
3. exercises similar to measures of creativity: name as many soft, round objects as you can, give titles to cartoons, list similes (clouds are like . . .), etc. Have students work both individually and in pairs.

Give students training and experience in becoming more aware and sensitive to their environment: the beauty of nature, how things look, feel, smell, sound, how things can be improved, what problems might be involved in trying to control one's physical environment, in establishing a business, etc. Give instruction and experience in the techniques of your field: control of variables and systematic experimentation in the sciences, expressing ideas in a clear, concise, but colorful style in creative writing, intuitive as well as logical thinking in mathematics, achieving good composition, perspective and balance in art.

Student Productions

Give students adequate time to complete projects and other creative productions (creativeness = inspiration + long hours of work). Allow them to carry out the full implications of their own ideas and encourage them to revise first drafts of their work, to rework and polish the results of their initial inspiration. Give them opportunities to work alone, not always in groups.

Deemphasize evaluation of your students' productions, particularly in the early stages. Encourage them to evaluate their own work, both constructively and critically. When you evaluate, do so as positively and constructively as possible with a compliment, a positive suggestion or a helpful question.

Give recognition to creative productions through classroom exhibits in which each student's work is shown, through a class newspaper or literary quarterly, and by reading or showing good stories, experiments, wood or metal work in class.

Remember that creativity is an individual matter:

1. evaluate student work according to individual progress, not group norms;

2. encourage students to pursue their own talents and the techniques that are best for them; avoid an emphasis on models and imitation;
3. emphasize the main characteristics of creative productions, not any one set pattern of creative thinking.

Measuring and Evaluating Creativity

Measuring Creative Ability

The two groups of standardized measures of creativity most widely used are: Guilford's Tests of Divergent Production and Torrance's Tests of Creative Thinking.

Some sample tests of the Guilford series are:

1. Alternate uses (Divergent production of semantic classes): list possible uses of an object, other than its common use, e.g., newspaper (used for reading). Sample answers: start a fire, swat flies, stuffing for packages, rain hat, etc.
2. Consequences (Divergent production of semantic units [obvious responses] and transformations [remote responses]): list different consequences of a given hypothetical situation, e.g., what would be the results if people no longer needed sleep? Sample answers: get more work done, alarm clocks not necessary, smaller houses, etc.
3. Possible Jobs (Divergent production of semantic implications): list possible jobs that might be symbolized by a given emblem, e.g., light bulb. Sample answers: electrician, light bulb manufacturer, a bright student, etc.

Besides the eleven published tests available, Guilford describes other measures of divergent thinking in several places, for instance the Plot Titles Test that measures originality.

> The Plot Titles Test presents a short story, the examinee being told to list as many appropriate titles as he can to head the story. One story is about a missionary who has been captured by cannibals in Africa. He is in the pot and about to be boiled when a princess of the tribe obtains a promise for his release if he will become her mate. He refuses and is boiled to death.
>
> In scoring the test, we separate the responses into two categories, clever and nonclever. Examples of nonclever responses are: African Death, Defeat of a Princess, appropriate but commonplace. The number of such responses serves as a score for ideational fluency. Examples of clever responses are: Pot's Plot, Potluck Dinner, Stewed Parson, Goil or Boil, A Mate Worse than Death, He Left a Dish for a Pot, Chaste in Haste, and A Hot Price for Freedom. The number of clever responses given by an examinee is his score for originality, or the divergent production of semantic transformations. (Guilford 1959)

The Guilford tests are not simple to score, but not impossibly difficult either. The director of testing in a school system can obtain the tests and manuals and either administer and score the tests himself or train interested teachers to do so. They are usually not available to individual teachers who have not had supervised training in their scoring.

Whereas the Guilford tests for the most part each measure a specific divergent thinking ability and are more appropriate with high school students, the Torrance Tests of Creative Thinking are designed to measure several components of creative thinking at once and are meant more for elementary school children, although they can also be used in high school.

The Torrance tests consist of two batteries:

1. Thinking Creatively with Words. For example, Ask and Guess test which presents an intriguing picture and asks the students to list: a) all the questions he would need to ask to find out what is happening, b) the possible causes of the action depicted, and c) the possible consequences of the action. These plus four more "activities," quite similar to some of the Guilford tests, are scored for the traits of fluency, flexibility, and originality.
2. Thinking Creatively with Pictures. For example, Lines, which provides many pairs of short parallel lines with the instructions to make as many different pictures as possible using the lines as the main feature. This plus two other "activities" yield scores for fluency, flexibility, originality, and elaboration.

The manuals accompanying the Torrance batteries provide detailed scoring guides with many examples, so that an interested teacher can master the scoring with a little practice.

Besides the standardized measures of creative thinking ability, there are other predictors of creativity that have been found useful such as checklists and observation scales. Some specific examples are:

1. A checklist of creative achievements or preferred activities such as The Creative Science Scale and The Creative Arts Scale used by the National Merit Scholarship Corporation.

The Creative Science Scale

1. Giving an original paper at a scientific meeting sponsored by a professional society
2. Winning a prize or award in a scientific talent search (or science fair)
3. Constructing a scientific apparatus on one's own initiative
4. Inventing a patentable device
5. Having a scientific paper published in a science journal

The Creative Arts Scale

1. Winning one or more speech contests
2. Having poems, stories or articles published in a public newspaper or magazine or in a state or national high school anthology
3. Winning a prize or award in an art competition
4. Receiving the highest rating in a state music contest

5. Receiving one of the highest ratings in a national music contest
6. Composing music that is given at least one public performance
7. Arranging music for a public performance
8. Having minor roles in plays (not school- or church-sponsored)
9. Having leads in school- or church-sponsored plays
10. Winning a literary award or a prize for creative writing
11. Having a cartoon published in a public newspaper or magazine

2. Systematic observation of students using criteria such as those on the following observation scale (Torrance 1969):

Intense absorption in listening, observing, doing
Intense animation and physical involvement
Use of analogies in speech
Intense bodily involvement in writing, drawing, etc.
Tendency to challenge ideas of authorities
Habit of checking many sources
Taking a close look at things
Eagerness to tell other about discoveries
Continuing in creative activities after the scheduled time for quitting
Showing relationships among apparently unrelated ideas
Follow through on ideas set in motion
Various manifestations of curiosity, of wanting to know, digging deeper
Spontaneous use of discovery or experimental approach
Excitement in voice about discoveries
Habit of guessing and testing outcomes
Honesty and intense search for truth
Independent action
Boldness of ideas
Low distractability
Manipulation of ideas and objects to obtain new combinations
Tendency to lose awareness of time
Penetrating observations and questions
Self-initiated learning
Tendency to seek alternatives and explore new possibilities
Willingness to consider or toy with a strange idea

More creative students will usually evidence more of these behaviors than less creative students, especially in a more open classroom that is amenable to such behavior.

3. Informal observation can also be used to evaluate creativity. For instance:

1. in group planning and brainstorming sessions, observe which students offer the most suggestions and seem to need the least guidance.
2. in problem-solving sessions, look for those who have a hopeful and

constructive attitude about reaching a solution as well as those who seem to intuitively anticipate a feasible solution.

Evaluating Creative Achievements

Although teachers regularly evaluate the creative productions of their students, it is not easy to evaluate them fairly and constructively. Such evaluation will of necessity be (and should be) more subjective than the evaluation of other intellectual processes. But teachers can develop criteria that will make their evaluation more helpful to students as well as somewhat more reliable. One such list of criteria for evaluating essays and papers follows.

Content
    Problem or issue well stated
    Positions, points of view
        clearly presented
        adequate in number
        evaluated sufficiently
    Main thesis, propositions well stated
    Evidence for thesis: reasons, facts, references
        accurate, tenable
        comprehensive, thorough
        presented with sufficient analysis, depth
        supportive of thesis (connection shown)
    Original thought evidenced

Organization
    Coherence, unity of structure
    Order in the development of content (logical, chronological, etc.)
    Continuity, transition between ideas, topics
    Summary included

Presentation
    Clarity in expressing ideas
    Conciseness of expression
    Originality in expression
    Choice of words
        color, vividness
        precision, correct terminology

Usage
    Grammar
    Spelling
    Punctuation
    Documentation

Finally, regarding evaluation of creative productions: Be positive. Emphasize several good points of a drawing or story (there will always be at least one or two), rather than stress mistakes or what the artist or author should have done. Most budding artists and writers need encouragement rather than criticism; they improve more by building on their strengths than by avoiding mistakes.

Where some critical evaluation is called for, it is better to pick out one or two things for a student to improve on rather than flooding a paper with red ink. Also, it is more helpful to show him how it might be done better rather than just to say that it is poor or needs improvement.

Ordinarily creativity is better assessed through paintings, projects, or stories done in a more leisurely way than under the pressure of an examination. However, including a creative item on a final examination, for instance, has the advantage of emphasizing—or in the view of many students, proving—the importance of creativity in classroom learning.

Examples of such items are (in art, social science, and English respectively);

> Make a tempera painting or a single figure. The painting is to have a mood or feeling of turbulence. The feeling should result from the attitude of the figure, from the use of colors, texture, lines, and shapes, and from the composition of the painting. (one hour) (Bloom et al. 1971)

> You are traveling on another continent and happen upon a country in which the majority of positions of influence and honor are filled by women. When you question people, they tell you that intelligence, kindness, and a respect for creative work are the ideal human attributes, and that women, by nature, excel men in these matters. Write an essay in which you describe what other social changes might accompany the situation described above.

> Write two descriptions of a single object located out of doors, e.g. a house, tree, car, or lamppost. The first should be a description of the object as it appears in one kind of weather or at one time of day; the second should be a description as it appears in a different kind of weather or at a different time of day. (Adapted from Bloom et al. 1971)

EXERCISE 10-3. Evaluating Creative Productions

The following composition was turned in by a tenth-grade girl to fulfill an assignment to write a "short-short story." How would you evaluate it? Read the story and then indicate your evaluation by checking a half dozen or so comments from among those suggested on the following page.

One day, I descended the stairs in my longest skirt, knee high socks,   1
loafers, and my red, bulky turtle-neck sweater. My paternal grandmother was sitting primly on our pink flowered chair, sipping a cup of tea. As I walked into the room, I thought she was going to spit the tea all over the wall.

"Beverly!" she screamed to my mother. "Beverly, you must do something 2
about this child. Why, the way she dresses is obscene! Just look at the length
of her skirt."

Her face was red and purple-striped, and since I had never seen her in such 3
a rage, I became frightened.

"Why, when I was a girl, if I had worn that outfit, people would have 4
suspected that I was of questionable morals. Why don't you buy that girl
some high-buttoned shoes and black stockings?"

My mother tried to calm her by saying, "Now, now, mother, that is the 5
fashion of the times, you know."

"Pshaw!" answered my grandmother and tottered grandly out of the 6
room.

I think the trouble with families is that they are not up with the times, 7
but I have no time to prove it. It takes me too long to button up those
high-buttoned shoes.

Par. 1	____	(1)	Lovely choice of details
	____	(2)	Too many commas
	____	(3)	Shattering contrast!
	____	(4)	Too much contrast
Par. 2	____	(5)	"Obscene" is well-chosen—in character
	____	(6)	"Obscene" is vulgar—for the context
Par. 4	____	(7)	Splendid! Sounds just like her
	____	(8)	Story becomes far-fetched here
Par. 6	____	(9)	I think grandma *could* "totter grandly"—like Charles DeGaulle
	____	(10)	A person cannot "totter grandly"—they are contraries
Par. 7	____	(11)	A snapper of an ending! Very effective to leave it like this.
	____	(12)	Too abrupt! You need to fill in some intervening steps before you conclude.
Whole	____	(13)	You make grandma come to life. A few bold strokes and everything in character.
	____	(14)	Your style is quite choppy. Each paragraph has only a sentence or two. You fail to delineate your characters sufficiently.

How many odd-numbered comments did you check? How many even-
numbered?

The odd-numbered comments were actually made by an experienced English
teacher who used to evaluate writing samples for the College Entrance Examination Board, Paul Diederich. They represent a positive, encouraging approach to
the evaluation of creative productions, an approach that is happily becoming
more and more common among English teachers. The even-numbered comments
are negative and represent an older approach to the evaluation of students'
writing that emphasizes correction rather than encouragement, elements rather
than the whole, and usage rather than creativity. Which do you prefer?

EXERCISE 10-4. Systematic Observation of Creativity in the Classroom

On the basis of the above analysis of the creative process, create your own systematic observation outline and then observe a class or two on your level of interest looking for creativity-oriented teaching strategies. (From your earlier observations you might recall a teacher who emphasized creative approaches.)

In your observation, for instance, you might look for activities that seem to be designed to develop one or more of the following abilities:

> sensitivity to problems
> fluencies
> flexibilities
> originality
> elaboration
> evaluation (in relation to creativity).

Or you might analyze the questions a teacher asks according to whether he or she

> asks open-ended questions
> asks questions calling for various answers (divergent thinking)
> asks for genuine information (not just "answers")
> accepts different answers (not just what he/she had in mind)
> encourages student questions.

Or finally, you might select some of the suggested applications for teaching listed above and formulate your systematic observation scale from them.

EXERCISE 10-5. Teaching Creatively

To apply some of what we have seen in this chapter, work up two teaching plans, one emphasizing creative teaching, the other teaching for creativity.

For the first, select a topic in your field that you think would be appropriate for teaching in a creative way. Plan a class session in which you teach it creatively by involving your students' creative thinking abilities for learning. State what you intend them to learn and then list the activities that you will have the students engage in to learn it.

For the second, plan a class session designed to improve your students' creative thinking abilities. From the suggestions offered in the chapter plus your additional reading and your own creative insights, decide on an activity that is designed to improve your students' originality, fluency, flexibility, etc. If the activity involves your asking them questions, draw up a list of specific questions and indicate which creative thinking abilities they are aimed at developing.

Suggested Readings

Barron, F. *Creative Person and Creative Process*. New York: Holt, Rinehart & Winston, 1969.

Gowan, J. C., Demos, G. O. and Torrance, E. P., eds. *Creativity: Its Educational Implications*. New York: John Wiley, 1967.

Guilford, J. P. *Intelligence, Creativity, and Their Educational Implications*. San Diego: Robert R. Knapp, 1968.

Mooney, R. L. and Razik, T. A., eds. *Explorations in Creativity*. New York: Harper and Row, 1967.

Parnes, S. J. and Harding, H. F., eds. *A Source Book for Creative Thinking*. New York: Charles Scribner's, 1962.

Smith, J. A. et al. *Creative Teaching in the Elementary School* Series (7 Vols.: Setting Conditions, Language Arts, Reading and Literature, the Creative Arts, Social Studies, Mathematics, and Science). Boston: Allyn and Bacon, 1966-1968.

Taylor, C. W., ed. *Creativity: Progress and Potential*. New York: McGraw-Hill, 1964.

Torrance, E. P. *Guiding Creative Talent*. Englewood Cliffs, N. J.: Prentice-Hall, 1962.

____. *Education and the Creative Potential*. Minneapolis: University of Minnesota Press, 1963.

____. *Rewarding Creative Behavior*. Englewood Cliffs, N. J.: Prentice-Hall, 1965.

____. *Encouraging Creativity in the Classroom*. Dubuque, Iowa: Wm. C. Brown, 1970.

____. *Creative Learning and Teaching*. New York: Dodd, Mead, 1970.

11

Problem Solving

The problem-solving process is our principal means of acquiring new knowledge and controlling our environment. We achieve new insights about the world around us mainly by being faced with a question or difficulty and then working toward an answer or solution; in other words, through problem solving. Similarly on a more practical level, we are able to gain greater control over our environment by testing out ideas on how to master a problematic situation in the physical or social world we live in, again through problem solving. In teaching, the problem-centered approach is usually found to be superior to a more didactic approach.

For many reasons, then, a knowledge of what is involved in the problem-solving process and how to help students solve problems more effectively is of utmost importance for a teacher. This is exactly what we will attempt to gain in this chapter: an understanding of the process of problem solving plus some ideas on how we can help students solve problems. First we should consider what a problem essentially is and some important types of problems. Next we will examine rather thoroughly various aspects of the process by which we solve problems, specifically the pattern or steps that we use, the intellectual abilities involved, plus some models that attempt to explain the internal process. Then we will be concerned with how we can help students solve problems more effectively, and will consider in this context both what the research states specifically and what can be derived by way of application from the general analysis, the theory and the research on problem solving. Finally, we will take a look at some ways to evaluate the problem-solving ability of students.

The Nature of Problems

Just what is a problem? And what are some of the main types of problems? Consider the mathematical problem:

Show that this statement is true: $(x + y) \ 15 = x \ 15 + y \ 15$

Some students will not be familiar with the three basic laws of algebra and hence must first learn them if they are to solve the problem. Other students will know the basic algebraic laws but will have to organize them and apply them to the problem before they can arrive at a solution:

1. $(x + y) \ 15 = 15 \ (x + y)$: using the commutative property of multiplication;
2. $(x + y) \ 15 = 15 \ x + 15 \ y$: by the distributive property;
3. $(x + y) \ 15 = x \ 15 + y \ 15$: by the commutative property.

Still other students (concrete operational thinkers) will simply not be able to handle unknowns in mathematics and so will not solve it because of an internal limitation in level of thinking. Similarly other students (present company excluded—hopefully) will throw up an emotional block at the very sight of an algebraic equation and so will not be able to solve it, again because of an internal limitation. We should add the student who is unable to do the problem because he lost his pen and no one around him has an extra one (an environmental block).

A problem, then, is basically a situation that involves a difficulty or need plus a gap between it and its solution. The gap can represent a lack of knowledge, an unstructured body of knowledge, or an inability based on personal limitations or environmental obstacles.

We can summarize the nature of a problem as follows:

a difficulty experienced or a need felt	a gap or obstacle of some kind, either lack of knowledge, unorganized knowledge, a personal limitation, emotional block, environmental obstacle	a solution found or a goal reached

Types of Problems

There are several types of problems:

1. Problems in which a question is presented and there is a standard method for solving it known to the student and guaranteeing a solution, e.g. (given the area of a rectangle $= b \times h$) "What is the area of the rectangle with the sides $8'$ and $5'$?" Actually, these are more exercises

or pseudo problems rather than genuine problems; they call for "repro-
ductive thinking" which requires little more than plugging data into a
formula or known method of solution.

2. Problems in which a difficulty is experienced but no procedure and/or
information for solving it is immediately known to the student, although known to others, e.g. "What is the cause (and cure) of elm
blight?" This is the most common type of an actual problem and the
one that we are mainly concerned with in this chapter. These problems
require productive thinking which involves the generation of new
knowledge from data that is either already known or is being currently
discovered.

3. Problems in which a difficulty is known but the method and/or the
data necessary for solving it are not known to the problem solver nor to
others. These are the problems with which scholars, scientists and
inventors who are at the cutting edge of their fields deal. They require
productive thinking that is characterized by original research and experimentation. Occasionally, a superior student in a science fair will
work on such a problem; but ordinarily they require more background
than that possessed by the average elementary or high school student.

EXERCISE 11-1. Some Types of Problems

Real problems, those requiring productive thinking, can be further divided,
depending on what type of thinking they require. Examine the following
problems and see if you can discern what intellectual processes they call for:
memory, convergent thinking, divergent thinking, or evaluation (some problems
will require more than one process).

1. 18-carat gold contains three times as much pure gold as copper. How much of
   each metal is there in 19.6 grams of 18-carat gold?

$$19.6 = 3c + c \qquad \text{copper--} \ 4.9 \text{ grains}$$
$$4c = 19.6 \qquad \text{gold--} 14.7 \text{ grains}$$
$$c = 4.9$$
$$3c = 14.7$$

2. On the basis of the following documents, did Senator Duckworth vote for or
   against the war?

   The Duckworth Documents

   New York *Call,* March 24, 1917. It is common knowledge in Washington
   that Senator Duckworth, that tool of the munitions mongers and Wall
   Street imperialists, will vote for war.

   Washington *Post,* March 26, 1917. Informed sources report that the vote
   on war in the Senate will hinge on Senator Duckworth of New York.

   New York *Herald,* March 27, 1917. (Columnist Drool Poison). I have
   learned from unusually reliable sources that Senator Duckworth told

Senator Lenroot that he would vote against war out of respect for his deceased mother who was born in Germany.

Duckworth to Katherine O'Reilly Duckworth, March 27, 1917, Duckworth papers, Library of Congress. Dear Mother: Greetings on your ninety-sixth birthday. Don't worry about the hospital bills. I have ample funds to meet them and to see to it that you are buried in your native Dublin.

Sen. George W. Norris to wife, April 1, 1917, Norris Papers, Lib. of Cong. Last night Duckworth and ten others attended our caucus of Senators, and although he complained about pressure from the Irish, he told us that he would vote for war.

Baltimore *Sun.* April 2, 1917, 1:4. Senator Duckworth, in a lengthy interview with *Sun* reporter, Samuel M. Scoop, said, "There is no reason to fight Germany until German submarines begin to attack our ships."

J. P. Morgan to Duckworth, April 2, 1917 (telegram copy), Morgan Papers, Wall Street Journal Office. If you haven't the guts to vote for war we'll call in our note for $100,000 and refuse you all further credit.

Diary of James Duckworth, Duckworth papers, Lib. of Cong. April 4, 8:27 a.m. What a night. The pressures converging on me are terrible. Not a wink of sleep. I must have laryngitis; I can't speak above a whisper.

Congressional Record, 65 Congress, 1 Session, p. 2364 (April 4, 1917), (final vote in Senate for war: 82 to 6) Senator Duckworth. Mr. President, I want to make it clear here and now that I voted as I did only for the most patriotic motives.

Milwaukee *Star,* April 5, 1917 (Editorial). The vote of that treacherous cur, Duckworth, can be viewed by right-thinking citizens only with anger.

Wall Street Journal, April 5, 1917, 6:1 (Editorial). Senator Duckworth finally came through as all decent citizens had hoped and expected.

I Stood Firm: By James Duckworth, p. 392. "When the hour came to vote, I rose in the Senate and declared in ringing tones that I acted solely for patriotic motives. No one had the effrontery to try to pressure me: Not Tammany, not the Irish-Americans, not Wall Street, not the White House—nobody.

3. (In the context of the Age of Discovery in the fifteenth and sixteenth centuries) Why does man seek to explore other parts of the world? Students offer many hypotheses:

> To obtain raw materials and wealth
> To get new land for his country
> To become famous
> To explore the unknown
> To spread religion
> To get better travel routes
> Better ships available
> To spread culture

Teacher suggests that they examine the possibilities, first for their logical validity and then evaluate them on empirical grounds. Students eliminate one or two hypotheses because they are conditions rather than real causes or reasons. On the basis of what they have read in their texts they put a few more aside as less important than others. Again on the basis of their text and from what a few students have read in addition, they select several as being major reasons, and then decide that obtaining raw materials and wealth was the main reason.

Check the one or two intellectual processes that are mainly involved in each of these problems.

	Memory	Divergent thinking	Convergent thinking	Evaluation
1. 18-carat gold	____	____	____	____
2. Duckworth papers	____	____	____	____
3. Why man explores	____	____	____	____

Most math and algebra word problems call for both convergent thinking and memory: convergent thinking or proceeding from given data to a conclusion; memory for standard ways of solving such problems.

In the Duckworth papers you were given all the data and simply had to figure out which conclusion it led to; so it involved almost pure convergent thinking.

In the question of why men explore other parts of the world, at first divergent production of hypotheses was called for, and then the evaluation of each of the hypotheses on the basis of logical and empirical grounds.

On the basis of the intellectual processes which are largely involved in the solving of a problem, then, we can distinguish among (1) problems that require convergent thinking and memory (many math problems), (2) those that require only convergent thinking, where the data is given or read about and a conclusion drawn, and (3) problems that call first for divergent thinking and then evaluation of the hypotheses or solution suggested. In addition, there are many complex problems that involve all of the intellectual processes, from cognition through explanation.

Finally, if we consider the content of the problem, we can distinguish among scientific, philosophical, mathematical, and practical problems. Scientific problems are those concerned with finding out "what is" on the basis of data; philosophical problems are those concerned with finding out "what is" on the basis of reasons; mathematical problems are concerned with relationships on the symbolic level; practical problems are concerned with the question of "how to" or "what should be done."

The Problem-Solving Process

How do we go about solving problems? What steps are involved in the problem-solving process? There are at least three ways of trying to answer this question:

(1) inductively, by examining how several different types of problems might be solved, (2) dialectically, by examining what some of the experts have said about the process, and (3) in a more expository way, by my explaining the essential steps involved in problem solving. Since each way adds a different dimension to understanding the process, we can afford to pursue all three, the first two in exercises 11-2 and 11-3, the third in the text.

EXERCISE 11-2. Problem Solving in Practice—An Inductive Analysis

What are the basic steps in solving different types of problems? Is there a general pattern or is the procedure relative to the specific type of problem? Given below are three problems of various types: practical, philosophical, and scientific. Analyze the episodes and try to discern the steps followed in the solving of the problems.

I. A wrecker tows a car into a repair garage. The problem is to discover what is wrong and fix it.

The mechanic will usually ask the driver what happened: did it fail to start, did it give out on the road? Using his knowledge of automobiles, he will then think of the several possible reasons for the difficulty: out of gas, faulty fuel line, worn spark plugs, dead battery.

He will then examine each of these possibilities—checking to see what happens when the starter is turned on, examining the fuel line and spark plugs, etc. When he discovers what seems to be the cause of the problem (e.g., a dead battery), he will repair the situation (recharge the battery) and see whether the car starts. If it does, then the problem is solved. If not, he examines another possibility, and another, and repairs each part of the car until it runs properly.

II. The problem is posed in class: Is man basically free or determined in his choices? The class then proceeds to try to arrive at a solution to the problem.

Someone asks exactly what is meant by the terms "free" and "determined"; a dictionary is consulted and the terms defined. Another student mentions that their efforts should concentrate on psychological freedom rather than political or economic freedom and determinism.

A plan of attack is chosen: students decide to look up what different writers have to say about the problem (the teacher suggests a few).

A discussion is held in which the main positions are examined, the reasons for each evaluated, and the best position, i.e. the one having the strongest reasons, is selected.

A student is asked to give a summary of the conclusion together with a review of the reasons supporting it.

III. A science class is reading about photosynthesis and one of the students asks, "Is sunlight absolutely necessary for plants to grow?" The teacher suggests, "Why not find out yourselves."

The students suggest experimenting with several possibilities: growing a plant in sunlight, inside with only a lamp, and in complete darkness.

The teacher asks them to state their specific hypotheses exactly (e.g., sunlight is necessary for plant life), which they do.

Several of the students prepare soil boxes and plant seeds, each using different light (sun, lamp, none). They water their plants every day with four ounces of water; after four weeks they compare their plants. They then select the hypotheses that are supported by the results of their experiments.

Analyze the foregoing problem-solving sequences: (1) identify which of the following steps are involved in any of them and (2) indicate when each step ordinarily occurs in the process.

		Initial	Early	Middle	End
___	1. Problem is perceived	___	___	___	___
___	2. Evidence is obtained	___	___	___	___
___	3. Teacher gives solution	___	___	___	___
___	4. Problem is delimited, clarified	___	___	___	___
___	5. Terms are defined	___	___	___	___
___	6. Evidence is evaluated	___	___	___	___
___	7. Possibilities, hypotheses are formulated	___	___	___	___
___	8. Solution is reached	___	___	___	___
___	9. Teacher explains reasons for solution	___	___	___	___

The problem-solving process involves each of the above steps except (3) and (9), which exemplify the expository approach, the inverse of the problem-solving or dialectical approach.

In the *initial* phase the problem is raised and perceived. Sometimes also the problem is clarified either through a definition of terms or through delimiting the problem, or both.

Early in the process the possibilities, hypotheses, or positions on the problem are formulated.

The main phase of the process (*middle*) is the collection and evaluation of evidence. Depending on the nature of the problem the evidence can take on several forms: in a practical problem (I) the possibilities are tried out; in a more philosophical problem (II) reasons are sought and evaluated; and in a scientific problem (III) data is collected by experimentation and then analyzed.

At the *end* of the process the solution is reached and accepted on the basis of the evidence. Sometimes by way of summary and review the solution or conclusion is stated together with the evidence supporting it.

The above pattern of problem solving seems to fit most types of problems with minor adjustments, for example, evidence takes different forms according to the type of problem and definition of terms is not usually necessary in a practical problem.

It should be noted that not all problems have one easy solution. Sometimes a problem is unsolvable either in itself or because of the limited resources available. In other instances, particularly in topics that are in the realm of opinion, there may be two or more tenable conclusions.

EXERCISE 11-3. The Problem-Solving Process—What Psychologists Say

There have been many attempts to analyze the steps involved in the problem-solving process, most notably those of John Dewey, but also Vinacke, Polya, Gagné and others. Consider the following comparative listing of the analyses of a psychologist-philosopher (Dewey), two psychologists (Vinacke and Gagné) and a mathematician (Polya).

Dewey	*Vinacke*	*Polya*	*Gagné*
1. Becoming aware of the problem	1. Confrontation by a problem	1. Understanding the problem	1. Stating and defining problem
2. Clarifying and defining problem			
3. Searching for facts and formulating hypotheses	2. Working toward a solution: a. calling on past experiences, analysis	2. Devising a plan for its solution	2. Recall of subordinate rules
			3. Searching for and selecting the rules relevant to problem
			4. Combining subordinate rules to form hypothesis
4. Evaluating proposed solutions	b. exploration, manipulation of materials	3. Carrying out the plan	
5. Experimental verification		4. Examining the solution	5. Verifying the provisional rule or solution
	3. Solution: understanding or modification of behavior		6. Solution rule acquired

Which of the problem-solving patterns do you prefer and why? Perhaps you like certain aspects of several of the analyses and prefer to formulate your own overall pattern. In any event it will be helpful to compare and evaluate them particularly on the basis of how comprehensive and explicit they are, or on a practical level, how helpful they would be in your teaching.

Check the pattern to which you think each statement applies most.

Positive Points   D   V   P   G

1. Emphasis on testing out hypotheses through experimentation makes it very applicable to scientific and practical problems.   ____   ____   ____   ____

	D	V	P	G

2. Emphasis on devising and executing a plan makes it applicable largely to mathematical problems, but to a lesser extent other types of problems, particularly practical. ___ ___ ___ ___

3. The general nature of the pattern makes it applicable to all types of problems. ___ ___ ___ ___

4. Stress on past knowledge can be used in most types of problems. ___ ___ ___ ___

Limitations

5. Omits any mention of hypothesis formulation and evaluation. ___ ___ ___ ___

6. Makes no provision for reasons as evidence as in philosophical problems; allows only for experimental evidence. ___ ___ ___ ___

7. Does not include a final step of arriving at a solution. ___ ___ ___ ___

8. Past orientation limits possibilities for solving problems. ___ ___ ___ ___

9. Lacks specific suggestions for most types of problems. ___ ___ ___ ___

Dewey. The emphasis on testing out the hypotheses through experimentation makes this pattern more appropriate for scientific and practical problems; for philosophical problems and many problems in the social sciences, the later steps of the process must be broadened to include evaluating the hypotheses on the basis of convincing reasons rather than simply experimental testing. Also, for purposes of closure, the pattern could be improved by adding the final step of reaching and understanding a solution.

Vinacke. The pattern is more general than any of the others. In this way it can encompass not only academic and practical problems but also behavioral and social problems. On the other hand, it lacks the steps of clarification of the problem and formulation of hypotheses, and it does not specify any kind of evaluation in its "working toward a solution" phase.

Polya. The pattern is most appropriate for mathematical problems, but can be helpful in other fields as well. It is fairly general: the main step of carrying out the plan specifies only that one should proceed step by step, checking and being able to prove each step as correct. On the negative side, other than its stress on a plan, it offers few specific suggestions for most types of problems.

Gagné. The pattern is based on the view that a problem is solved by bringing previously learned rules to bear on it and then combining them into a new rule that forms the solution of the problem. Unlike the present-oriented search and experiment approach of Dewey, Gagné's view emphasizes past rule learning and hence limits one's possibilities for solving problems.

If we combine the results of our inductive analysis of the problem-solving process (in exercise 11-2) plus the best aspects of the several patterns offered above (in exercise 11-3), we can derive a comprehensive pattern of problem solving which would take the following form.

1. Becoming aware of the problem
2. Clarifying and defining the problem
3. Searching for relevant information: facts, experiences, concepts, rules, relations, etc.
4. Formulating possible solutions or a plan
5. Evaluating the possible solutions through experimentation, manipulation, reasoning or follow through
6. Verifying the solution: proving it on the basis of evidence, checking it over
7. Solution accepted.

1. Becoming aware of the problem. The difficulty is perceived or realized; the student is aware of the lack of knowledge or the obstacle preventing an immediate solution. A feeling of perplexity, confusion, bafflement, or wonder often accompanies the awareness of the problem. This is an important step: realizing the problem fully, its background and importance, helps to interest and motivate students and eventually helps them to see the solution and its implications more clearly.

2. Clarifying and defining the problem. Before the students start working toward a solution, they should:

a. delimit the problem by deciding just what aspect(s) of the overall difficulty they should examine; this narrows the problem down to its essentials.

b. state the specific problem that they will be working on as clearly as possible; more than anything else, a clearly defined problem—preferably in writing—gives direction to the search for a solution.

c. define the key terms; this is very important, especially in group problem solving, for two reasons: if terms are defined, everyone will be talking about the same issue or concepts, and purely semantic problems, those based on different meanings for the same terms, will be cleared up and "solved" at this point (there is no need to go further because there is no real problem).

3. Searching for relevant information. In order to arrive at the most promising possible solutions, the problem solver does well to recall any related facts, personal experiences, rules or principles that he is aware of plus search for any ideas and findings of others that have a bearing on the problem. Taking advantage of what others have done will both give the students a broader base on which to construct better hypotheses and help them save time by avoiding the errors or blind alleys that others have fallen into.

4. Formulating possible solutions or a plan. On the basis of his search for

relevant information and ideas, the student thinks up several possible solutions to the problem. In a scientific problem these take the form of hypotheses: "The cause is. . . ." or "The result will be. . . ." In a philosophical or social issue problem, they will take the form of positions on the issue: "Man is. . . ." or "Society should not allow. . . ." In a mathematical problem, this step involves devising a plan, a step by step approach that should lead to a solution: "First, find the difference . . ., then . . ., etc." In a more practical problem, either the possible solution or the plan approach may be warranted, depending on the specific problem.

It should be noted that the high school student has the advantage of being able to think in terms of all or many possible solutions and then to select the most promising ones. On the elementary level, pupils will be more apt to think of one possibility at a time and then proceed using a trial and error approach. Similarly, in formulating a plan of attack high school students will be able to take into account many possible variations, whereas a plan devised by an elementary pupil will be much more specific and linear.

5. Evaluating the possible solutions. The most plausible solution(s) or plan(s) are examined or tried out with a view to determining which is most tenable. The emphasis here is on collecting and evaluating evidence, whether it is in the form of an experiment or other research in scientific problems, convincing reasons in philosophical and social issues problems, mathematical proof in mathematical problems, or manipulation and try out in practical problems. The main hypotheses or positions, and especially the evidence on which they are based, are compared and evaluated to see which solution is supported by the best evidence. If none of these original hypotheses or positions is found to be tenable, then some alternative possibilities, either newly formulated or from the original group, are examined. Similarly, if the problem calls for a plan of attack, the plan is carried out step by step with each step able to be supported by proof or other appropriate basis. If the plan is successful, fine; if not, another plan is tried. On the basis of this evaluation process, the solution with the best evidence or the plan that is most successful is chosen.

6. Verifying the solution. Closely related to the previous step—almost an integral part of it—verifying the solution. In mathematical problems this involves checking the solution and the proof for it; in scientific problems it can include a statistical analysis of the results or a replication of the experiment; in philosophical and issue-oriented problems it takes the form of summarizing the arguments for the most tenable position. Occasionally on the basis of this step, some clarification or revision of a point of evidence or of the accepted solution is made.

7. Solution accepted. Also closely related to the previous steps is the end result of the problem-solving process: a new relationship understood, an insight gained, a change made in one's behavior, a part of one's environment brought under control, in a word, a desirable goal reached. The basis for this solution to the problem is obviously the evidence that has been collected, evaluated and

checked, or the plan that has worked successfully in the previous steps of the process.

Intellectual Abilities Active in Problem Solving

What intellectual operations are at work in the various steps of the problem-solving process? Referring again to Guilford's schema of intelligence, we can identify the major processes and some of the specific intellectual abilities that are active in each phase. But first a general comment: Although it is usually most closely associated with convergent thinking, problem solving is a prime example of a process that can involve all of the intellectual operations. In fact, Guilford found in his factor analytical studies that there was no single problem-solving ability; rather problem solving calls for the interplay of many different abilities. Now let's take each step in order and try to identify the intellectual processes that are active in each.[1]

1. Becoming aware of the problem. The cognition process is involved mainly here, especially sensitivity to problems and to a lesser extent understanding the terms in the problem. Sometimes the divergent production of problems is active at this initial stage as well.

2. Clarifying and defining the problem. The cognition process is also the main one involved here: particularly verbal comprehension and the ability to structure the problem properly. Convergent thinking will come in if some analysis and classifying is called for, e.g. classifying a problem as psychological rather than political or economic. Evaluation frequently plays an important role, specifically when one judges whether the problem is real or merely semantic.

3. Searching for relevant information. Both memory and cognition are active in this step: memory in the recall of facts, ideas, and relations that one has learned previously; cognition of units, classes, and relations as well as the other abilities that are active in the reading (or listening) process.

4. Formulating possible solutions. Divergent thinking, coming up with a variety of possibilities, is the main process active here. In addition, memory for previously known relations is also active.

5. Evaluating the possible solutions. The evaluation process is largely at work here, particularly evaluation of systems and relations. In the preliminary phase of this step, the problem solver must evaluate the several possible solutions and select the most promising for further examination. In the main phase, he must evaluate the evidence as to both its truth and validity and its logical connection with the solution that it supports. In collecting evidence, where one must know and be able to use the appropriate research method, both the cognition and memory process and frequently some psychomotor abilities are involved. (Some-

---

1. For a full treatment, see Merrifield et al., 1962.

times if new techniques are constructed, divergent thinking, especially original-ity, is also active.)

6. Verifying the solution. Both evaluation and convergent thinking are active here: evaluation particularly of the system of reasoning or proof; convergent thinking in the form of ordering the ideas into a logical sequence, and—if some revision in the proof or solution is necessary—redefinition abilities (transforma-tion).

7. Solution accepted. Not only convergent thinking, drawing a conclusion from the data or convincing reasons, is involved here, but also cognition since the result of the problem-solving process is understanding a new relation.

In sum, all of the intellectual processes are active in the problem-solving process, usually two or three at each step. The summary in table 11-1 will show to what extent the various processes and abilities are at work in the different steps of the process. Again, the numbers indicate at which step a certain ability is active; parentheses indicate an ability that is only occasionally involved.

Table 11-1. *Abilities Involved in the Problem-Solving Process*

	Units	Classes	Relations	Systems	Transformations	Implications
Cognition	1, 2, 3	3	3, 7	2, 5		1
Memory	3	3	3, 4	5		
Divergent Thinking	4	4	4	1	(5)	
Convergent Thinking		2		6	(6)	5, 7
Evaluation	2		5	5, 6		

Theories of Problem Solving

How is the internal process of problem solving best explained? In other words, what goes on inside the person's mind as he solves a problem? Of the several models that attempt to explain the internal process of problem solving, two are in the tradition of the theories that we have seen previously, the S-R internal mediator model and the model provided by J. P. Guilford reflecting his structure of intellect plus some computer simulation.

First, consider how a class solved a particular problem, and then we will see how each theory would explain the process involved in its solution. Following a more technical analysis, we will examine how an understanding of the internal process will give your problem-centered teaching much more direction and effectiveness.

Problem: Pollution and Its Control

The following is a summary of a class session that was concerned with the problem of pollution, particularly what the students themselves could do to help control pollution. Analyze what took place in solving this problem. We will use the sequence presently to illustrate two major theories of problem solving.

1. As an introduction, teacher shows pictures of litter, haze, factory emitting smoke, 'greenish' stream, both photographed locally and from magazines.

2. Teacher asks: Is this a worthwhile problem? (S.: Yes!)
                 All right, what can we do about pollution?

3. One student suggests: Before we can decide on what we can do about it we have to know the cause of pollution.

4. Class agrees on the two subproblems:
   a. determine major causes of pollution;
   b. decide what can be done to stop pollution.

5. Students offer many possibilities regarding causes:
   automobiles
   industry
   non-recycled containers
   overpopulation
   overtechnological society
   electricity and power for extensive lighting, synthetic fabrics, etc.
   concentration of population in cities
   phosphates in soap, other chemicals
   physical features of certain geographical locations
   littering

6. To get away from the confusion of considering so many possible causes all together, students decide to distinguish among several areas of pollution and order the ideas accordingly:
   air
   water
   land

7. For air pollution the following possibilities were offered:
   autos
   industrial emissions
   physical features, e.g. mountains, altitude (class decided physical features were conditions that determined the degree of pollution)

8. Autos were determined to be the main cause on the basis of a state report supplied by one student. The statistics showed that air pollution was due 75 percent to autos, 15 percent to industry, 10 percent to other causes.

9. The problem was then raised: how to control air pollution from automobiles.

10. Several suggestions were made: public transportation, car pools, pollution controls on engines, engine check-up centers.

11. Engine check-up centers were decided on as the most workable and immediately effective. Plans were made to contact auto dealers for setting up free centers.

The S-R Internal Mediator Model

Among the few S-R models for problem-solving behavior, probably the best known and the one that is more closely related to the models we have examined in previous chapters is the internal mediator theory of Kendler and Kendler. In the context of problem solving, the S-R internal mediator model has two dimensions: a horizontal dimension that reflects the continuous behavior that is problem solving, $S - r \cdots s - R \quad \to S - r \cdots s - R$, and a vertical dimension that refers to the several independent S-R chains that may be operating simultaneously, e.g. as hypotheses for a workable solution, $S < \genfrac{}{}{0pt}{}{r \cdots s - R}{r \cdots s < \genfrac{}{}{0pt}{}{R}{R}}$. In addition, there can be some interaction between one chain and another, e.g., when one cue points up an important aspect of another response.

Recall the meaning of the symbols in the internal mediator theory. The basic unit is $S - r \cdots s - R$. S of course is the stimulus, most often a problem; r $\cdots$ s is the internal mediator between S and R, r—in the context of problem solving—representing the awareness of the basis for the possible solutions, s being a corresponding verbal cue; finally, R is the overt response. Of the several possible responses, the one that is selected as correct is the one that is reinforced in some way, for example, by the approval of the class, often after some trial and error activity.

In our pollution problem, we can represent the sequence that the students went through to solve the problem in the schema of figure 11-1.

For the behaviorist, problem solving is a compound of elementary S-R mechanisms (or in the internal mediator view, of S–r $\cdots$ s – R mechanisms). Not that problem solving actually consists of separate S-R units; as it actually occurs it is a complex process possessing continuity and flow. However, it can be represented (and, according to the behaviorists, better understood) as consisting of a number of specific S-R units which are linked together to form an integrated pattern of problem-solving behavior.

The S-I Model of Problem Solving

Incorporating both aspects of the traditional patterns of problem solving seen earlier in this chapter and computer simulation into his structure-of-intellect model, Guilford[2] has constructed a theory of problem solving that is presented in graphic form in figure 11-2.

The central activities in the process are the operations of cognition and production, both divergent and convergent; in addition the operations of evaluation and memory are constantly involved. The model provides for both input and exits. Input is in the form of information gathered from the environment (E) as well as from the person himself (S); for instance, his motivation and interests. Exits are in the forms of ignoring the problem (I), dropping it because it is too difficult or unimportant (II or IV), or solving it satisfactorily (III or V).

The general direction of the problem-solving process is indicated by the arrows going from left to right. The flow of information is represented by

---

2. Cf. J. P. Guilford 1966, 1967.

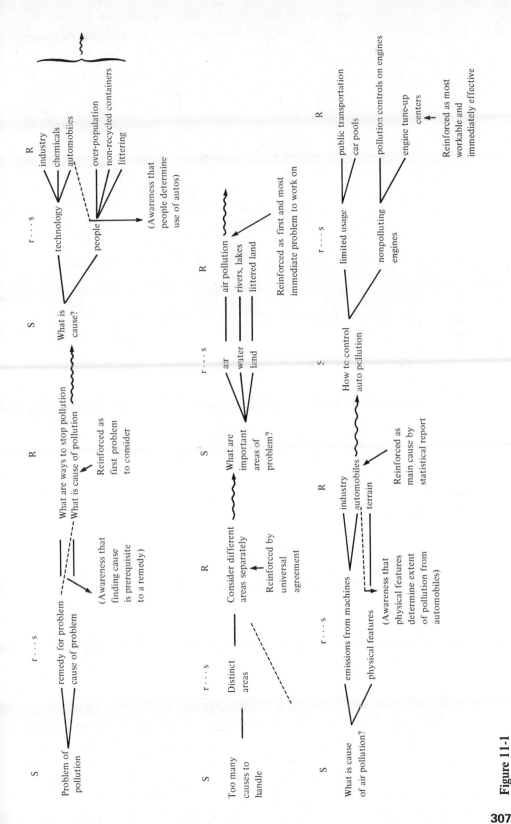

Figure 11-1

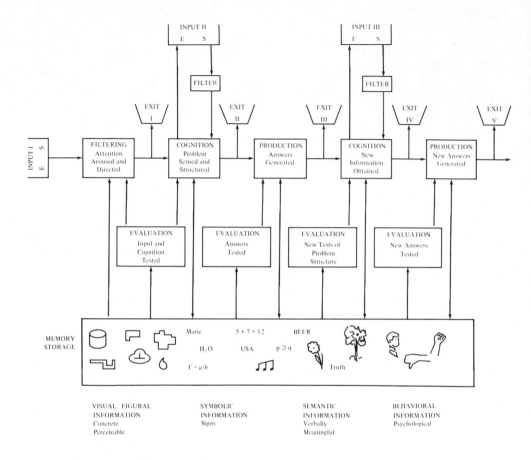

Figure 11-2. *Model for Problem Solving*

vertical arrows, sometimes one-way, sometimes two-way. Relevant information is searched for and obtained both from memory storage and from the environment. In both cases the information undergoes a selection process, sometimes through a judgment as to its relevance and value (evaluation), sometimes through our paying attention to it (filtering). In the pollution problem, the process can be organized as shown in figure 11-3.

The flow of the process is as follows. The person becomes aware that a problem exists and then structures it and draws up a search model designed to obtain the necessary data for a solution. Cognition is mainly at work here. Once the problem has been structured, the person searches for information from which a solution can be constructed. The kind of productive activity which is involved in the "generation of answers" will depend on the search model and the availability of information. If the problem is completely structured and if sufficient data are available for its solution, the production will be convergent; if there is insufficient information or if the problem is loosely structured, the

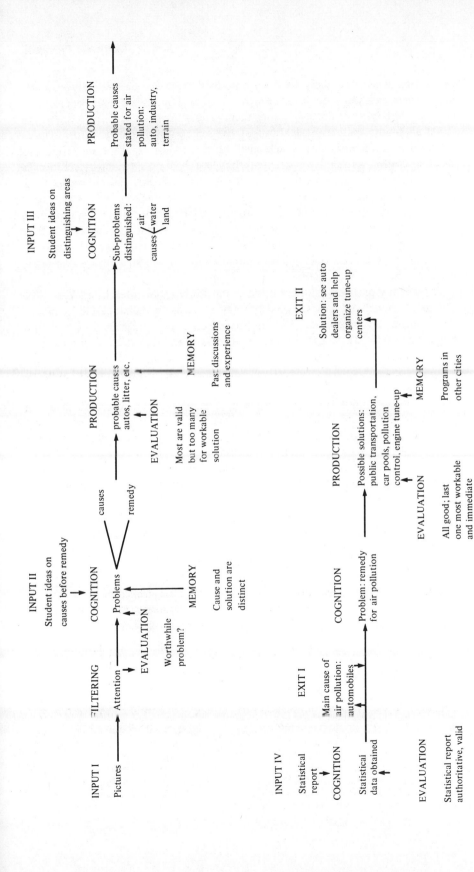

Figure 11-3

production will most likely be divergent. In the present case there were both kinds: some data were provided through the original pictures but students had to come up with most of the suggestions themselves.

At all points there is evaluation: of the search model,[3] of the information obtained from memory storage and environment, and of the solutions produced. When a solution is found and accepted, there is exit; if no satisfactory solution is found, a new cognition-production-evaluation cycle begins and continues until the problem is solved.

The S-I problem-solving model is flexible as far as order of events, providing of feedback information, and even occasional backtracking are concerned. It is admittedly a general model, needing some modification for specific types of problems. It represents one cognitive-oriented attempt to structure the internal processes involved in problem solving.

Is there any practical value for using a model in your own teaching? Yes.

First, a model can indicate what types of questions to ask at certain points in the problem-solving process, e.g. "Is this a worthwhile problem?" early in the sequence (Guilford). It also can help you to keep in mind the importance of a basis for possible solutions to the problem, e.g. the internal mediator "technology" for the responses "industry," "chemicals," and "automobiles" as possible causes.

Second, depending on your persuasion it can suggest an overall emphasis in your teaching through the problem approach, e.g. making sure each correct response or solution is reinforced (S-R), or encouraging students to evaluate both problems, data and solutions (Guilford).

Finally, a model can help your overall planning of a problem-centered lesson by suggesting a pattern and direction that the process and the lesson might follow.

Which of the models presented do you prefer and why? Do there seem to be worthwhile aspects in both of them? To help you decide, the following comparative listing should prove helpful.

	S-R	S-I
emphasis	selection of correct or best response	evaluation of possible solutions on basis of data
basis of solution	reinforcement	information
unique feature	internal mediator, which represents the basis for certain responses or solutions	productive thinking of possible solutions
direction	horizontal and vertical	horizontal and vertical
pattern	linear: one R leads to another S-R unit	cyclical: cognition − production − evaluation − etc.

---

3. Recall that in the present problem the original search model or plan for solution was found to be too general and to suggest an unwieldy number of hypotheses and was therefore reduced to encompass only one area at a time.

	S-R	S-I
interplay	between one internal mediator and another response	among processes especially cognition − production − evaluation
flexibility	allows for as many Rs and even internal mediators per unit as necessary	allows for either divergent or convergent production depending on availability of data

EXERCISE 11-4. Theories of Problem Solving in Practice

What are some specific ways in which the different theories of problem solving work out in practice? Given below are some comments and questions of teachers who follow either the S-R internal mediator model or Guilford's S-I plus computer simulation model of what goes on in the problem-solving process. Check the model on which you think each comment or question is based. You might also try to decide to which aspect of the model listed below each statement specifically refers.

S-R   S-I

1. "How about trying to analyze the topic and distinguish some of the more important aspects of it; maybe a solution will become clearer then." ____ ____

2. "Of the several mentioned, which do you think is the best approach to use in trying to solve this problem?" ____ ____

3. "How about in the area of minerals necessary for plant growth (one basis for hypotheses); are there any specific possibilities there?" ____ ____

4. "You mentioned it could be weight; what leads you to say that?" ____ ____

5. "You might check the *Reader's Guide to Periodical Literature* for some recent articles on the problem." ____ ____

6. "What do you think of that solution? It looks as though it has the strongest reasons supporting it, doesn't it?" ____ ____

7. "Can anyone think of additional information that may have a bearing on the problem?" ____ ____

8. "That approach is going to take a lot of time and effort; is it worth it to you?" ____ ____

9. "Why not try that possibility and see how it works out?" ____ ____

____ internal mediator (cue given)
____ internal mediator (response given)
____ reinforcement
____ trial and error activity
____ information from environment
____ divergent production of information

_____ production of a search model
_____ evaluating search model
_____ motivational input

The teacher who follows the S-R internal mediator theory will emphasize those mediators in two ways: first, he will give students suggestions that will serve as the basis (and cue) for further responses (3); second, he will make sure students are aware of the basis for responses that they have made (4). He will also encourage students to make responses, having them try the most probable ones first, then some others (9). He will always be conscious of the importance of providing reinforcement for the correct response, whether it be by class agreement on a solution or by his approval of one, or whatever is the best reinforcer for the specific problem (6).

The teacher who is more convinced of Guilford's model, combining information processing with his structure of intellect, would no doubt emphasize the formulation of a search model early in the problem-solving process (1) plus the evaluation and selection of the most appropriate model (4). Since information plays an important role in the process, he would very probably suggest some sources of information that students could consult (6) as well as encourage students to think up relevant information themselves (7). He also appreciates the motivational input of the student and the option of exit if the problem is too difficult and so might also refer to that possibility (8).

Factors Influencing Problem Solving

What factors help students to solve problems more effectively? Although the research on the conditions favoring problem solving has been somewhat limited as to the range of questions it has studied, most of the following conclusions are supported by a number of studies.

Information

The more relevant information a person has available to him, the more likely he is to solve a problem successfully (Saugstad and Raaheim 1957).

Even more important than the amount of information possessed is the degree to which students are able to bring relevant information to bear on the problem, particularly when the problem is somewhat different for them (Bloom and Broder 1950).

Approach

A hypothesis-testing approach is more effective than a hit or miss or "gambler's" strategy in problem solving, especially for students who are on or approaching a formal operational level of thought (Keislar and Stern 1970).

Flexibility

Flexibility or the ability and willingness to seek alternative approaches to a problem leads to greater success. On the other hand, rigidity or persistence in one plan of attack limits one's effectiveness (McNemar 1955, Luchins and Luchins 1959). Flexibility in thinking has been found to increase through experience with unusual uses of things (Flavell et al. 1958, Maltzman et al. 1958).

Objectivity and Openness

An objective attitude helps one to reason logically and to solve problems more effectively; prejudice and allowing one's strong personal opinions to color his thinking interferes with effective problem solving (Thistlewaite 1950). Open-minded persons solve problems more readily than dogmatic persons. Open-minded students are more content and evidence-oriented than authority conscious, and they are more apt to accept a novel solution when warranted (Restle et al. 1964).

Other Traits

Motivational traits such as drive, persistence and frustration tolerance help in solving problems (French and Thomas 1958).

Group Problem Solving

Groups often solve problems more efficiently than individuals because the probability of obtaining a satisfactory solution is higher with the group (Tuckman and Lorge 1962). However, some studies show no superiority for groups (Marquart 1955). When man-hours are computed, individuals are often much more efficient than groups (Moore and Anderson 1954).

When different types of groups are compared, less cohesive groups seem to be more efficient in solving problems than highly centralized groups, probably because of the greater degree of interaction possible (Phillips 1956).

Homogeneous groups are preferable to those of varied degrees of ability. Students are more satisfied in them and there are fewer signs of stress; the less creative students are more productive and show more self-confidence (Torrance 1961).

Improving the Problem-Solving Ability of Students

How can a teacher improve the problem-solving ability of his students? Combining what we have seen concerning the nature of the problem-solving process with the research on the conditions of problem solving, we can offer the following suggestions to the teacher who uses the problem approach in teaching and is concerned about developing his students' problem-solving ability. (Bear in mind that we are dealing with real problems rather than exercises or pseudoproblems and with typical classroom problems more than those requiring extensive original thinking.)

The suggestions are ordered according to the overall pattern of problem solving (p. 301) with the addition of a search model step as specified in Guilford's model (p. 308).

Becoming Aware of the Problem

Ask thought questions that require reading, inquiry, research. Or perhaps give a demonstration that baffles the students; present contradictory positions on an issue; call into question a common belief. Even more effective, have students project themselves into a problem situation, pretending that they are politicians, scientists, or business men. In addition, provide some background on the history and significance of the problem.

On a long-range basis, encourage a questioning and inquiring attitude among your students, positively by asking questions and having students ask questions about a topic, and by providing problem-oriented interest centers and group projects for them to work on; negatively by not stifling a questioning attitude through rigid lecture, textbook, or laboratory cookbook approaches.

Clarifying and Defining the Problem

Have students analyze the various aspects of the overall issue or question and encourage them to limit their efforts to the key aspect(s). (Further delimiting may occur when students begin to collect information about the problem.) Have students write out the problem; this forces them to state it clearly. Particularly in group problem solving, have them define the more important terms to make sure everyone is talking about the same thing.

Finally, it is important to give adequate time and effort to this step: the time spent in clarifying and delimiting the problem will result in time saved in later stages and will eventually help students to understand the solution more clearly. This is especially true if the students themselves take the major role in defining the problem.

Devising a Plan of Attack

Encourage students to draw up a search model or plan of attack. Have them decide what method or strategy the problem calls for: experiment, analysis, carrying out a plan, etc. Also have them decide whether the emphasis should be on drawing a conclusion from available information, searching for adequate information, or creating new approaches in order to solve the problem. In this regard encourage flexibility and willingness to try various approaches and search models, not just one or two.

On a long-term basis, give students instruction and practice in the different strategies for solving various types of problems: for example, the strict scientific method and philosophical analysis (making distinctions between important aspects of something), working both from the requirements of the problem and from the requirements of the solution, looking for a general principle that might be involved rather than several points of disconnected information.

Searching for Relevant Information

Make sure students possess the necessary library skills plus the skills of processing information: organizing, summarizing main ideas, outlining. Suggest sources of information, both general reference works and specific books and articles.

Encourage open-mindedness: students should be willing to use any source of information as long as it is relevant and valuable.

Formulating Possible Solutions or Plans

Accept all hypotheses and opinions that students offer. Once they have expressed all that they can think of, have them select the most promising hypotheses from the many that have been offered. Have students state the most promising hypotheses, positions or plans clearly, even in written form; they provide guidance for the rest of the process.

With regard to the formulation of hypotheses, there are some important long-range suggestions to consider. In general, encourage divergent production of ideas through such means as brainstorming. Give training particularly in flexibility, perhaps through exercises such as unusual uses of common objects or different ways of solving math problems. In addition, give students practice in systematic approaches to hypothesis formulation, such as starting with general possibilities and gradually constructing more specific possibilities, rather than coming up with too specific suggestions for solution at the beginning. At the same time appreciate the developmental level of your students, particularly their ability to formulate many possibilities systematically (high school) or their tendency to proceed on a trial and error basis (elementary school). Encourage high school students to think in terms of relevant possibilities.

Evaluating Possible Solutions

Emphasize valid evidence: proof, reasons, data; have students give not just statements or opinions but also the basis for them. During this phase ask penetrating questions; raise questions concerning the various positions; encourage students to raise objections to several possible solutions. Let the students do the evaluating; don't do it for them. In groups, encourage interaction, with students criticizing and supporting various positions. Structure groups somewhat loosely rather than center authority in the hands of one or two persons.

Encourage objectivity in reasoning and in the evaluation of evidence; encourage suspended judgment when the evidence is not convincing. Suggest that students be open-minded to all solutions; concentrate on evidence rather than who says it. Encourage flexibility: if one solution, originally thought best, doesn't work out, suggest there may be a better solution.

On a long-range basis, make sure students have developed critical thinking skills, e.g., ability to distinguish fact from opinion, truth from assumption, ability to evaluate primary, secondary, and hear-say sources of information. In addition give practice in "if-then" type of thinking, control of variables, grouping ideas into more abstract concepts, applying abstract principles to situations—especially in high school when students are more able to think in these ways.

Verifying the Solution

Have students summarize the proof and then check its logic and correctness. Where relevant, give instruction on statistical analysis of data, or perhaps have a student who is good in math do the analysis for the group.

Solution Accepted

Particularly in group problem solving, have someone state the conclusion reached as clearly as possible. Having students state the conclusion in their own words helps them to understand it clearly, allows the teacher to check for inaccuracies or misunderstandings, and helps the students remember and apply the solution more easily.

It is important never to omit this step of stating the solution or the new knowledge obtained. The purpose of the whole process is to reach a solution or new knowledge, and it should be made as explicit as possible.

Evaluating Problem-Solving Ability

How can a teacher evaluate the problem-solving process in his students? There are several ways ranging from observation, through essay questions, to objective test items. We will consider them each in turn.

Observation

A very useful technique is that of the informal observation of group problem-solving sessions or of board or seat work of individual students to see how well they solve problems. Seeing students in action in this way provides the best basis for evaluating the actual process of problem solving.

If you want to make your observation more systematic, you can make up a checklist based on the main phases or steps in the problem-solving process and use it as a guide in your evaluation.

Essay Questions

Essay items are appropriate for evaluating a student's ability to solve problems in a certain field and also for evaluating specific aspects of the problem-solving process. For instance, the following question is designed to evaluate a student's problem-solving ability in economics.

> A new country of three and one-half million people has just been formed in East Africa. It has rich natural resources, a poor but freedom-conscious population, and a moderately good school system plus one college. You have been called in as an economic consultant to help plan an economic system that will provide as high a standard of living as possible for all of the people. Using your knowledge of the various types of economic systems, draw up a system that will best help the new country reach their goal. Explain why you incorporate each element into the system.

Questions such as the following can be asked to identify how well students can do in one phase of the process—in this case becoming aware and sensitive to problems.

> A group of men are planning to start an importing business (wholesale) in a midwestern state. Draw up a list of problems they will have to consider before deciding whether the business will be profitable or not.

Finally, you should not undersell the take-home essay question consisting of a major or involved problem to be solved. This will allow the student to use the pertinent library resources and other sources of information important for solving the problem.

Objective Items

To some extent objective items can be used to measure your students' problem-solving abilities. For instance in math:

> A man wants to have a television set shipped to a city 250 miles away. He is told that railroad freight is the cheapest way to send it. The rates quoted him per 100 pounds are:
>
> | 100 miles | $1.85 |
> |-----------|-------|
> | 200 miles | 2.63 |
> | 300 miles | 3.47 |
>
> with rates in between pro-rated according to distance. The set in the carton weighs 175 pounds. How much will it cost to ship it by rail?
> a. $3.05
> b. $4.63
> c. $5.34
> d. $6.07

Of course the same problem could be given as a short answer question with the options omitted.

Some of the particular abilities or steps involved in the problem-solving process can also be measured through an objective format. For instance, the following item is designed to measure the ability to structure a problem.

> A man is hired at an annual salary of $8,500 with annual increases of $400. Which of the following expressions indicates his salary after X number of years?
> a. $400X + 8,500$
> b. $400(X + 8,500)$
> c. $8,500 + 400(X)$
> d. $8,500 (400 + X)$

A more complex objective item which is designed to measure problem-solving ability, particularly the evaluation of possible solutions, is the following.

> You are a member of the state legislature which is attempting to deal with the problem of marked inequality of income among the citizens of the state, but you also need money to finance the many state-sponsored programs. For each of the policies suggested below, indicate:
> A. If it would reduce the inequality of income
> B. If it would increase the inequality of income
> C. If it would have no effect on the distribution of income
>
> _____ Introduction of a 3 percent state sales tax
> _____ Increase in interstate trucking tax
> _____ Increase in the progression of income tax percentages

_____ Provision for a personal exemption on state income tax
_____ Increase in gasoline tax
_____ Provision for a tax on interest and dividends earned
_____ Tightened controls on business monopoly
_____ Provision for comprehensive medical services
_____ Increase in severance taxes (oil, timber, etc. going out of state)

EXERCISE 11-5. Individual Variations in Problem Solving

What are some of the ways in which individuals differ in their approaches to problem solving? What are some of the more productive approaches to the solving of problems?

The following experiments[4] should illustrate several dimensions of variation in the problem-solving processes of students. Indirectly they will also illustrate some conditions favorable to successful problem solving.

The experiments may be done in pairs or individually (at least some). If they are done in pairs, one student acts as subject, the other as experimenter and recorder. The subject thinks aloud in problem 1 concentrating on the problem rather than answering the experimenter. The experimenter records how the subject solved the problem. The other problems involve the experimenter directly, but he still notes how the subject proceeded.

If the student is working individually, he simply does problems 1 and 4 and then tries to remember how he went about solving them when he later analyzes some of the dimensions of variation in problem solvers. For problems 2 and 3 an individual can ask a friend to solve them while he acts as experimenter.

1. Some economists felt that there was danger of an extreme inflationary boom after World War II. It was the opinion of such economists that the government should control the boom in order to prevent a depression such as the one following the stockmarket crash of 1929. Below are a number of specific suggestions. For each of the following items check:

   A   if it would be *consistent* with the policy of controlling the boom;
   B   if it is directly *inconsistent* with the policy.

   A   B

   _____ _____ Lower the reserve that banks are required to hold against deposits.
   _____ _____ Reduce taxes considerably.
   _____ _____ Encourage the federal reserve banks to buy securities in the open market.

---

4. These problems are taken from the following sources:
(1) B. S. Bloom and L. J. Broder, "Problem Solving Processes of College Students," *Supplementary Educational Monographs,* No. 73 (Chicago: University of Chicago Press, 1950), pp. 1-31.
(3) R. H. Forgus, *Perception* (New York: McGraw-Hill, 1966).
(4) H. E. Durkin, "Trial and Error, Gradual Analysis, and Sudden Reorganization: An Experimental Study of Problem Solving," *Archives of Psychology* 30, No. 210 (1937): 18-84.

2. A car has gone off the road and has hit a tree. Find the cause of the accident by asking a maximum of ten questions answerable by "yes" or "no." The experimenter knows the cause (below).

3.

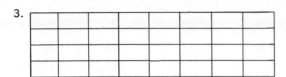

The experimenter thinks of one of the above squares. The subject must try to find out what square it is by asking no more than five questions.

4. Using a thin piece of paper, trace the four pieces of the puzzle, cut them out and make a square with them.

The Answers

1. B in all cases
2. A wheel came off
3. Experimenter's choice
4.

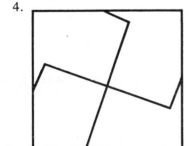

Dimensions of Variation. Cognitive. There are many ways in which students differ in their ability to attack and solve problems. The following dimensions[5] of variation are derived from the type of problems given above. Simply relate the

---

5. Adapted from B. S. Bloom and L. J. Broder, "Problem Solving Processes of College Students," *Supplementary Educational Monographs,* No. 73 (Chicago: University of Chicago Press, 1950), pp. 1-31.

aspect of the problem referred to with the given dimension of the problem-solving process. Most, though not all, of the variables included in the outline are illustrated in the four problems given above.

1. Understanding the nature of the problem
   a. ability to start the attack on the problem
      1. select a key idea, word, phrase
      2. comprehend directions
   b. ability to solve the problem as presented
      1. interpret problem directions, terms
      2. keep directions in mind while solving problem

#1: the problem is concerned with whether or not an action is *consistent* with the policy

2. Understanding the ideas contained in the problem
   a. extent to which one can bring relevant knowledge to bear on the problem
      1. apply knowledge at one's command to the problem
      2. relate readings, lectures etc. to the problem
   b. extent to which one can realize fully the implications of the ideas involved in the problem

#1: knowledge of terms: "inflationary boom," "reserve"

#2: knowledge of automobiles, mechanics

3. General approach to solution of problems
   a. extent of thought about the problem
      1. set up hypotheses, criteria, assumptions
      2. answer on the basis of several substantial rather than a few superficial considerations
      3. use reason rather than impressions and feelings
   b. care and system in thinking about the problem
      1. use systematic plan, method
      2. reorganize, simplify, pull out key terms, break down to subproblems
      3. organized, analytical approach versus hit or miss, trial and error approach

#3: what is necessary to narrow options down, viz. eliminate half of squares each time

#1: getting at the basic principle (amount of money in circulation) versus attacking each item separately

#2: begin with constraints or general hypotheses that will narrow down possibilities versus specific pot-shot hypotheses

#4: analysis and insight versus trial and error

EXERCISE 11-6. Attitudes in Problem Solving

How do individuals differ with regard to attitudes that are related to solving problems? What are some attitudes that help or hinder successful problem solving?

Work each of the following experiments individually (pairs are not necessary).[6] When you have completed all the problems relate how you went about solving them to the dimensions of problem-solving behavior on page 320.

1. In this item you are given two statements and four conclusions. Assume that the statements are true. You are to judge which of the conclusions then logically follows, which must be true if the statements are true. Put a check in the space before the one conclusion which logically follows. If none of the conclusions logically follows, put a check before the last option.

Statements:

Any action that threatens the security of the United States should be made illegal.
All strikes threaten the security of the United States.

Conclusions:

_____ All strikes should be made illegal.
_____ Some restrictions should be placed on the right to strike, but it would be unwise to make them all illegal.
_____ Some strikes should be made illegal.
_____ Unjustifiable strikes should be made illegal.
_____ None of the foregoing conclusions follows.

2. You are given eight coins that look alike but one is lighter than the other seven. Using a balance, determine in no more than *two* weighings which is the lighter coin.

3. Using one or more of the following empty quart jars: Obtain the following quantities of water (quarts) from a faucet:

a. 4	12	63	47
b. 8	10	59	41
c. 6	9	56	35
d. 8	16	48	24
e. 9	18	54	27
f. 7	15	52	22

The Answers:

1. All strikes should be made illegal.
2. Two groups of three, two coins on the side. (a) If the groups of three are of equal weight, then the lighter coin is on the table. When one weighs the two on the table, he sees which is lighter. (b) If the groups are not equal, take the lighter group, weigh two coins with one left on the table; if equal, the one on the table is lighter, if not, one sees which is lighter.
3. (a), (b), and (c) can only be solved by filling the largest first and then drawing off the smaller amounts to get the required quantity. (d) and (e) can be done

6. These problems are taken from: Bloom and Broder, 1950; Simmel, 1953; and Luchins, and Luchins, 1959.

in the same way or more directly and easily by simply filling the two smaller jars. (f) can only be done in the more direct way.

Dimensions of Variation: Affective.   Several dimensions of variation regarding attitudes that students bring with them to their problem solving activities are given below. Relate the given aspects of the experiment problems to the appropriate dimensions of variation in attitudes.

1. Confidence versus uncertainty

#1: reading only the first option versus reading all the options

2. Objectivity versus personal considerations and prejudices

#1: following the requirements of the problem versus allowing conviction on legality of strikes to enter in and color one's thinking

3. Persistence versus giving up

#2: trying different approaches versus giving up

4. Flexibility versus rigidity

#2: switching from an initial grouping of 4s to that of 3s

#3: solving the problem more simply and directly in (d), (e), and (f) rather than continue on with the approach established in (a), (b), and (c)

EXERCISE 11-7. Teaching for Problem Solving

Select a problem in your field, one that will require productive thinking. Plan a series of activities (1) that are aimed at helping the students improve their problem-solving abilities and (2) that reflect the analysis of the problem-solving process we have just gone through.

Suggested Readings

Bloom, B. S. and Broder, Lois J. "Problem Solving Processes of College Students." *Supplementary Educational Monographs,* 1950, No. 73. Chicago: University of Chicago Press.

Davis, G. A. "The Current Status of Research and Theory in Human Problem Solving." *Psychological Bulletin.*

Duncan, C. P. "Recent Research on Human Problem Solving." *Psychological Bulletin* 56 (1959): 397-429.

Johnson, D. M. *The Psychology of Thought and Judgment.* New York: McGraw-Hill, 1955.

Hudgins, B. B. *Problem Solving in the Classroom.* New York: Macmillan, 1966.

Kleinmuntz, B., ed. *Problem Solving: Research, Method and Theory.* New York: Wiley, 1966.

12

Critical
Thinking

If the analysis of the creative process has received extensive attention in research during the past two decades, perhaps the next intellectual process to be studied extensively by educational psychologists will be critical thinking. At present, however, there is a very limited amount of psychological information on critical thinking, certainly nowhere near commensurate with its importance in education and in society. Most of the writing on the topic is either by logicians, who consider more the products of logical thought than the process, or by educators, who offer some general analyses and suggestions for teaching critical thinking. However, critical thinking is so important as a process that we should venture into some analysis of it here, even though it will of necessity be rather limited as far as a basis in research is concerned.

Critical thinking is both an important kind of thinking in its own right and at the same time is integrally related to the other intellectual processes we have just studied. In the comprehension process, unless a person wants to accept everything he hears or reads, he must critically evaluate what he comprehends. In the creative process, evaluation and revision are essential facets of the elaboration phase in which the creative insight is worked out in the concrete. In problem solving, the problem is solved not when the person thinks it is solved but when a proposed solution is evaluated critically on the basis of an established criterion and found to be tenable.

No matter what our field of interest, we are constantly called on to think critically, whether it is to evaluate a defense as appropriate for a certain offense in athletics, to criticize a story, poem or other work of literature, or to judge the cogency of an explanation or theory in the physical or social sciences. Critical thinking can be stressed on any grade level, anywhere from the first grade teacher's "Did you like that story? Why?" to "Does Beard's theory of the frontier hold up against the facts of history?" of the senior high teacher of advanced placement students.

In this brief chapter, we will be limited to a general treatment of the nature and process of critical thinking, based more on a logical analysis than on psychological data, and to some brief suggestions gleaned from the available research on critical thinking as to what factors contribute to the improvement of critical thinking among students. We will have to omit any systematic treatment of theories or models of the process because there is not enough research on the topic for anyone to have braved the formulation of a theory that attempts to explain what goes on in the process of critical thinking. Finally, although both the experimental and the factor analytical studies of critical thinking abilities are still in their infancy, we will offer whatever suggestions for teaching and evaluating critical thinking that seem warranted by the data.

Specifically we will examine the following questions.

What is the nature of critical thinking?
How can the process of critical thinking be explained?
What intellectual abilities does it involve?
What conditions or factors are related to critical thinking?
How can a teacher help his students think more critically?
How can critical thinking be measured?

EXERCISE 12-1. The Main Elements in Critical Thinking

Read the following paragraph and see whether or not you agree with it.

The scope of educational psychology as an applied science might be regarded as practically coterminous with that of psychology itself. This is true for at least two reasons. There is hardly any aspect of the whole field of psychology which could not conceivably be brought into play in some educational problem, because the enterprise of education is concerned with many kinds of people—of different ages, degrees of ability and drive, and kinds of personality—as well as with many kinds of subject matter and skills. The description, analysis, and prediction of such diverse forms of behavior as may be encountered in education could demand findings, principles, and techniques from almost any phase of psychological science. Secondly, it can be claimed that the concept which unifies all psychology, and which is its central concern, is *learning*. Obviously, learning is the concern of education. (Carroll 1963)

Do you agree with the main proposition in the paragraph; on what basis did you go about deciding?

_____ 1. Whether the author offered any reasons in support of his main proposition

_____ 2. Whether the reasons are true or not, i.e. whether or not they are based on how things really are

_____ 3. Whether the reasons are logically connected with the statement which they are intended to prove

_____ 4. Whether the author is competent and knowledgeable in the subject

Actually any of these considerations can enter into your evaluation of the paragraph. Most relate to the reasons or evidence offered in support of the main proposition: initially (1) whether any reasons are offered at all, but mainly (2) whether the reasons are true and (3) whether they are logically connected to the proposition. Although your main concern was most probably the content of the paragraph, i.e. the main statement plus its proof, you may also have considered the authority of the writer (4) an important concern even though extrinsic and secondary to the actual content of the paragraph.

As far as the arguments themselves are concerned, the first one about the general applicability of psychology to education is generally true. The second argument about learning being the unifying factor to all branches of psychology (clinical, psychometrics, industrial as well as experimental, developmental, personality) is open to question. On the face of it, it seems to be a matter more of opinion than of fact and hence must either be proven more fully or be judged as a weak argument because it does not conform to the way things actually are.

In terms of whether or not the arguments are logically connected to the main proposition, it definitely seems that they are: both arguments deal with the close relationship between educational psychology and psychology in general.

As far as the degree of authority of the author there is no question: he is generally recognized to be one of the leading educational psychologists in the country.

The Nature of Critical Thinking

Critical thinking is not a unitary process. It is a complex of several abilities that involve a judgment about a communication or other information in the light of some criterion. Any act of critical thinking includes (1) a comparison of a production, a statement or a line of reasoning with a recognized criterion, and (2) a decision as to how well it measures up to that criterion.

The criterion used in such a judgment can be any one or more of the following: truth or fact, beauty or goodness, similarity or consistency, logic, clarity or necessity, accuracy or completeness, usefulness, appropriateness or effectiveness for a given purpose. The person who makes the judgment must have a knowledge of the criteria as they relate to the subject field of the statement or production as well as some knowledge of the subject field itself.

On a more immediate level, in order to critically evaluate any communication, a person must first comprehend it adequately: its main theme and propositions plus the evidence and line of reasoning offered in their support. Perhaps in addition he will have to analyze its various elements if it is at all complex. Only then is he in a position to evaluate it.

The actual evaluation of a communication includes two phases: (1) the evaluation of the main propositions plus the evidence offered for them, particularly how they measure up to the relevant external criteria; and (2) the evaluation of the internal line of reasoning used, whether it is valid and logical.

EXERCISE 12-2. Critical Thinking in the Classroom

Teachers often use articles from good newspapers or serious magazines as source of materials for teaching critical thinking. In the sample lesson given below,[1] the teacher first distributes mimeographed copies of a letter to the editor published in the *New York Times* and then bases the class session on an analysis and evaluation of the reasoning used in the letter.

Analyze the informal lesson plan, indicating which section or question plus expected answer relates to which phase of the critical thinking process: preliminary (comprehension), evaluation of the evidence offered, or evaluation of the line of reasoning used.

Right to Be Heard

To the Editor:

President Nixon has said that under no circumstances will he be affected by the campus demonstrations against the war in Vietnam. His rationale is that policy cannot be allowed to be made in the streets, for that would destroy "the democratic process." In taking this line of thought, the President misreads the Constitution and misunderstands the nature of the democratic political process.

For the same Constitution that provides for the election of the President and of the members of Congress also provides for freedom of speech, press, assembly, and petition for the redress of grievances. The democratic process by which our chief governmental officers are elected would not in essentials be different from the election process in the U.S.S.R. if we did not have—and use—the guarantees of the First Amendment.

But of what use are the freedom of assembly and the right of petition for the redress of grievances if our elected officials say to the people that they might just as well address their petitions to a blank wall? Implied in the First Amendment is the duty of the President and of the Congress to accept petitions when made peaceably, and to consider them on their merits. This does not mean that what is requested must always be granted. Of course not. But to say that the Government is indifferent to what people on the street, exercising their constitutional liberties, say are their grievances is in effect to tell them that their only resort is force and violence.

In constitutional contemplation, a document is not the only form petition can take. The Supreme Court has said that a march or a parade, or a peaceful mass meeting, or a silent and peaceful sit-in, in a public place where the protestants have a right to be, is an exercise of the constitutional right of petition. This, of course, is the intent of the Oct. 15 demonstrations—an appeal to the President and to the Congress regarding a matter of the gravest national concern.

Whether one is for or against the objectives of the Oct. 15 demonstrations has nothing to do with the exercise of the constitutional right, nor

---

1. Adapted from M. Finder, "Teaching to Comprehend," *Journal of Reading* 13 (1970): 581-86, 633-36. The letter appeared in *The New York Times,* October 19, 1969, p. E15. Copyright 1969 by the New York Times Company. Reprinted by permission.

with the constitutional duty of the President to listen, respectfully and sympathetically, to what millions of American citizens are desperately trying to say to him. They have a right to speak, and, what is more important in this context, a right to be heard.

Milton R. Konvitz
Ithaca, N. Y., Oct. 14, 1969

The writer of the above letter is a Cornell University professor and author of books on constitutional law and theory.

1. What is the writer's main theme and purpose?

   Main purpose: to persuade the reader that (1) citizens have a right to be heard on issues, and (2) they also have a right to demonstrate against government policy (war in Vietnam).

2. What line of argument does the writer present to support his theme?

   Constitution, 1st Amendment: freedom of assembly and petition for redress of grievances.

   useless if elected officials are unresponsive;

   —officials must consider petitions on their merits, otherwise they imply that the only resort is force and violence;

   —guarantee of 1st amendment is the difference between Communist dictatorship and democracy.

   Supreme Court: petition can be either a document or a peaceful demonstration.

3. How would you characterize the organization of the letter?

   Order: statement of problem, statement of fallacy, arguments for position, solution.

   Basis: logical

4. What is the tone or mood of the communication?

   Serious, one of concern. Clear from overall context, language, references.

5. Are the arguments used fact or opinion?

   Fact.

6. Are the proofs actually stated or are mere assumptions given?

   Stated.

7. Is the evidence fully documented? Why or why not?

   The 1st amendment argument is fully explained and even partially quoted.

   The Supreme Court reference is not fully documented because of the more or less informal nature of the communication, a letter to the editor.

8. What degree of authority does the writer possess?

   Editor's note indicates "expert in constitutional law."

9. Is there a logical connection between the main proposition and the arguments?

Yes, Both the main proposition and the arguments are concerned with the right to petition and to demonstrate. The arguments clearly relate to, and support, the main theme.

Indicate which section is related to which general phase of critical thinking given below. Put the proper numbers in the respective blanks.

_____ Preliminary: making sure a communication is understood in its important aspects.
_____ Evaluation of evidence: judging whether the evidence is true.
_____ Evaluation of logical reasoning: judging whether the reasoning is valid.

Before one criticizes a communication he must fully comprehend it. In the example, the teacher tried to make sure his students grasped (1) the author's theme and purpose, (2) his line of argument, (3) the organizational pattern used, and (4) the mood or tone of the letter.

The class session then turned to a critical evaluation of the letter, with the teacher asking questions both about the truth of the evidence—whether it was fact or opinion (5), whether it was fully documented (7), and what degree of authority on the matter the author had (8); and also about the validity of the line of reasoning—first, whether some proof was actually stated (6), and then whether there was a necessary connection between the proof and the main proposition of the letter (9).

The Critical Thinking Process

When we analyze the critical thinking process more fully, we can identify the mental activities which are important in an act of critical thinking.

Some *preliminary* activities which are often—though not always—involved in the overall process are the following.

1. Sensitivity to problems or a critical attitude toward the world around us, being aware that some things in our environment could stand improvement.
2. Judging whether or not an issue or problem has been fully identified and adequately defined, i.e. stated in terms sufficiently broad to include the whole problem, but also in a way that delimits it to a scope that will allow for a workable solution.
3. Judging whether the important terms of the issue are clearly defined, whether they are explained fully or the meaning is indicated sufficiently through a synonym or example.
4. Although it does not involve an evaluative ability, we should add as a preliminary activity what is often the necessary prerequisite for critical thinking, i.e., an adequate comprehension of the communication (as mentioned above).

The most *essential* activities of the critical thinking process consist of judgments about the truth of the evidence and the validity of the line of reasoning. The person makes a judgment about a communication or production in terms of the evidence offered in its support. This involves a judgment in the light of criteria that are external to the work or statement itself. The person examines the evidence and decides: (1) whether it is true, i.e. whether it has a basis in reality; (2) whether it measures up to the appropriate degree of certitude or standard of excellence for the subject field, e.g. demonstrated proof in mathematics, a high degree of statistical probability in the behavioral sciences, unity, balance and recognized technique in the fine arts; and finally (3) whether it is accurate and reliable, whether it is sufficiently precise given the methods of analysis or measurement available, whether it is carefully documented, and whether it can be corroborated or replicated by another person.

The person also makes a judgment about the connection between a statement and the evidence offered in its support. This entails an evaluation of the internal validity of the line of reasoning, whether or not it is logical and convincing. He must decide: (1) whether the statement has a satisfactory basis, i.e. that some proof is provided in the first place rather than simply assumed, and that the proof is sufficiently complete and is strong enough to support the statement; (2) whether the statement or conclusion follows either from the data (in inductive reasoning) or from the given premises (in deductive or "if-then" reasoning); conclusions derived from data usually possess a relative degree of certitude, whereas those deduced from premises should follow necessarily; (3) whether the connection between the proof and the statement is clear, whether the evidence is relevant and supportive of the statement and the line of reasoning contains no ambiguities.

On the basis of this double evaluation of the truth of the evidence and the validity of the line of reasoning, the person can arrive at one of the following decisions regarding the communication: (1) to accept it as convincing; (2) to accept it with some reservations; (3) to suspend judgment until further evidence is available; (4) to reject much of the communication as inadequate; (5) to reject the communication as invalid.

Intellectual Abilities Involved in Critical Thinking

What intellectual abilities are engaged in the process of critical thinking? Obviously it involves the operation of evaluation, particularly evaluation of relations, systems, and implications. The factor analytic work on the process of evaluation is minimal when compared to that on the other intellectual processes, most of the studies have used only the criteria of consistency and similarity. However, if we are allowed to interpolate from what is already known regarding the structure of intelligence plus the above analysis of the nature of critical thinking, we can derive the following hypotheses as to what abilities are active in an act of critical thinking.

First of all, although critical thinking is most closely related to the process of evaluation, it is not coterminous with it. For instance, sensitivity to problems is a critical attitude that consists in an awareness of deficiencies and implications of a current situation. Although originally thought to be an evaluation ability, Guilford has more recently classified this as a cognition factor, specifically cognition of implications. Similarly, judging whether a problem has been adequately identified and structured entails the awareness or cognition of a system.

The other phases of the critical thinking process, however, involve evaluative abilities, particularly the evaluation of:

> units (semantic): judging whether or not the important terms have been adequately defined
>
> relations: judging the truth and reliability of the evidence, whether it has a basis in fact or conforms to reality, and whether it is accurate and well-documented
>
> systems: judging the line of reasoning of a communication, whether a statement has a satisfactory basis offered in its support, and whether the connection between the statement and the proof offered is clear and unambiguous
>
> implications: judging whether or not a statement follows from the data collected or from the premises provided.

To summarize, the intellectual abilities that are involved in the critical thinking process appear in table 12-1.

Table 12-1. *Abilities Involved in Critical Thinking*

	Units	Classes	Relations	Systems	Transformations	Implications
Cognition				*		*
Memory						
Divergent Thinking						
Convergent Thinking						
Evaluation	*		*	*		*

EXERCISE 12-3. Questions Designed to Encourage Critical Thinking

The main way to encourage critical thinking in the classroom is to ask questions that call for the critical evaluation of problems, evidence, and patterns of reasoning. Given below are some questions that teachers who are concerned with developing the critical thinking abilities of their students might ask in different subjects. Indicate which aspect of the critical thinking process each question refers to; questions 1 through 4 represent preliminary activities, questions 5 and 6 have to do with the truth of evidence, and questions 7 through 11 refer to the validity of arguments.

1. Do you think the problem as Jake states it is comprehensive enough? Does it include all of the important aspects?

2. You say that the problem is about the epidemic of scarlet fever in the town. Should we pin it down a little more specifically, or can we solve the problem as it stands?

3. One of the major issues in recent history is the war in Southeast Asia. What are some of the problems that have been caused by the war?

4. Webster defines revolution as "a total or radical change." Does this definition fit the context of our problem?

5. The book states that seventy percent of the people of the state favor fluoridation. Is there anything you want to know further about this figure?

6. The author argues against war by saying that war is the main cause of famine, disease, and hardship among men. Is this true?

7. The author of the article states that the United States should avoid commerce with China because China does not want peace. Is this reasoning based more on fact or on an assumption that requires further proof?

8. The author argues that without the profit motive the owners of business and industry would soon lose their interest in producing and selling, business would decline, and eventually the whole economy would suffer. Is this a convincing argument for the necessity of the profit motive?

9. What do you think of Huck Finn's line of reasoning when he says: "Jim said bees wouldn't sting idiots; but I don't believe that, because I had tried them lots of times myself, and they wouldn't sting me."

10. On the basis of the facts presented in the case, the judge declared that the man was guilty. Was the judge's conclusion warranted?

11. The author presents many facts and documents them well. But do they actually prove his main thesis?

Preliminary activities
_____ sensitivity to problems
_____ problem delineated
_____ terms defined adequately

Truth of evidence
_____ basis in fact, reality
_____ possesses a degree of certitude
_____ accurate, documented

Validity of argument
_____ evidence is provided
_____ conclusion follows from data, premises
_____ connection between proof and statement is clear

Among the preliminary activities relating to critical thinking together with the teacher questions that are aimed at developing them are:

sensitivity to problems (in this case subproblems related to a major

problem): this is illustrated by the question on the problems created
by the war (3);

delineation of the problem: the problem must be broad and inclusive
enough to take into account all of the important aspects or variables
(1) and must also be delimited and specific enough to be workable,
i.e. with the necessary distinctions made (2);

adequate definition of terms: a judgment regarding how well the essential
terms have been defined is also in order (4).

One of the two main considerations in critical thinking is a judgment about
the truth of the evidence offered in support of a thesis. Specifically this involves
judgments concerning its

basis in fact or reality: whether it is based on or conforms to the real
world (6);

degree of certitude: whether it is certain or highly probable (degree of
statistical probability of the percentage in 5); accuracy, documenta-
tion: whether the data collected has been precisely measured or
carefully documented (5).

The second main consideration in critical thinking is a judgment about the
validity of the line of reasoning. This involves judgments concerning whether a
proposition has a sufficient basis or proof in support of it rather than no real
proof or simply an assumption (7); a conclusion follows from the data obtained—inductive reasoning (10)—or from the premises given—deductive reasoning (9); there is a clear and necessary connection between a statement and its
proof (8, 11).

Conditions Favoring Critical Thinking

What are some of the conditions favoring the development of critical thinking
that can be derived from the limited research on the topic? The following
conclusions seem warranted.

Explicit Teaching

If students are to improve significantly in critical thinking ability, critical
thinking must be taught for explicitly and students must be given practice in its
various aspects. It will not improve automatically through the study of a certain
subject matter (Barlow 1938, Zapf 1938).

Improvement in Critical Thinking

Critical thinking ability of students can be significantly improved through
materials and exercises designed specifically for training students in critical
thinking. The improvement in the ability to think critically seems to be rather
general, and applies to most of the problems, topics, and situations with which

the student deals. Such improvement is limited, however, to subject fields and problems that are within the person's experience and area of competence. For example, he must have a knowledge of the fine arts and of the relevant criteria before he can make critical judgments about works of art or music (Glaser 1941, Grener and Raths 1945).

Critical thinking ability can also be improved by special attention to it (examining assumptions, testing out hypotheses, etc.) in academic subjects such as science, mathematics and social studies (Anderson 1944, Edwards 1950, Zant 1952, Kastrinos 1964, Rickert 1967).

Propaganda Devices

Instruction in propaganda devices and how to detect them can be effective, but only if this instruction is related to the specific subject fields in which students are expected to improve. Simple instruction on the forms of propaganda unrelated to the appropriate content areas will not make students resistant to the influence of propaganda (Osborn 1939).

Critical Thinking and Intelligence

Critical thinking ability correlates to a moderate extent with "general intelligence" or cognition, around .50, with a range from .30 to .70. It correlates slightly lower with reading ability, around .45, give or take .10 points (Glaser 1941, Watson and Glaser 1952, American Council on Education 1953).

Teaching for Critical Thinking

How can a teacher help his students develop their critical thinking abilities? From our brief analysis above we can derive the following suggestions.

Explicit Teaching

Include training in critical thinking as an important objective in your teaching. Do not expect your students to improve in it automatically by simply studying a subject field; critical thinking must be taught for explicitly.

Background

A thorough knowledge of a subject field and specifically of the criteria for valid evidence or creative productions in that field is necessary for making critical judgments relating to a subject area. Impress on students the necessity of this broad knowledge for making informed criticisms and also give explicit instruction on the relevant criteria for judging statements and productions in your subject field(s).

Instruction and Practice

Provide instruction and practice in the critical thinking process both in itself and particularly in the context of your subject field as well as in relation to school and community issues. Stress such aspects as: clear definition of terms and problems; the strength and truth of evidence; accuracy and reliability of evidence; the recognition of assumptions and the necessity of supplying proof for statements; the necessity for a clear connection between proof and a statement; the requirements for deriving generalizations or conclusions from data and premises (inductive and deductive reasoning).

In addition, give students instruction and practice in detecting propaganda devices in the context of specific subject fields. Point out such devices as: glittering generalities ("freedom," "American"), name calling ("atheist," "Communist"), testimonial by a celebrity,. stacking the case by presenting only favorable facts, repetition of slogans, etc.

Measuring Critical Thinking

What techniques can a teacher use to evaluate the critical thinking abilities of his students? There are several, ranging from more informal observational techniques to standardized tests of critical thinking.

Informal Techniques

You might give your class a statement, a longer passage, a case plus a solution, or a work of art, and have them evaluate it either as a group or in half a dozen smaller groups. Then observe how they go about evaluating it: what criteria they use, how critical they are about the validity and accuracy of the evidence, and how thoroughly they examine the line or reasoning.

Similarly, problems or specific questions such as the essay and objective questions that we will examine below can be given orally to the class and the answers discussed briefly. This can serve both as an opportunity for the teacher to evaluate his students' critical thinking ability and also as a learning exercise in critical thinking for the students.

Essay Questions

An essay question designed to measure critical thinking usually begins with the presentation of a statement, longer passage or work of art and then asks the student to evaluate it in some way, e.g. criticize (+ and/or −), defend or refute, evaluate its line of reasoning, evaluate it in terms of suggested criteria. Consider the following question in science.

1. On the basis of your study of earth science so far this term, defend or refute the following statement, giving reasons and examples for your position.

    "Earth science is more of an observational science than an experimental science."

Or in literature, a typical question calling for critical thinking:

2. Evaluate *To Kill a Mockingbird* in terms of the criteria of good literature given by Aristotle in his *Poetics* (e.g. unity, universality, catharsis).

A similar question on the primary level would be the following oral question.

3. Tell what you thought of the story *The Hare and the Tortoise.* Was the story interesting? Why?

    Does it have a good beginning, ending?

    Are the words and phrases colorful?

Other types of essay questions are also available, depending on your ingenuity. The following question, for example, gives some arguments that students used in a class discussion on an issue and calls for a critical evaluation of them.

4. In our discussion about teachers being made to take an oath of loyalty to the government and to swear that they do not advocate any form of government alien to that of the United States, the following arguments were given for either side. Evaluate each of the arguments, showing (1) whether or not it is true and (2) to what extent it supports the position for which it was offered.

    Arguments offered in favor of a loyalty oath:

    It is dangerous to allow those who do not believe in the American way of life to teach in the public schools.

    Any person concerned about democracy should be willing to take an oath of loyalty to the government.

    Arguments offered against a loyalty oath:

    No government can make laws regarding a person's thoughts and convictions, only his actions.

    Anyone willing to overthrow the government will lie about his intentions anyway.

Objective Items

Objective items measuring critical thinking are very difficult to construct. If you are interested in trying your hand at it, you might profit from examining some of the items on one of the few available standardized tests of critical thinking. The most popular measure, the *Watson-Glaser Critical Thinking Appraisal,* includes such items as the following designed to measure the students' ability to evaluate the strength of arguments.

1. Indicate whether each of the arguments below is strong or weak in relation to the side of the issue it is offered in support of.

    Issue: Should groups in this country who are opposed to some of our government's policies be permitted unrestricted freedom of press and speech?

	Strong	Weak
a. Yes; a democratic state thrives on free and unrestricted discussion, including criticism. . . .	___	___
b. No; if given full freedom of press and speech, opposition groups would cause serious internal strife and make our government basically unstable, eventually leading to loss of our democracy. . . .	___	___
c. No; the countries opposed to our form of government do not permit the free expression of our point of view in their territory. . . .	___	___

An example of a more complex objective item measuring critical thinking is the following taken from the American Council on Education's *A Test of Critical Thinking,* an excellent test but more for the college level and unfortunately out of print. This particular item is designed to evaluate the students' ability to select the information pertinent to the solution of a problem.

2. In a radio broadcast the following story was told: "The people in a little mining town in Pennsylvania get all their water without purification from a clear, swift-running mountain stream. In a cabin on the bank of the stream about half a mile above the town, a worker was very sick with typhoid fever during the first part of December. During his illness his waste materials were thrown on the snow. About the middle of March the snow melted rapidly and ran into the stream. Approximately two weeks later typhoid fever broke out in the town. Many of the people became sick and 114 died."

Conclusion: The speaker then said that this story showed how *the sickness of this man caused widespread illness and the death of over one hundred people.*

Items (a) through (f) are statements which might appear in a discussion of this conclusion. Assuming that the story as told was true, mark each statement according to the following scale:
1. The statement argues *for* the conclusion.
2. The statement argues *against* the conclusion.
3. The statement argues *neither* for nor against the conclusion.

_____ a. Typhoid fever organisms have been known to survive for several months at temperatures near the freezing point.

_____ b. Good doctors should be available when an epidemic hits a small town.

_____ c. There may have been other sources of contamination along the stream.

_____ d. Typhoid organisms are usually killed if subjected to temperatures near the freezing point for a period of several months.

_____ e. Sickness and death usually result in a great economic loss to a small town.

_____ f. There may have been other sources of typhoid fever germs in the town, such as milk or food contaminated by some other person.

EXERCISE 12-4. Teaching for Critical Thinking

Select a passage or other communication in your field and plan a short class session listing the questions you will ask to stimulate a critical evaluation of the communication. The communication might take the form of a work of art or piece of music in the fine arts, a demonstration or product of a skill in the practical arts, or simply a passage, speech, or poem in the academic subjects.

For each question you plan indicate in the margin at which aspect of the critical thinking process you are aiming.

Suggested Readings

Ennis, R. H. *Logic in Teaching.* Englewood Cliffs, N. J.: Prentice-Hall, 1969.

Glaser, E. M. *An Experiment in the Development of Critical Thinking.* Teachers College Contributions to Education, No. 843. New York: Teachers College, Columbia University, 1941.

part five

Learning: Skills and Attitudes

In addition to the main types of learning that we have treated so far, there are two other very important types in education; namely learning psychomotor skills and learning attitudes and values. In fact, in some subject fields these are even more important than the types of learning with which we have been dealing. In any event, no matter what your field is you will be teaching some types of skills and will be trying to convey certain attitudes and values to your students. Hence, even though they are placed last among the types of learning, they are still important for you as a teacher.

Again, in these two chapters the outline we have used in the previous chapters will be followed for each type of learning, i.e. the nature, the process, the abilities involved, the conditions, applications and evaluation. However, for skill learning the important area of a task taxonomy will be added, and for attitudes and values some relevant dimensions will replace the usual section on abilities involved.

13

Skill
Learning

The main type of learning that students of the more practical and artistic fields are regularly engaged in is the learning of psychomotor skills. Doing a square dance or passing a football, operating a key punch or typing, making a soufflé or sewing a dress, stroking a canvas with a brush or playing the piano, operating a lathe or building a cabinet—all are familiar skills to be learned by the student of physical education, business, home economics, fine arts, or industrial arts. But other students as well are called on to learn psychomotor skills, whether it is learning how to write in script, how to enunciate words distinctly in language arts, how to read and make maps in social studies, how to bend glass tubes to the shape required for a chemistry experiment, etc.

How are motor skills learned? What psychomotor abilities do students bring with them to the learning of such skills? What are some factors that should be considered if skill learning is to be as effective as possible? How can teachers guide their students toward efficient learning of skills? And finally, how can psychomotor abilities and skills be measured? These are the main questions that we will examine in this chapter.

The Nature of Psychomotor Skills

In a sense, psychomotor skills are the most human things we learn. On one hand, they represent the blending of mind and body that is man; on the other hand, they allow man to achieve one of his key functions, the control of his environment.

Psychomotor skills are just what the name implies: organized patterns of activity that are as much intellectual as physical. Although we most readily observe the physical aspects, either the gross movements of the body or the manipulative movements of the hands, the intellectual aspects—the knowledge of how to do and the image or strategy of what to do (or make)—are actually more important. For the psychology of the intellectual side of skill learning and performance, you will have to apply much of what we have treated under creativity and factual learning; in this chapter we will be concerned mainly with the analysis of the physical side of psychomotor skill learning.

Actually, there are several types of skills: thinking, language, perceptual, and motor. The thinking skills of problem solving, creative and critical thinking were treated in chapters 10, 11, and 12. Language skills were treated to some extent in chapter 6 on verbal learning and chapter 9 on comprehension. The perceptual skills such as the perception of spatial patterns and relations, object discrimination, and the perception of speed, sound, and the like, have been omitted from this volume, not because they are unimportant in themselves, but because they have limited relevance for classroom learning.

We should note that often other types of skills are involved in the learning and use of one type. For instance, language skills are important in the initial stages of motor skill learning when students listen to a teacher or read about the skill; perceptual skills are included as an integral part of any motor skill that involves an object, either moving or stationary; thinking skills, both analysis, problem solving and creative thinking, are often involved in the use of motor skills, particularly those that involve several variables, competition, or creative production. One type of skill, then, while different and distinct from other types, is frequently interrelated with them either in its learning or its performance.

In this chapter, we will be concerned primarily with motor skills, both the gross body skills emphasized in physical education and the manipulative skills of the practical and fine arts.

Psychomotor Abilities

What psychomotor abilities can be identified and how are they related to learning skills? On the basis of the extensive factor analytical work of Fleishman and others on the identification of psychomotor abilities, Guilford has constructed a schema of motor abilities that is somewhat similar to his structure of intellect, except that it is two dimensional instead of three. Taking into account all the identified motor abilities such as manual dexterity, reaction time, leg speed, and general body strength, Guilford noted that there were two dimensions found in each of them, type of ability and part of body involved.

Some abilities essentially involved *strength,* others *speed,* and still others *coordination.* But there were other types discernable as well: (1) the rate at which bodily movement starts from a stationary position (*impulsion*),[1] (2) the

---

1. As distinct from speed, which pertains to the rate of movements after they have started.

accuracy of bodily position or of directed movements (static and dynamic *precision*), and (3) the extent to which the body is free to bend (*flexibility*).

These six types of psychomotor abilities form one dimension of the matrix, while the different parts of the body form the other. Some motor abilities involve the entire body; other factors involve certain parts such as the trunk, limbs, hands, or fingers. Finally, we might add the bodily complex that is involved in speech, although most of the relevant factors are only hypothetical at present. The two-dimensional schema of psychomotor abilities, adapted from Guilford (1958), is presented in table 13-1.

Table 13-1. *Matrix of Psychomotor Factors, adapted from Guilford (1958)*

| Part of Body Involved | Type of Ability | | | | | |
	Strength	Impulsion	Speed	Precision	Coordination	Flexibility
Gross	General Static & Dynamic Strength	General Reaction Time		Static & Dynamic Balance	Bodily Coordination	
Trunk	Trunk Strength					Extent & Dynamic Flexibility
Limbs	Limb Strength	Limb Thrust	Arm & Leg Speed	Arm Aiming & Steadiness	Multilimb Coordination	Leg Flexibility
Hand	Strength of Grip		Hand Speed	Hand Aiming & Steadiness	Manual Dexterity	
Finger			Finger Speed	Finger Aiming	Finger Dexterity	
Speech	Volume	Articulation	Rate	Enunciation		

Notice that such aspects of psychomotor functioning as agility and stamina are not found in the matrix. Agility is probably a complex of several abilities: impulsion, speed and coordination factors. Stamina or endurance seems to be a composite of physical and physiological characteristics plus a motivational factor, the will to produce maximum effort over a prolonged time in spite of physical discomfort.

A knowledge of the various psychomotor abilities is very important for a teacher since the first step in teaching a psychomotor skill is to assess the relevant abilities that are essential to that skill. On one hand, this will let the teacher know whether the student possesses the necessary abilities to a sufficient degree to acquire the skill with reasonable effort (he may be stronger in other abilities that are important for other motor skills, so that it would be more economical for him to expend his efforts at those). On the other hand, the assessment will make the teacher aware of the abilities that need further development before instruction in a skill actually begins. Finally, it will also give both the student and the teacher some idea of the level of proficiency at which to aim.

EXERCISE 13-1. Psychomotor Abilities and Various Skills

Different psychomotor abilities are essential for different skills. For the skills given below, try to analyze what specific abilities are necessary. Referring to the above matrix and, if necessary, the definitions of the basic types of ability on page 342, match the appropriate abilities with each skill by indicating 1A for General Strength, 2F for Dynamic Flexibility, etc. You can consider both the psychomotor abilities already identified, those actually contained in the matrix, and even the hypothesized abilities, those that would belong in the blank spaces if they had been identified.

	A	B	C	D	E	F
	Strength	Impulsion	Speed	Precision	Coordination	Flexibility
1. Gross						
2. Trunk						
3. Limbs						
4. Hand						
5. Finger						

_____ Running

_____ Throwing a baseball

_____ Lifting weights

_____ Gymnastics, modern dance

_____ Archery

_____ Typing, key punching

_____ Playing the guitar, violin

_____ A psychomotor skill in your field

Some of the psychomotor abilities that are essential for the skills listed are listed below. Perhaps you can discern additional abilities for the skills with which you are familiar.

Running—leg speed (3C) and limb strength (3A) for running in general, plus reaction time (1B) and limb thrust (3B) in the dashes and general dynamic strength (1A) (and stamina) in the distances.

Throwing a baseball—bodily and multilimb coordination (1E, 3E), arm and hand aiming (3D, 4D) plus limb thrust (3B).

Lifting weights—general strength (1A), trunk strength (2A), limb strength (3A), limb thrust (3B).

Gymnastics, the dance—bodily coordination (1E), trunk and leg flexibility (2F, 3F), plus static and dynamic balance (1D).

Archery—arm aiming and steadiness (3D), limb strength (3A), trunk strength (2A).

Typing, key punching—finger dexterity (5E), finger speed (5C), and finger aiming (5D).

Playing the guitar, violin—finger dexterity (5E), finger aiming (5D), hand and finger speed (4C, 5C) (finger flexibility) (5F).

It should also be noted that the relative importance of different abilities varies according to the phase of the skill-learning process. For instance, in the early phase, perceptual and cognition abilities are central. Also, in the earlier stages, the motor abilities of more general relevance are involved, whereas in the latter stages more specific and refined motor abilities are brought to bear. For example, in shooting a basketball, the emphasis shifts from perceptual and cognition factors as instruction begins, to hand aiming and limb thrust in the early practice sessions, to multilimb coordination and finger dexterity in later practice sessions.

Task Analysis

In addition to being aware of the main ability factors required for learning a skill, it is of equal importance for a teacher to analyze the essential characteristics of the skill itself. Such an analysis of the activities involved in a skill is usually referred to as a *task taxonomy*. Although an analysis of what is to be learned is valuable in any type of learning, it is particularly necessary in skill learning. Although a teacher does not have to be an expert at the skill itself, he should have a fairly thorough knowledge of both its general nature and its elements and characteristics before he attempts to teach it.

Some of the dimensions that might be considered in analyzing a psychomotor skill are:

1. Complexity: how many different abilities and types of activities are involved in the task sequence. For example, flying an airplane and directing an orchestra are very complex, whereas playing volleyball and soldering metal are relatively simple.

2. Degree of continuity: to what extent the skill entails continuous activity. For example, running, swimming, and driving a car are continuous tasks since they involve more or less flowing movement, while hitting a baseball and lifting

weights are more discrete since they have a clearly defined beginning and end. In between are serial-type skills such as typing, in which the units can be clearly identified but follow one another in rapid sequence.

3. Activity of the body relative to an object: whether the body and an external object are stationary or in motion at the beginning of the skill sequence. The obvious possibilities, plus typical examples, are:

    a. both the person and the object at rest initially; e.g., driving a golf ball, typing, and sewing;

    b. the body in motion and the object at rest, e.g., a running shot in basketball, skiing;

    c. the body at rest with the object in motion, e.g., hitting a volleyball or baseball, passing a football to a player in motion;

    d. both the body and the object in motion, e.g., most shots in tennis and handball, a pass on the run to a player in motion in football.

Once the teacher and the student are aware of the abilities important for learning a skill and the characteristics of the skill activity itself, they are in a position to start the actual teaching and learning of it.

EXERCISE 13-2.   Task Analysis

Select two or three psychomotor skills either from your subject field or from your favorite extracurricular activity. Analyze each of the skills according to their degree of complexity and continuity, and whether the person and/or the object is at rest or in motion.

Skill	Complexity			Continuity			Body—Object			
	Com-plex	Mod-erate	Sim-ple	Contin-uous	Serial	Dis-crete	Both at Rest	Body in Motion	Object in Motion	Both in Motion
_____										
_____										
_____										
_____										

The Process of Skill Learning

How are skills learned? How is the process best explained? In this section we will examine the various phases involved in learning a skill as well as the leading explanations of what essentially happens in the process of skill acquisition.

The Phases of Skill Learning

An analysis of how most skills are learned shows that basically there are three phases: an early cognitive phase, a lengthy practice phase, and a final autonomous phase. It should be emphasized that these are not completely distinct stages but rather emphases that reflect what mainly takes place during certain points in learning a skill. In other words, the phases overlap to a large extent with the progression from one to the other more continuous than distinct.

Even the order is not inflexible. At times the phases may not follow the sequence indicated, such as when an action is tried and practiced many times and only afterwards is consciously analyzed. However, in most cases of learning a skill, we can discern the order outlined below.

Cognitive Phase.   In the cognitive phase, the student attempts to understand the basic aspects of the skill and what it demands. The whole skill might be demonstrated by one who possesses it and then the essential components analyzed. Similarities and differences between the skill and those that students already possess can be pointed out to advantage, e.g. hitting a softball *and* the forehand in tennis, hitting a softball versus the golf swing.

Although traditionally the cognitive phase has emphasized thorough explanation and verbal exposition, more recently an emphasis has been placed on learner involvement and discovery even at this initial stage. For instance, early try-outs of the basic skill pattern interspersed with discussion sessions during which successful attempts are analyzed and difficulties diagnosed have been found to be extremely effective (Fitts and Posner 1967).

The student's initial trials during this stage are slow and unsure, and he is usually very conscious of each phase of the action pattern. Teacher acceptance and encouragement of attempts that even in some way resemble the correct pattern rather than negative criticism, are very effective in this early stage.

Practice-Fixation Phase.   During the long intermediate phase, the essential actions of the skill are practiced over and over until the student is able to repeat the correct pattern of action with very few errors. The student is still quite conscious of his actions as he attempts to perform them correctly.

Although he is mainly involved with practicing the skill pattern in this phase, the cognitive phase continues as the student becomes aware of the finer points of the skill and learns various ways to correct any errors that he has been making.

Autonomous Phase.   The mature phase of the skill is reached when the pattern of activity becomes practically automatic to the student so that he can perform the actions without concentrating on them.

This phase is characterized by many aspects: increased facility, speed and accuracy; proper timing, anticipation of most of the possible circumstances, knowledge of relevant strategy and of the finer points of the skill; also, the capacity to perform the skill well even in the face of distractions or while one's attention has turned to other matters.

Theories of Skill Learning

The two most popular theories as to what goes on in the skill learning process are the S-R chaining explanation and an information-processing explanation held by some cognitive-oriented psychologists. While both theories agree on the fact that there are three main phases in skill learning, the information-processing explanation places much more emphasis on the cognitive phase, whereas the S-R chaining explanation stresses the practice phase more. In terms of psychomotor skills themselves, the former theory emphasizes the "psycho-" and the later the "-motor" aspects. But before we get into a treatment of the theories themselves, analyze two approaches to teaching a skill that are based on them.

EXERCISE 13-3.   Teaching a Skill—Two Approaches

Given below are two approaches to teaching the forehand stroke in tennis. Analyze and compare them, trying to discern the pattern and emphasis that characterizes each.

I

Instruction	Activity
Show how to grip racket: "shake hands" grip.	Have students grip racket; reinforce correct grip.
Stand behind baseline ordinarily.	Have students stand in position.
Stance when hitting: perpendicular to net, parallel with ball.	Practice switching to position parallel with path of ball.
When ball has been hit, bring racket back.	Students practice backswing.
As ball approaches, keep eye on ball.	Have students look at imaginary ball coming.
When ball arrives, swing parallel to ground.	Students practice swing; comment on parallel swing.
When ball is struck, follow through on stroke.	Students follow through on swing.
Put elements together: grip, position, stance, backswing, eye, parallel swing, follow through.	Have students pair off, one with racket, one throwing balls from net.
	Have students practice complete stroke; give comments.

II

Instruction	Activity
Explain reason for parallel swing, ·i.e. so ball will go straight. It requires: a racket perpendicular to ground (therefore "shake hands"	Demonstrate stroke.
	Have students as a group review main elements.

Instruction	Activity
grip), body parallel to path of ball, full swing (requiring backswing).	Have students try stroke without ball.
	Commend strokes that are close; suggest ways to improve.
Stress position in back of line for ordinary deep shots, eye on ball from racket to racket to permit solid hit plus allow for speed of ball, etc.	Have students (as group) review steps: grip, position, stance parallel to ball, backswing, eye on ball, parallel swing, follow through.
	Have students pair off, one with racket, one throwing balls from net.
	Have students practice complete stroke.
	Give comments on how strokes compare to an adequate stroke.
	Have students try to figure out why balls do not go straight.

Check which approach you think is characterized by each statement.

                I   II

1. Essentials of forehand stroke are explained and demonstrated with emphasis on the stroke as a whole.   ____ ____
2. Forehand is broken down into basic elements, each one practiced separately.   ____ ____
3. Basic elements of forehand are taught in the sequence in which they will be used in the full stroke.   ____ ____
4. Teacher makes sure students grasp main elements of stroke before they attempt it.   ____ ____
5. Stroke as a whole is tried early in the session.   ____ ____
6. Once the elements of the forehand stroke are practiced, the students then practice the complete stroke putting the elements together.   ____ ____
7. Evaluative comments are made often: some correct errors, most commend correct performance.   ____ ____
8. Evaluative comments are made: both corrective and commending of good performance: emphasis is on comparing performance with a model.   ____ ____

The first approach, based on an S-R chaining theory of skill learning, emphasizes the basic elements of the skill, each of which is learned individually (2) and in the order in which they will be used to comprise the overall skill (3).

Once the elements have been learned, then they are put together in the proper sequence and the skill as a whole is practiced (6).

The second approach, based on an information-processing theory of skill learning, stresses an explanation of the skill in which the essential aspects are related to the whole (1), the learners grasp or "process" those essential elements (4) and then apply them in their initial attempts at performing the skill—more as a whole than as an assemblage of parts (5).

In both approaches, evaluation is an integral factor. In the first the stress is on positive comments as reinforcement of correct performance (7); in the second, the emphasis is on how well the students' performances compared with the model that was provided in an initial demonstration (8).

S-R Chaining Theory.   According to the stimulus-response explanation, skill learning consists essentially in connecting a set of specific motor responses into a sequence. In other words, it involves linking together several S-R bonds into a chain.

Each of the S-R units consists of a muscular-skeletal movement or motor response made on the occasion of a stimulus. A number of S-R units are combined into a chain which forms a part of the total response pattern that is the skill. The chain is the particular sequence in which the S-R units must be performed if they are to constitute a functional part of the motor skill. The pattern of an S-R chain is as follows (cf. Gagné 1970):

$$S \longrightarrow R \sim\sim S \longrightarrow R \sim\sim S \longrightarrow R \sim\sim S \longrightarrow R \sim\sim S \longrightarrow R \sim \text{etc.}$$

For instance, in the forehand stroke in tennis, the following S-R associations are combined into a sequence or chain:

S		R	S		R
racket	$\longrightarrow$	shake hands grip $\sim$	court	$\longrightarrow$	position behind base line $\sim$
ball hit	$\longrightarrow$	stance $\sim\sim$	ball over net	$\longrightarrow$	backswing $\sim\sim$
ball coming	$\longrightarrow$	eye on ball $\sim\sim$	ball arrives	$\longrightarrow$	swing parallel to ground $\sim$
ball struck	$\longrightarrow$	follow through			

A number of such chains, e.g. the backhand, the serve, the smash, the lob, combine to make up the overall skill of tennis.

In any skill, the S-R units, the chains, and the total response pattern are arranged in a hierarchical order:

1. We learn S-R units in order to combine them into a chain.
2. We learn each of the subordinate chains so that we can combine them into the total response pattern that is the skill.

The principles of contiguity, practice, and reinforcement are applicable both in forming the specific bonds and in learning the proper sequence of those bonds. In learning a skill, each stimulus and motor response must occur together several times; the S-R units must then occur together in the proper sequence several times so as to form a chain; and finally the chains must be combined together and practiced to form the overall skill. At each point in the process, both feedback that lets the learner know how well he is doing and how he can correct his errors, plus praise or reinforcement that helps to confirm his correct movements are extremely valuable. In the early stages, external feedback and reinforcement from a teacher is usually in order; during the later stages, the learner profits more from internal feedback, the right "feel" and effect of a movement.

An Information-Processing Model.   An interesting theory of skill learning that is more cognitive-oriented is the information-processing model proposed by Fitts (1964). In this model the stimulus is broadened and becomes *input* and the response becomes *output;* the counterpart of reinforcement is the more informational *feedback.* In addition, some intervening activities involving the processing of input or information are posited.

First, the learner acquires information regarding the skill: (1) instructions and probably a demonstration of how to perform it (a nonvariable model) and an analysis of the essential aspects of the skill and their relation to previously learned skills, plus (2) information regarding the circumstances (variables) that have some effect on the action pattern involved in the skill (in tennis, whether the ball is coming straight or on an arc, the effect of wind, etc.).

The learner processes this information in several ways: he transmits it to his motor areas, or in other words translates it into action; he synthesizes the data regarding the key variables and relates them to the basic model of how to perform the skill; he also stores all of this information and sometimes (later) elaborates on it to produce distinct patterns of his own.

Once the learner has processed the basic information he then tries the component actions of the skill, not separately, but more or less as a whole. He is given feedback by the instructor in the form of a comparison between his actions and the model.

The process continues with both new and sometimes repetitive information provided by way of further input, with further refinements suggested regarding the skill, both in terms of how to do it (model), e.g. in tennis, the importance of the backswing; and in terms of the variables affecting it, e.g. the strengths and weaknesses of the opponent (to be avoided and attacked respectively).

This information in turn is processed—transmitted, collated, stored, and sometimes elaborated on—with further trials and eventually whole action patterns attempted in which the various aspects of the skill become coordinated and integrated. Finally, there is additional feedback, largely external or by an instructor early in the learning process, shifting to mainly internal or by the person himself later in the process.

The process, which is clearly more circular than linear, continues the input-processing-output-feedback cycle until the skill is mastered. A schema of the information-processing model of skill learning is provided in table 13-2.

Table 13-2. *Information-Processing Model of Skill Learning*

Input ↓	→	Processing of Information ↓	→	Output ↓	→	Feedback ↓	→
1. model, instructions, information on how to do it correctly plus analysis of basic aspects of whole pattern		1. translation, transmission of information to motor areas		Actions, trials and action patterns		Output compared with input to see if output is best possible performance in view of model and variables	
2. information regarding variables, circumstances		2. collation of information regarding variables					
3. refinements		3. storing, elaborration of information					

EXERCISE 13-4.　Comparison of Theories of Skill Learning

Which theory do you prefer, the S-R chaining theory or the information-processing model? Perhaps you will use aspects of both in your teaching. To help you decide, the two approaches are compared here on the basis of their relative emphasis in each of the main phases of skill learning.

Theories

Phases	S-R Chaining	Information Processing
Cognitive	Instruction given on each aspect of the skill.	Instruction given on basic aspects of a whole skill or major part of an overall skill.
		Model provided.
		Processing of information.
Practice	Each element is practiced; elements are put together and practiced in proper sequence.	Whole action pattern is practiced.
	Feedback and reinforcement is given.	Feedback is given.
		Further instruction provided.
Autonomous	Whole skill is repeated until mastered.	Whole skill is repeated until mastered.

Which explanation, the S-R chaining theory or the information processing model, do you prefer for each aspect of the skill learning process listed below?

	S-R	Inf. Pr.
Instructions: each aspect separately versus essential aspects of whole skill.	____	____
Processing of instructions	____	____
Practice: parts put in sequence versus whole action pattern.	____	____
Feedback	____	____
Reinforcement	____	____

Obviously the information-processing model takes into account what the learner does with the instructions provided, and the S-R chaining theory allows for reinforcement. For the other components, instruction, practice and feedback, it is really up to your own preference. The research reported in the following section may help you a little in your decision, but it is largely a matter of your theoretical persuasion.

Conditions Favoring Skill Learning

How can skill learning be made most effective? The research conducted on the acquisition of psychomotor skills offers some helpful suggestions, many of which are summarized below.[2,3]

Initial Stages

Emphasis on the perceptual whole during the beginning stages of skill learning is much more effective than emphasis on specific aspects of a skill. For instance, perceiving pictures as a whole (insured by brief exposure) in drawing or listening to a brief explanation of an athletic skill that emphasizes only the basic essentials have been found to be far superior to gazing at pictures to discern all of their aspects or to being presented with a complete explanation of the skill (Sherman 1947).

Involvement or trial and error activity on the part of the learner early in learning a skill is more effective than some practice plus either much verbal instruction or demonstration. However, some brief demonstration and explanation of the skill as a whole, emphasizing its essential aspects is important in the beginning (Berlin 1959, Davies 1945, Fleishman and Parker 1962).

Extensive verbal explanation at the beginning of instruction in a psychomotor

---

2. You may wish to do Exercise 13-6 in conjunction with this section.

3. The research on skill learning can be thought of as belonging to four periods: early exploratory research (1890-1927), the beginnings of a systematic attack on some important problems (1927-1945), a period of extremely high productivity on the basic problems (1945-1957) and a period which stresses new theoretical orientations and more subtle variables (1957-present) (Irion 1969). As is true in several other types of learning, the research on the basic problems is of most interest and relevance to the beginning teacher; hence the older studies are reported here in more abundance than the more recent research.

skill is quite ineffective. In fact, demonstration of the skill with no verbal commentary is just as effective as demonstration with verbal explanation for both learning and retention. Verbal explanation is most effective when interspersed throughout the practice phase of the skill-learning process (Rivenes 1961, Robb 1966).

Providing students with information about the specific psychomotor abilities that are important for learning a motor skill and about the relation between specific components of the skill to one's overall proficiency in it results in improved performance of that skill (Parker and Fleishman 1961).

Practice

The whole training method in which the learner, after seeing a demonstration of the skill as a whole, receives practice on all aspects of the skill together is superior to the part training method in which instruction and practice is given on specific aspects of the skill one at a time. This is particularly true of tightly knit and less complex skills such as juggling, diving, and rifle. In loosely organized skill activities that are actually complex patterns of many component skills, e.g. baseball, tennis, preparing a meal, or performing secretarial duties, it is probably better to practice each component skill as a whole first and then integrate them into the overall pattern as soon as feasible (McGuigan and MacCaslin 1955, Knapp and Dixon 1952).

Although the exact length of the practice periods depends on the specific skill and on the degree of exertion expended, for the most part relatively short practice sessions over a longer period of time result in more effective learning than longer practice sessions over a shorter period of time. ("Relatively short" can range from 10 seconds in the 100-yard dash to half an hour or more in typing.) Similarly, a constant duration for practice periods is more effective than increasingly longer or shorter periods (Ammons and Willig 1956, Duncan 1951, Oxendine 1965).

Superior learning results when rest intervals are provided for along with practice sessions, whether the practice sessions are distributed over a period of time with considerable rest in between, or whether short rest periods are interspersed within a longer practice session. In fact, one study showed that when total time was equated, those who stopped for periodic rest periods learned the skill better than those who kept practicing—even though their total practice time was much less (Duncan 1951, Hilgard and Smith 1942, Irion 1949).

In many cases, an emphasis on practice under realistic conditions is more effective than practice under stylized or highly controlled conditions, e.g. typing real materials, working on defensive skills in a scrimmage, or using a jigsaw to make a part of a display (Crawford 1956).

Feedback

Feedback, or knowledge of results of how one's performance compares with some standard, is very effective in skill learning. A maximum degree of feedback, rather than intermittent, has been found to be most effective. Withdrawal of feedback after a learner is used to it results in a sharp drop in performance and a decrease in interest. Delaying feedback, even twenty seconds or so, also results in a reduced rate of learning and poorer performance. As a student advances to greater proficiency in the skill, he depends less on extrinsic feedback from an instructor and more on intrinsic feedback or his own judgment as to the quality of his performance (Elwell and Grindley 1938, Greenspoon and Foreman 1956).

Other Conditions

Should speed or accuracy be emphasized early in skill learning? For skills in which speed is important in the final performance, more effective results are gained through an emphasis on speed early in the practice phase. For skills in which both speed and accuracy are important, best results come from an equal emphasis on speed and accuracy. Finally, if accuracy is most important, early emphasis should be placed on accuracy. In this connection, it has been found that having students practice the movement pattern slowly is more a hindrance than a help to learning a skill (Robb 1966, Solley 1952).

"Mental practice," or thinking about the skill between practice sessions, is very effective, particularly in the advanced stages of skill learning, although not as effective as actual physical practice. The degree of effectiveness varies with the skill (Clark 1960, Jones 1965, Twining 1949).

If they continue to practice, individuals ordinarily show continual improvement in performance of a skill, at least until they approach their physical limit for that skill. The once-claimed plateaus or periods during which no progress was made have not been supported by the majority of studies (Crossman 1959, Fitts and Seeger 1953, Keller 1958).

EXERCISE 13-5. Skill Learning in Action

Earlier in the chapter we analyzed two approaches to the teaching of the forehand stroke in tennis. Given below is an account of a full session in a beginning tennis class in which many of the conditions and other important aspects of skill learning are applied. Analyze the account, looking for the specific approaches that the teacher uses.

Beginning Tennis Class

1. Teacher begins session by having pairs of students throw and catch a tennis ball several times; then he has each student pretend the racket is a softball bat and has them swing as if batting in softball.
2. For the students who show a lack of coordination or awkward motions, teacher provides special exercises to help them develop better coordination.
3. Teacher demonstrates the basic grip and the forehand stroke and briefly explains the essentials of the stroke: grip, stance, backswing, eye on ball, parallel swing, and follow through.
4. Teacher has students pair up, one throwing ball to the other who tries several dozen forehand strokes; teacher goes around offering suggestions to students.

5. Teacher encourages each student and mentions to each what he is doing correctly—or at least what is on the way to being correct.
6. Teacher brings students together and leads a discussion on what they did that seemed right and on problems they encountered and how to correct for them.
7. Students pair off again and practice the forehand stroke for most of the time remaining. Teacher goes around telling students what they are doing correctly, offering suggestions when needed and giving praise rather generously.
8. For the last few minutes, teacher gathers students together and reviews the essentials of the forehand stroke plus some of the more common difficulties observed and how to conquer them.

Analyze the sequence of this initial session in learning a psychomotor skill. What approaches does the teacher use? Match the sections with the approaches stated below. In a few instances there may be two sections that illustrate an approach.

_____ Informal assessment of some psychomotor abilities important for the skill.
_____ Development of essential psychomotor abilities.
_____ Student involvement and discovery learning.
_____ Emphasis on whole: the skill is explained and demonstrated as a whole.
_____ Session is varied to provide a rest from actual practice.
_____ Teacher provides feedback and reinforcement for students.
_____ Teacher spreads verbal instruction over the entire session rather than giving it all at the beginning.

Seeing how well students catch, throw and "bat" gives the teacher some idea of whether they possess the coordination required to learn a proper forehand stroke in tennis (1).

If some students are low in perceptual-motor and multilimb coordination, it is better to give them exercises to improve their coordination before attempting to have them learn the various strokes in tennis (2).

Right away the teacher got the students involved in trying out the skill. He realized that the best way for anyone to learn a skill is by doing it, by discovering what the basic elements of the action pattern are by actually experiencing it for themselves (4).

It is important to explain and demonstrate the action pattern of the skill as a whole at the beginning of any attempt to teach it. But the explanation should be brief and should highlight, not all facets of the skill, but only the basic essentials (3).

A short discussion session between practice periods actually serves two purposes: (a) it provides variation and some rest from physical practice, and (b) it is an integral part of the discovery approach in skill learning (students analyze and become aware of the basic components and problems involved) (6).

Knowledge of results plus encouragement are necessary ingredients of effective skill learning. Here the teacher is very positive and accepting rather than negative or critical. He does not look for perfection right away, but tries to reinforce any attempt that approximates the correct action pattern, realizing that the students will attain it only gradually (5, 7).

The teacher realizes that verbal instruction is most effective when it is offered when needed on appropriate occasions throughout the practice session rather than all at once at the beginning (4, 6, 7, 8).

Teaching a Skill

What do the research findings and the more theoretical analyses of skill learning mean in actual practice? Some direct applications that can be made for the teaching of skills are suggested below.

Preliminary

Analyze the skill both for the abilities that are essential for students to learn it relatively well and for the basic characteristics of the skill itself (degree of complexity and continuity, relation of body to object). On one hand, the analysis of the abilities will make you aware of what the components of readiness for the skill are; on the other hand, the analysis of the skill itself will help you design the best possible instructional plan for learning the skill.

Assess the degree to which students possess the requisite psychomotor abilities for the skill that you plan to help them learn (see the following section on evaluation for sample measures). If someone is low in an important ability, provide him with some exercises that will help him develop it further. If someone is extremely low in an essential ability, discuss with him the feasibility of learning another skill that is more in keeping with his psychomotor abilities.

Initial Stage

Give students a brief explanation and demonstration of the skill as a whole, stressing only its essential elements, plus perhaps some reference to how it is similar to skills they already possess. This will provide the students with the necessary model and general idea of how to perform the skill.

Emphasize student activity and discovery or trial and error learning in the early stages of motor skill instruction. A minimum of verbal explanation and a maximum of student involvement is the most effective approach.

Practice

Provide for extensive practice in the essential actions of the skill as a whole. Particularly for complex skills, but even in simpler skills, provide practice in the component parts of the skill when necessary.

Depending on how much exertion is involved in the skill, keep the practice sessions relatively short. If longer sessions are necessary, provide for short rest periods fairly often. In other words, distribute the practice sessions over a period of time rather than expect students to accomplish much in a few long sessions.

Feedback

Let students know how well they are doing as often as possible. In the initial stages give them encouragement if their attempts even approximate the model. In fact, whenever you make a comment, it will have more effect if it is positive and constructive rather than negative and critical. In the later stages particularly, but even before, have the students evaluate their own performance by asking themselves how a particular movement pattern feels plus how they think it compares to the original model.

Follow up initial trials as well as later practice with genuine discussions (*among* students and yourself) about what they did that seemed right and of what mistakes they are conscious. This discussion plus any further suggestions or explanation are best interspersed throughout the practice phase.

Other Suggestions

Among other things, make your students aware of the specific abilities that are important for the skill plus the relation between the basic components of the skill and their eventual proficiency in it. Gradually introduce them to the finer points of the skill as well as to its possible uses and strategies.

Regarding practice, have students practice the skill in realistic situations if possible. Even in the early stages, have students emphasize speed and accuracy to the extent to which each is important in the advanced stages. Finally, encourage students to think about various facets of the skill between practice sessions.

Evaluating Skill Learning

How can psychomotor abilities and skills be evaluated? Ordinarily the techniques used are either teacher observation or student performance of specified tasks or a combination of the two. Both observation and performance of tasks can be either informal or more systematic. We will take a look at some examples of each type in a variety of fields; you can use them as illustrations for designing evaluative techniques appropriate to your field.

Informal Observation and Performance Tasks

For both types of skills, the gross bodily skills of physical education and the more manipulative skills of the fine and practical arts, the ongoing, informal observation of student performance is one of the best and most commonly used methods of evaluation. Either a student's ordinary activities such as running or throwing are observed to assess his ability for learning a new skill, his attempts at the skill during practice sessions are analyzed to diagnose areas that need strengthening, or a student's actual performance in a skill is observed and compared with a model or standard to see how well he has mastered the skill. Usually a brief conference is held with the student afterwards to convey the teacher's judgment. In connection with the latter purpose, as has been mentioned previously, an emphasis on both the positive points or what a student is doing correctly and on constructive criticism or how his performance can be improved, is as effective as it is encouraging.

A teacher can set up his own performance tests to measure either the abilities that are important for the learning of a skill (a pre-test for predictive purposes), the degree of skill achieved at any point during instruction (formative or diagnostic evaluation), or the final level of achievement attained at the end of a unit or course (summative evaluation).

For example, in physical education the standing broad jump, measured to the closest inch with the best of three jumps used as a student's score, can be used as an indication of impulsion ability (leg thrust) or as an achievement test following a unit on the broad jump. Similarly, the student's time to tenths of a second in the sixty-yard dash can be used as a measure of either leg speed ability or of achievement during or following a unit on short distance running. Also, the number or percent of times a student hits an eighteen inch target from sixty feet away with a baseball can be used as a measure of precision ability (arm aiming) or of accuracy in connection with an instructional unit in accurate throwing.

Informal performance tests for the more manipulative skills are many and fairly obvious. For example, in business education the time plus the number of errors in typing a given group of paragraphs is most often used. In industrial arts, either the precision with which a student makes a bushing of 1.25″ within a given time, or the time it takes to make a bushing of 1.25″ ±0.0005 can serve as a measure of performance.

Systematic Observation and Judgment of Performance

Observation can be made more systematic in two ways: (1) by keeping specific aspects of the overall skill or specific subskills in mind as you observe your students, and (2) by using a rating scale to indicate the quality of performance for each student. Similarly, evaluation of performance in any field can be made more specific by means of a rating scale or a checklist, for which several examples are given below.

To make your observation more systematic in art, you might draw up a list of things to look for in your students' drawings or paintings such as the half dozen criteria at the left in table 13-3. Better still take an extra half hour and think up some capsule phrases that represent points on a continuum of excellence similar to the phrases used in the rating scale. Since you know your field fairly well, you should find it rather easy to come up with appropriate phrases that will serve your purpose more than adequately. In fact, you will probably be more satisfied with your own scale than with one that you find in the literature.

An even more concrete and objective type of rating scale that uses capsule phrases reflecting observable conditions rather than degrees of excellence is illustrated through the following items taken from a woodworking evaluation form in industrial arts (table 13-4), adapted from Baldwin (1971). Other areas or criteria together with appropriate phrases can be added.

Table 13-3. *Capsule Phrase Rating Scale for Evaluating Skills*

Criterion	RATING SCALE FOR ARTISTIC PRODUCTIONS Rating			
perspective	shows excellent perspective	perspective is well conveyed	there is some perspective, but more is needed	no relative distance or position is shown
unity	shows high degree of unity, purpose	unity and purpose is clear	shows only a moderate degree of unity and purpose	unity and purpose is really not clear
organization	very well organized; composition excellent	shows good composition and organization	composition and organization adequate; could be improved	shows lack of organization; composition is rather chaotic
variation	shapes are extremely well varied	shapes are varied for the most part	some variation is evidenced; but shapes are mainly similar	shapes are too similar; much more variation is needed
color	excellent choice and blend of color	shows good color; colors well prepared	color adequate; selection and blend needs improvement	much more work needed on choice and preparation of color
technique	application is extremely clear, distinct, consistent	technique shows distinctness and consistency	technique is all right, but clarity and consistency could be improved	much more work needed on technique; clarity and consistency are not good

The possible types of formats for rating scales are limited only by your imagination. For instance, a different type that contains opposite terms with several degrees in between is the one given in table 13-5 for use in home economics.

Table 13-6 shows a checklist that can be used to make either your judgment of student performance or your observation more systematic.

The checklist is designed to help the teacher evaluate the finished product; a similar one can be constructed to evaluate a student's on-going performance or technique. For instance, in typing a technique-oriented checklist would probably include such items as: finger placement correct, stroking smooth, consistent and even touch, shift for capitals made evenly, tabs placed properly.

Table 13-4. *Objective Rating Scale for Evaluating Skills*

RATING SCALE FOR WOODWORKING

Criterion	Rating			
gluing	glue not visible	some dis-coloration	much dis-coloration	bubbles of glue visible
nailing	fill and surface blend well	too much or too little fill	nail visible	damaged surface
clamping	no clamp marks show-ing	some evidence of clamps	deep impres-sions in surface	some splitting in surface
assembly	all parts fit well	some irregu-larities in fit	considerable distortion	parts do not fit

Table 13-5. *Rating Scale Using Opposite Terms*

RATING SCALE FOR CAKE

Criterion	Quality				
	1	2	3	4	5
taste	flat _____				delicious
appearance	irregular _____				attractive
weight	heavy_____				light
texture	uneven, large holes _____				uniform, smooth
crust	tough_____				tender
moisture	dry _____				moist (moderately)

Table 13-6. *Checklist Used for Evaluating Skills*

CHECK LIST FOR TYPING

_____	Proper margins used
_____	Letters centered horizontally
_____	Letters centered vertically
_____	Proper paragraph indentation
_____	Address placed properly
_____	Erasures made cleanly
_____	Titles centered
_____	Outlines neat and correct
_____	Footnotes spaced properly
_____	Tables typed attractively
_____	Quotations set off correctly

Finally, some of the performance tasks used as measures of various psycho-motor abilities, together with the specific abilities that they are designed to assess, are:

Ability	*Measure*
trunk strength	lying prone, S pushes body off floor repeatedly with arms
finger speed	S writes upside down π in squares
dynamic balance	S jumps up on the edge of a box and keeps his balance
bodily coordination	S jumps through a cable that he holds
leg flexibility	S touches toes with fingers without bending knees

Further examples of measures for other psychomotor factors are found in Fleishman (1964) and in Guilford (1958).

EXERCISE 13-6. Distributed Versus Massed Practice

The purpose of this experiment is to find out how people best learn a skill requiring motor coordination. Flip a coin to determine which half of the alphabet you will write first: heads, from A to M; tails, from N to Z. Then flip the coin again to determine what sequence you will follow first: heads, sequence I; tails, sequence II.

Sequence I: Print the letters of half the alphabet upside down four times in succession, not backwards but upside down. Work from left to right and concentrate on speed. When you finish one set, turn the paper upside down and check how many you got wrong. Then turn the paper over and continue on right away with another set until you have completed four sets of that half of the alphabet, using a new page each time and not looking at your previous attempts. When you have finished, do something else for about five minutes before going on to the other sequence.

Sequence II: Print the letters of half the alphabet upside down, not backwards but just upside down. Work from left to right and concentrate on speed. When you finish one set, turn the paper upside down and check how many you got wrong. Now rest for half a minute, turn the paper over so as not to look at your previous attempt and print another set upside down. Check the results quickly and take another thirty-second rest. Continue writing a set and then resting half a minute until you have done four sets, each one on a new side of paper so that you will not be able to look at your previous attempts. When you have finished, do something else for about five minutes before going on to the other sequence.

How did you do in either instance? Did you get all of them correct on the fourth trial in each case? If so, how about the third trial? The second? In other words, did you do better under the condition of massed practice or distributed practice? (If you are wondering about the equal difficulty of the two halves of the alphabet, a pilot study showed that on the average students find them of about equal difficulty.)

EXERCISE 13-7. Teaching a Skill

Select a skill that is important in your subject field and plan a set of activities that you would use in a half-hour session aimed at teaching that skill. Don't be concerned about any special format or lesson plan. Simply state the skill that you want to teach and list the activities you would use in having students learn it. The activities you plan should reflect the applications for teaching suggested in this chapter on the basis of the theory and research on skill learning. In fact it will be most helpful if you indicate in the margin the basis of each activity you plan to use.

Suggested Readings

Bilodeau, E. A., ed. *Principles of Skill Acquisition.* New York: Academic Press, 1969.

Fitts, P. M. and Posner, M. I. *Human Performance.* Belmont, Calif.: Brooks/Cole, 1967.

Fleishman, E. A. *The Structure and Measurement of Physical Fitness.* Englewood Cliffs, N. J.: Prentice-Hall, 1964.

Lawther, J. D. *The Learning of Physical Skills.* Englewood Cliffs, N. J.: Prentice-Hall, 1968.

Two articles by Fitts are also extremely valuable:

Fitts, P. M. "Factors in Complex Skill Learning." In Glaser, R., ed., *Training Research and Education.* Pittsburgh: University of Pittsburgh Press, 1962.

Fitts, P. M. "Perceptual-Motor Skill Learning." In Melton, A. W., ed., *Categories of Human Learning.* New York: Academic Press, 1964.

14

Attitudes and Values

Equally as important as learning facts and knowledge, skills and ways of thinking, is the acquisition of attitudes toward people and objects in our environment and especially the acquisition of a system of values that reflects the relative importance we place on the many facets of our lives and in turn helps to guide our behavior. If we devote only one chapter to learning attitudes and values it is not because they are any less important than the other products of our learning. It is because the school shares the responsibility of teaching them with other social agencies, particularly the home and the church, and also because our knowledge of how they are learned is relatively limited.

Attitudes and values are important both for our lives in society and our maturity as individuals. Our attitudes determine our relationships with the persons, groups, and institutions of society, whether they are harmonious or in conflict. Our values allow us to organize the complex input from our social and physical environment and also help to determine our interrelationships with that environment, how we view it, how we use it, and how significantly we contribute to it.

> What is the nature of attitudes and values?
> What are some main dimensions of attitudes and values?
> How are attitudes and values learned?
> What are some conditions that affect their learning?
> How can you teach attitudes and values?
> And finally, how can you measure them?

These are some of the questions that we will be concerned with in this chapter.

The Nature of Attitudes and Values

What are attitudes? Consider the following questions:

How do you feel about modern sculpture?
What do you think about socialized medicine?
What is your view on divorce?
In terms of credibility, how do you rate politicians? What do you think of your own congressman?
What is your attitude toward Orientals?

All of these questions are concerned about attitudes, about your emotionalized opinion regarding some object.

An attitude, then, can be defined as an emotionally toned disposition to respond in a certain way to a person, a group, an issue, a practice or a thing.

What are values?

Consider these questions:

How important to you is the enjoyment of art and music?
What is your view on such humanitarian activities as the Peace Corps and the Vista programs?
What is the place of a Supreme Being in your life?
What do you think of people who place financial gain above honesty and personal integrity?

These questions are concerned with values, with the relative importance or worth that you place on ideals, persons, aspects of life and behavior.

A value, then, is a meaning or ideal that is important to a person.

Attitudes and values are learned rather than innate; they are not observable in themselves but are inferred from a person's statements and behavior. They can be measured, but not as directly as can knowledge, skills, and thought processes.

Both attitudes and values have three components: cognitive, affective, and behavioral. The cognitive component of an attitude or value is the information that a person has regarding its object, whether factual or experiential knowledge of an attitude object or convincing reasons regarding the importance of a value object. The affective component consists in the emotional attraction or repugnance regarding the object of the attitude or value, the favorable or unfavorable feeling a person has toward it. The behavioral component is the action-tendency that is an integral part of an attitude or value: the person's disposition to be accepting and supportive or to be rejecting and negative toward the object of an attitude, or the degree to which a value influences the person's actions and his dealings with others.

Since the three components are simply three aspects of one value or attitude, we can expect them to be quite consistent with one another. This is in fact what happens; for instance, if one of the components undergoes a change, it is usually reflected by a corresponding change in the other components.

Both attitudes and values have similar components; both involve an evaluative function. How then do they differ? An attitude is basically a relation between the person and an object; a value is an ideal that has been made an intimate part of a person's life. As such, a value is even more permanent and resistant to change than an attitude, which is itself relatively stable. A value is also more general in its scope than an attitude; for example, a person can have an open attitude toward various forms of contemporary music and at the same time a value regarding music that makes it an important part of his leisure activities.

EXERCISE 14-1. Components of Attitudes and Values

Given below are some examples of behavior or experience that reflect the several components of attitudes and values. Indicate (a) whether each is an example of an attitude or value, and (b) whether it illustrates the cognitive, affective or behavioral component of that attitude or value.

	Att	Val	Cog	Aff	Beh
1. A person volunteers to work in an election campaign, studies the candidates' records, and (of course) votes for the best qualified candidate.	___	___	___	___	___
2. A person experiences a thrill from a well-played piano concerto.	___	___	___	___	___
3. A person does not believe every detail that the salesman mentions about a used car.	___	___	___	___	___
4. A person is convinced of the importance of becoming an authentic human being based on his reading of some existential philosophers.	___	___	___	___	___
5. A person becomes angry when reading a newspaper account of extensive destruction of human life in a foreign war.	___	___	___	___	___
6. A person befriends a minority group member who has just moved into the neighborhood.	___	___	___	___	___

Attitudes are illustrated by the piano concerto, the used car salesman, and befriending the new neighbor. The cognitive component of an attitude is clearly seen in the used car salesman example: perhaps the person either through personal experience or through reading about a recent survey that placed them twentieth out of twenty occupations in credibility, has arrived at the knowledge that used car salesmen are not to be completely trusted. The affective component of a favorable attitude toward classical music is illustrated by the emotional thrill experienced during a piano concerto. The behavioral component is exemplified by the person putting his conviction and feeling into practice and befriending his minority group neighbor.

Values are illustrated by the election campaign, the philosophical conviction, and the angry response to killing. The cognitive component of a value most often takes the form of a reasoned conviction, e.g. regarding becoming an authentic person based on philosophical reasoning. The affective component is illustrated by the person who has strong value regarding the importance of human life becoming angry over a newspaper account of its destruction in a war. The behavioral component of a value, specifically regarding the importance of the democratic system, is exemplified by the person who works in an election campaign and casts a knowledgeable vote at the polls.

Main Dimensions of Attitudes and Values

Of the many attempts to categorize values and attitudes and to identify their important dimensions, probably the most helpful to the teacher—as well as the best known—is the *Taxonomy of Educational Objectives, Affective Domain*. In the Taxonomy, values and attitudes are thought of as being on a continuum based on the degree of internalization of the affective behavior or outlook, that is, the extent to which it is incorporated into a person's cognitive and behavioral structure and becomes his own rather than imposed from outside. The continuum is as follows:

1. Receiving: awareness, openness, attention
2. Responding: participation, compliance, contribution, enjoyment
3. Valuing: acceptance, commitment, consistent behavior
4. Organization: interrelated system of values, philosophy of life
5. Characterization: consistent value system that determines behavior.

For instance, a person's favorable attitude toward a minority group can advance from (1) a willingness to listen to a more accepting attitude, to (2) participating in a rally for equal rights for the minority group, to (3) regularly supporting the rights and dignity of the minority group in discussions, to (4) integrating this attitude into his overall outlook on human dignity, to (5) regularly joining in programs to promote the rights of the minority group.

Similarly, a person's value regarding the welfare of his fellow man can develop from (1) an awareness of the need that some people have for a better life, to (2) a financial contribution to the United Fund, to (3) a commitment to work in a local tutoring program, to (4) incorporating the ideal of the greatest welfare of all men into his political, religious, and economic system of values, all of which then reflect a more humanitarian outlook, to (5) pursuing a career in social work out of a deep concern for the welfare of less advantaged members of society.

In terms of types of objects or content categories that an attitude or value can have, the most comprehensive list of dimensions is that of the German writer, Eduard Spranger. His six basic types of values together with their dominant concerns or interests are:

theoretical: discovery of truth, through observation (scientific truth) and reason (philosophical truth);

an order and system to one's knowledge

economic: the useful and practical affairs of the business world;
    wealth and surpassing others in wealth

aesthetic: expressions of form and harmony (music, art, nature, liter-
    ature);
    beauty

social: love of people;
    interest in the happiness and welfare of others

political: search for power; influence, renown

religious: comprehension of and unity with the cosmos as a whole;
    a unifying philosophy of life.

These types of values and attitudes are not all-inclusive, but they do represent the main ways in which men view their lives and the world around them. Most persons will have a value system in which one or two of these dimensions are more dominant than others.

The Process of Attitude and Value Learning

How are attitudes and values acquired; how can they be changed? How can the learning process best be explained? The learning of attitudes and values is a complex process that can involve many specific types of learning. In order to teach attitudes and values with any degree of effectiveness, you must gain some insight into that process. Two of the most popular explanations are the social learning and modeling theory of Albert Bandura and the cognitive dissonance theory of Leon Festinger. But before we examine these explanations systematically, consider two approaches to teaching attitudes, each of which reflects a different theory of attitude learning.

EXERCISE 14-2: Attitude Learning in Practice

Two teachers face the problem of teaching poetry to a class consisting mainly of boys whose attitudes towards poetry are far from positive. Analyze the two approaches and see if you can identify the main characteristics of each.

I	II
Teacher reads a poem by Robert Frost on the beauty of nature. Both from his reading of it and from his comments following, it is clear that he enjoys both the insights themselves and the way they are expressed.	Teacher and students read Kipling's "Gunga Din," with teacher as narrator, students reading some parts, and all students reading other sections in chorus.
Teacher has students select several short poems to read according to their	Teacher asks, "Did you enjoy it?" Why?"

I	II
interests. He has as many students as possible read one of their poems aloud and tell what it means to them.	He continues, after the majority claimed that they liked "Gunga Din": "But I thought you didn't like poetry. How come you enjoyed this?"
Teacher is generous in his praise for poems read orally and for the interpretative comments of students.	A lively discussion follows.

Indicate which approach is characterized by each statement.

		I	II
1.	Teacher provides himself as a model for his students.	___	___
2.	Teacher gives opportunity for students to do the same as he did.	___	___
3.	Teacher sets up an experience for students that will probably run counter to their ordinary attitude.	___	___
4.	Teacher gets students to discuss the difference between their present experience and their usual outlook.	___	___
5.	Teacher reinforces poetry read with meaning.	___	___

In the first approach the teacher provided a model (himself) for his students to follow (1) and gave them the opportunity to imitate what he did (2). He also gave reinforcement to the students whose reading of poetry seemed to show some degree of appreciation (5).

In the second approach, the teacher was more concerned about establishing a conflict or discrepancy, specifically between the students' present experience and their ordinary attitude toward poetry (3). He tried to focus their attention on this discrepancy by his questions and perhaps have them resolve it through some discussion (4).

The two approaches reflect two of the leading explanations of how attitudes are learned: (I) through imitation of a model and (II) through a discrepancy or "dissonance" between an attitude and a new experience.

Social Learning Theory

Albert Bandura explains his social learning theory as follows.

> Although it is generally assumed that social behavior is learned and modified through direct reward and punishment of instrumental responses, informal observation and laboratory study of the social learning process reveal that new responses may be rapidly acquired and existing behavioral repertoires may be considerably changed as a function of observing the behavior and attitudes exhibited by models.
>
> The latter type of learning is generally labeled "imitation" in behavior theory, and "identification" in most theories of personality. These concepts, however (can be) treated . . . as synonymous since both encompass

the same behavioral phenomenon, i.e. the tendency for a person to match the behavior, attitudes, or emotional reactions as exhibited by actual or symbolized models. (Bandura, Ross, and Ross 1963)

Bandura states that both social behavior and attitudes are learned largely through the person observing and imitating a model. Models can be either (1) parents, teachers, leaders in relevant fields (real-life models), (2) models presented through books or explained by teachers (symbolic models), and (3) models presented through movies, television, and other audio-visual means (representational models).

In attitude and value learning the model behaves in a certain way or makes value-oriented statements which are imitated by the learner. If the learner is rewarded—by approval, a smile or tangible reward—the attitude or value will tend to become a relatively permanent part of his outlook and behavior. In fact, even if the learner sees the *model* rewarded for such behavior, he will tend to take on the attitude or value as his own. Continued exposure to the model's behavior plus continued reinforcement will strengthen the person's attitude toward an object.

There are several variables that help to determine the degree of imitative behavior, particularly the following characteristics of the learner: moderate to low self-esteem, previous rewards for imitative or conforming behavior, perception of self as similar to the model, and degree of emotional arousal. All of these contribute to the person's tendency to imitate the model.

Bandura states further regarding the modeling process:

> Social learning theory assumes that modeling influences operate principally through their informative function, and that observers acquire mainly symbolic representation of modeled events rather than specific stimulus-response associations. In this formulation, modeling phenomena are governed by four interrelated subprocesses: attention, retention, motor reproduction and reinforcement. (Bandura 1971).

Bandura holds that there are several phases of learning through example, which he explains as follows.

1. Attention. The learner must attend to and recognize the distinctive features of the model's responses.
2. Retention. If the learner does not immediately perform the same behavior as the model, he can still acquire it later if he remembers the behavior itself, and especially if he converts its essentials into concise verbal terms and retains it through its verbal equivalents.
3. Motor reproduction. The learner must perform the behavior overtly, either in direct imitation of the model if he is present or through the guidance of the symbolic representations of the model's behavior (as in (2) above).
4. Reinforcement. Once an attitude or behavior pattern has been acquired, it will be activated into actual performance if some approval or other reward is offered to the person.

The process can be schematized as follows:

Modeled→ Attention to→ Retention   → Motor repro-   → Reinforcement →Matching
events   distinctive   through image   duction of   performances
         features   or verbal terms   modeled behavior

Cognitive Dissonance Theory

Festinger explains the basic elements of his theory as follows.

> It has frequently been pointed out that the individual strives toward consistency within himself. His opinions and attitudes, for example, tend to exist in clusters that are internally consistent. There is the same kind of consistency between what a person knows or believes and what he does. In the presence of an inconsistency, there is psychological discomfort.
>
> First, I will replace the word "inconsistency" with a term which has less of a logical connotation, namely, *dissonance*. I will likewise replace the word "consistency" with a more neutral term, namely, *consonance*.
>
> The basic hypotheses I wish to state are as follows:
>
> 1. The existence of dissonance, being psychologically uncomfortable, will motivate the person to try to reduce the dissonance and achieve consonance.
>
> 2. When dissonance is present, in addition to trying to reduce it, the person will actively avoid situations and information which would likely increase the dissonances. . . .
>
> In short, I am proposing that dissonance, that is, the existence of non-fitting relations among cognitions, is a motivating factor in its own right. By the term *cognition,* I mean any knowledge or opinion about one's behavior. Cognitive dissonance can be seen as an antecedent condition which leads to activity oriented toward dissonance reduction just as hunger leads to activity oriented toward hunger reduction (Festinger 1957, pp. 1-3).

For Festinger, attitudes and values change because of an inconsistency or dissonance either between two points of view regarding an attitude object or a value, or among the cognitive, affective, and behavioral components of an attitude or value. Any kind of inconsistency is disturbing to the person, and he will usually do something to reduce it and thus attain consistency of point of view and behavior.

There are many occasions for dissonance to occur: when a person becomes aware that two beliefs are logically inconsistent, when he changes group membership, when new behavior norms are imposed on him, when he obeys new laws of which he is not convinced, or when for some other reason—for example, to receive a reward or to avoid punishment—he behaves contrary to his beliefs.

The amount of dissonance depends on the degree of a person's commitment to a value or on the importance he places on the cognitive element of an attitude. The stronger the dissonance the more the person is motivated to reduce it.

A person may try to reduce the dissonance in a number of ways. If the inconsistency is between his convictions and his behavior, he will either change his convictions or his behavior or will search for new information to help him form his decision whether to change his attitude or value. If the inconsistency is between the cognitive elements of two conflicting attitudes or values, he will usually look for new information to help him judge between them and hence do away with the dissonance.

Festinger makes an important point regarding the permanence of attitude change. If an attitude change is to last, the environment must be supportive of the behavioral change that accompanied the change in attitude. If it is not, the person will probably revert back to his original attitude, particularly if it is more in keeping with his basic values.

As was mentioned above, Festinger holds that the greatest shifts in an attitude or value occur when the person experiences maximum dissonance. But consider the following situation. If a reward is given to a person to act in opposition to his beliefs, maximum dissonance will occur when the reward offered is just enough to get him to behave in a way contrary to his values or attitudes. A large reward ($20 bill) would result in very little dissonance ("there is no problem; it's worth going against one's beliefs for that"). On the other hand, a small reward that is just attractive enough to have the person act in the conflicting way creates a problem or discrepancy between belief and behavior. The result of these premises is that a greater attitude change should occur when one expects a small reward than when one expects a large one. This, however, is directly opposed to reinforcement theory in which larger incentives would be expected to bring a greater change in attitudes or values.

Of the numerous research studies that have attempted to solve this conflict between theories, some have supported the prediction of the dissonance theory, and some have supported an incentive theory. W. J. McGuire, a leading social psychologist, claims that the two theories can be reconciled in that the dissonance prediction deals with the *commitment* to action rather than the carrying out of the commitment, whereas the incentive theory deals with what happens when the person actually *carries out* the behavior. At least much of the evidence fits this attempt at reconciliation (Maguire 1969).

EXERCISE 14-3.   Evaluation of Theories of Attitude Learning

Which explanation of attitude learning do you prefer, Bandura's social learning theory or Festinger's cognitive dissonance theory? Given below are a few points of criticism; indicate which theory each point applies to.

	SL	CD
1. It explains how attitudes are learned originally better than how they can be changed.	____	____
2. It explains how attitudes can be changed better than how they were learned originally.	____	____

SL   CD

3. It does not account for the inner basis of an attitude or value, only the
   external cause.   ____ ____
4. It does not account for the social approval factor which is important in
   the formation of attitudes and values.   ____ ____

The imitation explanation fits initial learning of attitudes and values better than it does attitude change, since it does not account for a conflict in attitudes which is usually the case in any change of values or attitudes.

The dissonance theory explains attitude and value change better than the initial learning of an attitude, since for dissonance to occur an existing attitude or value with its several components must already have been formed.

Each theory has its strengths and limitations. The dissonance theory stresses the cognitive or informational basis for attitudes and values whereas the imitation theory does not. The imitation theory accounts for the importance of social approval and incentive motivation in the acquisition of attitudes and values whereas the dissonance theory does not.

Actually learning attitudes and values is so complex and allows for so many different types of learning that one or two theories cannot adequately explain it. A comprehensive explanation of how attitudes and values are learned would include both modeling, dissonance, and several other learning processes.

Other Explanations

Besides learning an attitude or value by imitation of a model, plus social reinforcement or changing an attitude or value by reducing the dissonance between its components or between the cognitive components of various attitudes, there are several other processes by which a person can acquire or change an attitude or value.

Most often a person acquires the informational component by listening to and talking with his parents, family, and friends. Similarly, the cognitive component of an attitude or value can be changed through new information provided by a teacher, friends or fellow students, or obtained from books or the mass media.

The groups that we belong to—both family and other groups—form a particularly strong influence in shaping the behavioral component of our attitudes and values. Often the price of membership in a group is adoption of the dominant point of view and behavior of that group; hence a person tends to take on the attitudes and the values that are evidenced by group members.

The affective component of an attitude or value is most often acquired by a process of conditioning or the frequent exposure to a pleasant or unpleasant object or situation.

We also learn attitudes or change our existing attitudes by direct experience with the object of the attitude. Although it accounts for a small percentage of the attitudes we learn, direct experience is probably the most effective technique since it usually causes a change in all three aspects of an attitude: cognitive, affective, and behavioral. For instance, a person who has had to work with some members of a minority group will usually acquire a more favorable attitude toward that group than he had in the past, especially if he has shared hardships and common problems with them.

Finally, we occasionally learn an attitude or value through a shocking or traumatic experience regarding an object or ideal. For example, a person who is robbed by a member of a minority group may tend to generalize his dislike to all members of that group. Although rare, a traumatic experience can bring an immediate and lasting change in an attitude or value.

EXERCISE 14-4. Attitude and Value Learning in the Classroom

How do the many ways of learning attitudes and values work out in practice? Given below are some ways in which teachers have attempted to teach values and attitudes. Match each strategy with the type of learning that it illustrates.

_____ 1. A social studies teacher has a student who expressed some feelings against legalized abortion help prepare a case and argue in favor of legalized abortion in a debate.

_____ 2. On group experiments and projects a science teacher arranges it so that the minority group members in the class are spread out among all of the groups so as to allow students of both majority and minority groups to work together.

_____ 3. A health teacher has several students whom he has seen smoking role-play a smoker who is the victim of lung cancer.

_____ 4. A science teacher shows a film on Madame Curie depicting some of the outstanding achievements of her life; a discussion follows in which students summarize her accomplishments and consider how they might follow her example in their study of science.

_____ 5. A homeroom teacher commends students regularly for their fair and democratic way of conducting class business.

_____ 6. A music teacher teaches a unit on jazz during which he stresses both the free and rhythmic nature of many blacks and especially the outstanding contributions of black musicians to the development of jazz as an art form.

_____ 7. An English teacher often plays music that is appropriate and that the students enjoy when he or a student reads poetry.

A. cognitive dissonance

B. imitation of a model

C. direct experience

D. information

E. social reinforcement

F. conditioning

There are two examples of cognitive dissonance: in the legalized abortion example (1), the cognitive component of one value is pitted against the cognitive component of its opposite; in the lung cancer example (3) the teacher tries to set up a dissonance between the affective and behavioral components of an attitude.

The teacher who shows the Madame Curie film (4) wants to provide a model or ideal for his students to imitate; the discussion which follows the film should help the students to put her achievements in verbal-symbolic form, which in turn has been found to be effective in guiding their behavior in the future.

Direct experience with members of a minority group is what the science teacher who assigned both majority and minority group members to working groups had in mind (2).

The music teacher provides information on a minority group (6) that should increase the students' appreciation and positive attitude toward that group.

The homeroom teacher emphasizes reinforcement for their democratic values as evidenced in their behavior (5).

Finally the English teacher tries to instill a liking for poetry—specifically a pleasant affective component—through a conditioning process, by associating a pleasant response (enjoyment of music) to his students' reaction to poetry (7).

Conditions that Affect Learning Attitudes and Values

What are some important conditions that are related to the learning of attitudes and values? Some of the research that pertains to this type of learning can be summarized as follows.

Imitating a Model

A student is more likely to imitate the attitudes and values of another person if he perceives him as similar to himself in some way, either in outlook, beliefs, interests, or other characteristics (Newcomb 1961, Byrne and Griffitt 1966, Kagan, Pearson and Welsh 1966). When a model is provided for them, students will be much more apt to imitate it if they categorize the various aspects of the model's actions in verbal terms. Short, concise verbal labels are more effective in this regard than general descriptions of the model's behavior (Bandura, Grusec and Menlove 1966, Gerst 1971).

Direct Experience

Direct experience with the object of an attitude can result in learning a positive attitude *if* the experience is pleasant or favorable. If the experience is unpleasant or if the person is hostile or aggressive, a negative attitude will probably result (Mussen 1950, Katz 1960).

When a pleasant experience is associated with the expression of an attitude, that attitude is strengthened, even though it might be inconsistent with one's overall attitudes and values. The pleasant experience can be, for instance, a compliment, an *A,* even a pleasant word (Staats and Staats 1958, Bostrom, Vlandis, Rosenbaum 1961, Calvin 1962).

Methods in Learning Attitudes and Values

Group discussion is much more effective than a lecture for changing a person's attitudes or values. In a discussion the person is more apt to participate actively and to make a commitment, both of which have been found to be important in attitude change. In addition, the discussion approach and the lecture affect the person not only through the cognitive component but through the behavioral component as well (Lewin 1947, McKeachie 1954).

Mere exposure to a model is not nearly as effective for learning attitudes as is seeing or reading about a model plus discussing various points about the model. For other communications regarding an attitude or value, e.g. a film, a follow-up discussion results in more permanent gains of positive attitudes than does simple exposure to the communication (Loban 1954, Taba 1955, Mitnick and McGinnies 1958).

Role playing in which the person assumes a role that is contrary to his attitudes or values is a very effective way to modify his attitudes, with the change often becoming relatively permanent. Role playing can involve one of several forms: the person acts out the feelings and behavior of a person who is the object of his unfavorable attitude; the person works out a problem related to the object of an unfavorable attitude, for example, housing for a minority group; the person defends a value opposed to his own values in a speech or debate (Culbertson 1957, Janis and Mann 1965, Mann and Janis 1968).

Having students participate vicariously in an emotional crisis of another, such as through reading a case, can lead students to reconsider their own attitudes and values relating to the situation (Toch and Cantril 1957).

The Impact of School and College

Although many studies concerned with the effect of college and high school experiences have shown little measurable value change, some studies have shown a decided liberalizing effect in most value areas. It has been found that students who are seeking independence from their families are most apt to change their values, whereas those who are overly dependent upon their parents tend to keep the values they developed while under their influence (Jacob 1960, Newcomb 1943, Lehmann 1963).

Teaching Attitudes and Values

How can you help students form positive attitudes and values? Applying what we have seen regarding the theories and conditions of attitude and value learning we can offer the following suggestions for teaching.

Based on the Nature and Dimensions of Attitudes and Values

Make students aware of the different degrees of internalization and commitment that attitudes and values possess (cf. Taxonomy, p. 367). Encourage them to analyze their positive attitudes and more important values and to realize the depth of their commitment to each. This may encourage some students to internalize their attitudes and especially their values more and to carry them over into their behavior to a greater extent than they had in the past.

Emphasize the reasons or bases for a particular value or attitude. Have students present reasons; contribute some reasons yourself; encourage students to evaluate critically the reasons that are offered. Do not attempt to impose a value or attitude, but through a genuine interaction among the students and yourself, encourage them to form their own positive attitudes and values based on convincing reasons.

Based on the Explanations of the Learning Process

To help students acquire more favorable or positive attitudes and values than they currently possess, create conflict or dissonance in their minds: either conflict between their outlook and the reasons underlying the more positive attitude or value, or discrepancy between their actual behavior and the ideas or rationale that underlies their stated value or attitude.

When possible, provide direct experience with the object of an attitude, but take the means to make the experience as pleasant as possible, since direct, *pleasant* experience fosters positive attitudes. For instance, involving students in cooperative attempts at solving problems together with minority group members, and giving a compliment for behavior that reflects a worthwhile value, are examples of attempts to make experiences pleasant.

In addition to direct experience, help students to acquire at least the affective component of attitudes and values by having them participate vicariously in the relevant and emotional experiences of others through cases, anecdotes, biographies, and the like. Provide models of positive attitudes and worthwhile values for students to follow, whether it be yourself as a teacher (most important), biographies of significant persons, appropriate anecdotes, or films. Hold discussions on the film or biography, and encourage the students to identify the attitudes or values evidenced in concise terms or labels.

Reinforce student statements and behavior that evidence positive attitudes and worthwhile values. A word of praise, a compliment, some encouragement can be very effective in learning attitudes and values.

Specific Techniques for Teaching Attitudes and Values

Use group discussion rather than lecture in attempting to teach attitudes and values. Involve as many students as possible in the discussion. In summarizing the discussion, try to establish the "sense of the group." Both personal participation and knowing how one's fellow students think helps students become committed to an attitude or value.

Use role playing frequently as an effective way to teach positive attitudes and values. Role playing is an informal, unrehearsed dramatization relating to social or psychological issues in which students act out the ideas, feelings, and behavior associated with an attitude or value. For example, have students act out the feelings of a person who is the object of an unfavorable attitude or set up a mock interview in which a student defends a worthwhile value that he does not actually hold.

The Measurement of Attitudes and Values

How can you as a teacher evaluate whether your students have acquired or changed an attitude or value? What are some of the available techniques for measuring attitudes and values? We will consider both some informal techniques plus some of the more objective measures that a teacher can use.

Observation

For the most part, attitudes and values are inferred from a person's statements and behavior. Hence your informal observation of a student's behavior or of his remarks in a discussion regarding the object of an attitude or regarding a particular value is one of the more direct as well as more convenient ways to evaluate his attitude or value.

To give some degree of system to your observation you might keep in mind the basic dimensions of attitudes and values outlined earlier in the chapter, or even a simple dimension such as positive–neutral–negative or changing with the times versus traditional.

Attitude Scales

Attitudes and values can also be measured through more objective scales. For instance, a commonly used type of instrument to measure the cognitive component of an attitude or value is one which contains statements about an attitude object or an ideal and then calls for the student to indicate the strength of his agreement or disagreement. For example, some items included on a "philosophy of life" scale (a value scale) are as follows:

1. One of the most important things for a person to come to grips with is the basic meaning for his existence.
   Strongly Agree   Agree   Undecided   Disagree   Strongly Disagree
2. If a man is fully involved in his business and his family, he really doesn't need to think about a philosophy of life.
   Strongly Agree   Agree   Undecided   Disagree   Strongly Disagree
3. A life lived with integrity is more satisfying to the person and is of more worth to society.
   Strongly Agree   Agree   Undecided   Disagree   Strongly Disagree
4. A man should be concerned about making a living and living life to its fullest and not worry about the reason for it all.
   Strongly Agree   Agree   Undecided   Disagree   Strongly Disagree

Usually twenty to thirty such items will form an attitude or value scale. Note that the scale can contain both positive and negative statements but all must pertain to the one value or attitude since they will all contribute to one score.

Another technique that is feasible for a teacher to construct is the capsule case plus multiple choice item that stresses the behavioral component of an attitude or value. For example:

You are visiting another city and a friend of yours invites you to accompany him to the local swimming pool. In front of you in the admission line is an athletic looking young man, a member of a minority group. As he is about to pay, the man at the gate says that they do not admit "your kind" to the pool. What would you do in this case?

_____ Voice your objection to the man over the policy and suggest to your friend that you and he should go elsewhere if this is the way they treat minority groups.

_____ Voice your disapproval to your friend loud enough so that the man will surely hear.

_____ Keep quiet about it then, but mention your displeasure at the situation to your friend later.

_____ Say nothing about the situation since it is the right of the pool owners to admit whom they wish.

You would want to include in such a scale at least several if not a dozen items having to do with the same attitude or value. As a guideline for options, you can use some or all of the basic dimensions of attitudes and values given earlier (receiving through characterization) or a four-point continuum such as the activist—liberal—center—conservative one used as a basis for the options in the above example.

There are other types of attitude and value scales similar to the scale provided as a measure of course interest in the chapter on motivation (p. 122), but they are quite complicated to construct and score. The two types offered above should suffice as workable measures for you as a teacher.

Suggested Readings

Bandura, A., ed. *Psychological Modeling.* Chicago: Aldine, Atherton, 1971.

Festinger, L. *A Theory of Cognitive Dissonance.* Palo Alto, Calif.: Stanford University Press, 1957.

McGuire, W. J. "The Nature of Attitudes and Attitude Change." In G. Lindzey and E. Aronson, eds. *Handbook of Social Psychology.* 2d ed. Reading, Mass.: Addison-Wesley, 1968. Vol. 3, pp. 136-314.

Triandis, H. C. *Attitude and Attitude Change.* New York: Wiley, 1971.

part six

Retention, Transfer and Evaluation

Now that we have analyzed the various types of learning that take place in the classroom, it is important that we look at three follow-up considerations to what we have seen so far: to what extent students retain what they learn, whether they are able to apply it to different situations, and how well they have learned it as indicated by different evaluation devices. None of these questions is brand new. For each type of learning above we considered ways to make learning more effective and—by implication—to make retention more lasting. Also, there have been several instances in which it was obvious that one type of learning could be used as an integral part of another type, for example, concepts in relations, comprehension in critical thinking, motivation in attitude learning. Finally, a regular part of our treatment of the various types of learning consisted of some suggestions on how to evaluate the quality of learning in each case. In the present section we will be considering the topics of retention and transfer more explicitly and systematically and the topic of evaluation more technically and practically than we did in the earlier sections of the book.

Although in the previous chapters we treated the theories that attempted to explain the learning process before the research regarding the conditions of learning, in the chapter on retention and transfer we will consider the research first and then the theories, mainly because in these cases the theories have grown out of the educationally oriented research more directly than in the case of the basic types of learning.

15

Retention and Transfer

Teachers are not only interested in students learning facts, concepts, and relations, they are even more interested in their retaining and using what they have learned. Recall our basic schema (table 15-1). As teachers, we hope that our students will remember some of the "products" we have taught them and that they will continue to think creatively and critically even after we have ceased to provide training in these processes. We also hope that they will apply what they have learned to other subjects and to situations outside of school that are not exactly the same as the context in which they learned it originally.

Table 15-1.

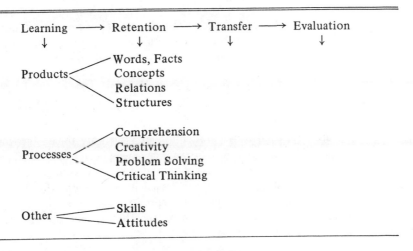

Retention

How can teachers help insure that learning will be fairly permanent? What makes students forget what they have learned in the first place? Even more basic: what is this thing we call memory? These are some of the questions we will treat in the first part of this chapter. The questions regarding the application or transfer of what has been learned will be treated in the second half.

Specifically, in this first part, we will consider the following points:

> The nature and types of memory
> Conditions influencing retention
> Theories of forgetting
> Applications in teaching
> Measurement of retention

The Nature and Types of Memory

What is memory? It is the intellectual process of storing and later retrieving what we have learned. Thus it serves two interrelated functions: (1) the conservation and retention of our knowledge, skills, and past experiences; and (2) the recall or recognition of what we have retained.

What is retained? In general, the products of information that we have acquired. Specifically, we retain anything that we "cognize": the units that we experience, the classes that we form, the relations that we arrive at, the systems that we construct or grasp, the transformations that we work out, and the implications that we draw. To some degree we probably retain everything that we learn: we can usually at least recognize it if we come in contact with it again.

Hence, the memory process is integrally related to the learning of information. In fact, we can think of the two processes as being on a time continuum:

1		2		3		4		5
Practice	→	Learning	→	Short-term memory	→	Intermediate memory	→	Long-term memory

After we have interacted with a certain product one or more times (1), we reach a point at which we can say we have learned it (2); it remains readily accessible for at least a few seconds to several minutes afterwards (3) and hopefully for several days or a few weeks (4); if we have learned it well and review it fairly often, we should retain it with relative permanence (5).

What is the difference between recall and recognition, both of which are retrieval functions of memory? Recall is a more demanding function that entails the active retrieval and reproduction of a memory trace. Recognition involves the identification of an idea or event as having been experienced previously; it is essentially a judgment that a past and present experience are the same. For instance, in testing for how well a student remembers what he has learned, an essay test requires the student to reproduce his knowledge whereas a multiple choice test requires that he recognize the correct option as the one that corresponds to what he has learned.

The more complex the original experience, the more difficult it is to reproduce it; on the other hand there does not seem to be such an increasing difficulty with regard to recognition. Similarly, it is important to have an intention to retain what is being learned and to learn it well if we wish to be able to recall it; much more so than if we simply wish to recognize it.

We often distinguish between rote and logical memory. Rather than representing distinct categories, they are probably better thought of as being on a continuum. For example, the following samples of material can be considered as being the objects of the corresponding points on the rote-logical continuum of memory:

jat   1832   ossify   verb   "heat expands metal"   evolution

rote $\longleftarrow$———————————————————$\longrightarrow$ logical

Jat, a nonsense syllable, is the object of pure rote or sense memory. Representing an event, 1832 is a factual unit, while ossify, representing an action, is a semantic unit; both require largely rote memory. Verb, a class which is the product of a mental grouping, is largely the object of logical memory but still requires some rote memory. The generalization "heat expands metal" (a relation) and the principle of evolution (the core idea of a system or structure) are objects of logical memory; the only rote element in these cases are the specific words used.

EXERCISE 15-1.   Retention—Kind of Material

What type of material is remembered best: verbal associations, elements of a class, or generalizations? In other words, which does a learner retain better: (1) verbal units, which are largely the object of rote memory, (2) a class of things which is remembered partly by rote and partly by logical memory, or (3) a relation that is mainly the object of logical memory?

Given below are three groups of ten short words each, one involving German-English vocabulary, one involving members of a class, and the third involving a generalization. Read through them with the intention of recalling them later. You can design the experiment in a few ways, but it is suggested that you read through each list three times, or—if you will—for fifteen seconds each, to control initial learning. For short-term memory, cover the lists and fill in the blanks; for long-term memory, finish the section on retention, and then go back and fill in the blanks.

1. tur—door
   weg—path
   auge—eye
   lied—song
   reise—trip

2. fruit

apple	pear
orange	lemon
peach	berry
grape	cherry
plum	

3. The early towns and villages were built near the ocean.

1. _____ \- _____
   _____ \- _____
   _____ \- _____
   _____ \- _____
   _____ \- _____

2. _____
   _____   _____
   _____   _____
   _____   _____
   _____   _____
   _____

3. _____ _____ _____ _____ _____
   _____ _____ _____ _____ _____

Which did you remember more of: the generalization, the class and its members, or the German-English vocabulary? This experiment should indicate that logical material is more readily retained than rote material and that in fact the degree of difficulty corresponds to the continuum of rote-logical material.

Conditions Influencing Retention

How can we help to insure that students will retain what they have learned? Actually, since the degree of retention depends to a large extent on the quality of initial learning, most of the suggestions regarding efficient learning that have been offered in previous chapters will also apply to retention—distributed practice, overlearning, and the others. Here we will state some specific conclusions from the research on retention that have some relevance for classroom learning. There are many factors that influence retention: our intention to remember, the nature of the material, how it is learned, and how often it is reviewed.

Intention to Remember. The intention to remember what is learned facilitates retention, at least if it is present before students learn something (if it is fostered after learning, it is not effective) (Ausubel, Schpoont and Cukier 1957).

A student's intention to remember can focus either on recognition or recall, with intent to recall being more effective than intent simply to recognize. For instance, if a student expects an essay test (recall) he will do better on such a test than if he expected an objective test (recognition) (Lester 1932).

The Nature of the Material. Meaningful material, the object more of logical memory, is retained more easily and longer than factual material, the object mainly of rote memory, particularly if the meaningful material is incorporated into a system or structure. One study showed that between the end of a course in biology and one year later the knowledge and application of principles was completely retained, the ability to interpret experiments actually increased by twenty-five percent, and relating the structure of organs to their function was retained to a large degree (almost eighty percent). On the other hand, naming structures in diagrams (recall) was retained only twenty-three percent, although identification of technical terms (recognition) was retained seventy-four percent. (All percentages represent the differences in test scores between the end of the course and one year later.) (Katona 1940, Briggs and Reed 1943, Tyler 1934)

Motor skills, both simple and complex, are retained to a very high degree; any losses that do occur are quickly recovered through relearning. Skills involving continuous motor activity (swimming, cycling) are retained much better than those involving discrete responses (rifle, flying a plane), probably because the former are usually learned to a higher degree (Eysenck 1960, Koonce, Chambliss and Irion 1964, Fleishman and Parker 1962, Ammons and Farr 1958).

Methods of Learning. Verbal and numerical material is retained much better if it is organized into categories or groups of some kind than if it is simply left in random order. Recall is even more effective when the categories are fairly narrow rather than broad (Bonsfield 1953, Miller 1956, Helson and Cover 1956).

Students remember verbal material better if they spend considerable time reciting it to themselves than if they just read it. About an 80:20 recitation to reading ratio gives the best results with pure rote material; much less recitation— about forty percent—is in order for meaningful material (here "recitation" should consist in stating the ideas in one's own words) (Gates 1917).

Review. Retention improves significantly with repetition and systematic review; considerable repetition and early review is particularly important when factual information is involved. Best retention is obtained through one early and one delayed review, such as after one day and then one or two weeks later (Tiedeman 1948, Gay 1971, 1973).

Interference. At least in the case of verbal-factual material, the degree of retention is lessened if students learn other similar material after or even before they learn the given material (retroactive and proactive inhibition respectively). The more similar the interpolated material, the greater the interference. The better the original material is learned, the less interference there will be (Mc-Geoch and McGeoch 1937, Underwood 1945, Slamecka 1959, Crouse 1970, 1971).

In the case of meaningful material, there is usually some interference of similar material on material that has already been learned, but not as much as in purely verbal material, particularly if the original material was sufficiently understood and the interpolated material was clearly discriminated from it. In fact, some studies have shown that the new material actually helps in the recall of the original material (retroactive facilitation); although other studies have not found such facilitation (Ausubel, Robbins and Blake 1957, Ausubel, Stager and Gaite 1968, Jensen and Anderson 1970, Wong 1970, Anderson and Myrow 1971).

EXERCISE 15-2.   Retention—Interference

Given below are the numbers from one to ten in four languages. Select one of the languages you do not know and spend one minute memorizing the list. Then relax for a minute thinking of two weeks at the ocean, skiing in the Rockies or in general how you would like to spend your next vacation. Then cover the lists and fill in the blanks with the numbers in that language.

English	French	Spanish	Italian
one	une	uno	uno
two	deux	dos	due
three	trois	tres	tre
four	quatre	cuatro	quattro
five	cinq	cinco	cinque
six	six	seis	sie
seven	sept	siete	sette
eight	huit	ocho	otto
nine	neuf	nueve	nove
ten	dix	diez	dieci

_____

_____

_____

_____

_____

_____

_____

_____

_____

_____

Now go back and select another language and spend one minute memorizing that list. When the minute is up cover the list and write the numbers from one to ten in the *first* language in which you learned them.

How did you do the second time as compared to the first? If you didn't do as well, it is most probably an indication that your learning of the second list interfered with your original learning. Interference of subsequent learning with original learning, termed retroactive inhibition, is particularly pronounced when the second material is similar to the first and/or the first material was not learned well—both of which were true in this experiment.

If the experiment had called for writing the numbers of the second language above, it would have been a study of proactive inhibition or the extent to which prior learning interferes with learning something. Just for kicks, see whether it did in this case by writing the numbers of the second language you learned below.

Again, if you had trouble remembering the numbers in the second language, it was probably due in part to the fact that you had learned a similar list in another language shortly before.

Theories of Forgetting

One of the more discouraging facts of life in a classroom is that students do not remember everything we try to teach them. Why do students forget some of what they have learned? This question is of obvious importance for teachers. If you know what causes forgetting, you will be more able to do something to help reduce it.

There are several possible explanations for forgetting, each of them having some basis in research. The early theories of Thorndike and the Gestaltists attributed forgetting to a weakening of memory traces either through disuse or through lack of cohesion. The most significant of the contemporary theories are those that attribute forgetting either to interference of other material that is learned or to the fact that the learner does not incorporate what he learns into an appropriate cognitive structure. We will consider each theory in turn.

Early Theories.   The earliest theory of forgetting was that proposed by Thorndike who claimed that a person forgot what he learned largely because of disuse or lack of practice with the passage of time. He stated: "In general . . . the disuse of a mental function weakens it, and the amount of weakening increases, the longer the lack of exercise" (Thorndike 1913, p. 243).

The Gestalt counterpart to the disuse theory is that forgetting occurs through the gradual decay of memory traces. Koffka hypothesized several ways in which memory traces could disappear, among them the proposition that they dissolve because they are not very well defined or organized. He described the process as the "autononous destruction of traces through lack of cohesion" (Koffka 1935, p. 507).

Although there is something to be said for these earlier theories, much more important for an understanding of why students forget are the contemporary theories of interference and integration into cognitive structure.

Interference.   The theory currently held by most stimulus-response psychologists is that of interference: we forget something because what we have learned either subsequently or previously interferes with (inhibits) the retention of that thing. The theory was originally stated by McGeoch:

> The data indicate that forgetting is a matter of the active blocking of the old by the new, rather than of a passive decay. . . . Retroactive inhibition or interference from interpolated activities is one of the major necessary conditions of forgetting; without the presence of inhibiting interpolated events forgetting would not in most cases appear. . . . Forgetting is then not a passive matter, but a result of an active interference from interpolated events. (McGeoch 1932, pp. 362-64)

According to the interference theory, if we did not learn anything after we learned, for instance, an idiom in French, we should remember that idiom without any difficulty. The problem is that we *do* learn other things and they tend to interfere with what we learned originally. This retroactive influence of subsequent learning upon original learning in which the one tends to inhibit the other is termed retroactive inhibition. More recently a second type of interference has been added to the theory, i.e. that what we have learned previously can inhibit our retention of what we have learned more recently (proactive inhibition). In other words according to the current view, forgetting can be due to interference that results either from previous or interpolated learning.

Integration into Cognitive Structure.   The most popular theory currently held by cognitive psychologists is that forgetting occurs because something has not been incorporated into one's cognitive structure. If something is understood and related to one's body of organized knowledge, it will be retained and will be readily available; if it is not so related but remains isolated, it will tend to be forgotten. A leading advocate of this theory is David Ausubel, who states:

> Subsumption of the traces of the learning task by an established ideational system provides anchorage for the new material, and thus constitutes the most orderly, efficient, and stable way of retaining it for future availability. . . . Rotely learned materials, on the other hand, are isolated from cognitive structure and are primarily influenced by the interfering effects of similar rote materials (Ausubel 1962)

According to the subsumption or integration theory, if we relate what we learn in some way to established cognitive structure, then we will tend to remember it. If we do not so relate it, we will tend to forget it. We can relate to our existing cognitive structures in at least two ways: by subsuming new ideas into our ordered knowledge of a topic, or by becoming aware of the differences and similarities between the new knowledge and our existing knowledge of that topic.

Both the disuse and the decay theories imply that forgetting is due to a change that occurs in the course of time, an internal weakening of the bond or trace itself. The interference theory claims that forgetting is due to the competition of events external to the original response or trace. The subsumption theory also explains retention and forgetting through a situation that is external to the learned information, whether or not it is incorporated into one's cognitive structure (even though "internal" to the person, cognitive structure is "external" to the information itself).

Which theory of forgetting is more tenable? Actually, there is evidence supporting each of them. Even though they are partly in conflict, they can be combined into an overall view of why a student forgets some of what he learns. Meaningful material that is understood and incorporated into one's cognitive structure is retained almost permanently. Meaningful material that is not so incorporated and rote material that is not learned well tends to be forgotten, mainly because of interference from other material but also because the memory traces tend to decay through lack of cohesion or repetition.

If this composite position is too eclectic for you, you may prefer to select one theory and build a case for its being the best explanation of forgetting. Note that on the basis of research, the two more current theories, interference and nonintegration into cognitive structure, have more support. On the basis of theory, recall that the interference explanation is more in keeping with the S-R approach, whereas most cognitive theorists prefer the cognitive structure explanation.

Applications in Teaching

Given what we have seen about the nature and conditions of retention, how can a teacher help insure that his students will retain what they have learned? The following suggestions are based on the research and theory we have just examined.

Intention.   Stress to students that they should have the intention to remember what they learned; encourage them to study so as to be able to recall what they learn, rather than simply recognize it.

Methods of Learning.   Have students organize concepts and relations that they learn into structures or interrelated knowledge, verbal-factual material into categories or other appropriate groupings.

Encourage students to recite to themselves what they are attempting to learn. For example, have them employ much more recitation than reading if it is a question of memorizing verbal material, or have them incorporate recitation into their study in the form of seeing whether they can summarize the main ideas if they are learning more logical material.

Have students relate new meaningful material that they are learning to what they already know about the subject, particularly the basic ideas or major structures of that field. Point out the similarities and differences with what they have seen previously, ask them to compare and contrast with a related topic. This will help eliminate any interference effect and promote permanence in retention.

Review.   Encourage frequent but distributed repetition and regular review of what has been learned, particularly if it is material that is more toward the rote end of the rote-logical continuum. This can be done by a short summary at the end of each class period, a brief review at the beginning of the next period, or shorter, more frequent tests.

Interference.   Try to prevent one subject from interfering with another by advising students (or administrators) that similar subjects with much verbal or factual material should be scheduled at different times of the day and by suggesting to students that they study similar subjects at different sittings rather than one after another. For example, someone taking two sciences or two languages should study one or two other subjects in between these classes.

The Measurement of Memory

What are some of the ways in which a teacher can measure retention of the various products that students have learned? Actually, he can use practically any of the evaluation techniques that have been suggested for the various types of learning in previous chapters. But specifically there are several ways to measure retention, each of which emphasizes a different aspect of memory.

Objective items such as those given below measure the recognition function of memory which is by far the easier of the two functions.

1. Match the following famous lines with the plays in which they occur.

    _____   "To be or not to be, that is the ques-   A   *Macbeth*
             tion."   B. *Romeo and Juliet*
    _____   "Out damned spot."   C. *Hamlet*

_____   "Goodnight. Goodnight. Parting is such   D. *Twelfth Night*
sweet sorrow . . ."
etc.

2. The famous farewell scene in which Romeo bids "goodnight" to Juliet
contains the words:

_____   "My love, goodnight; I shall not sleep til dawn shall break."
_____   "Parting is such sweet sorrow that I shall say 'goodnight' 'til it
be morrow."
_____   "Would that I could hold them in my arms forever and anon."
_____   "Would that you and I be joined in wedlock 'for too many
'goodnights' are said."

The more demanding function of memory, recall, would require written or
oral reproduction. For example:

3. How did Romeo say "goodnight" to Juliet? (Give verbatim)

In general, short answer items for verbal factual knowledge and essay questions
for concepts, relations, and structures measure the recall function of memory.
We have seen enough examples of these previously.

Ironically, the most sensitive technique for measuring retention, one that can
detect some degree of retention when recall measures cannot, is hardly ever used
in schools. This is the relearning method originally favored by Herman Ebbinghaus, the pioneer of memory studies, and still used in some psychological
laboratories. In the relearning method, the material is first learned to a criterion
level, usually one correct recitation; after a period of time, minutes to months,
the material is learned again to the criterion level. The time saved in the second
learning—more exactly the percent of the original time that was saved—represents the degree of retention of the material.

Although it is not too workable, if the relearning or "savings" method were
to be used in the classroom, it would go something like this:

1. Students learn the soliloquy "To be or not to be . . ." as well as they
wish. They record how long it took them.
2. After a period of time, if the teacher wishes to evaluate how well they
have retained it, he breaks the class into teams of two each and has
each student recite it to the other. If they find that they cannot recall
it very well, they study it again (in class) until they feel they can recite
it perfectly. Each student recites it to his partner who records the time.
3. The time saved (original time − second time) is an indication of the
degree of retention. The time saved is usually converted to percent:

$$\frac{\text{original time} - \text{relearning time}}{\text{original time}} \times 100 \quad \text{(to change decimal to percent).}$$

The savings method is probably more trouble than it is worth as a way of measuring retention in the classroom, but is outlined here mainly because it is a classic technique used in psychological studies of memory.

The teacher, realizing that multiple choice, matching, and true-false items measure recognition and that essay and short answer questions measure recall, will do best to choose between them according to his purposes.

Transfer

Besides retaining what they learn, teachers hope that students will be able to use their knowledge and skills in as many situations as possible, to apply them to subject fields and problems that are different from those in which they learned them originally. For instance, the scientific method learned in physics class hopefully will be applied later in the social sciences and in practical problems. Learning how to provide an exact proof to a solution in a geometry problem should carry over in writing expository essays and in preparing persuasive speeches. A knowledge of history can be of great help in the analysis of current international issues. One reason for studying a classical language such as Latin is to enrich one's knowledge of the etymology and nuances of the English language. The examples are endless, both for in school and out: a knowledge of mathematics applied to figuring proportionate amounts in a recipe, a knowledge of physics in fixing electrical applicances and making gadgets around the house, a knowledge of the culture of a country to make travel more rewarding and enjoyable, a habit of neatness acquired in a typing class carrying over to other school work.

These examples are all instances of what is called *transfer of learning*. Transfer of learning is a fact; it has been established by numerous experimental studies, particularly during the early decades of educational psychology (1920s and 1930s) and has been further substantiated by more recent replication studies.

There are some important questions to be asked about this fact of transfer, questions that we will take up in the second part of this chapter. What can transfer? How does transfer take place? What learning conditions make for the most transfer? How does one teach for transfer? How can we be sure that transfer will take place?

If we convert these questions to a list of subtopics to be treated in the remainder of the chapter, it will include the following:

> The nature and kinds of transfer
> Conditions influencing transfer
> Theories of transfer
> Teaching for transfer
> Measurement of transfer

The Nature and Kinds of Transfer

How is transfer of learning defined? What exactly can transfer? Before we get into the more important problems regarding transfer, we should answer these basic questions briefly.

From the examples given above, the meaning of transfer should be clear. It is simply the application of what is learned in one situation (history, Latin, school) to another situation (current issues, English, real-life problems).

What can transfer? Actually, we can transfer just about anything we learn:

psychomotor skills,	batting a softball to swinging a tennis racket;
verbal-factual learning,	French to Spanish, history to current issues;
concepts,	rhythm in music to creative writing, especially poetry;
relations,	proportionality in math to adjusting recipes in home economics;
structures,	evolution in biology to certain philosophical positions (pragmatism, cosmic evolution);
comprehension,	use of context in reading to understanding a painting;
problem solving,	scientific method in physics to practical problems;
creativity,	ideational and expressional fluency in English class to research report writing in social studies;
critical thinking,	deductive reasoning in geometry to speech writing;
affective learning,	appreciation of music and art in fine arts to a broader view of history (cultural as well as political history).

In other words, we can apply skills, knowledge, mental processes, values and appreciations to subject fields and contexts other than those in which we learned them originally.

Finally, transfer can be of two types:

1. We can apply what we learn to other subject areas and to various situations outside of school (horizontal transfer).
2. We can apply what we learn at one point in a course or subject field to learning a related topic later in the same course or subject field, making that topic more intelligible or more readily learned (vertical transfer).

We are concerned here with positive transfer or the case in which learning one thing *helps* in learning or performing something else. Negative transfer, or when original learning *interferes* with learning or performing another task, is actually the same as the interference or proactive inhibition that we considered in the section on memory.

Conditions Influencing Transfer

How can transfer of learning be fostered to a maximum degree? Some of the conclusions of the research on the question of the conditions of transfer are as follows.

Understanding. An emphasis on understanding concepts and principles results in much greater transfer than does an emphasis on memory and factual information, both for subject areas and situations different from the original subject and for further topics and problems within the same subject (Hilgard et al. 1953, McDougall 1958, Wittrock 1963, Mayer and Greeno 1972).

Practice.   Practice on a variety of problems and an awareness of possibilities for applying one's knowledge in various fields facilitates transfer more than practice on the same type of problem or on problems all in the same subject area (Lloyd 1960, Wittrock and Twelker 1964, Ulmer 1939).

On the other hand, practice on a series of tasks or problems of the same type improves an individual's ability to learn new material or solve new problems that are related or similar to the practice tasks. This progressive improvement in learning or problem solving within the same area is referred to as "learning to learn" (Harlow 1949).

Finally, the extent to which we are able to apply what we learn depends on how thoroughly we have learned it initially. Specifically, the amount of positive transfer has been found to increase as the amount of practice on the learning task increases (Mandler 1962).

Similarity.   At least in the area of verbal learning, the more similar one situation (in this case word) is to another, the more positive transfer is likely to occur (Bruce 1933).

Direct Teaching.   Transfer of what is learned does not take place automatically, but only if the possibilities of transfer are stressed in a course. For instance, if derivations are stressed in Latin, or principles of reasoning in geometry, then some transfer can be expected (Haskell 1923, Pond, 1938, Ulmer 1939). In addition learning skills that have wide applicability, e.g. study skills, outlining, have usually been found to result in higher grades and even in improved reasoning ability (Salisbury 1947, Howell 1950, Haslam and Brown 1968).

Individual Differences.   As might be expected, brighter children are able to discover generalizations and apply them more effectively than those of average intelligence or below. However, when the initial material is adapted to the ability level of students, there seems to be no difference among ability levels in their capacity for applying it (Ulmer 1939, Klausmeier and Check 1962).

EXERCISE 15-3.   Transfer—Learning to Learn

One kind of vertical transfer is learning to learn. Previous attempts to learn something should make later learning easier and more effective. For instance, practice in learning verbal associations of a certain kind will probably result in more efficient learning of similar verbal associations at a later date.

How would this work out in school learning? In learning the vocabulary of a foreign language, for instance, the first attempts to memorize a list will take a while, but after the fourth or fifth try the student should find learning the vocabulary list considerably easier.

You can actually design your own experiment to study this question. On pages 397-98 are provided five lists of English-German vocabulary combinations as material for your experiment. You will need to specify the exact conditions of your experiment. For instance:

1. Your hypothesis clearly stated: something like "the subject will be able to recall a greater number of vocabulary combinations on the fifth list than on the first."[1]
2. A measure of learning: for instance, you might use either the time taken to learn a list so you can recite it perfectly once or the number of associations you are able to learn in a specified amount of time, say twenty seconds.
3. Rest time between lists: at least several minutes, even more if you want, but it should be a fixed time for each list.
4. Testing: you should decide whether you want to use an oral or written test; also, to avoid tempting your "subject" to just memorize the German words in order, you will probably want to test for each list in random order (such a random list is provided following the vocabulary lists).
5. Difficulty of lists: although the words have been chosen so that each list is of comparable difficulty, you may wish to control for difficulty even further by randomizing the order in which you learn them.
6. Controls for studying one list at a time: somehow you should make sure you cannot see the other lists while studying the one at hand; either cut a square out in the middle of a sheet of paper and use it for the list you are learning, blocking out the rest, or cover the rest with your hands, or perhaps even cut out the lists and pick up one at a time.
7. Reporting results: a simple tabulation of times or number of words correct in each instance, perhaps put on a graph, is fine; if you decide to do this as a class experiment, after you all decide on the same experimental conditions and controls, you can put the data together and someone can do a t-test to see if the results support a significant improvement from the first to last list.

Once you have all of your controls worked out, begin the experiment.

1. happy — froh
   tree — baum
   thin — dunn
   path — weg
   table — tisch

2. solid — fest
   place — ort
   noise — larm

---

1. You will probably want to key on the learning to learn hypothesis as your primary one; however you should keep in mind the opposite possibility of former lists interfering with learning later lists (proactive inhibition), since the learning will not be very thorough.

dress — kleid
eye   — auge

3. beard — bart
   look   — blick
   time   — zeit
   part   — teil
   sound — schall

4. song   — lied
   small — klein
   gift   — gabe
   trip   — reise
   shirt   — hemd

5. favor — gunst
   clean — rein
   head   — kopf
   clock — uhr
   smoke — rauch

1. thin   — _____
   happy — _____
   table — _____
   path   — _____
   tree   — _____

2. place — _____
   eye   — _____
   solid — _____
   noise — _____
   dress — _____

3. sound — _____
   time   — _____
   beard — _____
   part   — _____
   look   — _____

4. small — _____
   trip   — _____
   shirt   — _____
   song   — _____
   gift   — _____

5. clean — _____
   favor — _____
   clock —_____
   head — _____
   smoke — _____

If you showed an improvement from the first through the fifth list, this supports a positive transfer or learning to learn hypothesis. If there was a decrease in efficiency, this would support a negative transfer or interference (proactive inhibition) hypothesis. If there was little or no change from the first to last list, this could indicate either that the positive and negative transfer effects cancelled each other out or that the experiment simply showed no influence one way or the other.

Theories of Transfer

How do we apply the products and processes that we have learned? In other words, how is transfer of learning best explained? Is it that our minds in general are strengthened by what we learn—particularly the more difficult subjects—so that they can operate well in all areas? Or is it much more specific, namely that we apply words, ideas, and skills to situations that are very similar to the original context in which they were learned? Or perhaps we transfer ideas, relations and mental processes because they possess a sufficient level of generality so as to be applicable to a wide range of related situations. These are some of the main explanations that have been offered over the years to account for the fact of transfer. We will examine these explanations more at length, giving some primary sources for each of them.

Formal Discipline Theory.   The prevalent theory before scientific psychology addressed itself to the problem was that transfer takes place because what we study sharpens or strengthens the mind in somewhat the same way as physical exercise strengthens our muscles, with the result that we are able to do better in practically any subject field or in any real-life problem. The explanation was called the formal discipline theory. One of its chief proponents was the educationist Joseph Payne, who claimed that instruction is "a species of mental gymnastics fitted to draw forth, exercise, invigorate and mature all the faculties." In particular, "the study of the Latin language itself does eminently discipline the faculties and secure to a greater degree than that of the other subjects we have discussed, the formation and growth of those mental qualities which are the best preparation for the business of life—whether that business is to consist in making fresh mental acquisitions or in directing the powers thus strengthened and matured, to professional and other pursuits" (Payne 1883, pp. 249, 250, 264).

Even well into the present century there were educators who held the formal discipline theory. In 1940 Bruce Barton stated:

Education . . . is trying to spread out and teach too much—a smattering of everything. We will live to see the time when there will again be more emphasis on mental discipline, on toughening the fibers of the mind, on subjects that make the mind tackle a hard problem and work it through to an accurate conclusion.

If you go through high school and college taking easy courses you are not cheating anyone but yourself. Put into your curriculum some hard courses—some courses that may have no relation to the work that you will do after but will exercise your mind, so that you can stand competition in the office or profession where you will eventually have to battle for a living. (Quoted in Garrett 1957)

The theory of formal discipline holds: (1) that transfer of learning is very broad and applies to all kinds of situations, (2) that it takes place because the powers of the mind are strengthened through exercise and "discipline," and (3) that the most effective exercise comes from the more difficult subjects in the curriculum such as Latin and mathematics.

Identical Elements Theory.   One of the most significant series of early experiments regarding transfer of training was that conducted by Thorndike and Woodworth at the turn of the century. In one experiment dealing with the perception of certain parts of speech, subjects were first tested for their ability to perceive and cancel verbs and adjectives, then given training in this ability, and finally tested with similar and different material. They found that the efficiency in marking the same parts of speech improved about twenty to twenty-five percent in speed and about sixty to seventy-five percent in accuracy as a result of the training. On the other hand, the ability to mark other parts of speech, while showing some increase in speed, often showed a decided decrease in accuracy.

From this and similar experiments, Thorndike derived a theory of identical elements in which he claimed that improvement or transfer occurs only when two situations are very similar. He stated:

One mental function or activity improves others in so far as and because they are in part identical with it, because it contains elements common to them. Addition improves multiplication because multiplication is largely addition; knowledge of Latin gives increased ability to learn French because many of the facts learned in the one case are needed in the other. The study of geometry may lead a pupil to be more logical in all respects, for one element of being logical in all respects is to realize that facts can be absolutely proven and to admire and desire this certain and unquestionable sort of demonstration. . . .

These identical elements may be in the stuff, the data concerned in the training, or in the attitude, the method taken with it. The former kind may be called *identities of substance* and the latter, *identities of procedure.*

Identity of Substance. Thus special training in the ability to handle numbers gives an ability useful in many acts of life outside of school classes because of identity of substance, because of the fact that the stuff of the world is so often to be numbered and counted. The data of the scientist, the grocer, the carpenter and the cook are in important features the same as the data of the arithmetic class. So also the ability to speak and write well in classroom exercises in English influences life widely because home life, business and professional work are all in part talking and writing. . . .

Identity of Procedure. The habit acquired in a laboratory course of looking to see how chemicals do behave, instead of guessing at the matter or learning statements about it out of a book, may make a girl's methods of cooking or a boy's methods of manufacturing more scientific because the attitude of distrust of opinion and search for facts may so possess one as to be carried over from the narrower to the wider field. Difficulties in studies may prepare students for the difficulties of the world as a whole by cultivating the attitudes of neglect or discomfort, ideals of accomplishing what one sets out to do, and the feeling of dissatisfaction with failure. (Thorndike, *The Principles of Teaching: Based on Psychology,* 1906, quoted in Thorndike 1913, pp. 276-77)

Thorndike held that the moderate amount of transfer that results from the learning of something is quite specific and occurs because of the presence of common or similar components in the two activities or situations. For Thorndike, transfer is specific because learning is specific; both must be described in terms of actual elements and particular connections.

Generalization Theory. Another significant experiment conducted only a few years after those of Thorndike and Woodworth is the well-known study of Charles H. Judd. Judd attempted to determine the effect of understanding the principle of refraction of light on the subject's ability to hit a target submerged in water. At first, all subjects practiced throwing darts at a target twelve inches under water; then one group was given a complete explanation of the principle. When the target was raised to four inches under water, the group that understood the principle of refraction of light adapted very quickly whereas the other group was confused.

From this experiment, Judd derived the explanation that transfer occurs because we have formed general ideas and methods of thinking that are applicable to many related instances or situations, not just those from which they were formed originally. Commenting on his experiment, he says:

[Those] who knew the theory of refraction adapted themselves rapidly to the second depth of water. Their ability to deal with the new situation grew out of the fact that they recognized the true relation between this and the earlier situation. The theory had put all their experiences . . . into a single general scheme or thought. . . . In other words, after they had mastered one practical situation and had comprehended it in the light of their theoretical knowledge, they were able to solve rapidly and with all the advantages of generalized experience a new problem which involved both practical adjustment and analysis. Theory is a kind of summary of many experiences. It makes possible the proper interrelating and interpreting of a whole body of varied experiences. (Judd 1939, p. 509)

Judd further explains his theory of transfer as follows.

> [A pupil] should be taught that the findings of science all group them-
> selves into related systems of generalizations. He should be taught that
> concentration of attention, analysis and discrimination are useful habits of
> mind that he can use in all the situations which he encounters. In short, he
> should be taught by every possible device to see the advantages of
> generalization.
>
> Generalization is another name for the relating of experiences in such a
> way that what is gained at one point will redound to the advantage of the
> individual in many spheres of thought and action. When a person fully
> grasps a scientific generalization or when he gains a view of a wide range of
> relations, he acquires independence and breath of intellectual power and
> becomes capable of transferring training to situations that are different
> from those in which he was first trained. (Judd 1939, p. 514)

In another place he states:

> Mental development consists . . . in equipping the individual with the pow-
> er to think abstractly and to form general ideas. When the ends thus
> described are attained, transfer of training . . . has taken place because it is
> the very nature of generalization and abstraction that they extend beyond
> the particular experiences in which they originate (Judd 1927, p. 441)

Judd held that most transfer of learning is moderately broad and occurs
because the two situations are related through a general idea or principle that
applies to both instances. Ideas and principles are abstracted from a certain
number of experiences but are in turn applicable to many more experiences,
even to those that are somewhat different from the original ones.

Which theory do you prefer and why? There seem to be several possible
reactions to the explanations of transfer:

1. You may consider them all to be quite ancient and look for more recent
theories to explain the phenomenon of transfer. You will probably be disappointed for at least two reasons: (a) theory building in the area of transfer has
not kept pace with the extensive research on the problem, and (b) the newer
theories such as stimulus predifferentiation, transposition, and learning set
theory, (cf. Ellis 1965) are based on laboratory research in perceptual or
paired-associate learning and have little relevance for education. At the present
time you will probably have to be content with the theories outlined here;
although old, they are still considered to be relevant to classroom learning.

2. You might consider the theories to be different, and then on the basis of
the experimental evidence and the rational pros and cons you might select the
most tenable theory as the point of view that you prefer.

3. You might conclude that at least two of the theories differ more by way
of emphasis and degree than substantially. Since in this view they are more
similar than different, it makes little difference which of the two you select.
(Although if you are an S-R theorist, you will probably favor identical elements

somewhat more; similarly if you are a cognitive theorist, you will tend more toward the generalization theory.)

4. Realizing that there are several types of learning, you might select one theory which, on the basis again of research and reason, best fits a certain type or types of learning and then another theory which best explains other types of learning. For instance, you might conclude that the identical elements theory is more applicable to verbal-factual material and probably psychomotor skills, whereas the generalization theory best explains transfer in relation to concepts, relations, and structures.

In any event the arguments provided in exercise 15-4 will probably be of some help.

EXERCISE 15-4. Theories of Transfer—Critique

The student's ability to apply what he learns is an important objective in education. The theory of transfer of learning that a teacher holds will to a large extent determine his emphasis in both the curriculum and teaching strategies. For instance, one who holds the formal discipline theory will argue strongly for the study of the classics, mathematics, and other difficult subjects and will stress drill and long assignments in his teaching. The teacher who favors the identical elements theory will be oriented toward vocational training and useful subjects in his view of the curriculum, stressing specific skills and information that students can use later on, e.g. typing, welding, social studies, and modern language. In addition he will stress real-life problems and the most commonly used words, skills, and principles in the academic subjects. The teacher who favors the generalization theory will be more oriented toward a liberal education (science, humanities, mathematics, social science), emphasizing an understanding of the basic concepts and structure of each subject as well as their widespread applicability.

You can readily see, therefore, that it is important for you to decide on a theory of transfer before you begin to teach, for it will greatly affect your approach to teaching and the curriculum. Given below are some criticisms of each theory of transfer that we considered in the text portion of the chapter; indicate which theory each statement criticizes. Then on the basis of the pros and cons for each, select the theory or combination of theories you think is most tenable.

	F.D.	I.E.	Gen.
1. If situations are identical or even very similar, there is no real transfer, only repetition. A criticism of . . .	____	____	____

2. Experimental evidence against it is strong, e.g. the early but excellent experiment of Woodrow (1927), who used three groups:

a. control—just took tests

F.D.   I.E.   Gen.

   b. practice–3 hours of practice in memorizing poetry and
     nonsense syllables
   c. training–1:40 hrs. of practice, 1:20 hrs. of instruction in
     methods of memorizing (by wholes, grouping, self-testing,
     use of secondary associations, etc.)

In the post-test with prose, Turkish words, and dates, the
training group showed large positive transfer (7.5 points), but
the practice group showed very little transfer (0.5 points).
Evidence offered against . . .   ____ ____ ____

3. The mind is not a material entity and so cannot be strengthened through pure practice or exercise like a muscle can. An
argument against . . .   ____ ____ ____

4. If general ideas are stressed, one can lose sight of specific
objectives and concrete, practical skills and information. An
argument against . . .   ____ ____ ____

5. The experimental evidence in its favor is narrow and consists
mainly of perceptual and verbal tasks; other experimental evidence shows something broader, the understanding of principles, to be the main basis of transfer. For instance the experiment of Craig (1953):

Task: for groups of words, all but one of which were somehow
related, subject had to select the word that did not belong.

Three groups:

   A. told to choose the word that did not belong;
   B. told that there was a reason or principle in each case for a
     word being inappropriate and not belonging;
   C. told what the reason or principle was connecting all of the
     words but one in each case.

Results: Group C which understood the principle involved
showed the most transfer with new lists; Group A showed the
least. (Cf. also experiments by Katona 1940, Hilgard et al.
1953) Evidence and criticism against . . .   ____ ____ ____

    The formal discipline theory has been under attack from psychologists ever
since the turn of the century. The experimental evidence against it is strong,
from the early experiments of Thorndike and Judd to the classic experiment of
Woodrow and beyond. The case against it is also supported by reason, particularly by the argument of the nature of intelligence. Man's intellect is something
more than a material entity; it is either a function of a person or an immaterial
power, depending on your philosophical outlook. Whereas an internal sense such
as rote memory, which is a physical part of the brain, can be improved to a slight
extent through pure exercise, the intellect cannot. Intellectual functions are
developed through the person's first becoming aware of the proper techniques of
analyzing, organizing, and remembering and *then* practicing these techniques.
    An early criticism of the identical elements theory was that if the elements in

the two situations have to be identical, there will be no genuine transfer, only a repetition of responses in a slightly different context. Thorndike responded by saying that the elements had to be similar, not exactly identical. The emphasis, however, was still on the presence of common or very similar components in the original and the new situations, and therefore little real application or genuine transfer takes place. This of course is in keeping with the findings of Thorndike's own experiments using perceptual and verbal material. But other experiments, such as those of Katona, Hilgard, and Craig, showed that considerable transfer does occur, mainly when the subjects understand a principle or underlying reason of something.

The experimental evidence has really favored Judd's more cognitive-oriented position of generalization. Judd admits that little transfer should be expected in "lower forms of experience: facts, dates, etc.," whereas in "higher forms of mental life: relations, ideas, transfer is great." In other words, he is saying that Thorndike's findings of minimal, specific transfer are exactly what is to be expected in Thorndike's area of research; but when experimentation is done using problems involving underlying concepts and principles, considerable transfer takes place and is due to the general nature of concepts, principles, and organized knowledge, in that they are applicable to a wide variety of related situations.

Behaviorists, however, will criticize the generalization theory because of the danger of neglecting specific behavioral objectives as well as practical, useful knowledge and skills in the curriculum. The cognitive theorists will counter the objection by saying that a true liberal education with its emphasis on broadly applicable concepts and structures (1) offers more possibilities for students to use their knowledge in a variety of situations and (2) respects man's dignity and freedom of choice much more than the delimiting emphasis on teaching for specific outcomes and the vocationally oriented curriculum that results from the identical elements theory.

It should be becoming clear that just as transfer of learning is only one, and not necessarily the most important, of the objectives in education, so within the question of transfer the psychological findings comprise only one dimension, along with the philosophical and social dimensions, that must be considered for a satisfactory solution of the overall problem. All that you can be expected to do in the context of educational psychology is to determine which position, or combination of positions, you prefer on the basis of the psychological considerations.

Teaching for Transfer

How can a teacher help insure that his students will be able to apply their knowledge and skills to a variety of situations once they have learned them? In a word, how can he teach for transfer? On the basis of what we have seen so far, the following suggestions can be offered.

Understanding.   Emphasize understanding of concepts, principles, and structures rather than learning facts and information; more transfer takes place by way of generalization of principles than anything else.

Explicit Teaching.   Teach directly for transfer as well as for other objectives, and suggest applications in a variety of fields and situations:

a. Give specific examples of how a concept or principle can be related to other topics and fields.
b. Point out similarities between words of different languages or facts of different eras.
c. Illustrate how a method of thinking, of research, or of making something can also be used in other contexts.
d. Suggest applications of values and attitudes to the life of the students both in and out of school.

Quality of Learning.   Make sure that students learn skills, words, concepts, and principles well in the first place by using the most effective approaches suggested in previous chapters: involvement, practice, induction and problem-centered techniques, and the like. Thoroughness of original learning will help promote its transfer.

Practice.   If possible, provide students with opportunities to use the principles and methods they learn in a variety of contexts. This is difficult, but the best insurance that transfer will occur later is that students realize what the possible applications are and then actually use what they learn in several different subject fields or other situations.

Individual Differences.   Make provision for individual differences in ability by providing more examples of possible applications of what is learned for those of average and below average ability; and varying the degree of difficulty of learning tasks to fit the ability level of students.

Measuring Transfer

How can teachers be sure that their students will be able to transfer their knowledge and skills? There are both informal and more objective techniques available as measures of transfer of learning.

In general, any measure of transfer has to include an example that is new and different from those that have been used in the original teaching of the knowledge or skill.

For instance, a case, either a capsule case or a complete version, can be given and students can be asked to analyze it or tell what the outcome will probably be. For example:

> Years ago the local radio station used to offer several programs with "live" music, but for the past ten years it has only used recorded music. A long-standing contract with the musicians' union provided for several musicians to continue to be employed by the station even though they no longer played. Recently, when the contract expired, the station refused to

renew it and the union went on strike, picketing the station and running ads in the local paper. When all attempts at settlement failed, the station, annoyed at the continued picketing, took the case to court. What will the court probably rule regarding the picketing?

Such a case can be used in several ways:

1. As an introduction to an informal discussion aimed at seeing how the class in general is able to apply their knowledge of the Taft-Hartley Act.

2. As an introduction to an essay question that asks the students to support their opinion as to what the court will decide.

3. As the beginning of an objective item that would continue by offering several choices such as:

    a. Illegal. Featherbedding is not allowed.

    b. Illegal. The union is no longer under contract with the station.

    c. Legal. The musicians can use any peaceful means to protect their jobs.

    d. Legal. Strikes are allowed against unilateral actions of employers.

4. As part of a more extended case which can then serve as the basis for several multiple choice or other types of questions.

To a large extent, testing for transfer of learning through an objective item involves having the student relate a principle or concept with a novel example that is taken either from the same or a different subject field, or that represents a practical application to something outside of school. There are several possible formats.

The example can be given first, i.e. in the stem, with the possible concepts or principles that it illustrates listed as options. For instance:

John Raskin, a good but not outstanding miler from Denver (mile high) whose previous best time was 4:09, competed in a meet in Los Angeles against some of the leading collegiate milers in the country. He not only improved on his time but won the race in 4:02. What is the most plausible reason for his excellent performance?

    a. Greater expenditure of effort results in greater speed in blood circulation.

    b. More red corpusles bring more oxygen into the blood stream.

    c. Higher air pressure forces more oxygen into the lungs.

    d. Greater density of air makes one's body seem relatively lighter.

Or the concept or principle can be given in the stem with capsule examples comprising the options. For instance:

When a current is induced by the relative motion of a conductor and a magnetic field, the direction of the induced current is such as to establish a magnetic field that opposes the motion. This principle is illustrated by

    a. a magnet attracting a nail.

    b. an electric generator or dynamo.

    c. the motion of a compass needle.

    d. an electric doorbell.

Finally, a case or an example can be given together with some specific solutions, the correct one calling for the application of a certain concept or principle, such as in the radio station case above. Although the principle is not mentioned explicitly, the student must be aware of it if he is to arrive at the correct solution.

In each instance, of course, an essay or short answer question can be substituted for the multiple choice item. For variety, either several true-false items or a series of statements or examples from which the student checks the applicable ones can be used.

Any appropriate format is usable; the important points in the evaluation of the capacity to transfer learning are that the students associate a principle with an example and that there be an element of novelty in the example(s).

EXERCISE 15-5.   Teaching for Retention and Transfer

Given below are some specific approaches used by teachers in different subjects. Indicate whether each approach mainly illustrates a condition favoring retention or a condition favoring transfer of learning.

	Reten.	Trans.
1. Physics teacher has students use the actual scientific method in lab experiments rather than follow a cookbook approach.	____	____
2. Math teacher gives a twenty-minute test each Friday containing problems on topics covered during the week.	____	____
3. Geometry teacher suggests similarities between a geometric proof and establishing a case in a debate.	____	____
4. French teacher often refers to common roots of words in French and English.	____	____
5. Biology teacher constantly stresses the function of each organ, how it is similar to those of organisms studied previously and how it is an advance over the organs of lower species.	____	____
6. Geography teacher encourages students to group countries in various ways: by region, by products, by climate, etc.	____	____
7. History teacher stresses importance of obtaining sufficient evidence for a thesis or opinion, of withholding judgment until evidence is convincing; he indicates how this attitude is also important for the physical and social sciences as well.	____	____
8. History teacher holds a discussion on a current international issue each week during which he constantly ask questions about the background of the problem and about parallels with what other countries have done in similar situations.	____	____
9. Counselor schedules senior social studies electives in both morning and afternoon so students will not have two such classes back to back.	____	____

Having students use the scientific method insures a high quality of learning which is an important condition of transfer.

Stressing similarities and possibilities of application—in geometry, French, etc.—is teaching directly for transfer; so is suggesting the importance of a demanding attitude toward evidence in other fields as well as one's own.

Having students actually use what they learn in another context, e.g. history-current issues, is one of the best ways to promote transfer.

Frequent tests encourage distributed study and regular review, both of which help retention.

Relating material to cognitive structure or basic ideas, e.g. functions of organs, greatly aids retention; grouping or classifying factual knowledge also helps one remember it (6).

Removing occasions for interference (9) also helps students to retain what they learn.

Suggested Readings

Adams, J. *Human Memory*. New York: McGraw-Hill, 1970.

Ellis, H. C. *The Transfer of Learning*. New York: Macmillan, 1965.

Grose, R. F. and Birney, R. C. *Transfer of Learning*. Princeton, N. J.: D. Van Nostrand, 1963.

Katona, G. *Organizing and Memorizing*. New York: Columbia University Press, 1940.

16

Evaluation of Learning

Throughout our treatment of the many kinds of classroom learning, we have seen a number of ways for evaluating learning outcomes. We have included evaluation techniques in each chapter rather than leaving it all until now for two reasons: first, each type of learning has its own most appropriate methods of evaluation, and second, evaluation is—or should be—an integral part of the learning process.

What is evaluation? What are some of the more important types of evaluation and evaluation techniques? What characteristics do all good evaluation techniques possess? How can you as a teacher construct quality tests and other evaluation techniques? Finally, how should you report the results of any evaluation of your students? These are the specific questions that we will be concerned with in this final chapter. But first, do a quick review of the evaluation techniques we have seen so far in the book.

EXERCISE 16-1. Review of Evaluation Techniques

We have seen many evaluation techniques that can be used for the various types of learning we have considered. By way of review, indicate which two or three techniques you would prefer to use for each type of learning.

_____ Words, facts	1. Essay
_____ Concepts	2. Oral questions
_____ Relations	3. Short answer
_____ Structures	4. True–false

_____	Comprehension	5. Matching
_____	Creativity	6. Multiple choice
_____	Problem Solving	7. Complex objective item
_____	Critical Thinking	8. Informal observation
_____	Skills	9. Systematic observation
_____	Attitudes, values	10. Rating scale
_____	Transfer	11. Checklist
_____	Motivation	12. Attitude scale
		13. Project
		14. Production
		15. Interview

Each teacher has his own preferences regarding evaluation techniques, but some of the most appropriate ones for each type of learning (plus transfer and motivation) are the following.

Facts, words:	Short answer, matching, multiple choice
Concepts:	Essay, oral questions, multiple choice
Relations:	Essay, multiple choice, complex objective items
Structures:	Essay, oral questions, complex objective items
Comprehension:	Oral questions, essay, complex objective items
Creativity:	Productions, checklist or rating scale, essay
Problem solving:	Informal or systematic observation, project, essay
Critical thinking:	Informal observation, essay, complex objective items
Skills:	Informal observation, rating scale, checklist
Attitudes, values:	Attitude scale, rating scale, observation
Transfer:	Essay, multiple choice, complex objective items
Motivation:	Interview, attitude scale, checklist

The Nature of Evaluation

Evaluation is a judgment either about (1) a person, his abilities, his interests, his personality, or (2) his learning or performance, how well he has learned the knowledge and skills that form the essential objectives of a subject area.

There are many techniques that you as a teacher can use as a basis for making such a judgment. Some are more informal such as observation, an interview, evaluating a creative production; some involve assigning a numerical value to the performance or to a quality of the person according to some rule, in other words, measurement. In this latter category are included the following:

1. tests—measures which involve problems or questions relating to knowledge or ability;
2. assignments—papers, projects, homework which students work on individually or in groups;

3. inventories—measures which contain questions about one's interests or personality;
4. rating scales and checklists—measures that contain statements or phrases which reflect various aspects of performance or behavior;
5. other (laboratory) techniques that are not ordinarily used in relation to classroom learning (and therefore will not be considered here).

The relation then, between evaluation, measurement, tests, etc. is summarized through the schema (figure 16-1).

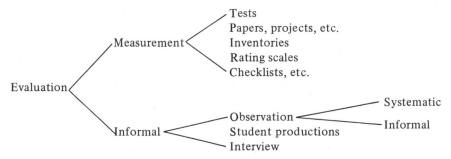

Figure 16-1. *Evaluation Techniques*

In teaching, the most commonly used type of evaluation technique is the test that calls for the student to answer a number of problem-type questions. The various types of tests used in the classroom can be thought of as being on a continuum depending on the degree of generality or specificity in the content.

1. General intelligence tests: content is general, supposedly familiar to most students of a certain age or grade level; emphasis is on thought processes and how one compares with others in basic mental ability.
2. Multiple aptitude: content is general within specified areas such as number, space, vocabulary; emphasis is on thought processes and how one *will* perform in certain subject areas.
3. Special aptitude tests: content is related to one subject area such as art, law; emphasis is on the thought processes necessary for that subject and how one will achieve it.
4. General achievement tests: content is related to several subject areas; emphasis is on broad knowledge and basic skills that are considered representative of the several subject areas covered.
5. Course-oriented achievement test: content is specifically related to the topics and objectives emphasized in a course; emphasis is on the knowledge and skills that are considered important for that course.

The first four types of tests are practically always standardized tests constructed by experts.[1] The last is most often constructed by a teacher for a

---

1. Standardized tests are published tests that: (1) have been constructed by experts, with the validity and other important qualities of the test established; (2) have been

specific course (although there are a few standardized tests of this type available for certain courses).

Basic Types of Evaluation

Evaluation traditionally has been done by the teacher. But besides teacher-centered evaluation, there is also self-evaluation and teacher-student cooperative evaluation. For instance, in evaluating creative productions, you may prefer to encourage students to evaluate their own work rather than always depending on you for criticism. Or in evaluating the learning outcomes of a section of the course, you might try having a conference with each student to discuss how well he has been achieving the objectives for that part of the course—with both you and the student providing input to the discussion.

Which type is preferable? They all have advantages. On one hand the teacher will possess the better background in terms of both experience and level of competence in the subject. On the other hand, if the student is brought into the evaluation process, he will most likely develop a more mature and independent outlook toward his own learning and achievement in school. Cooperative evaluation, if really done cooperatively, will take advantage of the teacher's competence and will also shift at least some responsibility for evaluation to the student. The student will contribute a dimension to the evaluation that would probably escape the teacher; at the same time the teacher can temper the overgenerous judgment of some students.

The purpose for which you use the evaluation techniques in relation to learning form another important basis for distinguishing types of evaluation. Depending on your specific purpose for using an achievement test, we can distinguish among several types of evaluation: preliminary, diagnostic, and summative evaluation plus evaluation for mastery. Each type uses a different kind of achievement test. Each type of evaluation also addresses itself to a specific concern of a teacher, employs a specific emphasis in a test itself, and calls for a special kind of follow-up once the results are known. We will consider each of these points for the several main types of evaluation as it relates to learning.

Preliminary Evaluation

Before a topic is treated this type helps the teacher decide what background students have in the topic to be covered. Do students possess the necessary cognitive structures on which to base a more advanced treatment of a topic? To find this out, a teacher can give a pre-test, a fairly easy general test which stresses the main ideas of the topic to be treated, especially the ideas that will be taken for granted as the topic progresses. If you find that some students do not

---

administered to a large enough group so that norms or standards have been established to which you can compare your students; (3) have exact or standard instructions for administering and scoring plus interpreting the results.

understand some prerequisite material, it will pay you to fill in the gaps before proceeding. Of course if most of the class shows up weak in one or two areas, you will want to treat these as preliminary points with the class as a whole before getting into the topic itself.

Diagnostic Evaluation

During a topic or section of a course, this type discovers if students are learning the topic sufficiently well. Are the teaching approaches that have been used effective? What particular difficulties are some of the students having? What sections bear further review or reteaching?

A quiz or other measure of moderate difficulty, covering one portion or subtopic within a broader topic, and stressing the main points that have been treated can help the teacher answer these questions. The measure should also include any points that seemed to have given students particular difficulty when they studied them. If most students do poorly on an item or two, you will want to reteach that specific section of the topic. If only a few students are weak on certain items, you can give them review work on those points.

Evaluation for Mastery

At the end of a specific topic, this type detects how well students have mastered the essential content and objectives of a particular section of the course. Do they possess the basic knowledge and requisite skills to go on to the next section? For this purpose a teacher gives a test or other measure which covers the knowledge, skills, and other learning outcomes that all students are expected to achieve. The level of difficulty is minimal and students are expected to get practically all items correct.

If a student's test score shows that he has not mastered the essentials of the topic, he reviews the topic—either individually or with the help of the teacher or even with the help of a student who *has* mastered it—until he makes a near perfect score on a similar test of essentials given several days or a week later.

Summative Evaluation

At the end of a major section of a course, this type measures how well students have learned the topics covered in a section of the course. Putting their classwork and outside reading together, what is the extent of each student's knowledge and skill regarding several major topics of the course?

For this type of evaluation, traditionally the most common, a comprehensive test or other instrument (or combination of instruments) is given when a major section of the course is completed. It should include items of varying degrees of difficulty, some fairly easy, most of moderate difficulty, and a few quite difficult.

This type of evaluation is designed to inform you of the relative standing of each student in the class in terms of the overall learning outcomes for a section of the course. At this point it is too late to provide any remedial help to students; the results are merely reported to those who have a right to know them (students, parents, counselors, administrators).

Characteristics of Measuring Instruments

What are some important characteristics that you will want to make sure any test or other measure you plan to use possesses? You will certainly want to know exactly what it measures, how accurately it measures it, and whether it gives scores that will tell you something.

What Does It Measure?

Your most important concern is what the test or other instrument measures, or more generally, whether it actually does the job which you intend it to do. Do you want to evaluate your students' knowledge of relations and structures? You will want to construct a test that includes questions regarding principles and theories, not facts and concepts. Do you want to measure your students' aptitude for mathematics? You will want to use a test that has proven successful in predicting math grades for your grade level. Do you want to find out how thoroughly your students have learned the content of your course as a whole? You will want to either select a standardized achievement test that covers the same topics and objectives that you have stressed, or else construct your own test, making sure that your relative emphases on content areas and types of learning are reflected in the makeup of the test. In general, since you have a purpose for any measure you use, you will want to make sure that the measure is *valid* and does the job for which it is intended.

In any measure of learning outcomes the most important consideration is to what extent your measure gets at the content and objectives that you have emphasized in a course.[2] In other words the most important type of validity is content validity. For example, a test is given after a three-week segment of a fourth-grade math class that covered fractions, decimals, and percent. One week was spent on each, and in both class and homework, twice as much emphasis was put on solving word problems than on pure computation. A twenty-five item test that had about five or six word problems and about three computation items for each topic could be said to possess content validity. A content validity study for such a test would consist of a matrix of content and objectives plus the number of test items pertaining to each category (table 16-1).

Table 16-1

		Objectives	
		Ability to solve word problems	Computation ability
Content	Fractions (1/3)	6	3
	Decimals (1/3)	5	3
	Percent (1/3)	5	3

2. Recall that before chapter 6, when the parallels between types of learning, intellectual abilities, and educational objectives were analyzed, the three were seen to be very similar—differing more in a person's way of looking at them than in substance. In the context of evaluation, we can use the three almost interchangeably.

For the most part, whether a measure possesses content validity or not depends on your judgment that it corresponds with the content and objectives of your course. Setting up a tabulated comparison such as in the arithmetic example above will usually help you in making this judgment. Note that the correspondence does not have to be perfect, but it should be reasonably close.

For intelligence and aptitude tests, you will want to have some assurance that the test compares well with a recognized test of intelligence, such as the Stanford-Binet, or that it has actually been found to predict school achievement to a reasonable degree. The manual accompanying the test will give validity data, usually in terms of correlations with other tests or with school grades. Validity coefficients, as they are called, of about .50 or better are usually considered good; coefficients of .70 or better are considered excellent.

EXERCISE 16-2. Planning a Test for Content Validity

Given below are the types of learning objectives that have been emphasized in a biology course plus their relative weight in terms of percent. The teacher has already constructed some items and has ideas on several more; all of these items are summarized below. There are obviously too many items. Which ones would you select so that the time spent on the items corresponds to the relative emphasis placed on the various types of learning during the course? In other words, plan a test that will have a high degree of content validity.

The total test will take one full fifty-minute period. In terms of time you can figure that essays take approximately ten minutes, short essays five minutes, complex objective items five minutes, matching items five minutes, and multiple choice items one minute each.

Knowledge of biological facts	15%
Understanding of basic concepts in biology	15%
Knowledge of principles and relations	30%
Skill in using the scientific method to solve problems	15%
Skill in using laboratory apparatus	10%
Application of biological knowledge to practical situations	10%
Critical thinking regarding data and theories in biology	5%

_____ 1. Fifteen multiple choice items on names and characteristics of various chordates.

_____ 2. Matching item on varieties and characteristics of mammals.

_____ 3. Essay on the relation between structure and function of organs.

_____ 4. Five multiple choice items on the relation between the embryo and the mature organism.

_____ 5. Five short essays on basic concepts or processes of organisms: reproduction, nutrition, respiration, circulation, excretion.

_____ 6. Eight multiple choice items on basic concepts or processes of organisms.

_____ 7. Short essay on structure of a micro-organism that calls for viewing slide on compound microscope (which instructor will unfocus after each student uses it) (seven min.).

_____ 8. Complex objective item on safety on a camping trip. An essay calling for an analysis of a case concerning family nutrition.

_____ 9. Short essay on what procedure a student would use to solve a problem regarding the cause of a disease in a plant.

_____ 10. Essay evaluating Lamarck's view of evolution.

_____ 11. Complex objective item evaluating Darwin's and Lamarck's views of evolution.

For knowledge of facts—fifteen percent or seven and a half minutes—you would probably prefer a five-minute matching item (2) to fifteen minutes of multiple choice items. On one hand a few minutes or percentage points either way doesn't really matter; on the other hand, the student will no doubt bring his knowledge of factual material into his answers to other questions later in the test. Seven or eight multiple choice items would be all right, but fifteen would be too many for the weight given to the knowledge of facts.

For understanding of basic concepts, eight multiple choice items (6) would fit the emphasis intended much better than half the test devoted to short essays on basic concepts.

Knowledge of principles and relations is considered the most important single type of knowledge for the course. Therefore fifteen minutes worth of questions consisting of an essay (3) plus five multiple choice items (4) is just right.

The skill of using the scientific method should be measured; a short essay (9) will serve nicely. The skill in using laboratory apparatus can be incorporated into a test through a question calling for the use of a microscope (7).

Both applications and critical thinking are considered relatively less important than some of the other objectives, so shorter questions such as a complex objective item (8 and 11) are more appropriate to their weight than the longer essay questions.

We have keyed on the various types of learning or objectives in this attempt to plan a test in biology. The other important dimension, content, must also be considered if a teacher is to achieve complete content validity. He would apportion the various topics to be evaluated according to their relative weight or emphasis in the course in a way similar to what we have just done with the objectives.

Is the Measure Accurate?

Besides knowing to what extent a test measures what you want it to measure, you will want some idea of its accuracy. In other words, if you were to give it again, how close would the second set of scores be to the first set. In the context of testing, this accuracy and consistency of test scores is termed *reliability*.

With standardized tests of intelligence or achievement, reliability is usually established by retesting the same group within a few weeks after the original testing and then correlating the two sets of scores. (There are other techniques, but this is the basic way to determine reliability.) As in the case of validity the test manual will contain data on the consistency or accuracy of the test. Depending on your purpose, you should require rather high coefficients of reliability: at least .80 but preferably around .90 if you are using the test score of an individual student, particularly for grouping or other important decisions; at least .60 but preferably .70 or better if you are using the test to get an idea of the class as a whole or if a decision regarding an individual student is only tentative or of little consequence.

For the tests you construct yourself, you will probably not compute a reliability coefficient. However, you should be aware of several ways in which you can make your tests more accurate:

1. Make sure that there are no ambiguities of phrasing and that the correct answers are definitely correct, i.e. supported by fact, authority, etc.
2. Apply a uniform standard and use the same expected or model answer for all students as you correct the test papers. Of course this latter suggestion will restrict your latitude for asking different types of questions somewhat, e.g. questions calling for divergent thinking cannot ordinarily be scored by using a model answer. In this case you have to decide which is more important: to measure creativity or to maintain reliability of measurement (better to opt for the former and then strive for accuracy in other test items).
3. Have enough items or questions on the test so as to remove the chance factors as much as possible. For example, with fifteen spelling words rather than five you will get a more accurate indication of your students' spelling ability; with three shorter essays rather than one long one you will get away from the possibility that you may be testing one of the few weak areas of a student who has otherwise learned most of the course topics well.
4. Include questions of varying degrees of difficulty on the test. Too many easy questions will result in everyone bunching together at the top end of the score scale; too many very difficult questions will put most students toward the lower end of the scale. In both cases the coefficient of reliability will be considerably less than if there was a good spread of scores due to a corresponding spread of degree of difficulty among the test items.

Does the Measure Give Meaningful Scores?

You will find when you are correcting any test or other measure that if the first student whose paper you correct gets 45 out of 60 questions correct—for example on a multiple choice test—you have little idea of how well he actually did until you correct quite a few other papers. To get an even better picture of his performance you will want to correct the whole set of papers and then see how he rates among all of the students in your class. If the highest score was 58 and the average 35, he did very well; if the highest score was 58 and the average 51, he didn't do so well compared with the other members of the class.

If you are against making comparisons among students, you will at least want to compare his present score with his scores on similar tests in the past to see whether 45 is good for him or is below par. In the same way, if you are operating in a nongraded, task-based program or on the contract system, you will want to compare the student's performance with the expected or agreed-on standard of performance that you and he set up for that section of the course.

If you gave a standardized aptitude or achievement test and knew that one of your students answered two-thirds of the items correct on a foreign language aptitude test or a little over half of the items correct on the science part of a standardized achievement test, what would you know about his aptitude or achievement? Not very much, until you were able to compare his scores with those of a larger group.

A score from a test or other measure means something only in the way it compares with other scores, either previous scores that a student received on similar tests—if we are concerned with the growth or improvement of an individual—or with the scores of other students of comparable age and background, either the other students in his class for a teacher-made test or the students included in a more national sample for a standardized test.

The number of items a student gets correct on a test can be converted into many types of scores to give the results more meaning. The easiest, of course, is to convert the raw score into a percent of the maximum possible number correct and report the student's score in terms of percent. But this does not tell you much more than the raw score did, for you still have no basis for comparison.

For teacher-made tests, the most common technique for obtaining a meaningful score is to divide the raw scores into five categories: excellent, good, average, below average, and unsatisfactory. For short you can assign some symbols to the categories, A, B, C, D, F. In most classes a large percentage of the students are of average ability and will be expected to achieve to an average degree; in other words more students will be around the middle or average score (C) than at the extremes (A and F). In a typical class you would expect about thirty or forty percent of the students to score in the average or C category. There will probably be a few students at either extreme, maybe ten to fifteen percent doing excellent work and one or two students doing very poor or unsatisfactory work. A somewhat larger proportion, anywhere from fifteen to thirty percent, can be expected to do good work and a similar percentage to do below average work, and to be in the B and D categories respectively.

A five-category scoring system provides a general framework for conveying greater meaning to a student's raw score in a test. It allows for enough flexibility so that you are not imposing a score scale on your class. Instead, you are using approximate, expected percentages to categorize performance and at the same time making judgments when necessary, particularly with regard to what is excellent and what is unsatisfactory work. There are many current issues regarding marking systems that you should be aware of before adopting one specific system, but rather then open this particular Pandora's Box here, suffice it to say that the five-category system is the most popular of those in use today.

Standardized tests use several different score scales, most of them based in some way on a mid-point or average.[3] The most popular in order are: percentile, grade equivalent, quotient, and standard score. Let's consider them each in turn.

Percentile.   Percentile scores are most widely used for any type of test. A percentile simply refers to what percent of a group performs below a given score. When a raw score is converted to a percentile, first the position of that score in relation to the group is determined, e.g. tenth out of thirty, and then that ranking is expressed in percent, e.g. sixty-sixth percentile.

Grade Equivalent.   Grade norms, which are most often used to report achievement test results, are based on the average score that students of particular grade levels achieve on a test. For instance, if the average score of fourth graders in the standardization group of an achievement test given in February was 38, then the raw score of 38 would be assigned a grade equivalent of 4.6 or fourth grade, sixth month. Any student taking the test and getting 38 items correct would receive a grade score of 4.6.

Quotients.   Intelligence tests frequently report scores in terms of a quotient or ratio of mental age over chronological age. For example a ten-year-old child who got as many questions correct as the average twelve-year-old would have a score of 12/10 or an intelligence quotient of 120 (with the decimal removed). Obviously if his score was the same as the average ten-year-old it would have been 100. Actually, ratio I.Q.s are no longer used for reporting intelligence test scores. A deviation I.Q., which is a special type of standard score, is used.

Standard Scores.   A few intelligence or aptitude tests are reported in terms of standard scores. If you know what standard deviation is, then standard scores are easy to understand; if you don't have a real grasp of standard deviation, they are impossible. (You may want to consult the section on standard deviation in appendix C at this point.)

Standard scores represent the number of standard deviations a person scores above or below the mean in terms of an agreed upon score scale. For instance, in an intelligence test the raw score mean of the standardization group is converted to 100 and the standard deviation ordinarily to 15. Hence a person who is one S D above the mean will have an I.Q. (the deviation type) of 115. Similarly on the College Entrance Examination Board Test, the agreed upon mean is 500 and the standard deviation converted to 100. For example, a student who was ½ S D below the mean of the standardization group would have a college board score of 450. Most of the tests that you will encounter use one of the other types of scores, so you need not be too concerned about standard scores.

EXERCISE 16-3. Interpretation of Test Scores

Your school system has administered the SRA Achievement Test to all fourth-grade students in February and you now have the profile of scores for each student. A portion of the score sheet is as follows. What does it mean?

---

3. In the area of statistics and measurement, arithmetic average is called the mean.

SRA Achievement Series

Language Arts

	Cap & Punc		Gram Usage	
	GE	Pctle	GE	Pctle
	Raw Score	Sta	Raw Score	Sta
Smith, Sam	6–3	81	5–2	60
	39	7	30	5
Stillman, Al	4–9	55	3–7	20
	33	5	22	3

                      Sam   Al

1. Scored the same in capitals and punctuation as the average sixth grader would in a November testing. ____ ____
2. Almost a full year below grade level in grammar. ____ ____
3. Scored very high in capitals and punctuation; only nineteen percent of the standardization group did better. ____ ____
4. Only one-fifth of the students in the country scored below him in grammatical usage. ____ ____
5. About average—or slightly above—in capitals and punctuation. ____ ____
6. Answered thirty questions correct on the grammatical usage subtest. ____ ____
7. With the total score scale divided into nine segments, he scored in the second from the top in capitals and punctuation. ____ ____

GE is SRA's (Science Research Associates) abbreviation for grade equivalent, the grade level corresponding to a certain raw score. Sam's thirty-nine items correct in capitals and punctuation made him even with a typical sixth grader in the third month of school (6–3, or more commonly 6.3). Al, on the other hand, was almost a year below average in grade equivalent; he was in the fourth grade when the test was given in February (sixth month), but he scored the equivalent of third grade, seventh month.

We have seen previously that percentiles indicate the percent of the standardization group that scored below an individual. On capitals and punctuation Sam is in the eighty-first percentile, with only nineteen percent scoring above him. Al is in the twentieth percentile in grammatical usage, with four-fifths scoring above him and only one-fifth below. In capitals and punctuation, Al is at the fifty-fifth percentile, or slightly above average.

To give some idea of how many questions students answered on each subtest, SRA gives raw scores. For example, on grammatical usage Sam answered thirty items correctly.

"Sta" is short for Stanine, a type of score system in which the total score scale is divided up into nine segments, with five as the mid-category. Sam received a stanine score of 7 on capitals and punctuation, putting him into the second category from the top.

Constructing Evaluation Instruments

We now turn to the question of how to construct the different evaluation instruments that will help you measure the learning outcomes of your students. First we will consider essay questions, then various types of objective items, and finally several miscellaneous evaluation techniques.

Essay Questions

Constructing Essay Items.   What are some ways that will help you as a teacher to construct quality essay test items? A few important suggestions are offered.

1. First of all, as you write an essay question, keep both the content and the types of learning or course objectives in mind. As you are going over the text, your notes or other course material, keep the various products of learning (facts, concepts, relations, structures) and the several thought processes (comprehension, problem solving, creativity, and critical thinking) in the back of your mind. In this way you will be more apt to think of a question that will cover an important topic plus involve one or more types of knowledge or thought processes. (Recall that for the test as a whole to have content validity, both the topics covered and the types of learning involved should correspond to the content and objectives of the course, with each weighted according to their relative importance.)

2. Keep in mind the appropriate key words that relate to the specific type of learning or objective you wish to measure. Here are a few suggestions; you no doubt can think of others that are relevant to your field.

Words	define, what is the meaning
Facts	state, identify, describe
Concepts	explain, distinguish between
Relations	explain giving reasons, examples
Structures	explain the interrelationships, show how it is organized
Comprehension	give the meaning, summarize
Creativity	write a theme, develop a play, suggest
Problem solving	what was the cause
Analysis	compare, contrast, distinguish
Critical thinking	criticize (on the basis of . . .), evaluate (in the light of . . .)
Application, transfer	(given an example or case) explain in terms of . . .

Keeping various types of learning plus appropriate key words for each in mind will help you avoid starting all questions with "give and explain" or "discuss." It will also help you achieve greater content validity for your test.

3. Phrase each essay question so that it is clear to the student what you intend by the question. For example, which do you prefer?

Discuss the Bill of Rights in the Constitution.

or

Analyze the Bill of Rights covering the following points:
   a. its basic purpose
   b. the rights it insures
   c. how it grew out of the constitutions of the various states.

The first is too general. "Discuss" means "talk about" and leaves the student wide open to write whatever he wants. The second gives the student specific guidelines by suggesting some essential considerations about the Bill of Rights. It certainly is not vague (as "discuss" is) but neither is it *too* specific (as "list" would be).

Often an intermediate point between general and specific is the ideal in essay items. The scope of the question can be restricted, and the clarity in turn increased, by either giving a brief outline in the form of subquestions (as above) or by including some fairly specific guidelines in the statement of the question itself. For example, "Explain the concept of tragedy as exemplified in Shakespeare's *Macbeth* and *Romeo and Juliet.*"

4. Decide on how much structure you want to provide the students with and phrase the question accordingly. Which do you prefer and why?
   Compare Jefferson's and Hamilton's concepts of the structure of federal government.

or

   Compare Jefferson's and Hamilton's concepts of the structure of federal government covering the following points:
   a. states rights
   b. make-up of population
   c. finance.

You can make a case for either item. If you want the student to organize his own answer, judge for himself what the more important bases of comparison between the two men's views are, plus give him flexibility with regard to how much emphasis to give to each basis of comparison, you will prefer the first way of phrasing the question.

If you want everyone to write on the same points, or perhaps if you feel your students need more structure to get them started, or if you are more interested in their knowledge of those particular areas of comparison, you will prefer the second way. In other words, the degree of structure you provide for your students in an essay question depends more on your particular purposes than on any specific set of rules or suggestions.

Scoring Essay Items. One of the main problems connected with essay questions is the relative lack of objectivity and reliability in their correction. How can you correct your essay items more objectively and with greater reliability? There are several important suggestions that we will summarize here.

1. Frame the question so that it is clear what is called for in a complete answer, in other words, so that everyone will be writing on the same question. This is the same as the third point mentioned above on the construction of essay

items, but it is worth repeating because if a question is phrased clearly and contains adequate guidelines, half the problem of reliability in its correction is solved.

2. Draw up and use an outline of a model answer that includes the main points you expect in a complete answer. This will serve as a standard against which all of the students' papers can be judged. With a little practice your model answer will be fair and not too demanding; however this should not be of great concern since objectivity is achieved from comparing all answers to a single standard—your model answer.

3. Determine how many points you will give for each part of the model answer and grade accordingly. For example, if you ask a question calling for the students to explain a relationship and to give two reasons that support it, you can, in a ten-point question, give four points for a full explanation, and three points each for the reasons offered. If the explanation is limited, you might give three or two points (even one if it is sketchy); similarly if the reasons are not very strong or are not fully stated, you might give half credit. However, the established point scale should be flexible; for example, if you asked for three reasons and the student gave only two but explained them thoroughly, you could give full credit.

4. You will probably find it easier to read through all of the answers to one essay question at a time. The shuffling of papers involved is minimal and the advantage of staying in the same frame of mind for all of the answers is great. By concentrating on only one standard for all the students rather than switching your conscious awareness of model answers back and forth from one item to the next, you greatly increase your objectivity in scoring.

5. It is often recommended that you not look at the students' names as you correct the papers. Try it; it may help you achieve greater objectivity. But it will not always work, since you will find it hard not to notice some names and will also find yourself recognizing some students' handwriting. In any event, you can make a case for knowing who wrote an answer in that you can become more aware of the strengths and deficiencies of individual students.

Objective Items

What are some of the essential characteristics of multiple choice and other objective items that you should keep in mind as you attempt to construct them? And what are some of the ways you can use to construct quality objective items? The following analysis and suggestions should prove helpful. We will emphasize multiple choice items since they are most versatile, but we will also take a brief look at other commonly used types.

Multiple Choice.   First, by way of definition we speak of the problem or *stem* and several answers or *options,* one of which is correct and the rest *distracters.* Most often four options are used; three allows too much for guessing; a fifth good option is usually very difficult to think of.

You should also be aware of the several types of multiple choice items available, for instance:

1. a. correct answer: with one definitely correct answer based on fact or absolute certitude.

   b. best answer: with one answer judged the best from among several; it uses such words as main, most important, primary, most likely. With the best answer type of item, the multiple choice format is not limited to content that is absolutely true or correct.

2. a. positive: the ordinary item phrased positively where one chooses the correct answer.

   b. negative: the item is phrased in terms of "which is *not*," or "all of the following *except*," with the person choosing the option that is *not* correct. Although most multiple choice items are phrased positively, the negative type of item is useful for something that has several characteristics or reasons. It is much easier to construct a quality item by including three characteristics or reasons plus one distracter than by selecting one characteristic and trying to think of three good distracters.

3. a. Incomplete statement in stem, with sentence to be completed by correct option.

   b. Question in stem, i.e. self-contained interrogative sentence, with possible answers as options. If your options are fairly long, your students will be less confused if you use the question format; also if the stem is long, it will usually be clearer if you phrase it as a question rather than juggle the sentence around so that it is completed by an option. Other than that, you should use whichever sounds clearer to you.

There are three important rules that will help you to construct quality multiple choice items:

1. State the problem clearly and completely in the stem. Use almost a full statement with subject and verb. For example: "the main result of the Industrial Revolution on the economy of England was. . . ." Do *not* use just a phrase: "In the aftermath of the Industrial Revolution in England. . . ." A full problem is called for in the stem; otherwise your item becomes a series of true or false statements.

2. Make sure that the correct option is phrased correctly and that you can support it as being *the* correct answer. This is particularly important in the best answer type of question. You must be able to defend your correct option by commonly recognized fact, most convincing reason, authority, or the like.

3. Think of several plausible, attractive distracters that will help your item discriminate between those who know the answer and those who might try to guess. Coming up with plausible distracters is the most difficult problem in the construction of multiple choice items; for some specific suggestions, do exercise 16-4.

EXERCISE 16-4.   Different Bases for Distracters in Multiple Choice Items

What are some bases you can use to think up some plausible, attractive distracters for your multiple choice questions? Given below are some sample questions; try to discern the bases for the distracters in each item. Match each item with a basis given at the right. A few examples illustrate more than one basis. Also, to save you reading all the way through the bases, the first five items go with the first six bases; the next seven items with the last six bases.

1. The complex organic substances that are essential to   _____ Similarity in time
   the normal nutrition of animals and are found in
   small quantities in natural foods are called

    calories   _____ Similarity of area or field
    vitamins
    minerals
    nutrients

2. A synapse is the point at which   _____ All related to one object
    a. a dendrite is attached to a nerve cell body
    b. an axon passes an impulse to a dendrite   _____ Similar words to key
    c. a dendrite passes an impulse to an axon   word in stem
    d. the cell body connects to an axon

3. The south pole was discovered by
    Richard E. Byrd
    Roald Amundsen   _____ Opposite of correct answer
    Robert F. Scott
    Robert Peary

4. The fifth president of the United States was   _____ Opposites used as distracters
    John Quincy Adams
    John Madison
    James Monroe
    Andrew Jackson

5. Transformers are used in electric power plants to
    a. change water power to electric power
    b. transform alternating current to direct current
    c. transform direct current to alternating current
    d. raise or lower the voltage in a power line

6. What part of the dictionary would you consult to find   _____ Part of the
   the origin of the term *habeus corpus*?   whole
    a. the main part
    b. the list of foreign terms and phrases   _____ A related
    c. the section on the history of the English lan-   aspect of a key
       guage   word
    d. the section that deals with special legal terms

7. The main theme of Shakespeare's *Othello* is:
    a. jealousy
    b. treachery
    c. innocence
    d. anger

8. "In three wealthy northern states the average salary of teachers is three times that in the three poorest southern states of the United States. However, the three poorest states have a higher tax in proportion to their income than do the wealthy states." For which of the following propositions is this statement the best evidence?
    a. The southern states are not as interested in quality education as the northern states.
    b. Teachers in the northern states are overpaid in relation to their profession.
    c. State governments in the poorer states should increase their contributions to local school districts.
    d. Federal financial aid to education is necessary.
    e. Education should be controlled more by the national government.

9. What is the main purpose of the United Nations?
    a. To provide a forum for interchange of ideas among the peoples of the world.
    b. To maintain peace among the nations of the world.
    c. To help new nations maintain their independence from other nations.
    d. To help newly formed nations to establish responsible forms of government.

_____ Secondary considerations

_____ Common misconceptions

_____ Common errors that students make

10. What is the ratio of 25¢ to 5¢?
    a. 1/5   b. 5/1   c. 20/1   d. 1/20

11. Which of the following is the chief characteristic of the wise consumer?
    a. He knows that the least expensive goods are the best buys.
    b. He knows that the more expensive something is the higher its quality.
    c. He realizes that he must plan his spending.
    d. He realizes that advertising is generally misleading.

_____ Most or all of the possibilities

12. Which of the following would be most likely to cause a fog?
    a. A layer of warm dry air meeting another layer of cool moist air.
    b. One layer of warm moist air meeting another layer of warm moist air.
    c. Cool air meeting a layer of warm moist air.
    d. Cool air meeting a layer of cooler moist air.

Similarity is a commonly used basis for distracters:

similarity of options in time, e.g. presidents (4);

similarity of options with regard to area or field (1, 3);
all options related to one object or topic, e.g. food (1) or nerve cell (2);
similarity of distracters to word in stem, e.g. transform and change (5), and nutrient (1).

Opposites can also be used effectively as distracters:

the opposite of the correct answer (2); or
two opposites used as distracters (5), figuring that the unassuming student will go for at least one.

Part-whole or primary-secondary relationships can suggest attractive distracters:

part of a story but not the main theme (7);
based on part of the stem but not the whole statement (8a,b,c);
secondary aspects, purposes, but not primary (9).

A specific reason can be the basis for distracters, for example:

an aspect of a key word(6): foreign language (b), historical origin (c), legal term (d).

Common mistakes can also serve as effective distracters:

common misconceptions (11);
common errors (10).

Sometimes there is no special basis other than all or most of the reasonable possibilities (12).

Short Answer Items.   Because short answer questions test recall rather than recognition, they are more difficult than other objective-type items. They also do away with the problem of guessing. They are useful for vocabulary, factual information, mathematical problems, and even knowledge of simple relationships.

First consider the several types of short answer items.

1. Question: How many legs do insects have? _____
2. Completion: Ivanhoe was written by _____.
3. Association: Pennsylvania _____ (Capital)
                    fromage (French) _____ (English equivalent)
4. Problem: Joe went to the store to buy the following items: one loaf of bread (39¢), one can of peas (26¢), and a candy bar (10¢). Counting in a 4 percent sales tax, how much change did he get from a dollar?
   _____
5. Identify: Who was Stonewall Jackson?
6. List: List the steps in the process of mitosis.
      Give three reasons for the decline of England as a colonial power.

      _____
      _____
      _____

Note that the last two or three types are midway between the usual short answer item and an essay question. Realizing that there are many types of short answer items, you can select the type that best fits your particular purpose or subject matter.

How can you make your short answer questions more effective? Since they are the easiest type to construct, we will only consider a few basic suggestions here.

1. In a completion item give most of the statement first; this sets up a problem for the student which he in turn answers.
2. Leave only one or two blanks at or near the end; in this way you will not end up with a mutilated sentence.
3. It is sometimes appropriate to be explicit as to what type of answer or degree of exactness you are looking for:

   The Pilgrims first came to America in the year _____.
   Or in math and the sciences: feet and inches, two decimal places, etc.

True-False.   Although objective items with only two options leave themselves open to guessing (a chimpanzee with a coin will get fifty percent correct), they are much more versatile than you would probably imagine. Consider some of the main types.

1. True-false. The pressure in a fixed quantity of gas varies directly as its volume if the temperature remains constant. T F

   This is the most commonly used type and is appropriate for almost all subject fields. As in the above item, it is not limited to the purely factual, but can be used to test knowledge of relationships as well.
2. Right-wrong. If I was to tell you, you would be worry. R W

   This is very usable in grammar study.
3. Correct if false or wrong. The oldest permant settlement in the "New World" is *Plymouth, Massachusetts.*

   This is a more demanding type of question and also minimizes guessing.
4. The cluster of items. The volume of a given quantity of gas

can be increased by increasing temperature	T F
can be increased by using pressure	T F
can be held constant by increasing pressure when temperature increases	T F
can be decreased to zero by increasing pressure and decreasing temperature	T F

   Note that this is somewhere between the true-false and the multiple choice item. It is different from the multiple choice item in that (a) the introduction includes only a phrase rather than a full problem, and (b) the student indicates a choice for each option. It is a convenient format if you want to ask several true-false questions about the same topic.

5. The sometimes true-sometimes false item. If a person is living at a latitude of 20 degrees, he is living north of the equator.   T   F   TF

    Ordinarily a true-false item has to be unambiguously true or false. The "sometimes" item allows circumstances to be brought in and gives the true-false format a little more flexibility. If you use it, you would include some items keyed for "sometimes" with a group of regular true-false items, but use T   F   TF as the options for all the items.

6. Fact-opinion.   F   O   Labor unions have helped the economic growth of the United States.

    This type of the alternative choice item can be used to evaluate critical thinking. Except for this type of item, opinion—even *your* opinion—has no place in true-false questions.

This listing of the types of alternative response items may open up possibilities that you had not thought of regarding true-false questions before. You may even come up with further types of alternative response items yourself; as is true in most other types of evaluation techniques, the possibilities are limited only by your imagination.

What are some guidelines regarding the construction of true-false type of items? Other than clarity and fairness, the maxims are mainly "don'ts." For example:

Don't lift sentences out of textbooks; often they are not sufficiently clear or qualified when taken out of context.

Don't use double negatives; they are confusing.

Don't use two statements in one item, e.g. one true and one false; use two separate items if you must.

Don't make an insignificant part of a statement false; trickery is not the way to find out whether students know something or not.

Beware of tip-offs, or "specific determiners" as they are called; e.g. "all" and "never" usually indicate that the item is false; "sometimes," "usually," "often" are tip-offs that the item is probably true. (It's all right to use these if an "all" item *is* true, or a "sometimes" item *is* false.)

Beware of using ambiguous or partly true statements, e.g. "The degree of nourishment that our bodies assimilate depends on the amount of food we eat." This is true, but it is not the whole story; hence it's a poor T   F question, in fact even a poor T   F   TF question.

Matching.   A very convenient and concise way of testing for a large amount of factual knowledge is through the matching item. Names, dates, terms, titles, objects, statements, definitions, parts of a diagram can be used as premises or responses. It is most important, however, to have the same type of content in each matching item, e.g. all titles to be matched with all authors. We have seen examples of matching items above, particularly in the chapter on verbal-factual learning, so there is no need to repeat one here. Instead, let's consider some suggestions for constructing matching items.

1. Have all homogeneous items in each column. Otherwise students can figure out which response goes with which premise without knowing anything about the topic.
2. Premises, usually the longer phrases, go at the left, the responses or shorter phrases, go at the right. This reduces the amount of reading since the student has to look through the shorter phrases each time for the response to a premise.
3. The responses should outnumber the premises; in other words you want a few extra responses as distracters so that students will not be able to match the final premises with one unused response. About one and a half times as many responses as premises can be used as a guideline.
4. Matching items should be relatively short; five or six premises for younger pupils, and ten or twelve for junior and senior high students. It is better to break up the material than have students fish through dozens of responses looking for the correct one.

Complex Objective Items. In a few of the preceding chapters we have seen different types of more complex objective items. As they are generally extensions of the simpler objective items we have just treated, there is little further to say about their construction. If you are aware of some basic formats together with their requirements, you can construct them without too much trouble. By way of review we will specify the basic types here.

1. The interpretative item. A passage, poem, a case, picture, cartoon, map, diagram, graph, table or the like is presented first. Then a series of multiple choice or true-false items is asked about the passage. A teacher can include questions that measure various types of objectives: comprehension of general theme and the meaning of specific sections, ability to interpret and draw conclusions from data, to recognize warranted and unwarranted generalizations, to recognize assumptions and inferences, and the ability to apply principles and other knowledge.

The interpretative item can either be self-contained, where all of the data necessary for answering the questions is given in the introductory passage or data; or it can require knowledge over and above what is given in the introductory material. In the latter case, the emphasis is usually on applying one's knowledge to a new situation or example.

2. The complex matching item. After a brief introductory statement, several generalizations theories, policies, or processes are provided and then a list of examples, statements, characteristics, criticisms, quotations or the like are given—each one to be matched with one (or more) of the generalizations given above it.

3. The extended multiple choice item. The problem is stated in the stem and then a list of options is given, with the instructions to check as many as are appropriate. The options can be reasons, conditions, or characteristics.

More than in any other type of item, the complex objective format is flexible and open to many varieties and combinations, limited only by your creativeness.

Other Evaluative Techniques

In several of the previous chapters we have seen examples of rating scales, checklists, attitude scales, and other evaluation techniques. A teacher learns how to construct these more by taking the lead of a model and then trying his hand at it rather than from a definite list of prescriptions on how to construct them. However, there are a few suggestions pertaining to these techniques that are worthy of mention.

Rating Scales.   Of the several recognized formats probably the best is the capsule phrase format in which several points on a continuum from most to least favorable are specified through specific concrete statements. For example, in a speech rating scale you might include a dozen or more points such as the following, with the rater checking the appropriate phrase.

Opening Statement

Arouses audience attention and interest in topic	Gains the attention of most listeners	Commonplace. Does not attract attention	Not appropriate. In fact, distracts from topic

Another related format is the continuum with fewer statements but an opportunity to rate between the capsule phrases. For example:

Opening Statement

Captivating Arouses great interest	Ordinary Audience is neither attracted nor distracted	Distracting Causes attention to wander

A capsule phrase rating scale gives you as the rater something much more tangible on which to base your judgment than the usual "excellent," "good," etc. Even for one teacher, one day's "good" might be another day's "excellent"; but if the ratings of several persons are being compared, the use of capsule phrases rather than general words is all the more essential if the raters are to all use the same bases for rating.

Checklist, Observation Scale.   In drawing up a checklist or observation scale, your main step is to identify the steps in a sequence, the characteristics of satisfactory performance or the like. List or describe each step or characteristic identified. You might also include some common errors or qualities of a faulty performance, perhaps in a separate section of your scale. Finally, you will want to arrange your list or scale so that there is a convenient way of checking each item as it occurs.

Attitude Scales.   The easiest type of attitude scale to construct is the one in which you present either favorable or unfavorable statements to students and they indicate the extent of their agreement or disagreement with each statement. For instance:

Mathematics is very interesting.

Agree Strongly   Agree   Undecided   Disagree   Disagree Strongly

Mathematics is a waste of time and effort.

Agree Strongly   Agree   Undecided   Disagree   Disagree Strongly

For favorable statements, agree strongly gets five points, agree four points, etc. For unfavorable statements agree strongly gets one point, agree two points, etc. A student's score is the sum of his points on each item, with the higher score indicating a more favorable attitude. For this type of attitude scale you can only use statements that are clearly favorable or clearly unfavorable; neutral or moderate statements cannot be included. Also, you must be certain that all of the statements have to do with the same thing, since they will all contribute to one score relating to that thing. There are other types of attitude scales that are useful but considerably more difficult to construct, and so they are not worth going into here. Suffice it to say that since most attitude scales are designed for a specific purpose and context, you will do better to construct your own rather than searching for one in the literature.[4]

Reporting Results of Evaluation Instruments

Once you have administered and scored one or more of the measures treated above, what do you do with the scores? How do you report them to those who will profit from the knowledge of the results: students, parents, counselors, and administrators? In this section we will examine several ways of reporting evaluation results and then discuss which way is preferable given a specific purpose or type of measure.

Ways of Reporting Results

Raw Score or Percent.   You can either indicate how many items a student got correct out of a total number, or you can convert this to the percentage correct and report the results in terms of percent. This tells you how well the student himself did in relation to the maximum possible performance level.

Symbols Representing Standing in Relation to a Group.   If in addition you wish to report how each student performed in relation to the others in the class, you can divide the raw scores into several categories ranging from outstanding to inadequate, and then let each category be represented by a symbol. The most common division is into five categories: excellent, good, average, below average,

---

4. Shaw and Wright's *Scales for the Measurement of Attitudes* (1967) is an excellent source book for attitude scales.

and unsatisfactory, which are represented by A, B, C, D, and F respectively. Sometimes, twelve categories are used with the corresponding symbols A, A−, B+, B, B−, etc.; and sometimes only two, satisfactory and unsatisfactory.

If symbols from several measures are to be added together and averaged, they can be easily converted to numerical values: A = 4, B = 3, C = 2, D = 1, F = 0. Of course first each value should be multiplied by the relative importance or weight of the measure: e.g. an A (4) on a final exam worth 25 percent of the overall grade = 100 points; a C (2) on a project worth 10 percent of the grade = 20 points, etc. The total of all the weighted values is eventually divided by the total weight or 100 percent. Once all of the scores are weighted, they are averaged, and the average becomes the student's overall grade, e.g. an average of 3.1 is converted back to a B.

A Checklist of Content or Objectives.   If you want to report a more detailed analysis of a student's performance than one symbol can give, you might prefer using a checklist specifying different aspects of performance. For instance, in arithmetic you could specify:

1. shows understanding of basic concepts
2. solves word problems calling for numerical reasoning
3. does computations accurately.

For each aspect, you can either indicate: outstanding, satisfactory, or needs improvement, or the traditional categories represented by A, B, C, etc.

The objectives or types of learning stressed in a course can serve as the basis for a checklist that you draw up. If your course is task-oriented you can use the tasks that were set up for the student to master; similarly for specific topics or content areas that you expect your students to master.

Written Analysis.   A more in-depth analysis of a student's performance, his strengths and achievements plus his weaknesses and areas in which he needs improvement, is possible through the written report. The written report is fairly difficult and time-consuming. However, if a teacher both keeps the stated objectives and standards of the course in mind and is also conscious of the specific contributions and accomplishments of each student, he should be able to write a perceptive and personal report that conveys more helpful information than any form of reporting we have seen so far.

Conference.   A teacher-student or teacher-parent conference allows for a dimension of reporting on a student's performance that is not possible with other methods. Since it provides for input from both parties plus an interaction between them it makes possible an even more complete analysis of a student's strengths and shortcomings than in the case of the written report. In addition it can highlight areas of accomplishments not encompassed by course standards or requirements. Finally it can help to identify causes or reasons for a student's low achievement. A list of tasks, standards, or objectives to be achieved in a course can serve as a basis for at least the first part of the conference; special achievements or problems can be discussed in the latter part.

Methods for Various Types of Evaluation

Which reporting techniques are appropriate for the various types of evaluation and the different types of learning?

For student self-evaluation, in which the prime responsibility for judging the quality of his work is up to the student himself, the basis for any evaluation has to be the student as an individual: his abilities, his background, his aspirations, and his past achievement. For this type of evaluation, either the student-teacher conference or a written report by each student is the more appropriate reporting method.

For teacher-centered evaluation, in which the teacher makes the judgment about the quality of his students' performance on the various tests and other measures used for the course, the basis for the evaluation can either be (1) the student himself: his abilities, background, aspirations, and past achievement, or (2) the group: how each student's performance compares with that of the class as a whole, or (3) the percent scores that the student achieved on the various measures.

With all three bases, first the course standards and objectives are set up, then they are measured and a raw score or percent score obtained. If the teacher uses percentage of material mastered as the basis for his overall evaluation of student work, he goes no further. If he uses the individual as the basis he compares this raw or percent score to what he thinks the student should be able to do or what the student aspired to at the beginning of the term, and makes his judgment accordingly. If he bases his evaluation on the group, he compares the raw or percent score with the scores of the rest of the class, and assigns a relative grade to the student, possibly one of the five categories mentioned above: A, B, C, D or F.

If the teacher decides on the individual student as his basis for evaluation, he can use either a checklist, a conference, or a written report as his method of reporting to student and parent. If he prefers the group as the basis, then the appropriate reporting method is a symbol system such as A through F which represents categories of performance level; or if his course is structured on a task basis, then a checklist plus symbol system is appropriate. Finally, if he uses percentage of material mastered as his basis for evaluation, he simply reports student performance in terms of percent.

For cooperative student-teacher evaluation, in which the teacher and student share the responsibility of evaluating the quality of the student's performance jointly, the basis again has to be the student as an individual: how his performance measured up to his abilities, his past achievement, and his stated aspirations at the beginning of the term. The appropriate method of reporting is the conference, specifically the final portion of the conference in which the cooperative evaluation takes place. In conjunction with the conference, a checklist of tasks or objectives or a written report can be used as a supplementary method and for reporting to parents.

To review, the several types of evaluation together with the appropriate bases used and the reporting techniques that they call for, are shown in table 16-2.

Table 16-2. *Types, Bases and Methods of Evaluation*

Type of Evaluation	Basis for Evaluation	Method of Reporting
Self	individual	conference or written report
Teacher	individual	checklist, written report or conference
	group	symbol system or checklist plus symbol system
	percent	percent
Cooperative	individual	conference, perhaps checklist or written report in addition

We should consider briefly a few points on what the more appropriate reporting methods are for different types of learning and different types of evaluation techniques.

A checklist or rating scale that is used to evaluate a skill such as reading, psychomotor skill, laboratory procedures, can be reported in its raw form with or without a summary report or symbol representing relative performance. Scores on an arithmetic, grammar or spelling test can very well be reported in terms of percent, particularly if your chief concern is with each student's mastery of the material, or in terms of a symbol system if you prefer to compare each student with the group. Evaluations of individual projects or creative productions are best reported in a brief statement or through a rating scale that is constructed for the purpose. Symbol systems have little place in the evaluation of creative productions.

For most types of learning and the techniques used to evaluate them, a teacher can use whichever reporting method he prefers: conference, written report, checklist, symbol system or percent. Your choice should be based on what you feel contributes most to your main function as a teacher: the most effective learning of your students.

EXERCISE 16-5. Construction of Evaluation Techniques

Among the most commonly used techniques in the evaluation of classroom learning are the essay question, the multiple choice item, and the rating scale.

1. Construct an essay item in your field that reflects the suggestions given in the chapter. Indicate the type of learning or objective that you intend to measure.
2. Construct a multiple choice item in your field, indicating (a) the type of learning or objective you intend to measure, and (b) the basis for each distracter.
3. Construct a rating scale for a skill or creative activity in your field, emphasizing the essential aspects of that skill or activity, and allowing for some way of checking each item on the measure.

Suggested Readings

Anastasi, A. *Psychological Testing.* New York: Macmillan, 1968.

Bloom, B. S., et al. *Taxonomy of Educational Objectives: Cognitive Domain.* New York: McKay, 1956.

Bloom, B. S., Hastings, J. T. and Madaus, G. F. *Handbook on Formative and Summative Evaluation of Student Learning.* New York: McGraw-Hill, 1971.

Gronlund, N. E. *Measurement and Evaluation in Teaching.* New York: Macmillan, 1971.

Thorndike, R. L. and Hagen, E. *Measurement and Evaluation in Psychology and Education.* New York: Wiley, 1969.

Appendix A
The Structure of Intellect

(J. P. Guilford)

PRODUCTS

PROCESS	UNITS	CLASSES	RELATIONS
COGNITION	Perception of figures, sounds*	Recognition of figures, symbols and words as belonging to classes, i.e., having a property in common	Seeing or grasping relationships
	Recognizing symbolic units		"
	Verbal comprehension		"
MEMORY	Visual and auditory memory		Memory of relationships between:
	Rote memory	Memory for word or number classes	words/numbers
	Logical memory	Memory for class names	ideas/things
DIVERGENT THINKING	Figural fluency	Ability to classify figures and words in various ways	
	Word fluency		Fluency for number/ letter combinations
	Ideational fluency	Spontaneous flexibility	Associational fluency
CONVERGENT THINKING		Classification of objects	
			Education of correlates
	Ability to name abstractions	Classification of ideas, words	"
EVALUATION	Perceptual speed		Judging similarity or consistency of symbols or words used in analogical or syllogistic form
	Judging identity of series	Evaluation of symbolic and semantic classes	
	Comparison of ideas		

*The upper third of each box represents figural content, the middle third symbolic content, and the lower third semantic or ideational content.

SYSTEMS	TRANSFORMATIONS	IMPLICATIONS
Seeing order or arrangement of objects in space	Visualization	Foresight in figures
Grasping order of symbols		Ability to extrapolate with symbolic data
General reasoning	Seeing similarities by a shift of meanings	
Remembrance of the order of: objects in space, list of numbers, sequence of events		
	Memory for word transformations	Memory for symbolic and semantic implications
	Memory for transformation of meanings	
Fluency in production of objects and symbol systems	Adaptive flexibility	Drawing out implied forms
Fluency in production of sentences problems, theories		Drawing out symbolic and semantic implications, elaborating given information
	Originality	
	Redefinition abilities: changing use of part of unit and giving it new use in new unit	
Ordering of symbols or ideas into operational, logical or temporal sequence		Deduction, reasoning
		"
Judging internal consistency and conformity of systems with a principle		
	Judgment of symbolic and semantic transformations	Judging of symbolic implications
		Judging of logical inferences

Appendix B

Summary of the Taxonomy of Educational Objectives: Cognitive Domain
(B. S. Bloom et al.)

Knowledge

Knowledge involves the recall of specifics and universals, of methods and processes, or of patterns and structures. It can involve the mental processes of remembering and/or relating into an order or system.

1.10 Knowledge of specifics
The recall of specific bits of information, e.g. words, technical terms, events, persons, places, etc.

1.20 Knowledge of ways and means of dealing with specifics
Knowledge of characteristic or conventional ways of treating ideas and facts,
Knowledge of temporal sequences and trends,
Knowledge of basic classifications and categories,
Knowledge of criteria by which facts and ideas are tested or judged,
Knowledge of the methods of inquiry and investigation of problems in a field.

1.30 Knowledge of universals and abstractions
Knowledge of the major patterns by which ideas and phenomena are organized, e.g., the generalizations which summarize our observations, the theories that provide a systematic view of a field.

Intellectual Abilities and Skills

Abilities and skills refer to organized ways of thinking and dealing with materials and problems. They emphasize the mental processes involved in organizing either given material or one's own ideas to achieve a particular purpose.

2.00 Comprehension
The understanding of a communication together with the ability to make use of the material by translating it, summarizing it or drawing implications from it.

3.00 Application
The use of ideas, principles or methods in particular situations.

4.00 Analysis
The breakdown of a communication into its several aspects or parts, plus grasping the relationships between the parts or the systematic arrangement which gives the communication unity.

5.00 Synthesis
Putting together elements to form a whole, e.g., a communication of one's ideas, a plan of operation.

440

6.00   Evaluation
           Judgment about the value of ideas, methods, or material in terms of
           whether they measure up to certain criteria, either internal criteria such as
           logical accuracy or consistency, or external criteria such as recognized
           standards, established facts, or the given purpose of an activity.

Appendix C

Statistical Techniques

There are a few basic statistical techniques that you may wish to use in the course of doing some of the experiments contained in the book. Here we should not try to become experts at statistics, but should simply attempt to grasp the nature of each statistic plus how to perform the necessary calculations involved.

Mean: the average of several scores.

> To compute the mean:
> 1. add the individual scores, i.e. ΣX;
> 2. divide the sum by the number of scores, i.e. $\dfrac{\Sigma X}{N}$.

Median: the middle score or mid-point in a group of scores.

> To compute the median:
> 1. line the scores up from lowest to highest;
> 2. divide the number of scores by 2; and
> 3. count up to that number.
>> (a) with an odd number of scores, add 0.5 to $\dfrac{N}{2}$; this will give the position of the mid-score or median (e.g., $\dfrac{7}{2} = 3.5; 3.5 + .5 = 4$)
>> (b) with an even number of scores, the median will be at a point half way between $\dfrac{N}{2}$ and the next higher score (e.g. 2 4↑6 7; median is 5).

Standard deviation: a kind of average of the differences between each score and the mean. The actual average of these differences or deviations would be found by subtracting the mean from each score, finding the total of the differences and then dividing this total by the number of differences. The standard deviation, in order to avoid some mathematical limitations of the average deviation, is similar but adds the steps of squaring each difference and then ultimately taking the square root of the total.

> To compute the standard deviation:
> 1. square each score, i.e., X^2;
> 2. find the sum of these squared scores, i.e., ΣX^2
> 3. divide by the number of scores, i.e., $\dfrac{\Sigma X^2}{N}$;
> 4. from the result in (3) subtract the mean squared, i.e., M^2;
> 5. find the square root of the result in (4), i.e., $\sqrt{\dfrac{\Sigma X^2}{N} - M^2}$.

Test of significance (t-test): a way of determining whether the diffierence between the means of two groups is real and not just due to chance.

To compute a t-test:
1. find the standard deviation for each group;
2. divide each SD by the square root of the number in the group minus 1, i.e.,

$$\frac{SD}{\sqrt{N-1}}$$ for each group;

3. square each value obtained in (2), i.e., $\left(\frac{SD}{\sqrt{N-1}}\right)^2$;
4. add them together and take the square root of the sum, i.e.,

$$\sqrt{\left(\frac{SD}{\sqrt{N-1}}\right)^2 + \left(\frac{SD}{\sqrt{N-1}}\right)^2}$$

5. find the difference between the means of the groups, i.e., $M - M$;

6. divide this difference by the result of (4), i.e., $$\frac{M - M}{\sqrt{\left(\frac{SD}{\sqrt{N-1}}\right)^2 + \left(\frac{SD}{\sqrt{N-1}}\right)^2}}$$

   The result is called the t-ratio.
7. For the most part, if the t-ratio is greater than 2, this indicates that the difference between the means of the two groups is due to something more than sampling or chance differences, e.g., it is due to the experimental variable applied to one of the groups. At least we can be 95 percent sure of this; in technical terms, the results of the experiment are significant at the .05 level of confidence.

Chi square: a means of determining whether there is a real difference between the number of persons or scores in two (or more) groups. This is done by seeing whether the difference between the numbers in the groups varies significantly from the case in which there is no difference (chance or 50-50).

To compute Chi square:
1. add the numbers in each group and divide the total by 2 to determine what a 50-50 situation would be, i.e., the number *expected* if there were no difference (*e*);
2. for each group, subtract the "expected" number [in (1)] from the actual or "observed" number in the group, i.e., $o-e$;
3. square each difference and divide by the expected number, i.e., $\dfrac{(o - e)^2}{e}$;

4. add the results [of (3)] for each group, i.e. $\Sigma[\dfrac{(o - e)^2}{e}]$. The result is termed Chi square.
5. With two groups, if the value of Chi square is greater than 3.84, this indicates that the difference between the numbers in each group is too large to be due to chance and is very probably (95 percent) due to there being a real difference between the groups, e.g., because of an experimental variable applied to one. Again, the result possessing this 95 percent degree of probability is referred to as being significant at the .05 level of confidence.

Bibliography

American Council on Education. Test of critical thinking. 1953.

Ammons, R. B. and Farr, R. G. Long-term retention of perceptual motor skills. *J. exp. Psychol.,* 1958, 55, 318-328.

Ammons, R. B. and Willig, L. Acquisition of motor skill: IV. Effects of repeated periods of massed practice. *J. exp. Psychol.,* 1956, 51, 118-126.

Anderson, G. L. Quantitative thinking as developed under connectionist and field theories of learning. In *Learning theory in school situations.* Univ. Minn. Stud. Educ. Minneapolis: Univ. of Minnesota Press, 1949, 40-73.

Anderson, H. R. et al. An experiment in teaching certain skills of critical thinking. *J. educ. Res.,* 1944, 38, 241-251.

Anderson, I. H. and Dearborn, W. F. *The psychology of teaching reading.* New York: Ronald Press, 1952.

Anderson, R. C. and Hidde, J. L. Imagery and sentence learning. *J. educ. Psychol.,* 1971, 62, 526-530.

Anderson, R. C. and Kulhavy R. W. Imagery and prose learning. *J. educ. Psychol.,* 1972, 63, 242-243.

Anderson, R. C., Kulhavy, R. W. and Andre, T. Conditions under which feedback facilitates learning from programmed lessons. *J. educ. Psychol.,* 1972, 63, 186-188.

_____. Feedback procedure in programmed instruction. *J. educ. Psychol.,* 1971, 62, 148-156.

Anderson, R. C. and Myrow D. L. Retroactive inhibition of meaningful discourse. *J. educ. Psychol.,* 1971, 62, 81-94.

Angell, G. W. The effect of immediate knowledge of quiz results on final examination scores in freshman chemistry. *J. educ. Res.,* 1949, 42, 391-394.

Atkinson, J. W. The mainsprings of achievement-oriented activity. In Krumboltz, J. D. (ed.), *Learning and the educational process.* Chicago: Rand McNally, 1965.

Ausubel, D. P. *The psychology of meaningful verbal learning.* New York: Grune and Stratton, 1963.

Ausubel, D. P. A subsumption theory of meaningful verbal learning and retention. *J. gen. Psychol.,* 1962, 66, 312-324.

Ausubel, D. P. The use of advance organizers in the learning and retention of meaningful verbal material. *J. educ. Psychol.,* 1960, 51, 267-272.

Ausubel, D. P. and Fitzgerald, D. The role of discriminability in meaningful verbal learning and retention. *J. educ. Psychol.,* 1961, 52, 266-274.

Ausubel, D. P., Robbins, Lilliam C. and Blake, E. Retroactive inhibition and facilitation in the learning of school materials. *J. educ. Psychol.,* 1957, 48, 334-343.

Ausubel, D. P., Schpoont, S. H. and Cukier, L. The influence of intention on the retention of school materials. *J. educ. Psychol.,* 1957, 48, 87-92.

Ausubel, D. P., Stager, Mary and Gaite, A. J. H. Retroactive facilitation in meaningful verbal learning. *J. educ. Psychol.,* 1968, 59, 250-255.

Baldwin, T. S. Evaluation of learning in industrial education. In Bloom, B. S. et al., *Handbook on formative and summative evaluation of student learning.* New York: McGraw-Hill, 1971.

Bandura, A. (ed.) *Psychological modeling.* Chicago: Aldine, Atherton, 1971.

Bandura, A., Grusec and Menlove. Observational learning as a function of symbolization and incentive set. *Child Devel.,* 1966, 37, 499-506.

Bandura, A., Ross, D. and Ross, S.A. A comparative test of the status envy, social power and secondary reinforcement theories of identificatory learning. *J. abn. soc. Psychol.,* 1963, 67, 527-534.

Barbe, W. B. The effectiveness of work in remedial reading at the college level. *J. educ. Psychol.,* 1952, 43, 229-237.

Barlow, M. C. Transfer of training in reasoning. *J. educ. Psychol.* 1938, 38, 122-128.

Barron, F. *Creativity and psychological health.* Princeton, N. J.: Van Nostrand, 1963.

Bereiter, C. and Englemann, S. *Teaching disadvantaged children.* Englewood Cliffs, N. J.: Prentice-Hall, 1966.

Berlin, Pearl. Effects of varied teaching emphases during early learning on acquisition of selected motor skills. Unpublished doctoral dissertation. The Pennsylvannia State University, 1959.

Berlyne, D. E. Conflict and information-theory variables as determinants of human perceptual curiosity. *J. exp. psychol.* 1957, 53, 399-404.

_____. *Conflict, arousal and curiosity.* New York: McGraw Hill, 1960.

Bloom, B. S. and Broder, Lois J. *Problem solving processes of college students.* Supplementary educational monographs, 1950, no. 73, Chicago: Univ. of Chicago Press.

Bloom, B. S., Englehart, M. D., Furst, E. J., Hill, W. H. and Krathwohl, D. R. *Taxonomy of educational objectives: I. cognitive domain.* New York: McKay, 1956.

Bloom, B. S., Hastings, J.T., and Madaus, G. F. *Handbook on formative and summative evaluation of student learning.* New York: McGraw-Hill, 1971.

Blyth, J. Teaching machines and human beings. *Educ. Record,* 1960, 41, 116-125.

Bonsfield, W. A. The occurrence of clustering in the recall of randomly arranged associates. *J. genet. Psychol.,* 1953, 49, 229-240.

Boroff, D. The three r's and pushbuttons. *New York Times Magazine,* Sept. 25, 1960, pp. 36 ff.

Borrow, S. A. and Bower, G. H. Comprehension and recall of sentences. *J. exp. Psychol.,* 1969, 80, 455-461.

Bostrom, R., Vlandis, J., and Rosenbaum, M. Grades as reinforcing contingencies and attitude change. *J. educ. Psychol.,* 1961, 52, 112-115.

Bourne, L. E. *Human conceptual behavior.* Boston: Allyn and Bacon, 1966.

Bourne, L. E., Goldstein, S. and Link, W.E. Concept learning as a function of availability of previously presented information. *J. exp. Psychol.* 1964, 67, 439-448.

Bourne, L. E. and Jennings, P.E. The relationship between contiguity and classification learning. *J. gen. Psychol.,* 1963, 69, 335-338.

Bower, G. H., Clark, M.C., Lesgold, A. M. and Winzenz, D. Hierarchical retrieval schemes in recall of categorized word lists. *J. of Verbal Learning and Verbal Behavior,* 1969, 8, 323-343.

Briggs, L. J. and Reed, H. B. The curve of retention for substance material. *J. exp. Psychol.,* 1943, 32, 513-517.

Bruce, R. W. Conditions of transfer of training. *J. exp. Psychol.,* 1933, 16, 343-361.

Bruner, J. S. The act of discovery. *Harvard educ. rev.,* 1961, 31, 21-32.

_____. *The process of education.* Cambridge: Harvard University Press, 1960.

Bruner, J. S., Goodnow, Jacqueline J. and Austin, G. A. *A study of thinking.* New York: Wiley, 1956.

Bruning, R. H. Short-term retention of specific factual information in prose contexts of varying organization and relevance. *J. educ. Psychol.,* 1970, 61, 186-192.

Bulgarella, Rosaria and Archer, E. J. Concept identification of auditory stimuli as a function of amount of relevant and irrelevant information. *J. exp. Psychol.,* 1962, 63, 254 257.

Burt, C. The structure of the mind: a review of the results of factor analysis, *Brit. J. educ. Psychol.,* 1949, 19, 100-111, 176-199.

Buss, A. H. and Buss, E. H. The effect of verbal reinforcement combinations on conceptual learning. *J. exp. Psychol.,* 1956, 52, 283-287.

Byrne, D. and Griffitt, W. A developmental investigation of the law of attraction. *J. Pers. soc. Psychol.,* 1966, 4, 699-702.

Cahill, H. E. and Hovland, C. I. The role of memory in the acquisition of concepts. *J. exp. Psychol.* 1960, 59, 137-144.

Calvin, A. Social reinforcement. *J. soc. Psychol.,* 1962, 56, 15-19.

Carlson, T. The relationship between speed and accuracy of comprehension, *J. educ. Res.,* 1949, 42, 500-512.

Carroll, J. B. *Language and thought.* Englewood Cliffs, N. J.: Prentice-Hall, 1964.

_____. The place of educational psychology in the study of education. In J. Walton and J. Kruthe. *The discipline of education.* Madison: Univ. of Wisconsin Press, 1963, 105-119.

_____. Words, meanings and concepts. *Harv. educ Rev.,* 1964, 34, 178-202.

Child, I. L. and Whiting, J. Determinants of level of aspiration: evidence from everyday life. *J. abnorm. soc. Psychol.,* 1949, 44, 303-314.

Chomsky, N. Review of Skinner's Verbal behavior. *Language,* 1959, 35, 26-58.

Christensen, P. R., Guilford, J. P. and Wilson, R. C. Relations of creative responses to working time and instruction. *J. exp. Psychol.,* 1957, 53, 82-88.

Clark, D. C. Teaching concepts in the classroom. *J. educ. Psychol.,* 1971, 62, 253-278.

Clark, L. V. Effect of mental practice on the development of a certain motor skill. *Research Quarterly,* 1960, 31, 560-569.

Clark, R. W., Research studies in automated instruction. Report presented to the Pennsylvania Advisory Committee on Self-Instructional Devices. Harrisburg, Pa., 1961.

Cohen, S. R. Influence of organizing strategies and instructions on short term retention. *J. educ. Psychol.,* 1973, 64, 199-205.

Craig, R. C. *The transfer value of guided learning.* New York: Teachers College, 1953.

Crawford, T. J. The effect of emphasizing production typewriting contrasted with speed typewriting in developing production typewriting ability. Unpublished doctoral dissertation, University of Pittsburgh, 1956.

Crossman, E.R. A theory of the acquisition of speedskill. In *Ergonomics.* London: Taylor and Francis, Vol. 1, 153-166.

Crouse, J. H. Retroactive interference in reading prose materials. *J. educ. Psychol.,* 1971, 62, 39-44.

_____. Transfer and retroaction in prose learning. *J. educ. Psychol.,* 1970, 61, 226-236.

Crowder, N. A. The rationale of intrinsic programming. In DeCecco, J. P. (ed.), *Human Learning in the School.* New York: Holt, Rinehart and Winston, 1963.

Culbertson, F. M. Modification of an emotionally held attitude through role playing. *J. abnorm. soc. Psychol.,* 1957, 54, 230-233.

Cumming, Allana and Goldstein, L.S. The effect of overt and covert responding on two kinds of learning tasks. In *Technical Report 620919.* New York: Center for Programmed Instruction, 1962.

Davies, Dorothy. The effect of tuition upon the process of learning a complex motor skill. *J. educ. Psychol.,* 1945, 36, 352-365.

Dervin, D. and Deffenbacher, K. Effects of proportion of positive instance and degree of restriction on the induction of a principle. *Psychonomic Science,* 1970, 21, 79-80.

Dewey, J. *How we think.* Boston: Heath, 1910.

Dooling, D. J. and Lackman, R. Effects of comprehension on retention of prose. *J. exp. Psychol.,* 1971, 88, 216-222.

Duncan, C. B. The effect of unequal amounts of practice on motor learning before and after rest. *J. exp. Psychol.,* 1951, 42, 257-264.

Dunkel, H. B. Testing the precise use of words. *Coll. Engl.,* 1944, 5, 386-389.

Ebbinghaus, H. *Memory, a contribution to experimental psychology.* 1885. Translated by H. A. Ruger and C. E. Bussenius. New York: Teachers College, 1913.

Edwards, M. D. and Tyler, Leona E. Intelligence, creativity and achievement in a nonselective public junior high school. *J. educ. Psychol.,* 1965, 56, 96-99.

Edwards, T. B. Measurement of some aspects of critical thinking. *J. exp. Educ.,* 1950, 18, 263-278.

Egan, D. E. and Greeno, J. G. Acquiring cognitive structure by discovery and rule learning. *J. educ. Psychol.* 1973, 64, 85-97.

Ellis, H. *The transfer of learning.* New York: Macmillan, 1965.

Elwell, J. L. and Grindley, G. C. The effect of knowledge of results on learning and performance: 1. a coordinated movement of the two hands. *Brit. J. Psychol.,* 1938, 29, 39-53.

Eysenck, S. B. G. Retention of a well-developed motor skill after one year. *J. gen. Psychol.,* 1960, 63, 267-273.

Fenton, E. *The new social studies.* New York: Holt, Rinehart and Winston, 1967.

Festinger, L. *A theory of cognitive dissonance.* Palo Alto, Calif.: Stanford Univ. Press, 1957.

Fitts, P. M. Perceptual-motor skill learning. In *Categories of human learning,* ed. A. W. Melton. New York: Academic Press, 1964.

Fitts, P. M. and Posner, M. I. *Human performance.* Belmont, Calif.: Brooks/Cole, 1967.

Fitts, P. M. and Seeger, C. M. S-R compatibility: spatial characteristics of stimulus and response codes. *J. exp. Psychol.,* 1953, 46, 199-210.

Fitzgerald, H. T. Teaching machines: a demurrer. *School review,* 1962, 70, 247-256.

Flavell, J. H. *The developmental psychology of Jean Piaget.* Princeton, N. J.: Van Nostrand, 1963.

Fleishman, E. A. *The structure and measurement of physical fitness.* Englewood Cliffs, N.J.: Prentice-Hall, 1964.

Fleishman, E. A. and Parker, J. F. Factors in the retention and relearning of perceptual motor skills. *J. exp. Psychol.,* 1962, 64, 215-226.

Forehand, G. A. and Libby, W.L. Jr. Effects of educational programs and perceived organizational climate upon changes in innovative administrative behavior. In *Innovative Behavior.* Chicago: Univ. of Chicago, Center for Programs in Government Administration, 1962.

Frase, L. T. Questions as aids to reading: some research and theory. *Am. Educ. Res. J.,* 1968, 5, 319-332.

French, Elizabeth. The effects of the interaction of motivation and feedback on task performance. In Atkinson, J. W. (ed.), *Motives in Fantasy, Action and Society.* Princeton, N. J.: Van Nostrand, 1958.

French, E. G. and Thomas, F. H. The relation of achievement motivation to problem solving. *J. abnorm. soc. Psychol.,* 1958, 56, 45-48.

Friedman, M. P. and Greitzer, F. L. Organization and study time in learning from reading. *J. educ. Psychol.,* 1972, 63, 609-616.

Fryatt, M. J. and Tulving E. Interproblem transfer in identification of concepts involving positive and negative instances. *Canadian J. of Psychol.,* 1963, 17, 106-117.

Gagne, R. M. *The conditions of learning.* New York: Holt, Rinehart and Winston, 1970.

_____. Context, isolation and interference effects on the retention of facts. *J. educ. Psychol.,* 1969, 60, 408-414.

_____. Human problem solving: internal and external events. In B. Kleinmentz (ed.), *Problem solving: research, method and theory.* New York: Wiley, 1966.

Gagne, R. M. and Brown, L. T. Some factors in the programming of conceptual learning. *J. exp. Psychol.,* 1961, 62, 313-321.

Gagne, R. M. and Wiegand, V. K. Effects of a superordinate context on learning and retention of facts. *J. educ. Psychol.,* 1970, 61, 406-409.

Garrett, H. E. *Great experiments in psychology.* New York: Appleton-Century-Crofts, 1951.

Gates, A. I. Recitation as a factor in memorizing. *Arch. Psychol.,* 1917, 6, no. 40.

Gay, L. R. Temporal position of review and its effect on the retention of mathematical rules. *J. educ. Psychol.,* 1973, 64, 171-182.

Gerst, M. S. Symbolic coding processes in observational learning. *J. Pers. soc. Psychol.,* 1971, 19, 9-17.

Getzels, J. W. and Jackson, P. W. *Creativity and intelligence.* New York: Wiley, 1961.

Gibbons, Helen D. Reading and sentence elements. *Elem. Engl. Rev.,* 1941, 18, 42-46.

Glaser, E. M. *An experiment in the development of critical thinking.* New York: Teachers College, 1941.

Grant, D. A. Perceptual versus analytic responses to the number concept of a Weigl-type card sorting test. *J. exp. Psychol.,* 1951, 41, 23-29.

Gray, W. S. and Holmes, Eleanor. *The development of meaning vocabularies in reading.* Chicago: Univ. of Chicago Laboratory School, 1938.

Greenspoon, Joel and Foreman, Sally. Effect of delay of knowledge of results on learning a motor task. *J. exp. Psychol.,* 1956, 51, 226-228.

Grener, N. and Raths, L. E. Thinking in grade III. *Educ. Res. Bull.,* Ohio State Univ., 1945, 24, 38-42.

Gropper, G. L. and Lumsdaine, A. A. Experiments on active student response to televised instruction, an interim report. Pittsburgh: Am. Inst. Research, 1960.

Guilford, J. P. Intelligence: 1965 model. *Amer. Psychologist,* 1966, 21, 20-26.

_____. *The nature of human intelligence.* New York: McGraw-Hill, 1967.

_____. A system of psychomotor abilities. *Am. J. Psychol.,* 1958, 71, 164-174.

_____. Three faces of intellect. *Amer. Psychologist,* 1959, 14, 469-479.

Hammer, B. Grade expectations, differential teacher comments, and student performance. *J. educ. Psychol.,* 1972, 63, 454-458.

Harlow, H. F. The formation of learning sets. *Psychol. Rev.,* 1949, 56, 51-65.

Harootunian, B. Intellectual abilities and reading achievement. *Elem. Sch. J.,* 1966, 66, 386-392.

Haskess, R. I. A statistical study of the comparative results produced by teaching derivations in the ninth grade Latin classes and in the ninth grade English classes of non-Latin pupils in four Philadelphia high schools. Unpublished doctoral dissertation, Univ. of Pennsylvania, 1923.

Haslam, W. L. and Brown, W. F. Effectiveness of study-skill instructions for high school sophomores. *J. educ. Psychol.,* 1968, 59, 223-226.

Haygood, R. C. and Stevenson, M. Effects of proportion of positive instances upon concept learning. *Psychol. Reports,* 1967, 20, 179-182.

Heidbreder, Edna. The attainment of concepts: II. The problem. *J. gen. Psychol.,* 1946, 35, 191-223.

Helson, R. M. and Cover, A. Specificity-generality of classificatory categories as a variable in recall. *Percept. mot. skills,* 1956, 6, 233-236.

Herbert, J. and Ausubel, D. P. (eds.) *Psychology in teacher preparation.* Toronto: Ontario Institute for Studies in Education, 1969.

Hermann, G. D. Egrule vs. ruleg teaching methods: grade, intelligence, and category of learning. *J. exp. Educ.,* 1971, 39, 22-33.

Hilgard, E. R. Teaching machines and programmed learning: what support from the psychology of learning? *Nat. Educ. Assoc. J.,* 1961, 50, 20-21.

Hilgard, E. R. and Bower, G. H., *Theories of learning.* New York: Appleton-Century-Crofts, 1966.

Hilgard, E. R., Irvine, R. P. and Whipple, J. E. Rote memorization understanding and transfer: an extention of Katona's card-trick experiment. *J. exp. Psychol.,* 1953, 46, 288-292.

Hilgard, E. R. and Smith, M. B. Distributed practice in motor learning: score changes within and between daily sessions. *J. exp. Psychol.,* 1942, 30, 136-146.

Hill, W. F. *Learning: a survey of psychological interpretations.* San Francisco: Chandler, 1971.

Hoepfner, R. Intellectual aptitude involvement in thinking skills. *J. Res. Dev. in Educ.,* 1969, 3, 43-52.

Hoepfner, R., Guilford, J. P. and Bradley, P. A. Transformation of information in learning. *J. educ. Psychol.,* 1970, 61, 316-323.

Hoffman, M. L., Mitsis, S. B. and Protz, R. E. Achievement striving, social class, and test anxiety. *J. abn. soc. psychol.,* 1958, 56, 401-403.

Houtz, J. C., Moore, J. W. and Davis, J. K. Effects of different types of positive and negative instances in learning "nondimensional" concepts. *J. educ. Psychol.,* 1973, 64, 206-211.

Hovland, C. I. and Weiss, W. Transmission of information concerning concepts through positive and negative instances. *J. exp. Psychol.* 1953, 45, 165-182.

Howell, W. J. Work-study skills of children in grades IV-VIII. *Elem. School J.,* 1950, 50, 384-389.

Hull, C. L. Conditioning: outline of a systematic theory of learning. In *The psychology of learning,* 41st Yearbook of the National Society for the Study of Education. Chicago: Univ. of Chicago Press, 1942.

_____. *Principles of behavior.* New York: Appleton-Century-Crofts, 1943.

Hunt, E. B. and Hovland, C. I. Order of consideration of different types of concepts. *J. exp. Psychol.,* 1960, 59, 220-225.

Hurlock, Elizabeth B. An evaluation of certain incentives used in schoolwork. *J. educ. Psychol.,* 1925, 16, 145-159.

Hyman, R. Knowledge and creativity. In *Widening horizons in creativity,* (ed.) C. W. Taylor. New York: Wiley, 1964.

Inhelder, Barbel, and J. Piaget. *The growth of logical thinking from childhood to adolescence.* New York: Basic Books, 1958.

Irion, A. L. Historical introduction. In *Principles of skill acquisition,* (ed.) Bilodeau, E. A. New York: Academic Press, 1969.

_____. Reminiscence in pursuit-rotor learning as a function of length of rest and of amount of pre-rest practice. *J. exp. Psychol.,* 1949, 39, 492-499.

Jacob, P. *Changing values in college.* New York: Harper & Row, 1957.

Janis, I. L. and Mann, L. Effectiveness of emotional role playing in modifying smoking habits and attitudes. *J. exp. Res. Pers.,* 1965, 1, 84-90.

Jensen, L. and Anderson, D. C. Retroactive inhibition of difficult and unfamiliar prose. *J. educ. Psychol.,* 1970, 61, 305-309.

Johnson, D. M. and Stratton, R. P. Evaluation of five methods of teaching concepts. *J. educ. Psychol.,* 1966, 57, 48-53.

Jones, J. G. Motor learning without demonstration under two conditions of mental practice. *Research Quarterly,* 1965, 36, 270-281.

Judd, C. H. *Educational psychology.* Boston: Houghton Mifflin, 1939.

_____. *Psychology of secondary education.* Boston: Ginn, 1927.

Jung, J. A cumulative method of paired associates and serial learning. *J. verbal learning and verbal behavior,* 1964, 3, 290-299.

Kagen, J., Pearson, L. and Welsh, L. Modifiability of an impulsive tempo. *J. educ. Psychol.,* 1966, 57, 359-365.

Kastrinos, W. The relationship of two methods of teaching to the development of critical thinking by high school students in advanced biology. *Science Educ.,* 1964, 48, 187-195.

Katona, G. *Organizing and memorizing.* New York: Columbia Univ. Press, 1940.

Katz, D. The functional approach to the study of attitudes. *Public Opinion Quart.,* 1960, 24, 163-204.

Keislar, E. R. and Stern, C. Differentiated instruction in problem solving for children of different mental ability levels. *J. educ. Psychol.,* 1970, 61, 445-450.

Keller, F. S. The phantom plateau. *J. exp. anal. Behavior,* 1958, 1, 1-13.

Kendler, H. H. and Kendler, Tracy S. Vertical and horizontal processes in problem solving. *Psychol. Rev.,* 1962, 69, 1-16.

Kendler, H. H. and Vineberg, R. The acquisition of compound concepts as a function of previous training. *J. exp. Psychol.,* 1954, 48, 252-258.

Kerfoot, J. F. Reading in elementary school. *Rev. educ. Res.,* 1967, 120-133.

Kersh, B. Y. The adequacy of "meaning" as an explanation for the superiority of learning by independent discovery. *J. educ. Psychol.,* 1958, 49, 282-292.

_____. The motivating effect of learning by discovery. *J. educ. Psychol.,* 1962, 53, 65-71.

Kittell, J. E. An experimental study of the effect of external direction during learning of transfer and retention of principles. *J. educ. Psychol.,* 1957, 48, 391-405.

Klaus, D. J. Some observations and findings from auto-instructional research in newer educational media. University Park: Pennsylvania State Univ., 1960.

Klausmeier, H. J. and Check, J. Retention and transfer in children of low, average, and high intelligence. *J. educ. Res.,* 1962, 55, 319-322.

Knapp, C. G. and Dixon, W. R. Learning to juggle: II, a study of whole and part methods. *Research Quarterly,* 1952, 23, 398-401.

Koffka, K. Principles of Gestalt Psychology. New York: Harcourt, Brace, 1935.

Kolb, D. A. Achievement motivation training for underachieving high-school boys. *J. Pers. soc. psychol.,* 1965, 2, 783-792.

Koonce, J. M., Chamblis, D. J. and Irion, A. L. Supplementary report: long-term reminiscence in the pursuit-rotor habit. *J. exp. Psychol.,* 1964, 67, 498-500.

Kornreich, L. B. Discovery versus programmed instruction in teaching a strategy for solving concept identification problems. *J. educ. Psychol.,* 1969, 60, 384-388.

Krathwohl, D. R., Bloom, B. S. and Masia, B. B. *A taxonomy of educational objectives: affective domain.* New York: David McKay, 1964.

Kreuger, W. C. F. The effect of over-learning on retention. *J. exp. Psychol.,* 1929, 12, 17-78.

Krumboltz, J. D. and Weisman, R. G. The effect of intermittent confirmation in programmed instruction. *J. educ. Psychol.,* 1962, 53, 250-253.

Kurtz, K. H. and Hovland, C. I. Concept learning with differing sequences of instances. *J. exp. Psychol.,* 1956, 51, 239-243.

Lehmann, I. J. Changes in critical thinking, attitudes and values from freshman to senior years. *J. educ. Psychol.,* 1963, 54, 305-315.

Lester, O. P. Mental set in relation to retroactive inhibition. *J. exp. Psychol.*, 1932, 15, 681-699.

Lewin, K. Group decision and social change. In T. H. Newcomb and E. L. Hartley (eds.), *Readings in social psychology*. New York: Holt, Rinchart and Winston, 1947.

Lloyd, K. E. Supplementary report: retention and transfer of responses to stimulus classes. *J. exp. Psychol.*, 1960, 59, 206-207.

Loban, W. *Literature and social sensitivity*. Champaign, Ill.: National Council of Teachers of English, 1954.

MacKinnon, D. W., (ed.) *The creative person*. Berkeley, Calif.: Univ. of California, 1961.

_____. The highly effective individual. *Teachers College Record*, 1960, 61, 367-378.

_____. Personality and the realization of creative potential. *Am. Psychologist*, 1965, 20, 273-281.

Mager, R. F. Preliminary studies in automated teaching. *IRE Trans. on Education*, 1959, E-2, pp. 104-107.

Maguire, W. J. The nature of attitudes and attitude change. In *Handbook of social psychology*, 2nd ed. (ed.) G. Lindzey and E. Aronson. Reading, Mass.: Addison Wesley, 1969, Vol. 3, 136-314.

Maltzman, I., Brooks, L. O., Bogartz, W. and Summers, S. S. The facilitation of problem solving by prior exposure to uncommon responses. *J. exp. Psychol.*, 1958, 56, 399-406.

Mandler, G. From association to structure. *Psychol. Rev.*, 1962, 69, 415-427.

Mann, L. and Janis, I. L. A follow-up study on the long-term effects of emotional role playing. *J. pers. soc. Psychol.*, 1968, 8, 339-342.

Marquart, D. I. Group problem solving. *J. soc. Psychol.*, 1955, 41, 103-113.

Maslow, A. H. *Motivation and personality*. New York: Harper and Row, 1954.

Mayer, R. E. and Greeno, J. G. Structural differences between learning and outcomes produced by different instructional methods. *J. educ. Psychol.*, 1972, 63, 165-173.

McConnell, T. R. Discovery vs. authoritative identification in the learning of children. *Univ. of Iowa Stud. Educ.*, 1934, 9, no.5.

McCullough, C. and VanAtta, L. The use of miniature programs to supplement conventional teaching techniques. Presented at the American Psychological Association, Chicago, Sept. 1960.

McCullough, C. M. Implications of research on children's concepts. *Reading Teacher*, 1959, 13, 100-107.

McDougall, W. P. Differential retention of course outcomes in educational psychology. *J. educ. Psychol.*, 1958, 49, 53-60.

McFee, J. K. Creative problem-solving abilities of acaðemically superior adolescents, a preliminary report. Tempe, Ariz.: Arizona State Univ., 1964.

McGaw, B. and Grotelueschen, A. Direction of the effect of questions in prose material. *J. educ. Psychol.*, 1972, 63, 580-588.

McGeoch, J. A. Forgetting and the law of disuse. *Psychol. Rev.*, 1932, 39, 352-37.

McGeoch, J. A. and McGeoch, G. O. Studies in retroactive inhibition: X. The influence of similarity of meaning between lists of paired associates. *J. exp. Psychol.*, 1937, 21, 320-329.

McGuigan, F. J. and MacCaslin, E. Whole and part methods in learning a perceptual motor skill. *Am. J. Psychol.*, 1955, 68, 658-661.

McKeachie, W. J. Individual conformity to attitudes of classroom groups. *J. abn. soc. Psychol.*, 1954, 49, 282-289.

McNaughton, A. H. The ability of seventh grade children to infer meaning and to generalize from two selections of written history materials. Unpublished doctoral dissertation, Univ. California, Berkeley. 1960.

McNemar, Olga. An attempt to differentiate between individuals with high and low reasoning ability. *Am. J. Psychol.*, 1955, 48, 20-36.

McNemar, Q. Lost: our intelligence? why? *Am. Psychologist*, 1964, 19, 871-882.

Meadow, A., Parnes, J. J. and Reese, H. Influence of brainstorming instructions and problem sequence on a creative problem-solving test. *J. appl. Psychol.*, 1959, 43, 413-416.

Merrifield, P. R. An analysis of concepts from the point of view of the structure of intellect. In *Analyses of concept learning,* (ed.) Klausmeier, J. H. and Harris, C. W. New York: Academic Press, 1966.

Merrifield, P. R., Guilford, J. P., Christensen, P. R. and Frick, J. W. The role of intellectual factors in problem solving. *Psychol. Monogr.*, 1962, 76, no. 10 (whole no. 529).

Merrill, M. D. and Stolurow, L. M. Hierarchical preview versus problem oriented review in learning an imaginary science. *Amer. educ. Res. J.*, 1966, 3, 251-262.

Meyer, W. J. and Seidman, S. B. Relative effectiveness of different reinforcement combinations on concept learning of children at two developmental levels. *Child Devel.*, 1961, 32, 117-127.

Miles, Catherine C. Crucial factors in the life history of talent. In *Talent and education,* (ed.) E. P. Torrance. Minneapolis: Univ. of Minnesota, 1960.

Miller, G. A. The magical number seven, plus or minus two, some limits on our capacity for processing information. *Psychol. Rev.*, 1956, 63, 81-97.

Mitnick, L. L. and McGinnies, E. Influencing ethnocentrism in small discussion groups through a film communication. *J. abnom. soc. Psychol.*, 1958, 56, 82-90.

Mittman, L. R. and Terrell, G. An experimental study of curiosity in children. *Child Devel.*, 1964, 35, 851-855.

Montague, W. E., Adams, J. A. and Kiess, H. D. Forgetting and natural language mediation. *J. exp. psychol.*, 1966, 72, 829-833.

Moore, J. W. and Smith W. I. Role of knowledge of results in programmed instruction. *Psychol. Reports*, 1964, 14, 407-423.

Moore, O. K. and Anderson, S. B. Search behavior in individual and group problem solving. *Amer. sociol. Rev.*, 1954, 19, 702-714.

Mussen, P. Some personality and social factors related to changes in children's attitudes toward negroes. *J. abnorm. soc. Psychol.*, 1950, 45, 423-441.

Newcomb, T. M. *The acquaintance process.* New York: Holt, Rinehart and Winston, 1961.

_____. *Personality and social change.* New York: Holt, Rinehart and Winston, 1943.

Osborn, W. W. An experiment in teaching resistance to propaganda. *J. exp. educ.*, 1939, 8, 1-17.

Oxendine, J. B. Effect of progressively changing practice schedules on the learning of a motor skill. *Research Quarterly*, 1965, 36, 307-315.

Page, E. B. Teacher comments and student performance. *J. educ. psychol.,* 1958, 49, 173-181.

Parker, J. F. and Fleishman, E. A. Use of analytical information concerning task requirements to increase the effectiveness of skill training. *J. applied Psychol.,* 1961, 45, 295-302.

Parnes, S. J. Can creativity be increased? In *A source book for creative thinking,* (ed.) S. J. Parnes and J. F. Harding. New York: Scribner, 1962.

Pavlov, I. P. *Conditioned reflexes.* London: Oxford Univ. Press, 1927.

Payne, J. *Lectures on education.* 1883.

Peeck, J. Effect of prerequisites on delayed retention of prose material. *J. educ. Psychol.,* 1970, 61, 241-246.

Phillips, B. N. Effect of cohesion and intelligence on the problem solving efficiency of small face to face groups in cooperative and competitive situations. *J. educ. Res.* 1956, 50, 127-137.

Piaget, J. *The science of education and the psychology of the child.* New York: Orion Press, 1970.

Piaget, J. and Inhelder, Barbel. *The psychology of the child.* New York: Basic Books, 1969.

Pikas, A. *Abstraction and concept formation.* Cambridge, Mass.: Harvard Univ. Press, 1966.

Polya, G. *How to solve it.* Princeton, N. J.: Princeton Univ. Press, 1954.

Pond, F. L. Influence of the study of Latin on word knowledge. *School Review,* 1938, 46, 611-618.

Porter, D. Some effects of year-long teaching machine instruction. In *Automatic teaching: the state of the art,* (ed.) E. H. Galanter. New York: John Wiley, 1959.

Postman, L. Retention as a function of degree of overlearning. *Science,* 1962, 135, 666-667.

Postman L. Short-term memory and incidental learning. In *Categories of human learning,* (ed.) A. W. Melton. New York: Academic Press, 1964.

Postman L. and Goggin, J. Whole versus part learning of paired-associate lists. *J. exp. Psychol.,* 1966, 71, 867-877.

Poulton, E. C. Previous knowledge and memory. *Brit. J. Psychol.,* 1957, 48, 259-270.

Pressey, Luella C. and Pressey, S. L. A critical study of the concept of silent reading ability. *J. educ. Psychol.,* 1921, 12, 25-31.

Ray, W. E. Pupil discovery vs. direct instruction. *J. exp. Educ.,* 1961, 29, 271-280.

Rathkopf, E. Z. and Bisbicos, E. E. Selective facilitative effects of interspersed questions on learning from written materials. *J. educ. Psychol.,* 1967, 58, 56-61.

Reed, J. C. and Pepper, R. S. Interrelationship of vocabulary, comprehension and rate among disabled readers. *J. exp. Educ.,* 1957, 25, 333-337.

Reid, Florence. Films provide a rich source of vocabulary study. *J. educ. Res.,* 1958, 51, 617-623.

Restle, F., Andrews, M. and Rokeach, M. Differences between open- and close- minded subjects on learning set and oddity problems. *J. abnorm. soc. Psychol.,* 1964, 68, 648-654.

Rickert, R. K. Developing critical thinking. *Science Educ.,* 1967, 51, 24-27.

Rivenes, R. S. Effect on motor skill acquisition and retention of teaching by demonstration with and without verbal explanation. Unpublished master's thesis, Pennsylvania State Univ., 1961.

Robb, Margaret. Feedback. *Quest,* 1966, Monograph VI, 38-43.

Roberts, G. R. A study of motivation in remedial reading. *Brit. J. educ. Psychol.,* 1960, 30, 176-179.

Ruddell, R. B. Effect of the similarity of oral and written patterns of language structure on reading comprehension. *Elem. Engl.,* 1965, 42, 403-410.

_____. Second and third year of a longitudinal study of four programs of reading instruction with varying emphasis on the regularity of grapheme-phoneme correspondences and the relation of language structure to meaning. U. S. Dept. of Health, Education and Welfare, Office of Education. Cooperative Research Projects nos. 3099 and 78085, 1968.

Salisburg, B. A. A study of the transfer effects of training in logical organization. *J. educ. Res.,* 1947, 28, 241-254.

Sanders, N. M., DiVesta, F. J. and Gray, G. S. Effects of concept instance sequence as a function of stage of learning and learner strategy. *J. educ. Psychol.,* 1972, 63, 235-241.

Saugstad, P. and Raaheim, K. Problem solving and availability of functions. *Acta Psychol.,* 1957, 13, 263-278.

Scandura, J. M. and Voorhies, D. J. Effect of irrelevant attributes and irrelevant operations on rule learning. *J. educ. Psychol.,* 1971, 62, 352-356.

Scherer, G. A. and M. Wertheimer. *A psycholinguistic experiment in foreign language teaching.* New York: McGraw-Hill, 1964.

Schooley, M. and Hartmann, G. W. Role of insight in the learning of logical relations. *Amer. J. Psychol.,* 1937, 49, 287-292.

Schultz, C. B. and DiVesta, F. J. Effects of passage organization and note taking on the selection of clustering strategies and on recall of textual materials. *J. educ. Psychol.,* 1972, 63, 244-252.

Schvaneveldt, R. W. Concept identification as a function of probability of positive instances and number of relevant dimensions. *J. exp. Psychol.,* 1966, 72, 649-654.

Schwartz, S. H. Trial-by-trial analysis of processes in simple disjunctive concept attainment tasks. *J. exp. Psychol,* 1966, 72, 456-465.

Sears, Pauline. Levels of aspiration in academically successful and unsuccessful children. *J. abnorm. soc. Psychol.* 1940, 35, 498-436.

Serra, Mary C. How to develop concepts and their verbal representations. *Elem. sch. J.,* 1953, 53, 275-285.

Shaw, M. E. and Wright, J. M. *Scales for the measurement of attitudes.* New York: McGraw-Hill, 1967.

Sherman, H. L., et al. *Drawing by seeing.* New York: Hinds, Hayden and Eldredge, 1947.

Shores, J. H. and Husbands, K. L. Are fast readers the best readers? *Elem. Engl.,* 1950, 27, 52-57.

Silberman, C. E. *Crisis in the classroom: the remaking of American education.* New York: Random House, 1970.

Silberman, H. R., et al. Fixed sequence versus branching autoinstructional methods. *J. educ. psychol.,* 1961, 52, 166-172.

Singer, H. and Ruddell, R. B. *Theoretical models and processes of reading.* Newark, Delaware: International Reading Association, 1970.

Skinner, B. F. *Science and human behavior.* New York, Macmillan, 1953.

_____. The science of learning and the art of teaching. *Harv. educ. Rev.,* 1954, 24, 86-97.

_____. Teaching machines. *Science,* 1958, 24, 969-977.

_____. *Verbal behavior.* New York: Appleton-Century-Crofts, 1957.

_____. Why we need teaching machines. *Harv. educ. Rev.,* 1961, 31, 377-398.

Skinner, B. F. and Holland, J. G. *The analysis of behavior.* New York: McGraw-Hill, 1961.

Slamecka, N. J. Studies of retention of connected discourse. *Am. J. Psychol.,* 1959, 72, 409-416.

Smedslund, J. The acquisition of conservation of substance and weight in children. III. Extinction of conservation of weight acquired "normally" and by means of empirical controls on a balance scale. *Scand. J. Psychol.,* 1961, 2, 85-87.

Solly, W. H. The effects of verbal instructions of speed and accuracy upon the learning of a motor skill. *Research Quarterly,* 1952, 23, 231-240.

Spearman, C. *The abilities of man.* New York: Macmillan, 1927.

Staats, A. W. and Staats, C. K. Attitudes established by classical conditioning. *J. abn. soc. Psychol.,* 1958, 57, 37-40.

Stendler, Celia, Damrin,D. and Haines, A. Studies of cooperation and competition: 1. The effects of working for group and individual rewards on the social climate of children's groups. *J. genet. Psychol.,* 1951, 79, 173-197.

Strom, Ingrid M. Does knowledge of grammar improve reading? *Engl. J.,* 1956, 45, 129-133.

Suchman, J. R. Inquiry training: building skills for autonomous discovery. *Merrill-Palmer Quart. of behavior and development,* 1961, 7, 148-169.

_____. Inquiry training in the elementary school. *Science Teacher,* 1960, 27, 42-47.

Taba, H. *With perspective on human relations.* Washington: American Council on Education, 1955.

Taft, R. and Gilchrist, M. B. Creative attitudes and creative production. *J. educ. Psychol.,* 1970, 61, 136-143.

Tanner, R. T. Expository-deductive versus discovery-inductive programming of physical science principles. *J. res. Sci. Teach.,* 1969, 6, 136-142.

TEMAC, Programmed learning materials. Wilmette, Ill: Encyclopedia Britannica Films, 1961.

Tennyson, R. D. Effect of negative instances in concept acquisition using a verbal learning task. *J. educ. Psychol.,* 1973, 64, 247-260.

Tennyson, R. D., Wooley, F. R. and Merrill, M. D. Exemplar and nonexemplar variables which produce correct concept classification behavior and specified classification errors. *J. educ. Psychol.,* 1972, 63, 144-152.

Thelan, H. A. Programmed instruction: insight vs. conditioning. *Education,* 1963, 83, 416-420.

Thistlewaite, D. L. Attitude and structure as factors in the distortion of reasoning. *J. abnorm. soc. Psychol.,* 1950, 45, 442-458.

Thompson, G. G. and Hunnicutt, C. W. The effect of repeated praise or blame on the work achievement of "introverts" and "extroverts." *J. educ. psychol.*, 1944, 35, 257-266.

Thorndike, E. L. *Educational psychology.* New York: Teachers College, 1913.

Thurstone, L. L. Psychological implications of factor analysis. *Amer. Psychologist*, 1948, 3, 402-408.

Tiedeman, H. R. A study of retention in classroom learning. *J. educ. Res.*, 1948, 42, 516-531.

Tinker, M. A. Rate of work in reading performance as measured by standardized tests. *J. educ. Psychol.*, 1945, 36, 217-228.

Toch, H. and Cantril, H. A preliminary inquiry into the learning of values. *J. educ. Psychol.*, 1957, 48, 145-156.

Torrance, E. P. *Creativity.* San Rafael, Calif.: Dimensions, 1969.

_____. *Guiding creative talent.* Englewood Cliffs, N. J.: Prentice-Hall, 1962.

_____. *Rewarding creative behavior.* Englewood Cliffs, N. J.: Prentice-Hall, 1965.

_____. *Rewarding creative thinking.* Minneapolis: Univ. of Minnesota, 1960.

_____. Stimulation, enjoyment and originality in dyadic creativity. *J. educ. Psychol.*, 1971, 62, 45-48.

Traxler, A. E. Improvement of vocabulary through drill. *Engl. J.*, 1938, 27, 491-494.

Tuckman, J. and Lorge, I. Individual ability as a determinant of group superiority. *Hum. Rel.* 1962, 15: 45-51.

Twining, W. E. Mental practice and physical practice in learning a motor skill. *Research Quarterly*, 1949, 20, 432-435.

Tyler, R. W. Some findings from studies in the field of college biology. *Science Educ.*, 1934, 18, 122-142.

Ulmer, G. Teaching geometry to cultivate reflective thinking: an experimental study with 1239 high school pupils. *J. exp. Educ.*, 1939, 8, 18-25.

Underwood, B. J. The effect of successive interpolations on retroactive and proactive inhibition. *Psychol. Monogr.*, 1945, 59, no. 3.

_____. Laboratory studies of verbal learning. In *Theories of learning and instruction*, 63rd Yearbook of the National Society for the Study of Education, Part 1. Chicago: Univ. of Chicago Press, 1964.

_____. Ten years of massed practice on distributed practice. *Psychol. Rev.*, 1961, 68, 229-247.

Van Wagenen, R. K. and Travers, R.M.W. Learning under conditions of direct and vicarious reinforcement. *J. educ. psychol.*, 1963, 54, 356-362.

Vernon, P. E. *The structure of human abilities.* London: Methuen, 1950, 1960.

Vinacke, W. E. *The psychology of thinking.* New York: McGraw-Hill, 1952.

Wallas, G. *The art of thought.* New York: Harcourt Brace, 1926.

Watson, G. and Glaser, E. M. Watson-Glaser critical thinking appraisal. New York: Harcourt, Brace and World, 1952.

Watts, G. H. and Anderson R. C. Effect of three types of inserted questions on learning from prose. *J. educ. Psychol.*, 1971, 62, 387-394.

Weisberg, P. S. and Springer, K. J. Environmental factors in creative function. *Archives of General Psychiatry*, 1961, 5, 554-564.

Wertheimer, M. *Productive thinking.* New York: Harper, 1945.

Wittrock, M. C. Focus on educational psychology, *The Educational Psychologist,* 1967, IV, 7, 17-20.

_____. Verbal stimuli in concept formation: learning by discovery. *J. educ. Psychol.,* 1963, 54, 183-190.

Wittrock, M. C. and Twelker, P. A. Verbal cues and variety of classes of problems in transfer of training. *Psychol. Report,* 1964, 14, 827-830.

Wong, M. R. Retroactive inhibition in meaningful verbal learning. *J. educ. Psychol.,* 1970, 61, 410-415.

Woodrow, H. The effect of type of training upon transference. *J. educ. Psychol.,* 1927, 18, 159-172.

Worthen, B. R. Discovery and expository task presentation in elementary mathematics. *J. educ. Psychol. Monogr. Suppl.,* 1968, 59, 1-13.

Youness, J. and Furth, H. G. Learning of logical connectives by adolescents with single and multiple instances. *J. educ. Psychol.,* 1967, 58, 222-230.

Zapf, R. M. Superstition of junior high school pupils, part 2: effect of instruction on superstitious beliefs. *J. educ. Res.* 1938, 31, 481-496.

Zigler, E. and Kanzer, P. The effectiveness of two classes of verbal reinforcers on the performance of middle- and lower- class children. *J. personality,* 1962, 20, 157-163.

Index

Abstraction, 197-98
Accommodation, 85, 234
Achievement motive, 134-38
Assimilation, 85, 234
Atkinson, J., 134-38
Attitudes: nature of, 365-67; dimensions of, 367-68; teaching of, 376-77
Attitude learning: process of, 368-75; research on, 378-79
Ausubel, D. P., 103, 391

Bandura, A., 369-71
Behaviorist view of intelligence, 23
Bruner, J. S., 102-3
Burt, C., 30-33

Carroll, J. B., 157-58
Certitude, 213-15
Chaining, 350-51
Chomsky, N., 164-66
Classifying, 43-44
Cognition, 36-39
Cognitive dissonance, 371-72
Cognitive theory: of learning, 67-68, 73-77, 83-86; of concept learning, 197-99; of relations and structures, 223-26
Comprehension: nature of, 248-50; types of, 250-51; process of, 254-56; research on, 262-64; teaching for, 264-65; evaluation of, 265-68

Concepts: nature of, 184-85; types of, 185-90; teaching of, 203-4
Concept learning: process of, 190-94; theories of, 194-200; conditions of, 201-2; evaluation of, 204-5
Concrete operations, 43-46, 50-51
Conditioning, 66
Connectionism, 70-73
Conservation, 44-45
Contingent programs, 115-18
Convergent thinking, 36-39
Coordination, 44-45
Correlation, 16-17
Creativity: nature of, 269-70; process of, 270-74; in teaching, 276-79, 281-84; research on, 279-81; evaluation of, 284-89
Critical thinking: nature of, 324-28; process of, 328-29; research on, 332-33; teaching for, 333-34; evaluation of, 334-36
Crowder, N. A., 115, 118

Decentering, 44-45
Deductive approach, 97, 192
Development of thought processes, 43-54
Dewey, J., 299-300
Dialectical approach, 97
Didactic approach, 97
Discovery learning, 95-108
Discrimination, 192-98

Disuse, 390
Divergent thinking, 36-39
Drive theory, 133-34, 137

Education, 3-6
Educational psychology: nature of, 2-6;
    content of, 6-7; type of knowledge,
    8-9
Emotions, 125-26
Equilibration, 86
Essay tests, 422-24
Evaluation: of verbal-factual learning,
    178-80; of concept learning, 204-5; of
    relations and structure, 240-42; of
    comprehension, 265-68; of creativity,
    284-89; nature of, 411-13; types of,
    413-14; of problem solving, 316-18; of
    critical thinking, 334-36; of skills,
    258-62; of attitudes and values, 378-
    79
Evaluation ability, 36-39
Evaluation instruments: essay items,
    422-24; objective items, 424-31; rating
    scales, 432; attitude scales, 432-33;
    reporting results of, 433-36
Experiential approach, 97
Experimental approach, 97
Expository teaching, 95-105

Factor analysis, 29
Factual learning: process of, 159-61;
    research on, 172-74; teaching for,
    176-77; evaluation of, 178-80
Festinger, L., 371-72
Fitts, P., 351-52
Foreign language learning, 171
Forgetting, 389-91
Formal discipline theory, 399-400
Formal operations, 46-56

Gagne, R., 91, 226-30, 299-300, 350
Generalization, 192, 198
Generalization theory of transfer, 401-2
Gestalt theory, 67-68, 73-76
Grammar, 153-55, 170-71
Guided discovery, 99-101, 105-8
Guided learning, 99-101
Guilford, J. P., 33-41, 53-54, 157, 306-
    12, 342-43

Hull, C. L., 133-34
Hypothetico-deductive thinking, 46-47

Identical elements theory of transfer,
    400-401

Illumination, 274
Incubation, 274
Individual differences in problem solving,
    318-22
Inductive approach, 97, 192
Information processing model, 351-53
Intellectual abilities: in verbal-factual
    learning, 171-72; in concept learning,
    200; in learning relations and struc-
    tures, 235-36; in comprehension, 259-
    61; in creativity, 275; in problem
    solving, 303-4; in critical thinking,
    329-30
Intelligence: definitions of, 23-25; mea-
    sures of, 25-28, 33-35, 54-57; theories
    of, 30-41; development of, 43-51
Interference, 387, 388, 390
Internal mediation theory, 197, 306

Judd, C. H., 401-2

Knowledge, 211, 216, 223-25

Language: nature of, 152-53; structure
    of, 153-55; meaning in, 155-58; learn-
    ing of, 161-67; in the classroom, 167-
    71
Learning: nature of, 63-64; classical
    theories of, 64-76; contemporary
    theories of, 77-91
Learning hierarchy approach, 226-28
Linear programs, 114-17

McGeoch, J., 390
Memory: nature, 36-39, 384; types, 384-
    85
Motivation: motivating factors, 122-26;
    motivating techniques, 126-28; in-
    trinsic, 128-30; extrinsic, 128-30;
    theories of, 131-38; research on, 138-
    40; applications in teaching, 140-42;
    measurement of, 142-45

Needs, 124-25, 128

Objectives, 5-6, 147-49
Objective tests, 424-31
Operant conditioning, 80-83
Operational view of intelligence, 24
Ordering, 43-44

Piaget, 43-54, 83-91, 223-24
Polya, G., 299-300
Pragmatist view of intelligence, 24
Proactive inhibition, 387-90

Problem-solving: nature of, 293; types of, 293-96; process of, 296-303; theories of, 304-12; research on, 312-13; teaching for, 313-16; evaluating, 316-18; individual differences in, 318-22
Programmed instruction, 109-21
Psychology, 3
Psychomotor abilities, 342-45

Reading, 167-70
Reception learning, 95-105
Reinforcement, 80-82
Relations: nature of, 212; types of, 212-13; learning of, 221-30; research on, 236-37; teaching of, 238-40; evaluation of, 240-41
Relational concepts, 185, 193-94
Reliability, 417-18
Reporting techniques, 433-36
Research methods, 12-17
Retention: research on, 386-88; theories of, 389-91; teaching for, 392, 408-9; evaluation of, 392-94
Retroactive inhibition, 387-390

Score scales, 420-21
Scores of tests, 418-19
Second order concepts, 47, 189
Shaping, 81
Skills: nature of, 341-42; characteristics of, 345-46; teaching of, 357-58
Skill learning: phases of, 347; theories of, 348-53; research on, 353-55; evaluation of, 358-62
Skinner, B. F., 80-83, 87-90, 115-17, 163-66
Social learning, 369-71
Spearman, C., 30
Statistical significance, 15
Stimulus-response theories: of learning, 66-67, 70-73, 80-83; of problem solving, 306, 310-12; of verbal-factual learning, 163-64; of skill learning, 350-51; of concept formation, 197-200

Structures, 83, 213; nature of, 213-19; types of, 219-20; learning of, 221-32; further development of, 232-35; research on, 237-38; teaching of, 238-40; evaluation of, 241-42
Structure of intellect, 33-39; model of problem solving, 306-12
Subsumption theory of retention, 391

Task taxonomy, 345-46
Taxonomy of educational objectives, 148-49, 367
Teaching: attitudes, 376-77; concepts, 203-4; comprehension, 264-65; creativity, 276-79, 281-84; critical thinking, 333-34; factual learning, 176-77; problem solving, 313-17; relations, 238-40; retention, 392, 408-9; structures, 238, 340; skills, 357-58; transfer, 405-9; verbal learning, 174-77; values, 376-77
Teaching machines, 109-21
Tests, 411-12
Thorndike, E. L., 70-73, 390, 400-401
Thurstone, L. L., 30
Transfer of learning: nature of, 395; types of, 395; research on, 395-96; theories of, 399-405; teaching for, 405-9
Transformation, 37, 39

Validity, 415-17
Values: nature of, 365-67; dimensions of, 367-68; teaching of, 376-77
Value learning: process of, 368-75; research on, 375-76; evaluation of, 378-79
Verbal learning: process of, 161-67; in the classroom, 167-71; research on, 172-74; teaching for, 174-77; evaluation of, 178-80
Vernon, P., 30-33
Vinacke, W., 299-300

Wallis, G., 275-76
Wertheimer, M., 73-76, 86